Enjoy your journey with the
Dad - He ... Like
go through ...
2010

RIGHT PLACE, RIGHT TIME!

The inspiring adventures of STANLEY A. MOE, Trailblazer
world traveler, architect, storyteller

Making the most of life's possibilities...

Writings of Stanley A. Moe ✧ *Produced by Billie Moe Crouse*

Right Place, Right Time, ***The Inspiring Adventures of Stanley A. Moe, Trailblazer world traveler, architect, storyteller***

Writings by Stanley A. Moe and others
Produced and commentary by Billie Moe Crouse
in collaboration with Susan Baldwin Stroh, writer/editor/book coach

Published by Billie Moe Crouse, Sandia Park, New Mexico

ISBN 978-1-7354051-0-0 — First Color/B&W Print Edition
ISBN 978-1-7354051-2-4 — First KDP Print Edition
ISBN 978-1-7354051-1-7 — First eBook Edition
First Printing 2020
Printed in the U.S.A. by Gorham Printing and Kindle Direct Publishing
Library of Congress Cataloging-in-Publication Data

Cover, typesetting and interior page design by Randall Michael Tobin at
Theta Media Group, Inc.
Family Tree Graphics by Kelly Graphics

First edition (perfect bound) includes: Foreword, Table of Contents, Dedication, Preface, 18 Parts and 58 Chapters, Acknowledgements, Epilogue, Appendices, photographs, graphics, newspaper article excerpts.

Credit goes to the following photographers and companies:
Condé Nast: to Toni Frissell, Vogue © Condé Nast
Fortune Magazine, December 6, 1942, photos by
The Minneapolis Star Journal
Engineering News-Record, "Reprinted courtesy of Engineering
News-Record, copyright, BNP Media, 2020, all rights reserved."
S.S. Normandie burning: photo courtesy of The New Jersey
Maritime Museum, Beach Haven, New Jersey
Photos of the Sea Cloud yacht are courtesy of Sea Cloud Cruises, GmbH,
Hamburg, Germany

Photographers: Richard Siminski, Robert Laetare of Artistic Image, Leilani Roberts, Stanley A. Moe, Billie Moe Crouse, and others credited under their photos.

Dedication

This book is dedicated to the heirs of Stanley Allen Moe who was father to me and Myra; grandfather to Lisa, Tambralyn, and Keith; great-grandfather to Quinn, Madison, Kaelyn, Kaila, and Terran.

Dad hoped that this book would be shared with family and friends, colleagues from work, veterans, members of Rotary and other organizations to which he belonged in an active way, and with all who enjoy travel, adventure, architecture, hunting, reading, and photography—in other words YOU!

Enjoy the adventure,
Billie Moe Crouse

***Work Is Love Made Manifest* — Kahlil Gibran**

Foreword

By Ray Landy, former President and CEO of Daniel, Mann, Johnson & Mendenhall, (DMJM), the architecture firm that brought Stan Moe and Ray together.

What motivates a young kid in a tiny town in North Dakota to reach out to the entire world—that resulted in his working in 43 countries and visiting 100? Was it that he wanted to "get out of Dodge?" I don't think so—he returned to the community of his youth to help it and his family time after time. Was it poring over *National Geographic* like so many other kids? I'm sure that inspired him. But most likely it was simply his early and intense interest in people and places, and his ambition to be the best at everything he did, that motivated him not only to contribute so much but also to grow into what I would call a Renaissance man.

Why was Stan Moe so able to produce, not only as an engineer/architect/project manager and partner, but also as a storyteller, writer, husband, father, grandfather, hunter, photographer, friend? You will find out the answers to these and other questions as you dive into his diary entries, letters home from early projects in Yellowstone, from a ship he wasn't allowed to name, from Africa during WW2, from Japan in the early 50s. And you will enjoy his filling in historical and cultural details and observations while reading his reflections about work and life from the 40s through the 90s.

What to expect from all these writings? His letters home were not only descriptive, colorful, and often humorous—wonderful windows into the times, they were love letters to his wife that revealed the admiration, respect, and trust that grew over the 65 years of their marriage. In those letters, he spared her much of the violence and turmoil of his journey—revealed in his personal diary entries—where we are privy to all the emotional and physical challenges of working and living in war-torn countries and other difficult environments.

I learned in this memoir, that no matter where Stan was or how hard the task, he always managed to get himself in a place of greatest potential to get the job done.

✧ ✧ ✧

I got to know Stan in Algeria when our project director had to return to the US after many, many months of managing this large team of over 50 architects and engineers as well as a complex client organization—neither very easy. Our director was a tough boss, but we loved him and were not happy to see him leave, and we were sure not happy to see this guy, Stan Moe, show up as his replacement. I mean, how could this new guy ever match up? Stan was retired for God's sake! I could easily have made a case against Stan.

- I distrusted "suits."
  Stan wore a suit every day.
- AIA (American Institute of Architects) was an anachronism for me.
  AIA was a professional keystone for Stan.

- Stan was known for his management of military and corporate projects. I wanted to work on so-called socially relevant projects.
- I had just left three tough years in the Peace Corps. Stan was living the good life in L.A.
- I was a Democrat. Stan was a Republican.

But, put a couple of opposites in a tough place to work such as on the renovation of a major airbase in Algeria, and put them there for many months working 14-hour days, seven days a week, people get to know each other in ways not always available to them in conventional circumstances. Stan didn't care that we were suspicious. He had a job to do. He was now our leader. And the fact that we were all taller than him didn't deter him—it never did!

A lesser person could have failed, but not Stan. And one reason he didn't fail was because he was such a *gentleman*—a gentleman in the sense that he was always up-front and honest, always there for his colleagues, always quick to both compliment as well as offer constructive criticism, always prudent in his behavior, always respectful, always confident, and always confidential. And within weeks of Stan's arrival in Algeria, we were all in line behind Stan.

And it wasn't easy for me, as Stan always wore a damn suit and tie every day, even when it was over 100 degrees outside. I hated that, but I would never have told Stan as, by then, my respect for him, what he had accomplished, and his terrific character had begun to impress me immensely. We would have done whatever Stan had asked by the end of the job.

I am forever thankful to Stan for doing what he so loyally did—give up a good part of the first several years of his retirement—to give us what we will forever remember: *the gentleman, Stan Moe.*

He gave so much to so many of us: mentorship, leadership, an understanding of commitment and remarkable perseverance. I personally owe Stan much more, as he reinforced in me the qualities of what it meant to be a gentleman. My career would not have been the same had I not met and worked for Stan. And because of what I had learned from Stan, I proudly wore a suit for the next 30 years at DMJM—even when it was 100 degrees outside.

Ray Landy

TABLE OF CONTENTS

Introduction

By Billie Moe Crouse (Stan Moe's daughter)

I have chosen to follow through on Dad's request to build on what he's written (his prolific writings about his life) and to turn them into a memoir. *Right Place, Right Time!* covers the years 1914 to 2010. I have created a book following his specifications. You see, my father kept diaries since he was eleven years of age. During his World War II travels abroad, he not only kept a diary, but he also wrote daily letters to my mother. We have chosen to include many excerpts from these diaries and letters, but there were way too many to include them all. The same story is true of the letters from Japan. We had to be selective and we needed to abbreviate them.

Dad was an amazing storyteller and his writing is alive with wit, keen observation, and glimpses of history as his life unfolded on several continents during his seven decades of work and travel.

My job, along with my collaborator-editor, Susan Baldwin Stroh, was to organize all his stories, diary and letter writings, his photography, audio interviews, newspaper and magazine articles covering career, family, church, humanitarian efforts into the book he envisioned. I have had invaluable help from students, editors, my sister Myra and her children, my cousin Kathy, friends Jim Daniel, Pat Gillick, and Lee Jackman. I will mention all who helped accomplish this massive task in the acknowledgement page at the end of this book.

Expect enticing stories, expect revelations; his and yours! Look forward to learning things you didn't know before. This book is his odyssey, in his voice and from his point of view. It is also your passport, an invitation to travel with my dad. Perhaps you will realize, like I have, that Stanley Allen Moe was spiritually and materially successful; a fully realized individual, a true renaissance man. Anticipate inspiration.

Not only will you learn about my dad's successful actions as an artist, businessman, photographer, traveler, family man, and leader of many organizations, but also you may be inspired, after reading this book, to seize the possibilities in your own life for greater fulfillment and expansion.

As my editor, Susan, and I organized this book, we found places where transitions and explanations were sometimes needed for clarification and enrichment. I have aimed to provide illumination for you with special notes that separate my comments from his writings.

The parts of *Right Place, Right Time* are identified and in some chapters there's a section, Looking Back, where my dad, in his later years, summarizes, reflects and provides missing pieces that his letters and diaries did not provide. For example, when the government during World War II didn't allow employees working for them in other countries to disclose their locations, Dad could now provide the names of those places and offer historical, geographical and cultural observations.

Dad loved people and people loved him. He had many friends—too many to mention in this book. But some of his most dearest family and friends or their children, including my sister Myra Parsons and her children, will add their memories in a special section towards the end of the book.

One note about Dad's letter writing philosophy—one he related to Mom as they carried on their correspondence over the years. He told Mom that even in a journal entry, you want to tell a tale about what's happening. He disclosed that when they wrote each other, this was a way to keep their minds alive and alert—to heighten curiosity and stoke interest. He said that saying, "I'm having fun; wish you were here," is empty writing. You want to make each letter a story and include the who, what, where, when and why of a scene or event or a day as much as you can. You give a full description of everything from an overview to the details to make the whole story vivid and relatable. To my dad, writing was storytelling.

Thank you for taking this journey with us. May you have fun, learn, be moved and inspired to go after your own dreams with gusto!

Billie Moe Crouse, eldest daughter (Christened: Willa Joanne Moe)

PREFACE

By Stanley Moe

For many years I have thought about writing my memoirs. From time to time, I have written brief notes for material I might include in such an effort. My memories of the past tend to fade a bit, so the recollection of names may not be as good as I would like. Still, the stories remain vivid in my memory and I feel I should share them with others.

I have had the good fortune of being in interesting places at the right time to see history unfold. Though my role in many of these events has been mostly as an observer, on occasion I have found myself drawn in as a participant. These experiences have served me well during my lifetime and added to my ability to live an active and productive life.

Being at the right place at the right time and making the best of the opportunities on hand was the basis for what I look upon as the secret of what success I have achieved during my life.

There was no grand plan with special stated goals to guide my efforts. I merely responded to the pressures and challenges that seemed to appear without any real planning.

In the more than nine decades of life experiences, the most significant and rewarding experiences were those that resulted from forces outside my control. I discovered it was wise to respond quickly to opportunities. When travel was involved, I did not hesitate to tackle a new challenge.

Growing up in a small country town in North Dakota, with little knowledge of the world outside, may have been an advantage. My knowledge was limited to what I had gained from books in my father's small library and his subscription to *National Geographic.* At its inception, you were required to apply to be a member of the National Geographic Society. My father applied for membership in 1928 and was accepted. I still remember reading the letter from National Geographic formally accepting his membership in the Society.

Because our world is constantly changing, I hope my recollections will provide future generations a better understanding of the colorful times and places of my lifetime.

Hello there! Welcome to my life!

PART I

1914-1930

Launching the Journey

Imagine...

Picture a boy in the year 1924 sitting at a slanted wooden desk affixed to the floor of a one-room schoolhouse in Ross, North Dakota. He's drawing a map of the world, perhaps occasionally glancing at the large one hanging at the front of the room.

Can you see him? Feel his fascination and excitement? Had he embraced the entire world with his mind at that moment? Was the rest of his life a natural consequence of that embrace, the revealing of a dream that was designed and built with each stroke of his pencil?

Whether he knew it or not, the boy was already an architect—a builder of his own amazing life that years later he very much wanted to share.

It's as though he is saying, *I had a good, adventurous life and learned some things you might find interesting and saw fascinating parts of the world you might want to see. Share in my wonder without taking a step — by just turning the page.*

Stanley reaches through time and invites you to come along.

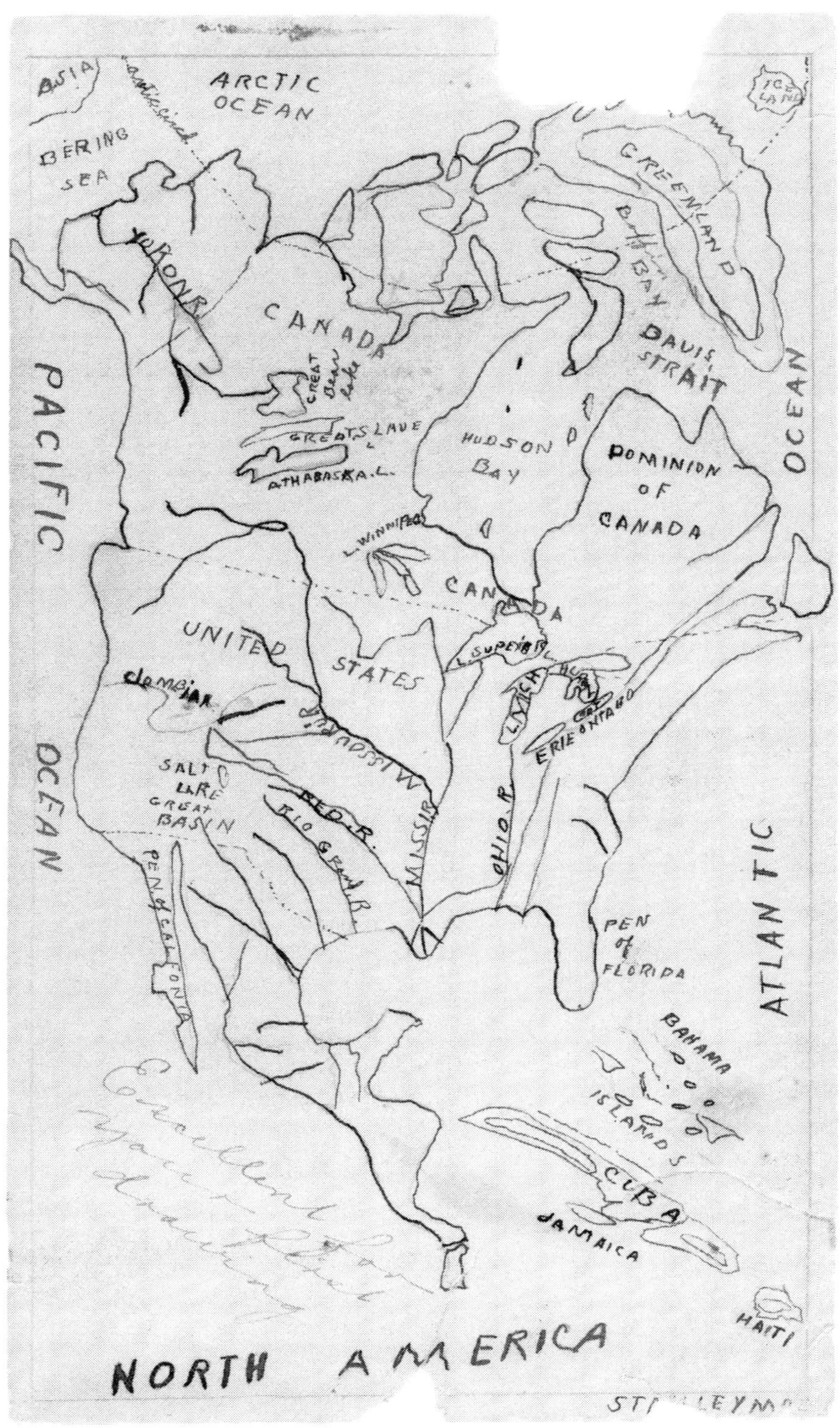

Stanley Moe drew this map in the 4th grade

CHAPTER 1

Origins of the Moe Family

Train station in Braskereidfoss, Norway

Looking Back (from Audio tapes by Stanley Moe, circa 2005)
In 1955, during our Christmas holidays, my fifteen-year-old daughter, Billie, who was living with me in England, accompanied me to Braskereidfoss, Norway. We went to meet Carl Gisti, my father's second cousin, to see if we could find some pieces to the picture of our family background that were puzzling us back home. My dad had never met his Norwegian relatives, though he spoke and wrote in Norwegian as well as in English, so his family story was shrouded in mystery. Billie and I were excited to see what we could discover.

When we were all settled in their living room with tea and hot chocolate, which Carl's wife Anna had served, I asked cousin Carl, "How is it you and I are related on the male side of the family and yet your last name is Gisti and mine is Moe?"

Carl's explanation was a bit startling.

The old man said, "There lived an unmarried woman who had three sons out of wedlock; one of which was my father, one was your grandfather, and a third boy. Each son had a different father and was born on a different farm. Your great-grandma named each son after the name of the farm on which he was born."

Carl added, "My father was born and grew up on a farm named Gisti, therefore my last name is Gisti."

Billie's face was lit with interest. "Wait, what did she do?"

Carl continued, addressing Billie, "Your great, great-grandmother had worked on the Gisti Farm and another two farms, one of which was 'Moen' and the other, a name I can't recall. Billie, your great-grandfather, your father's grandfather was born on the Moen farm and so was given the last name of Moen."

Billie jumped in, "So, our name Moe, and it comes from Moen."

Carl smiled and said, "Yes! Billie, when your great-grandfather Arne immigrated to America, he shortened the name to Moe. By the way, one of the meanings of the word 'Moen' means 'very attractive place' or 'beautiful valley.'"

I said, "This is so interesting. My great-grandmother named each son after the name of the farm on which the child was born! One of her sons, my grandfather, was named Arne Moen and his half-brothers each had different last names when they emigrated from Norway to America in the late nineteenth century. One was Gisti, and what was the other brother's last name?"

Carl said, "I forget but his first name was Theodore."

I said, "I love knowing all this."

Carl told us that Arne's father had been employed on a large farm near Hamar, Norway. In those days, farm laborers and artisans in general, had a difficult existence. They were little better than serfs.

He continued, "Farm laborers had to work hard for their lords and were paid very little. They would tackle just about anything. Most men were involved in farming and forestry."

And so, that day in the warm parlor at Carl Gisti's home, we had found the missing piece that clarified the rest of the story that I had been told.

✧ ***Billie: The following is a letter from my father to his parents after our visit to Norway.***

Smestad Hotel
Oslo, Norway, Dec. 31, 1955

Dear Mom and Dad,

Another year almost gone. I'm spending a quiet evening and will probably go to bed early. There are a few Americans in the hotel who may consider it essential that I join them. I'll wait and see. Billie has gone to a party with the general's son and won't be home until one.

Billie and I came in from Lillehammer on a train this afternoon. It was a pleasant ride down (four hours) and we found no snow here.

We had a long day yesterday. Got on the way 10:00 in the morning and got home at 11:00 in the evening. We took three trains and finally took a single electric coach to Braskereidfoss. The station agent in Elverum knew Carl Gisti and called ahead to the station at Braskereidfoss, so a taxi was there to meet us. We finally got out to Carl's house at 2:15 p.m.

Carl has remarkable pep for his age and after five minutes we were talking like old friends. He sold his farm but is still living in his house which was built sixty years ago. He built an addition to it and so has a large living room and bath upstairs for him and his wife. A young Norwegian couple lives downstairs and takes care of all the housework.

His wife Anna is very nice and also peppy but does not speak a word of English. She had to leave for a church rummage sale shortly after we arrived. Carl said he would like us to have lunch and reached into a cabinet and brought out a bottle of brandy. He said he couldn't drink. "The doctor said not to!" In a few minutes we went downstairs for "lunch." Beautiful linen, silver, china and table decorations—beat the finest hotels we have visited in Scandinavia. He was a gracious, relaxed host. He apparently has a small but adequate income, so he lives well.

Carl and Anna Gisti of Braskereidfoss, Norway

I found that Carl was well informed on the Moes in America and had a big collection of pictures from Great-Uncle Louis, his wife Emma and their children: Cora, Edgar, and Thelma. He has maintained a lot of interest in the family. I am not too keen on visiting distant relatives, generally, but this was so worthwhile. He and I hit it off very well and it was most pleasant visiting with him. He was almost in tears when we left. Guess we are the only visitors from America he has ever had. He is a rattling good conversationalist with a great memory and sense of humor. He chuckled a lot. Nothing dottery about him. He was annoyed over his eyesight as he needs half-inch thick glasses to see anything. Still, he is not morose and does get around.

I got a lot of information on the background of the family and the whys and wherefores of the Moe name. I'll tell you about it when I see you.

We stayed about 2-1/2 hours and then had to rush to take the taxi and three trains back. We left a wool scarf with him and he seemed very happy and pleased at the gesture. Billie is very attentive to older people and had picked it out in a shop. She thinks he is grand. He dug out his gold nugget watch chain for Billie to see. When she mentioned how large the nuggets were, he said, "Oh, these aren't big; a lot are about the size of the end of your finger!" (Carl had mined gold in the Alaska gold rush around 1896.)

There aren't many towns in Norway but there are many crossroads where there is a store or two and a train stop. Carl said that Braskereidfoss was established only 20 years ago (in the 30s). The station and post office are in one. Anyhow, if Doris comes over, we will go to Norway again and will visit Carl, too. He would really enjoy it and I know we would as well.

We are leaving for Paris on Monday morning and then will go on to London after a day. I have some business to transact which will help charge off some of the trip to my business account.

We got in one good day of skiing up in Lillehammer; two feet of soft snow was very nice. The Norwegians do less of the downhill type of skiing, they concentrate on cross-country. It was a rare, quiet and sunny day so we had a wonderful time up in the big hills, or small mountains as they seem to be here. We all got home safely without sprains or scratches.

Billie skiing in Lillehammer, Norway

The Norwegians make the most of the holidays. They close all stores at 2 p.m. during the week between Christmas and New Year's. I think they are wise.

Oh, Billie finally bought a big stack of lefse[1] up at Lillehammer. She carries some with her when she goes to eat in a hotel—when they don't have it.

Hope you are all well and that I will hear from you when I get back to London.

Love, Stan

1. Lefse is a traditional soft Norwegian flatbread. It is made with potatoes, flour, butter, and milk or cream.

Looking Back
When growing up in North Dakota, I was aware of a few members of the Moe family tree. It did not seem to be a very big tree. I never heard very much about the various relatives. I don't remember Grandmother Mina's maiden name, nor my wife's grandmother's maiden name. I do believe she was Norwegian as well.

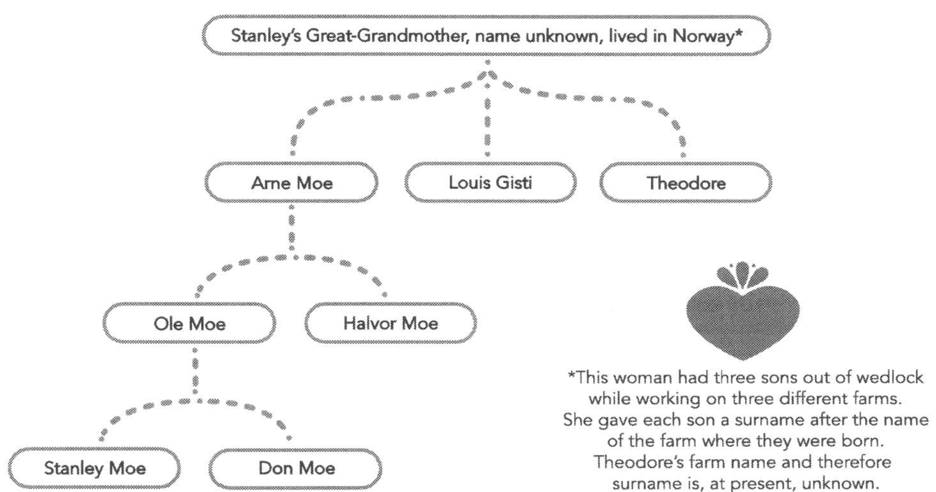

My grandparents emigrated from Europe during the period right after the end of the American Civil War. Economic and social conditions in both the USA and in Europe were not good. America seemed to offer more opportunities. The West was opening up and it was possible to get free land from the US government by merely improving it through cultivating what had been wild prairie land inhabited by Indians and buffalo (bison). There were many factories being built and vast stands of forest with timber to be harvested. Railroads were being built all over. There were many employment opportunities for anyone with a strong back.

Looking back, it seems to me that young women did not so readily immigrate to this country at that time. Those in the Moe and Pape families had limited education in Norway and Germany. As such, they were told they didn't have much chance to gain employment as teachers or nurses. Those were the usual occupations for educated women. Instead, they would work as domestic servants, nannies, or seamstresses in the garment trades. Those that did immigrate most likely had as their common objective to marry and have a family.

The conditions which attracted each pair of my grandparents were somewhat different, however.

My maternal grandfather, Wilhelm Pape, came from an area along the Moselle River near the city of Trier in Germany. He was learning the brick-making trade when he reached the age (late teens) when he became eligible for the draft into the German army. Not long after he came to America he went to northern Illinois near Rockford. Thereafter, he lived in several communities where there were many German immigrants: Iowa, Minnesota, Wisconsin, and finally, North Dakota.

My maternal grandmother Wilhelmina Winter arrived at the Port of Baltimore with several other German immigrants. It was through one of the other young German ladies on shipboard that she later met Wilhelm and soon they were married. They accumulated quite a family before they settled on what was to be their final family farm in North Dakota. The youngest living member of that family of at least eighteen children was my aunt Lila. My mother Frieda, was, I believe, next to the oldest.

My paternal grandfather Arne Moe had a similar history of moving around before settling down in a final location. Arne was one of three half-brothers who came to America about the same time that Grandfather Pape did. In those days, farm laborers and artisans, in general, had a difficult existence. Craftsmen were under the apprentice system and found it hard to accumulate enough capital to start a business. They were accustomed to hard work and would tackle most anything. Most were used to farming and were also familiar with the woods. The forests and lands open to claims for farming attracted them to Minnesota and Wisconsin where the climate and activities were not too different from Norway.

Grandfather Arne Moe went to northern Minnesota and took up farming in a Norwegian community—near the village of Newfolden, north of Thief River Falls.

My paternal grandmother, Mina, met and married Arne and they had two boys: Halvor and my father Ole. Mina had come to America when only 19 years old with only a trunk and a suitcase. The trunk contained a disassembled spinning wheel which worked up until the time of this writing.

Times were tough. Through hard work and frugal living, our Moe and Pape grandparents managed to acquire small farms. Arne never used a single piece of power equipment. Windmills, horses, and humans provided the only power on most farms. Oxen pulled the wagons and heavy plows.

Medical care was not good. It was a rare occasion when old people visited a doctor. Grandfather Pape went only once, when he was sixty-five. He died the next day of a stomach ulcer.

Arne Moe's two half-brothers went separate ways. Theodore, the oldest, went to Canada and farmed near Olds, Alberta. There was little contact with Great-Uncle Theodore and his family in Canada. As I recall, there was a daughter named Clara with whom I exchanged Christmas cards in the early thirties. We never visited one another.

Great-Uncle Louis, the younger, was a very outgoing person and had a colorful career in North Dakota. Louis' wife was Emma and the mother of Edgar, Cora, and Thelma. We felt quite close to them when we all lived in Ruso and later after we all moved to Minot and then to Ross. They were all very kind to me and my brother Don.

I had been in close contact with my grandfather Arne during my early years. This was memorable for me because he brought me into close contact with those pioneer spirits who were somewhat reluctant to change with the times.

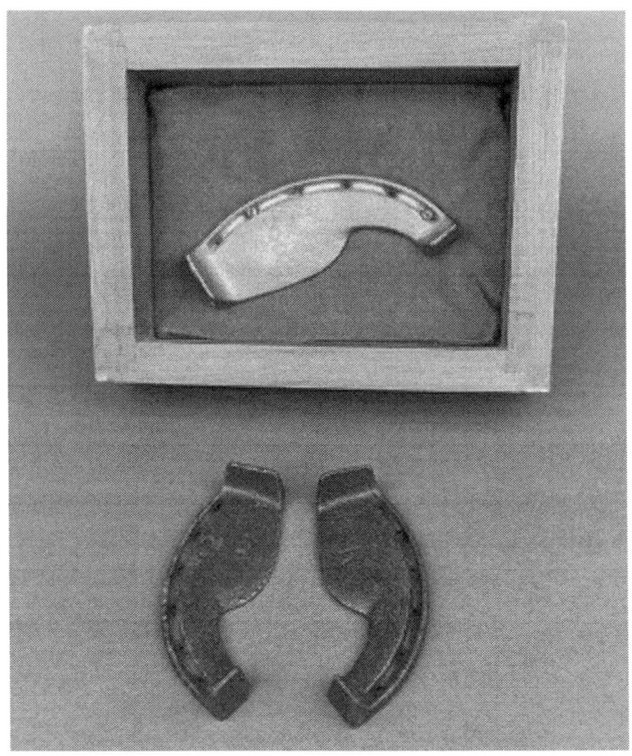

✧ *Billie: We have several oxen shoes (different from horseshoes) around our house today. Grandpa used them for paperweights at the bank. I have one that he painted gold.*

***The people who lived in small towns in those days were always looking out for us little ones who chose to explore the area. The mothers didn't seem to worry about anyone harming their small offspring. We were allowed enormous amounts of freedom.* — Stan**

CHAPTER 2

Dad, Mom, and Geography

My father Ole spent his early years working on the family farm for his parents—performing all the usual farm tasks. He did so all through his teen years. Then, determined to have a better life without the drudgery of manual labor, he attended the schools available in the area. Fortunately, he obtained the necessary prerequisites to enter the University of North Dakota in Grand Forks. Although he did not earn a degree, the formal training in accounting provided an opportunity to work in banks. His first significant job in a bank was in Fargo, North Dakota.

(from left to right) Ole and Halvor Moe

Ole met and married Frieda Pape, the daughter from the family of German immigrants I mentioned above. In due course they had a baby — me! As is usual with the increase in family responsibility, the father finds it very important to increase his income. Banks, then as now, were not known for their generous pay and promotions for the rank and file employee.

My parents: Ole and Frieda Moe

Dad chose the course of buying a bank. I became the son of a young banker when I was about two years old. The bank that my father acquired along with his partner, Lee Crowell, was located in the village of Ruso.

Ruso was a village in the center of the state. It was one of dozens of similar communities that grew up at the turn of the century. Most had a population of a hundred or so. These communities were the key to the development of farming in the area.

Land, acquired under the Homestead Act of 1862, encouraged the development of small farming communities. Ruso was located on the plains in central North Dakota and had the advantage of being on a major north/south highway. In addition, the town was on a branch line of a railroad running east and west. The

Ruso zip code 58776 - July 17, 1906-1981

Ruso School and Church

land was ideal for growing grain. And so, the Central Plains became known as the "Breadbasket" of the United States.

These railroad companies built branch lines to serve the general countryside. Towns were located along these lines to serve the farming communities. They were spaced in such a way as to accommodate the farmers who would haul their grain by horse-drawn wagons into town. A farmer wanted to be able to drive to a grain elevator, dump his grain, and get back home before dark. Trucks did not come into common use until the late 1920s.

The "quarter section" per the Homestead Act of 1862 was defined as the one-fourth square mile. That size of plot had been considered by the government as about all the land a family could manage in the days of hand and horsepower for planting and harvesting. Hilly country attracted cattle raisers. Lack of transportation discouraged anyone from dairy operations or truck farming. North Dakota was a grain producing area.

The Twin Cities flour milling operations were hoping to be supplied with vast quantities of grain from the North Dakota plains. The key to the development of the farms was the means for transporting the grain to market. Railroads were the answer. North Dakota was served by two main railroads: The Great Northern and The Soo Line.

Our Family: 1900s through 1920s

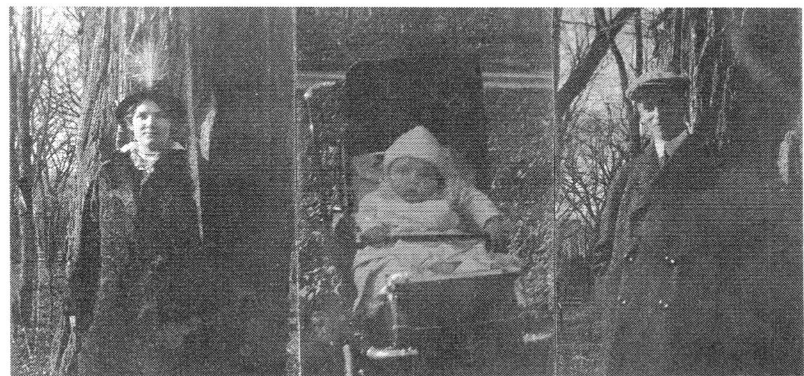

Frieda Moe, Stanley and Ole Moe circa Autumn 1914

Growing up in small town U.S.A. in the early 1900s was an adventure. I was born Stanley Allen Moe, in Fargo, North Dakota, on May 28, 1914. My brother, Donald Owen Moe, was born in Ruso on June 8, 1916, when I was two years old.

Even though I must have been only about two to seven years old at the time, I moved freely about on every street in the town and never encountered any memorable danger. The people who lived in small towns in those days were always looking out for us little ones who chose to explore the area. The mothers didn't seem to worry about anyone harming their small offspring. We were allowed enormous amounts of freedom.

Stan and Don circa late 1917 in fancy attire

Don and Stan in sailor suits

Though only a small town, Ruso had all the basic requirements for a pioneer town in the early 20th Century. It had a post office, a bank, a couple of grain elevators, and a railroad depot on a branch line of a major railroad. It had a school, a jail, a church, and a small hotel/rooming house. The town had been established in 1909. It had a population of 141 in 1910. (In 2020, the population was 4!)

As a child in a small country town, I had great opportunities to acquire lots of knowledge that remained with me. Before our family moved to Minot when I was seven, I had a great time. I still can remember the location of virtually every house and business establishment and the names of its occupants. It was high adventure.

One of the most interesting people I visited with was Dan Kaedus, the blacksmith. Dan had come from Russia. He had left his wife behind. I thought he was a fascinating person. He allowed us young boys to turn the crank on the forge and heat the iron until it glowed. We were mesmerized as he hammered the red-hot metal into tools and horseshoes.

Near to the blacksmith shop was the livery stable. It was owned by Pete Severson, a jolly fellow, who had had nice buggies and carriage horses for hire when the town was first established. Since they had to have their hooves shod from time to time, Dan Kaedus was handy. Since cars had put the buggy hire operation out of business, Pete Severson concentrated on heavy duty work horses used on almost every farm. Pete had one or more large stud horses of the Percheron or Clydesdale variety on call for breeding purposes. He also had a lot of chickens and an enormous red rooster who used to chase me whenever I was foolish enough to take a shortcut through his yard during my travels.

The Post Office was run by Ed Sargent, a young man who graduated from Princeton Theological Seminary. Ed stopped in Ruso on his "way out west to earn a fortune" and never left. Quite the character, he would frequently wear a tin can on his head.

In addition to Ed Sargent, there were several other colorful characters. The daily doings of "Ma" Broonsock were often the subject of my father's stories that entertained us at dinner in the evening. She was a very talkative person and dressed in an outlandish manner.

Phyle Wipple owned the general store where a wide variety of things were available for sale. Groceries, produce, and pots and pans were there. Guns and ammunition were also stocked. My father was a good sports consumer. Our house was always well supplied with ammunition for shotguns and small rifles.

The only clothing store in town was owned by Dave Kraman. It was located on Main Street and had an elevated wood sidewalk. To walk from this store to reach my dad's bank, which was across the street, one could use a plank sidewalk laid on the dirt road. It kept one's feet out of the mud but was a bit of a hazard since the cars driving over it caused it to split. It was soon covered with large splinters. One day I fell on it and got a sliver in my hand. This was treated by a surgeon in Velva and was my first memory of any medical treatment.

Because of its strategic location, the grain elevators, and railroad depot, Ruso became a center of commerce. All the homesteaders in the area brought their grain to our town to be shipped to the mills for processing.

We left Ruso when I was seven and Don was five and moved to Minot for two years and then to Ross. Soon thereafter, my father established a bank in Ross, a small town (population of 52-57) which sits high on the prairie in Mountrail County, North Dakota.

Our Main Street was typical of an upper Midwest small town. We had a hotel and lunch counter, the Alpha Drug Company, the hardware and furniture store, a clothing store, the local bank/post office (which processed land and farm loans), Ross Promoter (the local newspaper that was eventually absorbed by The Stanley Promoter), the General Merchandise Store, two or three saloons, and at the end of Main Street stood the essential train station and grain elevator.

One side of the street in Ross, North Dakota

The other side of the street in Ross, North Dakota

The schoolhouse and the church were situated on the road connecting Ross to the nearby town of Stanley.

My parents owned a small, two-bedroom home on First Street East. It had a room at the back of the house with a sink to wash up and brush our teeth. Mother used this sink to wash our clothes since the water pump was just outside the back door. The outhouse was out back across from the chicken coop. My father would walk across our back yard, cross the alley to get to his office, his bank, on Main Street every morning.

Our house when Mom and Dad bought it

PASS BOOK
OF
STATEBANK OF ROSS
NO. DAK
1924, & 1925

At age 10, I made a passbook at my father's bank

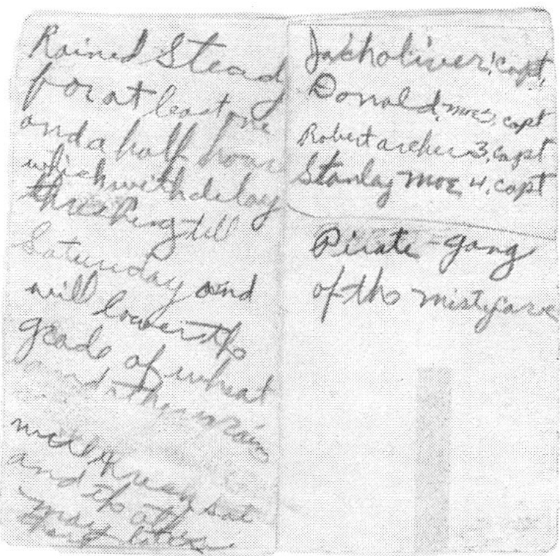
Rained Steady
for at least one
and a half hours
which with delay
threshing till
Saturday and
will lower the
grade of wheat

Jack Oliver, 1 capt
Donald moe, 2 capt
Robert archer, 3, capt
Stanley moe, 4, capt

Pirate-gang
of the misty cave

Mimicking my dad, I wrote the weather and grain reports in my diary

Me at age 10, my mother, and Don at age 8

Billie: I don't know how many projects my dad might have designed in his youth, but he told me the first plans he made up were for his dog Curly. During these years, from age 11 to 15, Dad was hanging out at the bank; making deposit books for the family; helping Grandpa on the farm and Grandma with the chickens.

Ole Moe, Frieda Pape Moe, Don & Stanley Moe
Circa 1927

PART II

1930s: Exciting Passages

Billie: At the end of the school year autograph books were used to share thoughts and feelings with fellow classmates. Most messages were silly, but Pauline wrote a prophetic message to Dad.

CHAPTER 3

Growing in Mind and Heart

Stan's high school graduation photo

In 1930, I graduated from Ross High School. There were 10 students in my senior class: 5 boys and 5 girls. I was the youngest in the class. The last day of class I was 15, and on graduation day, two days later, I was a year older!

Ross
High School
THIS CERTIFIES THAT
Stanley A. Moe
has completed the Course of Study prescribed by the Board of Education for the High School Department and is therefore entitled to this
DIPLOMA
Given at Ross, North Dakota, this twenty-ninth day of May, 1930.

Stanley's high school diploma, 1930

Military Training Certificate
RESERVE OFFICERS' TRAINING CORPS

This is to certify that Stanley A. Moe
has successfully completed the prescribed course of instruction in the Basic course, Infantry Division, Reserve Officers' Training Corps, in which he was enrolled from September 17th, 19 30, to June 7th, 19 32, and that he is qualified to perform the duties of a Corporal in the Organized Reserves.
Given at University of North Dakota, this 7th day of June in the year of Our Lord One Thousand Nine Hundred and Thirty- Two
Remarks:

E.V. Smith
Major, Infantry, (DOL)
Professor of Military Science and Tactics.

Military training certificate

I was busy the summer of '30 getting things ready for college. In August, I enrolled as a freshman at the University of North Dakota in Fargo. It was quite a change going from my family's small house in the tiny town of Ross to a large campus. I enrolled in the School of Engineering and loved it. The drafting tools were wonderful. The professors gave us many assignments which required using the tools in various ways. I still have many assignments saved in a 27" x 21" portfolio from when I was a 16-year-old freshman.

My pencil drawing (15 x 27.5 inches)

My garden drawing in pencil and watercolor (27.5 by 15 inches)

Detail 1 from the above drawing

Detail 2 from the above drawing

I was the youngest in all my classes at the University of North Dakota, and I pledged a fraternity, DELTA TAU DELTA, to make friends. However, before I went to college, I'd already met a girl, Doris Anderson, who would change my life. I couldn't get her out of my mind, so at every vacation my freshman and sophomore years, I'd hitch a ride from Ross to Stanley to see Doris.

Billie: Daddy told the story about how he first noticed Mother at a basketball game at Stanley High School. He saw that she had a problem with her cheerleader outfit. One of her uniform straps kept slipping revealing her bare shoulder. Daddy kiddingly talked about this being the moment he fell in love!

1st Row: MISS GUNTER, MISS LARSON
2nd Row: B. PEEK, C. MEDBERY, M. NELSON, S. BROOKS
3rd Row: A. LASSESSON, L. GILLESPIE, F. ST. CLAIR, L. JOHNSON
4th Row: C. CORY, D. ANDERSON, G. HANSON

Doris is on her right knee on the right side of frame

I would get into Stanley (about seven miles away from my home in Ross) a few times a month. I wanted to see Doris as often as possible. She worked in her father's store—Anderson's General Store in Stanley. He sold stoves, iceboxes, refrigerators, fabric for custom suits, some farm equipment, shoes and shoelaces—all items essential for the farming families in rural North Dakota. I went there often to visit with Doris when she was working there, but her father was not pleased, and visits were discouraged. Finally, seeing my persistence, her father insisted I buy something each time I was there! So, I bought a package of shoelaces each visit. Each pair cost from five to ten cents!

My sweetie pie graduated from Stanley High School in 1932 and the following term she enrolled in Macalester College in St. Paul, Minnesota.

Doris's high school graduation picture

Billie: In 1932, in the <u>La Concha</u> yearbook under "Senior Prophesy," Doris wrote,""I predict that in 1957, I will be running the Orphans Home for Communist Children whose parents have been deported to Russia."

After two years at the University of North Dakota, I transferred to the University of Minnesota in Minneapolis to major in architecture. After two years at Macalester, Doris transferred to U of M and changed her major to Architectural Interior Design.

Now that we both lived in Minneapolis, our relationship grew.

Courting at a sock hop!

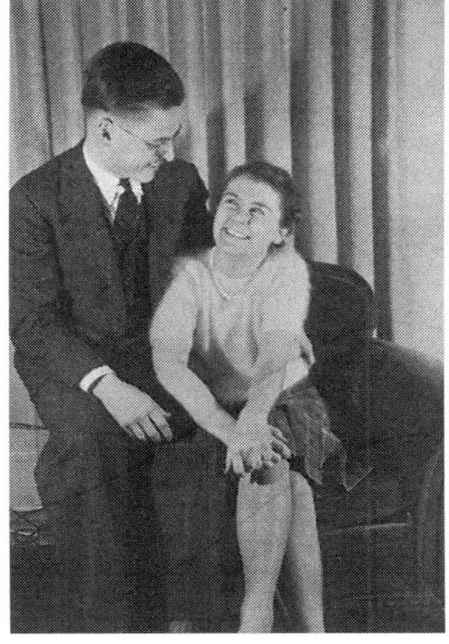

Falling in love!

We had a wonderful group of friends, many of whom attended U of M, and the group became known as "The Gang." At the U of M, I decided to join a professional architectural fraternity—The Scarab. (Many universities had chapters.)

Scarab · Fraternity · united · by · the common · devotion · of · its · members · to architecture · extends · by · these presents · her · rights · and · privileges to · Stanley · A · Moe · of · Khons · temple of · the · University · of · Minnesota · [illegible]
We · of · the · national · council · hereto · affix · our signatures · and · seal · this [illegible] · day · of · February · 1934 ·
Hiram · Sphinx ·
Hiram · Papyrus ·
Hiram · Horakh ·

The Scarab—The 17th of February 1934

I graduated from U of M, June of 1936.

My college graduation photo
(I didn't need glasses but wore them to look older!)

Doris and I became engaged my senior year of college (her junior year) and planned to marry after she graduated from the U of M. In order to be able to afford marriage and a future family, I needed a job.

CHAPTER 4

Career Beginnings

Don't stay in one place without learning something new and significant each day. Don't close your mind to doing things in new ways and growing each day. — **Louis Bersbach, architect**

Looking Back

In finding work, I was faced with a major problem that both young and old people faced during the Depression—to find employment. The self-employed, like the farmers, small business owners, such as merchants and other tradespeople were all suffering. Business was at a low-ebb activity.

I was fortunate. I found a paying job in an architect's office within one week after graduation. I make special note of the fact that it was a "paying" job. It was not uncommon in the mid-thirties for architects to pay no wages for newly graduated "would-be" architects. Architectural firms assumed new graduates had no knowledge of the practical application of their education. Therefore, a non-paying apprenticeship, or a very low wage of thirty-five to fifty cents per hour was offered. Some of the firms with elite clientele expected the new graduate to pay the architectural firm for the "honor" of working there.

My first boss, Louis Boynton Bersbach, paid me fifty cents an hour. Moreover, I was put to work on a drafting board the first day. In a forty-hour week, I could earn twenty dollars. Louis was a bachelor, a graduate of Harvard University, and a very pleasant person. He loved to talk and explain the lore of architecture. He would often stand by my drafting board with his elbow on the end of my T-square telling interesting tales of his early experience. When Louis started talking, my production time would end. I would be "off the clock." On occasion, I would be his captive audience for two hours. I learned a lot despite the many unproductive and uncompensated hours.

Most of the work in the office was residential. One of my first assignments was to prepare a detailed plan of a mansion on Lake Harriet for our client, Mr. Groves. The exterior of the house was plain in comparison with its neighbors. The owner wanted a Mediterranean look. Almost overnight Louis created a set of sketches inspired by the Spanish Revival design popular in California. The plans were readily approved by the owner.

I was given a peek into the world of the rich and famous. While I measured and sketched, I garnered bits of information from the upstairs maid, downstairs maid, and the cook about our client, Mr. Groves. He was particular about his dress. His suits were custom tailored by Herman of Minneapolis. Because Mr. Groves was color-blind, shirts, ties, and socks were stored side-by-side according to color combination.

I was fascinated by the process and was enjoying doing some of the research involved. This was followed by my drafting the details prescribed by Louis. Some of our references were books on the architecture in California. Santa Barbara and Pasadena had established a favorite architecture style, a style imported by wealthy people who had moved to California from the eastern part of the United States. They were prominent citizens who built impressive homes and exercised influence over the architectural style for their large homes and civic buildings. They had the means to hire outstanding architects who have left some fine examples of their work. Among these are such names as: Reginald Johnson, George Washington Smith, and Myron Hunt.

Another interesting assignment I had was to do some work for the Minneapolis airport. It was under the administration of the Department of Parks. It was classified as an entertainment facility. Residents and visitors would spend an evening or weekend afternoon watching planes land and take off. These activities were exciting for the public. I was to design a check-in counter complete with built-in baggage scales and lots of drawers. The front was "modernized" with black glass and chrome strips. Little did I ever expect to have any further contact with the air travel industry, except, possibly as a passenger. However, in 1942-43, I became both an airline passenger and an airport designer in Africa.

✧ **Billie: Dad designed many airports in several countries throughout the world.**

The architectural profession in the thirties was not thriving. There was relatively little new construction. This had the effect of discouraging young people from getting an education in the building design field. Quite a few graduates had gone into other fields as well. Those of us who had stayed with it kept in close contact with one another. We had a grapevine going. Now they call it "networking." We learned through our friends which firms needed some additional drafting help. We knew who was getting what salary. I can remember hearing about a person whom I never met having the reported weekly salary of $135. It was my goal to exceed it, which I did in a few years. But I never knew how much more he might have been making when I finally attained that number.

This calls for a bit of explanation. In spite of the level of training one received in an institution with an architectural department, school or college, the graduates generally started out in an architectural design office as a "draftsman." When women graduates became more numerous, the term was changed to "drafter." Few were so presumptuous as to call himself or herself an "architect" until he or she had qualified and obtained a license to practice as an architect.

Because most of my contemporaries were male, I will choose the male form for any further description of the profession of which I was and am still a part.

The people with their names on the door to the company office were the business owners. They were the "partners." As a matter of fact, it was illegal to practice architecture as a corporation until the 1970s, as I recall. The courts were very fussy about the matter of personal liability in the practice of professions. Architects also were forbidden from advertising in the usual business fashion until the1970s or so, as well. Employer architects discouraged even their senior people from getting licenses. They were protecting their ivory tower.

Job titles provided some means for architectural office production staff members to distinguish themselves. There were chief draftsmen, job captains, project directors, specification writers, estimators, delineators, and others. Nowadays, they have several categories of architects in the production organization. Most are not licensed.

After a period of time, I finally followed the advice I had been getting from Louis Bersbach. I learned that Louis was a slow-pay employer and with a growing family responsibility, I decided to move on.

I went to work for a small firm of two partners, Cyrus Peseck and Glen Shifflet. One of my former classmates at the university gave me the tip on the opening. He was Gordon Schlicting, a talented artist and versatile designer. The lead draftsman was Clair Armstrong who had been at the University several years before I attended.

The office was on the second floor of a two-story building on Marquette Avenue. It was not more than a quarter mile from my first job location. While the work was interesting in its variety, the atmosphere of the office was not pleasant. Peseck sat in his office behind a large mahogany desk and ran things. He also did the marketing.

When I arrived, the office had a large, high-school building in the plan-production phase as well as some small commercial buildings. Shifflet managed production, but in a strange fashion. For one thing, he was thrifty and went to extreme lengths to keep costs down. As an example, he required us draftsmen to turn in our pencil stubs to him before we were issued a new pencil! Good drafting pencils produced by several different manufacturers cost about 10 to 15 cents each. When a pencil got short from sharpening, it was customary to put the stub in an extender where it would serve well until about two inches long. H.A. Rogers, an architect and engineer supply store, was just across the street from the office. We draftsmen suspected that Shifflet would buy pencils only by a dozen or less each time he shopped because he was afraid we would take pencils home!

Pesek was a very attractive fellow who dressed well and carried himself like a man of some means. We heard that his mother, a widow, had invested the cash she inherited in a successful business venture. She had a substantial interest in a little company up in Two Harbors on Lake Superior. The company made sandpaper and was called Minnesota Mining and Manufacturing Co. It is now known as 3M. The last I heard of Cy Pesek, he was an executive vice-president of the company and was directing their world-wide facilities program.

✧ ***Billie: I grew up hearing about 3M. It sticks in my mind because they invented Scotch Tape and Post-It Notes.***

The office finally completed the large projects and I was surplus. Within a couple of days of being laid off, I found another job in an interesting industry. It was with a well-known and highly regarded woodworking mill. I had always enjoyed working with wood, both as carpenter and cabinet maker.

Meanwhile, Doris was about to graduate from the University of Minnesota.

UNIVERSITY OF MINNESOTA COMMENCEMENT CONVOCATION:
WINTER QUARTER 1937

THURSDAY, MARCH 18, 1937, ELEVEN O'CLOCK

DEPARTMENT OF ARCHITECTURE:
BACHELOR OF INTERIOR ARCHITECTURE

DORIS LUCILLE ANDERSON

Doris graduated in early spring of 1937. I was so proud of her.

There were between 1 and 20 candidates for graduation in each of several departments. However, in her department, there was only one—my Sweetie Pie!

CHAPTER 5

Starting our Life together

We were so much in love we didn't want to wait anymore, and I had a good job. We got married July 25, 1937. We set up housekeeping in Minneapolis.

(By that time, I had two shoe boxes full of shoelaces!)

✧ **Billie: Mom's dress was hand-stitched by one of her aunts. My grandmother, Mother, and Myra all wore this dress.**

From the *Stanley Promoter* (local Newspaper):

Miss Anderson Wears Mother's Bridal Gown

Doris Lucille Anderson, daughter of Mr. and Mrs. A.L. Anderson of Stanley, N.D., became the bride of Stanley Allen Moe of Minneapolis on Sunday, July 25…

The Bride's dress of white peau de sole had been worn by her mother at her marriage 28 years ago. It was of floor length fashioned with a tunic. The high collar and square yoke were trimmed in embroidered net…Mrs. W.W. Andersgord of Turtle Lake was matron of honor and Donald Moe of Minneapolis; brother of the bridegroom, was best man…

The family gathers in Doris' childhood home—in the front yard

After our wedding, we had a one-week honeymoon at Doris' family cabin on Lake Lida, Minnesota. Then, we both went to work in earnest—Doris as an interior designer for a very successful interior architectural decorator, and I in the woodworking mill.

Lake Lida, Minnesota

Mother and Dad Creating Together (by Billie)
After Mother and Dad married, they lived in a basement apartment that belonged to a lady named Myra Ward, after whom my sister Myra was named. This was in an area of Minneapolis called Prospect Park.

Despite the depression, Mother and Dad keenly wanted to design a house together, so built one in the middle of 1939 in St. Louis Park, Minnesota. I can only imagine the synergy and excitement they created combining the talents of Mother as an architectural interior designer and Dad as an engineer/architect. They always worked well together, creating houses, inside and out, and found great joy in doing so.

The following are photos from 1939 in the area.

I was born July 31, 1939, and moved into the new house when it was ready, October, 1939. The world was in turmoil then and there were rumblings about possible war. Dad switched employment from the woodworking mill to work for a highly respected architect, Frank Moorman, who became a life-long friend. As there wasn't enough for Dad to do there, he signed on with the Quartermaster Corps and was sent to West Yellowstone, Montana.

Even though their friends were anxious about getting their careers started amidst worrisome times, their "gang" was so important to each of them, they actively kept in touch and created many pleasure moments together.

***We always made time for fun stuff with the gang!* — Stan**

CHAPTER 6

Fun Times with the Gang!

Looking Back (written July 12, 2001— age 87)
One satisfying aspect of becoming more "mature" (never old) is recalling past adventures and friendships. I have many happy memories of the times spent with a fine group of friends while in college in the thirties and subsequent decades.

A small group became fast friends during college days. Dating couples that later, and not surprisingly, became married couples: Hop (Phillip) and Vi (Violet) Layman, Dave and Gladys Hamrin, Norman and Harriet Fugelso, Bert and Mae Larsen, and Stan and Doris Moe. In addition to those couples, there was, Billie Irwin, who had been one of Doris's college roommates and became Billie's godmother, and later became Mrs. Cyrus Guss. Other couples came and went over the years. Among those were Leonard and Edwina Larsen, the Franklins, and the Mortensons (Laurie, another one of Doris' college roommates, and Mort). Our friendships remained constant even though some couples scattered.

Dr. Billie Irwin Guss & Billie Crouse
Circa 1985

Gatherings were often arranged around University of Minnesota Homecoming, Fourth of July, New Year's Eve, Memorial Day, or any other good reason for having a party. In the early days, there were weekend or one-day excursions. Low-budget affairs initially, which became more ambitious as we became more prosperous.

I remember one episode when we decided to canoe on the St. Croix River. We picked up rental canoes at a place in Stillwater, Minnesota. Because there was a nice breeze from the south, we held blankets up as sails in order to go upstream without paddling. The idea was to travel upstream, have a picnic, then drift with the current back to Stillwater. All went well until it began to rain. We quickly divided up the food and blankets and turned the canoes over. Each couple then had a picnic shelter. When the rain stopped, we headed for home but now the breeze from the south was brisk. We had to paddle our way home.

Harriet and Norm Fugelso had moved to Duluth, Minnesota in 1938. Because Duluth and the North Shore area were favorite destinations for people from the Twin Cities, the Fugelso's home became a popular gathering place. Later, their cabin on Eagle Lake in Wisconsin became another favorite. Harriet continued to encourage our visits after Norman passed away.

Whenever I think of Eagle Lake, I am reminded of the "cannon episode." One Fourth of July, the Fugelsos had invited the group to Eagle Lake. Doris and I had flown in a few days early. On our way to Duluth we stopped in to visit with the Laymans in St. Louis Park, Minnesota. Because we were going to Eagle Lake a few days before the group would arrive, we asked if we could transport anything to Eagle Lake for them. Hop suggested we take his cannon to the lake for a field test. Sounded like a good idea, so we put the cannon in our car, bought a can of black powder, and headed for the lake.

When we reached Eagle Lake, Norm Fugelso and I evaluated the cannon. It was a most unusual device. The steel barrel had been made from an old railroad axle. The carriage was heavy timber mounted on small steel wheels. The cannon was painted solid white. This was most unconventional, we thought. Norm and I had a full day before the other guests arrived, so we thought we might improve the cannon's appearance. We decided to add some decorations. Adhesive plastic tape in red, white, and blue became spiral strips around the barrel. We devised British Flags for the sides of the carriage. We studied old *National Geographic* magazines for the design. The results were quite dramatic.

The next day was the Fourth. When the rest of the group arrived, we were all ready to celebrate. To add to the festivities, we made up a few batches of "moose milk:" 1-part Crème de Cacao, 2-parts Canadian Club whiskey, and 3-parts skim milk. The concoction is whipped up in a blender filled with crushed ice and is very smooth and refreshing!

Firing the cannon was great fun. Small charges of powder and wrapping-paper wads stuffed in the barrel produced beautiful sounds and impressive clouds of smoke. I still remember the wonderful echoes. It attracted neighbors, who were quite eager to try the "moose milk." The noise annoyed some of the neighbors on the other side of the lake. Even though no formal complaints were filed, we decided it wise to tone things down after firing a dozen or so shots during the day.

For many years I had pictures of Norm, Bert, Leonard, and Hop standing at attention and saluting, with flags in hand, when we fired the cannon!

PART III

1941: Career Moves in Wild Idaho and Montana

Photo of an old Mormon barn with the Grand Tetons behind it
(photo courtesy of Ken Edgein)

CHAPTER 7

1941: Exploring the Wilds

Great Falls, Idaho; Yellowstone, Montana; Idaho Falls, Idaho

✧ **Billie: Dad was hired by the Quartermaster Corps which was to oversee the construction of a military camp planned for the Henry's Lake basin in Idaho. At that time, the Quartermaster Corps was part of the Army.**

Looking Back (from audiotapes circa 2006-2009)
My friends and I had draft cards and were eligible for military duty. We told ourselves the United States was not at war, but we were still aware of the White House's support of England.

Henry's Lake Military Camp Project in Great Falls, Idaho
I met with Van Teylinger (Van T.) who offered me a position on the Henry's Lake Project in Great Falls, Idaho. I called some friends who had signed up for the project and finally decided it would be wise to take the job.

When I got home and told Doris about my meeting with Van T., she was shocked. We had felt so comfortable with my work at Moorman's. Doris and I had lived in the home we'd designed and built for only seven months. Billie would be turning two years old in July. The prospect of changing jobs that would necessitate separation was more than we could deal with in a rational way. I don't think I had a full night's sleep for days.

I notified the Moorman office of my decision to leave. Frank Moorman, who headed the company, flew back from St. Louis to talk me out of leaving. However, he could see the "handwriting on the wall" and acknowledged that he had limitations put on his design projects as a result of the war. We parted friends.

Now, I had to pack for Great Falls. We got a trunk out of the basement. It was a fine steamer-wardrobe trunk, one that Doris had with her in college. (Billie took this trunk to college seventeen years later.) It seems strange today to even consider burdening oneself with a trunk to take any trip, even when one might be away for months.

I had never been to Great Falls. I went by train and it involved sitting up overnight. The seats in coaches were not comfortable—bench type with backs that could be tilted forward and back. This was to make it possible to arrange seating that was easily adjusted to suit the direction of the travel of the train. The candy vendor had pillows for rent. I took advantage of that touch of comfort and rented one. I took my shoes off, so I must have taken a nap using the whole width of the bench seat. The trains were not often packed with passengers.

When I arrived at the Great Falls train station about mid-morning, I noticed that my shoes seemed to have shrunk in size overnight. It was difficult to get them on. Then I recovered my trunk that had been delivered to the baggage room. Since I didn't know where I would be staying, I checked the trunk.

After having a snack of breakfast near the station, I became painfully aware of my tight shoes. The many hours of inactivity on the train and the increase in altitude at Great Falls had caused my feet to swell. This might not have been much of a problem if I had been wearing old shoes. I was, however, wearing a new pair of shoes. I suppose I felt a little "flush" with my new job and wanted to make a good impression. They were cordovan leather (noted for its stiffness). These shoes needed some "breaking in" and I was in a poor place to handle that chore. I removed my shoes and socks and walked down the street barefoot looking for a shoe repair shop. I felt like a fool. Luckily, I found one nearby. It took about an hour for the shoe repairman to soften and stretch my new footgear.

Great Falls was a modest-sized city. I was happy to note that the office was only a short walk from the train station. When I reported for duty, I quickly realized that Van T. had done quite a recruiting job. As I looked around the drafting room, I saw many old friends. Architects' offices in the Twin Cities must have been de-populated.

The men I saw were old classmates and others who had graduated from the University of Minnesota in the years surrounding my graduation. I doubt if any of them were more than thirty years old. Because of business conditions and the slowness in recovery of the construction industry in the 1930s, people with architectural training were vulnerable to shifts in business. We changed jobs quite often. That accounted for Van T.'s success in recruiting. Most young couples with children relied on a single wage-earner for support. A surprising number of the crew from Minnesota had brought families with them to Great Falls. Those with working wives like mine traveled single status.

After learning more about the project and my technical assignment, I felt certain I would be kept very busy.

A day or two after I arrived in Great Falls, I managed to find a rental room in a house not too far from the office. The home was owned by a middle-aged couple who seemed distant, but I surmised the reason. Renting rooms might have been new to them and they didn't quite know how to talk to a stranger in their home. The room was convenient to the office, and the rent was twenty dollars per week. I retrieved my trunk from the rail station and settled in for what I assumed would be several months of concentrated effort.

A Letter Excerpt from Stanley to Doris

Saturday, 3 p.m.

Hello Sweetheart,

I am settled at last in a room for $20.00. (In Great Falls.) Some rooms could be had for $15, but they were holes.

I would rather be at Moorman's, but I just don't know if the income would be enough.

The job is so mixed up here that it will likely last quite a while and so will the income.

I just got back from the office and it is a little after nine. Walked by several cheap saloons and dance halls. A very refined atmosphere, as you can imagine. It must be tiresome for those who live here all year round.

We were monkeying with a large Photostat machine they just got at the office. No one knows how to run any of the stuff and the government furnishes the finest equipment for them to play with. It really is a shame. When they need one thing here, they buy a dozen or a hundred. It seems of no consequence if no one uses them. Fine Stuff! Taxpayers' money all for nothing.

So long, Sweetheart. All my love forever and ever and longer than that.
Stanley.

Looking Back (continued)
Great Falls was a "western" town. Ranchers, cowboys, and farmers were well represented in the saloons in town on weekends.

One of the most prominent bars was the Silver Dollar Saloon. The name was appropriate since it was a large establishment with silver dollars inlaid in the floor and bar tops. A main feature was the fine collection of Western paintings and sculptures on display in glass showcases. Charles Russell and Frederick Remington works were the most prominent. I was told that this was the best and largest collection of Russell's work in existence at that time.

The Quartermaster Corps expected us to develop plans for a military training camp. However, the Quartermaster Corps sent us drawings from World War I! They had been used as a basis for the construction of facilities in the Panama Canal Zone. But how could the facilities for the Canal Zone be adapted as a "winter training camp" in the mountains? This construction seemed to be totally inappropriate for a setting in the mountains for what was to be a winter training camp, where soldiers were to be trained in arctic warfare involving skis and so on.

We had heard that West Yellowstone, Montana, had been chosen for a field operation headquarters. It was the residential community nearest the campsite in the Henry's Lake basin of Idaho. Van T. walked into the office one afternoon and said that his partner, Mr. Shanley, needed some help in the field office in West Yellowstone. There was one position open. He invited anyone who might be interested to put his name on a slip of paper and put it into his hat.

Without hesitation, I put my name in the hat along with a half dozen others. One of the secretaries was asked to pull out the winning name. I was happily surprised my name was drawn. My landlady was kind enough to store my trunk at her home. For some reason I found it easy to limit my baggage to one suitcase of clothes and essentials.

Van T. congratulated me. Then, he drove me to West Yellowstone a few days later.

I learned that Van T. was an immigrant from the Netherlands and really studied American history, particularly of the West. He seemed to know a great many interesting things about this part of the country. His constant commentary on the geography, geology, Indians, frontiersmen, and the flora and fauna of the region kept me spellbound and made the trip seem quite short.

We arrived in West Yellowstone in late afternoon. The setting was so very pleasant with its heavy wooded surroundings and mountain resort atmosphere. Van T. knew just where to go. We checked in at the Madison Hotel on the entrance street leading to the park. It was, perhaps, the only real hotel in town. It was a picturesque place with a log cabin entrance, a large fireplace in the lobby and cozy rooms. It was to be my "home away from home" for quite a long time, but at the time I thought it might be a short time. It was only a block away from the office where I would be working. Several nearby restaurants seemed to be prospering in this little tourist town.

CHAPTER 8

1941: Letters & Reflections from Yellowstone

For one who has led something of a quiet life in one spot,
I am getting around like a nomad. — Stan

✧ **Billie: Dad's bosses were Van Teylinger (Van T.), Bill Jones, and Mr. George Shanley.**

Letter Excerpt from Stan to Doris - 1941

Sweetie Pie,

I have been transferred to West Yellowstone for a week or so. It is 6,700 feet high here among the clouds and is it cold! I was the only one asked to come here—the envy of the office. We came down in Van T.'s Cadillac. Some buggy! The job is not dull, that's for sure. I am going through Yellowstone Park this weekend with some of the boys and will get some color pictures. Continue to send my mail to my Great Falls address, for now.

Looking Back

The next day I reported to the field office and met Mr. George Shanley, Van T.'s partner. Both the office and Shanley were a big surprise to me. The office was in what had been an auto repair garage. It was quite primitive as some of the construction was of logs. The building was heated by what were called "chunk stoves." These were, simply, old steel drums that had been used for oil or other material that had been fitted with some cast-iron parts such as legs, a door to the stove and a chimney pipe outlet for the smoke. The stove was operated in a horizontal position and was fueled by wood, preferably large pieces with knots.

Across the street from my hotel was a large and impressive rustic structure owned and operated by the Yellowstone Park agency. In addition to a large dining room and other public accommodations, it was also the railway station. Major national parks that had been established and had grown up in the early part of the twentieth century, were closely related to train travel. Before the popularity of automobiles and the development of a good national road system, most park visitors arrived by train. They were then bussed around among the several large and impressive hotels in the parks. The regular arrival and departure of the trains always seemed to attract a lot of attention. This was the end of the rail line that entered the area from the east.

Hello Sweetheart, (no date was provided)

Some town—really a nice one—quite picturesque. It will be pleasant working here and very interesting. There are now about 15 men in the office and there's talk of 100 more! Frankly, we don't know what we are doing and maybe never will. There will be some 1000 buildings; some of them are over 400 feet long!

The camp is 14 miles west of the town of West Yellowstone. Really, it is in Idaho. The camp-town will occupy a space some six miles long. It will be about twice the size of Minot. It will be made to withstand temperatures which are expected to be about 50 degrees below.

The government quartermaster will be in here soon to take charge.

Francis (Frank) Meisch (a friend from the University of Minnesota) and I may go up to Glacier Park over some weekend before the snow closes it up. I would like to take some color pictures and he wants to paint.

We will have a nice time here. I find that I can stay in a decent hotel for what I can pay for a room in a home.

To be perfectly honest, I see the mistake in the prospect of your coming here. I would never have come here knowing what I know now. It seems that a lot of the reputable boys from Minneapolis said they would come but didn't, so, I would not be so badly off if I had turned it down.

I will write Moorman in a few days, when I hear from you.

I spotted a covey of partridges on the way in. We are making friends with some of the local boys for hunting.

Love you, Honey.

Be sure to send me my social security card as there is no pay without it.

Sweetheart,

It's a wild, wild, life here in West Yellowstone. I have teamed up with a fellow who came from Holland four and a half years ago. His name is Menno Broadman, the nicest fellow you can imagine. He has a second-hand Chevrolet of 1936 vintage and he is going to take us through the park Sunday. This will be an experience I'll never forget. Perhaps that is ample compensation for the inconvenience that I am undergoing.

I wish you could be up here with me.

There was a sprinkle of rain this p.m. and we had an enormous vivid rainbow right across the street! Can you imagine it? It is really cloud-land here.

The weather of the country seems to start out right here. The elevation is 6,700 feet compared with about 720 feet in Minneapolis. Mr. Shanley, who I am working with here, in appearance is a typical character out of a Dickens novel. He is short and stubby and a little like W.C. Fields. He wears the loudest checked coat and vest I have ever seen. On top of that he wears a pork-pie hat. Really a comical sight, but he has a disposition like a wounded lion. This place would be too much for an extended period, but for a while, it can be fun.

I miss you and little Bill more than I can tell you. But I have been covering so many miles in the last weeks, I feel like a globe-trotter.

For one who has led something of a quiet life in one spot, I am getting around like a nomad.

Love to you and Little Bill, Stanley

Looking Back

As the weeks went by, I could see that things were getting slow. The tourists had almost disappeared. But a few businesspeople hung on. Our project employed a few dozen land surveyors and other field engineers who had to have a place to live. Some were locals with family; others were married people from other towns who took up residence in tourist cabins.

Letter Excerpts (not necessarily in order because there were no dates)

Saturday Evening (approximately September 2, 1941)

Sweetie Pie,

I'm back from work today. We were engulfed by "Brass Hats" this afternoon so I worked right up to five o'clock.

Billie: Brass Hats refer to those Army and Navy Military officers who have lots of brass on their hats.

Tomorrow morning, we go to Yellowstone.

My friend here, Menno Brackman, the Dutch boy I told you about, got a hold of the payroll scale today and we checked up on the wages. Jones was tops with $500 a month. There were two men (old ones) who are sort of engineers at $300. One fellow from Hoxley and Bissell in Minneapolis at $280, and down in the $225 and $250 range…no names. I know Andy got $250. Frank Meisch is listed at $225. I thought Vic was given $350, but now I doubt it. I wasn't on the list, but I am being paid $285, so I think that I must be a key man (whatever that means).

The architects in Montana are somewhat like its cow punchers—rough and poorly paid. Normal wages here are about $150. Minneapolis sure is high.

So far, I've only received your special delivery letter. There's no service out of here except by airmail. So please write me a line. If you continue to send them to Great Falls it takes a day longer, but they will reach me, anyway. But this next week (September 8th onward) you can write me here by way of Shanley, Wandelingen, & Hemmingson. That way if I leave here my letters will follow me around the country.

Hotel Madison, West Yellowstone, Montana
September 9, 1941

Sweetheart,

I think you would get quite a kick out of all the people around here. Literally, hundreds of dudes. It seems as if everyone who comes out here first buys cowboy hats, pants, and belts. Then, they try walking down the street bow-legged. Some of them don't do a very convincing job.

A little boy, four years old, left his piggy bank in the middle of the room downstairs here. Now he just yelled down the stairs for some of the people to watch his pennies and nickels for him. It makes me homesick for Billie. I have a feeling that I will see her soon.

The hotel here is filling up with red-nosed people who are tired of travelling. The county has only a few stragglers left. The main tourist crowd has gone to warmer climes. I am doing okay and am very busy now.

We are planning this project at a much larger scale. My plot plan covers a mile and a half. There are over a thousand individual buildings—about 100 different types. I am laying out railroad tracks and all that sort of thing, kind of strange work for an architect draftsman, but I seem to be the only man who Shanley can get to do this sort of thing. None of the rest of them seem to accomplish anything. The lobby is full of engineers and officers—talking shop, of course. That is all they do around here.

I am quite sure that Frank Moorman would like me back anyway, even if he had someone else. He can use all the competent men he can get. I am doing okay here for now, and the main thing is, they apparently like my work.

I have been waiting for word from you before I write back. So far, I haven't had any. This is certainly the end of the world. It takes 24 hours to get to Great Falls by bus (275 miles) and two days by train. Can you imagine? The plane is the only thing.

We are going trout fishing up here tomorrow evening. I am going to try to get some black and white movies of it. For now, I am going to mail this and go out for a Coke and then to bed. Be a good girl.

All my love, Stanley

P.S. I am sending a little package for you and Billie, but it may take a week to get to you.

Thursday Evening (date not found)

Hello Hon!

I just got your letter and am already answering it. It is only 5:15. I just finished talking to Mr. Shanley and he said that I would be here for two or three weeks longer. I think it will be nearer to five weeks.

I still haven't been able to cash my check. One hundred fifty people with an average of $50 a week or so really depletes the town's cash. That's about $7500.00 worth of cash a week.

I haven't got my camera bag yet. I may try for a better deal in Great Falls this weekend. It certainly is a funny place to live. Well, will "see you soon" in another letter. I must go out to eat and will finish later this evening. I am going to find a cheaper room if possible. I am tired of living like a duke! Even so, it isn't so swell.

Hello again!

—I'm back after working an hour and talking with Menno the remainder of the evening. I just figured out my finances (old stuff, eh?) and am sending you about $40 Friday and will send about $60 on the next pay day. I have some laundry bills to pay and will have to stand some of the gas to Great Falls. I am buying a meal ticket at another restaurant and am checking out of the hotel tomorrow night.

September 14, 1941

Hi Honey,

As the boss, Mr. Shanley, lives in the same hotel here, I intend to move to the TEEPEE across the street. (The lobby was built as a teepee and the name of the hotel is in all capital letters.) I have had to work all day Saturday and late in the evening because I have been too handy.

We saw Yellowstone Park today. The day broke wet and cold (40 degrees). We crossed the Continental Divide while it was really snowing. I had hoped to visit Tom McCort but found that he is stationed at Mammoth Springs. It is in the north part of the park and too far away for one day. We may go in again before the snow gets too deep. I hope the sun will shine just once. The colors defy description. You would really like them. Billie would like the bears, I am sure. Some of them come and put their paws on the car! They are really big up here.

Wed. Evening

Hello Honey,

Today was payday and now I think I will stay awhile. I was very unhappy last night and was all set "to throw in the sponge." I prayed for guidance to do the right thing. (You know me.) A solution sort of presented itself. I received my regular weekly check of $66.00. I told Mr. Shanley I wanted to be transferred back to Great Falls this weekend and he asked why?

You see, I have kept my room for $20 a month there because I planned on being here only a short time and I wanted a nice safe place to headquarter and leave my stuff. So far, I have had to pay $1.50 a day for a room here. This is a tough place to stay by the week. I plan on getting a cabin someplace and have my own stove. I told Mr. Shanley that I couldn't afford to stay as I would go broke.

He went on to tell how we are getting along so well, and he would like me to stay on until all the site planning was finished. That may be a matter of weeks or months, even, who knows?

The red tape makes everything take longer. He told me if money was the main thing, he would change my classification, so now I am earning $360 a month with the new raise (at least I get a raise of $75 we hoped for).

I feel sorry for some of the engineering draftsmen who have come here from Omaha to work. One tonight shared that he has a wife and two children and sent home only $25 of his weekly $40 check. I am one of the highest paid fellows around. I must have something, as one of the architects from Minneapolis, for them to offer me over $200.

Times are tough and I guess I am lucky.

All my love and kisses, Stanley

Sweetie Pie,

I found a cabin with bath and innerspring mattress with a wood cookstove for $1.00 a day which is cheap in these parts. That will keep me until snowfall, and it freezes. Then it will be the Army's problem to take care of us.

I certainly look forward to your very newsy letters. They give me great comfort and enjoyment. It's almost as good as being home. Be good and write as often as you can, Sweetheart.

There is a great commotion upstairs—a woman started screaming because a "night bug" got in her room. They are the size of a bat and look like a June bug. They are quite horrible and terrifying. I hope I don't run into one. I have seen them dead on the street during the day but never saw one on the "fly," as it were.

I have no trouble covering miles of paper, do I? Well, you have wanted letters and here they are by the dozen. I always do chatter, you know, even on paper.

All my love to you and Billie,

Stanley

P.S. There is an awful influx of inexperienced draftsmen. "Cats and dogs," Van calls them. They are hired for the routine work.

✧ ✧ ✧

Hi Honeybunch,

I'm home by my fire (a usual beginning). I got your sweet letter today and I'm so happy to hear that everything is okay. I'm lonesome for you and Bill, too, but I'm trying not to let it get to me. A couple of times I almost packed my bags and went to the train. I gave up my room in Great Falls but packed my trunk and had it ready to be picked up. Somehow, I get more tied up here each day.

Mr. Shanley said this morning that we would be here perhaps a month or more. I'm glad that Bill Jones said that last Saturday night they all celebrated in Great Falls because they thought they wouldn't have to move. But Sunday, the quartermaster wired, and they moved yesterday. Some of the fellows lost as high as $90 in rent paid in advance. Really tough (the Army is tough).

Bill said that while planned work would likely be done on Dec 8th, that making tracings of it might consume the rest of the winter for a good crew. He seems as uncertain about it as any one of us, though. I found that I knew more about the job than any of them. It seems that our work really has more importance now than theirs. They have a lot of individual buildings to take care of and to arrange them all as they should be. Our drawings here are 3' x 6' and at a scale of 100' to 1." At that, it takes six of the sheets side by side to take care of the whole containment.

The engineering staff here is bidding for my services as architectural consultant, for their building. Power plant, sewage disposal, water, and so on, for a city the size of St. Cloud; or 35,000 people. Some responsibility, but I suppose I can take it.

If Mr. Shanley agrees, I will be here at the site until the end and pretty much as my own boss. I will have, as a structural man, a professor of structural engineering at Montana University. I'm a little shaky in my boots, but of course don't let on. Now, what do you think of your hubby? But don't get me wrong, I'm not bragging. I'm going to do my best, no matter what.

Menno and I had Bill Jones tell us to keep track of our overtime and he will try to get it for us. If that is the case, I might get another hundred or so. We'll see.

I'm really glad you're not here. You couldn't get used to the cold. Gas heat spoils a person.

Menno and I went to see Sargent York. It wasn't bad, but it cost 55 cents. Big city prices here. Then everybody walks home down the middle of the street just like in Ross! All the sidewalks are covered with ice.*

I think I'll be home before Christmas for sure. Or else, I'll have to stake a claim and build my own cabin. I've paid enough rent to own one.

My supply of paper is running low so will say good night.

Your honey, Stanley

P.S. I often dream of you.

Sept 15, 1941, Monday evening

Hi Sweetheart,

I received my billfold and my pictures of Billie in the mail from Great Falls. Billie is a little sweetheart, all right. I have been showing the pictures to everyone.

I put plenty of sentimental value on the billfold. It was like finding a long-lost friend.

All the trains and planes have stopped, and mail now goes by stage to Idaho Falls and Bozeman. We can really consider ourselves isolated.

Tuesday evening

Hello Honey,

I am now officially getting $81.00 per week or $360 a month. While I think it will last about six weeks here at the most, we can pay some bills, Sweetheart. We will feel like new people when the bills are all paid, won't we?

Contrary to popular belief, this mountain water is not good to drink. It all comes from wells and is so full of mineral salts that it is not good for the stomach. It's like Epsom salts. So, all we drink is coffee—by the gallon. Milk is 10 cents a glass, so we don't drink much of that. Last night I became quite sick to my stomach and rolled and tossed in misery for a couple of hours.

Menno and I went out for a couple of milkshakes tonight. Now, we have enough calories for today. These people around here are mostly heavy liquor consumers. Not a decent single woman in town according to reports and obvious appearances. Morals here might put a monkey to shame. I don't know what makes them that way. A person would have a very low opinion of the female tribe, if he had to judge by the material here.

My social life, however, doesn't involve them, so I get along very well.

We have new management in our favorite restaurant. The waitress, while attractive, has a following like a female dog and for no better purpose, we are quite sure.

Off to bed while my room is still warm.

Love, Stanley

P.S. There are a lot of moose and bear around here. Plenty wild. We are 30 miles to Bozeman (the nearest town), 80 miles to St. Anthony, and a hop, skip, and jump to Salt Lake City. They are preparing for six or eight feet of snow and a mean temperature during the winter of 50 below. It is rated as one of the coldest spots in the U.S. and has gotten as low as 72 below in the last 10 years.

*When Stan wrote longhand in his diary or letters about books or movies, he could only underline the titles. In his **Looking Back** pieces in this book, titles of books and movies are italicized, as is the current style.

Sept 22, 1941: Still in Yellowstone

Hi Sweetheart,

It was so cold last night that I got up several times during the night to get my fire going. I caught a nasty head cold over the weekend and am sitting by the fire doctoring it tonight. Things seem okay, otherwise.

My trunk is all packed and sitting in my closet in Grand Forks. I will send for it if I don't go back. I brought my books and camera equipment back here with me to do a little work. I hope I get a chance to accomplish great things. I have a half-roll of color film that ought to be good for now.

Sept 26, 1941

My Honey,

It's Saturday noon and because Menno and I put in a long day yesterday (11:30 p.m.) I will write you now. We had to revise the camp layout—a tough job—so many people had made mistakes that we had to go over the whole thing.

My darling Honey-Pal,

I got your wonderful letter and just finished reading it. I started reading at dinner and Mr. Shanley sat down with us, so I couldn't finish. I was so pleased because it was so long and newsy. Almost as if you were here. I think you are the best letter writer in the world. No foolin!

You would die laughing if you could see me here writing with my hat and topcoat on. It isn't quite so cold today, so I didn't wear my sheepskin. When the sun does shine the skies are probably bluer than any place in the world.

I'm sorry Billie's slippers didn't fit. Mrs. Eagle (what a name) who operates the store where I got them said I could have them exchanged. She is very nice. The Eagles own more than half the town. They have sent eight children through college: Stanford, Columbia, MIT, etc. They have two more to go. Menno and I have really been sweating trying to check 1200 or more buildings with the new War Department lists. But since we finally got our books to balance this p.m., we are taking an evening off. I wish you could see our office—an old auto-repair shop and the heating plant consists of an old oil barrel. The stove either overheats or doesn't heat at all. All they burn is pine logs cut last summer and are they ever hard to start a fire. Oh Boy! Incidentally, that's what I'm trying to burn in my cabin. They crackle, pop, and sputter with all the sap and pitch in them.

Got a letter from Mom tonight. They have had a snowstorm on some of their uncut grain. Don and Helen were down, and they all went hunting. They came upon your dad out hunting with Dave Handy. They were stuck in a mud hole and Don and my dad pulled them out with some barbed wire. Primitive, eh? It was very wet, but Dad got six pheasants. It makes me lonesome for home and hunting.

Poor Meisch. He'd have fits if he knew that I was making $360. It would help a lot if we buy some tax bonds. It would help when we pay our punishment for big earnings.

I'm proud of you, Sweet! You really must be going to town, $2000! That ain't hay! Keep it up and we'll go to Bermuda! "Make it while the sun shines and salt it away" is a good policy.

✧ **Billie: Mother worked for a large interior designer. She must have in one month sold $2000 worth of work. In those days people didn't buy new upholstered furniture, they reupholstered what they had. And, they didn't buy curtains, they had draperies made.**

DAMN my fire. I sit and coax it like an old car. I have to do all but push it. Say, will you do me a favor? It's a bit off the subject, but I just thought of it. I can't get my Home Movies magazine here. Will you buy current copies and send them to me? I am trying to digest all I can now, while I have time.

That book you sent really is a WOW! Of course, it's "history," but I like it. The North's side of the Civil War and it is just as interesting as Gone with the Wind for me.

I sure wish I could see the house. I'll certainly be glad to see it filled with nice accessories. We needed some more furniture and decorations. It must be very nice. How is Billie at "un-decorating"? Or has she "outgrown" that phase already.

Be a good girl and get to bed earlier. I worry about your health. I'm afraid you chase too much and get too little sleep, Beautiful! Because, you're most important to me.

All my love forever, Tootsie Snooks! Stanley

Sunday, Sept 28

Sweetie-Pie,

Here I am again and without my darling! We returned safe and sound from Bozeman last night. We ran into three snowstorms on the way and arrived there in a downpour of rain. I couldn't find anything I wanted except a necktie and a couple pairs of wool socks.

We went out to the site today and took a lot of colored pictures of the valley. I'm soft, I guess, for I was panting badly after climbing up a lesser mountain. We got a view of the Grand Tetons of Wyoming. Truly wonderful. Some time I'm going to venture into them for some pictures. I found that they received their name from a striking resemblance to a reclining figure with a marvelous pectoral development. Hence the French name for the Grand Tetons is "The Big Teat" and the Tetons mean the 3 breasts. HA HA, some stuff! We drove around Henry's Lake and stopped for a bottle of Budweiser beer at a dude ranch. Tonight, we went to see Dive Bomber—a wonderful color picture full of flying shots.

Love, Stanley

P.S. I miss you and Bill so. I never knew I could love anyone so much. I think you write the best letters in the world, My Sweet!

A Photo of an old Mormon barn with the Grand Tetons behind it on a stormy day (photo courtesy of Ken Edgein)

Letter from Frank Moorman (prior employer from A. Moorman and Company, Minneapolis, MN, Architect and Construction Managers of Bank Buildings.)

September 30, 1941

Dear Stan,

We were surely glad to get your letter which was very interesting and indicates that your work at Yellowstone is most unusual and on a big scale. The others read it also and they join me in sending our best wishes.

We all will always be glad to see you, when you return to the cities. We are still very busy and up to the present time are still able to get steel.

We are planning to commence work at Escanaba in a few weeks.

With kind regards,
I remain sincerely yours,
Frank Moorman

Dear Doris,

Menno and I have spent a pleasant evening studying reinforced concrete. The plan is to continue all the way through the structural stuff. It is surprising what one can forget but is easy to recover.

It's cold and raining. The little wood range keeps it comfortable in here. More so than the hotel, except I can see my breath in the morning. I usually rise at 6:30 to start a fire, then jump back in bed to snooze until 7:15 or so.

Sweetheart,

Menno and I walk up to town every evening which is about a mile and a half round trip. He lives a block from my place, so we get together often. We have no appetite and think maybe the exercise will help us out. The food is either getting monotonous or we are hard to please. It may be both.

Friday evening, we are going to attend a large banquet of the office force. There will be about one hundred people there at least. Some affair. Some of the boys are even getting up an orchestra and are looking for a girl singer. They now have several bowling teams, etc. One of the ambitious bowlers is a power plate engineer who has been state bowling champ of Nebraska several times. But with only a couple of bowling places in town, and plenty of local leagues, it is hard to find a place to indulge in the sport. It is the same here as elsewhere. The sport interest is way ahead of the facilities. By the time they are increased to capacity, the sport will be on the decline.

Menno has been busy having his car overhauled. A '36 Chevrolet takes a lot of tinkering and he wants it to be sound and run like new. He is very fussy.

Say, how do you like the '42 Chevy? Looks like a young Cadillac, don't you think? If we were to fall into a million, it would be nice to get one. I've seen a few on the street lately and they look plenty smooth.

Tonight, I have made up my mind to write Moorman to come back to his office. I am convinced that it will be best if he has the same set up as before.

If I lived here all year, I couldn't really be contented. I feel as if I can't stand this cockeyed government set up; not one minute longer. No overtime pay, but no limit on overtime hours. It is too impersonal. I liked Frank Moorman and his immense sense of fairness. That is not known around here at all. Everyone works like the devil and everyone is griping. I'll be glad when I leave here.

I wanted to write this soon enough to get to you at the same time my last letter arrived. It was a very grumpy one, since I was not very happy. I'm sorry if it made you unhappy. Here, I'm so grouchy sometimes, so, that is why I don't write more often. I try to write only when I'm in good humor. You are so sweet, Honey, you don't deserve to hear naughty things from me.

Today was the opening of hunting season! And it's a wonderful, cloudy, snowy day. Some people got their limit before breakfast—geese too! I wish I wasn't a working man. However, I'll wait until Saturday or Sunday and go with some of the fellows.

My fire is very slow, so I still am wearing my coat. NOW, I'm blowing on my fire! Darn it anyhow! As soon as I get this place warm, I'm going to bed so I might as well continue this letter until that thing happens.

Will you do me a big favor, Sweetheart? Get me some Russell "Bird Shooter" boots. They have them at Rothchild's, I think. I need them for hunting and for the cold, wet weather. I've worn rubbers every day here. I'm sending you an outline of my foot. You may find some of my shoes around the house for size, of course. Figure on heavy wool socks and send some with them. I really keep you busy, you little angel. I don't know if I deserve you.

My Sweetheart,

We've had quite a time the last couple of days. They fired the coordinator here who had been receiving $90 per week. He is under investigation by the FBI for stirring up unrest in the offices. We had to make affidavits of what he had told us. Menno and I sure hated to do it, but Mr. Van and James requested it and we couldn't renege. A messy business.

Looking Back (Stanley Moe, circa 2005)
This is what I want to write about: hunting season, elk, exploring the Park, fishing the Madison, the grizzly bears and rubbish cans, black bears, buffalo, social life, parties, Henningson's visit, Bull Durham, Bob Richardson, cowboy surveyor, and fly fisherman.

The military camp would be located in an area west of Targhee Pass, near the west entrance to Yellowstone Park. A mountain basin several miles wide extended further west and north. Within this area is Henry's Lake, an important landmark and sports fishing location. North of the lake is a steep mountain slope up to the Continental Divide.

The existing maps of the area were very general in scope and detail. They could only serve for a rough location of a camp. Detailed surveys were necessary before any construction drawings for site development could be made.

When I arrived on the scene there were dozens of surveyors in the field. Some were up near the Continental Divide trying to refine the site data for layout of gunnery ranges. Others were down in the lower areas doing detailed topographic surveys suitable for locating buildings, streets, and utilities.

The survey work was being done on a crash-basis. It was intended that some buildings in the camp be under construction before winter set in. Work up at the higher elevations had a lower priority. They weren't going to build anything at the Continental Divide anyway. The men and equipment were moved around on mules at the Divide. It was not surprising when it was determined the work must be stopped for the season when the snow got too deep for the mules to get around.

Shanley and I kept busy with the planning of the overall development of the camp. We had a small staff in our log cabin office that had been an auto-repair garage at one time. In addition to me, we had one other site-planner, my young Dutch architect friend, Menno Brackman.

We had a fair number of young ladies on the staff oriented to the more social aspects of our existence. As a result, cocktail parties and bar-b-ques were organized. These were always pleasant affairs and well attended. I never knew just how these were financed but was told of a ready source of organizational funds. There were soft drink machines. It seemed that in every large room where people worked, there was one of these large red Coke machines. These were the equivalent of the water cooler as a place for people to gather for relaxation and gossip throughout the day. I can't believe the machines really produced the funds reported.

There were also several dances organized that were well attended. It was at one of these that the third partner of my employer appeared. He was Mr. Henningson from Omaha. At first, he appeared to be what we called a "Blue Serge Suit" person. After a couple of cocktails, he relaxed and entered the light-hearted conversation of our group. Henningson told about his early days as a young cowboy on a ranch north of Yellowstone Park. He said it was customary in those days to pay ranch and farm hands at the end of the season rather than weekly. Since they had full board and room on the ranch, they didn't need much pay along the way. At least that is what the bosses thought. Henningson told of an experience that had a great impact on his life.

At the end of a long and hard season on a ranch (it ended in the fall after the calves were weaned and shipped off to market) Henningson and other ranch hands went into Billings, Montana, for a bit of relaxation. Among the diversions, there was gambling. Henningson had the good fortune of winning a lot of money. Rather than blow it, he put it in the bank. Someone suggested that he might get a college education rather than live the rough life of a ranch hand. This idea appealed to him, with the result that he went to Iowa State and got a degree in civil engineering.

Henningson had a very successful career. He had become one of the leading figures in the engineering field in Nebraska. Some of the details were filled in by his son-in-law, Charles Durham, who was the lead man on the field operations out of West Yellowstone. Chuck was a dignified, quiet person. Tall and handsome, he was quite impressive when dressed up in his dark overcoat and gray fedora hat when not dressed in rough field clothes. Chuck, too, was a graduate of Iowa State.

That brings to mind another interesting person from Iowa State who was on our project. That was Bob Richardson, a civil engineering professor who spent the summer with us on the project. He was a very pleasant and energetic person who added a lot of color to our field operations. He was an expert on many civil engineering matters. I had occasion to use some of the techniques I learned from him in testing water-well production in Algeria many years later. (I think that was about 1984).

I must get ahead a bit with my recollections about Henningson. In the 1980s, there was a very well-known firm of architects and engineers in the Midwest. I believe they were headquartered in Omaha. The firm was known as Henningson, Durham & Richardson. We had friends who knew Durham, but who always spoke of him as Bull Durham. (Remember the tobacco cowboys used to "roll their own"?)

I remember seeing pictures of him in later years and he appeared to be a big burly person. Not quite like the Chuck I had known.

With the onset of real winter, life in West Yellowstone was becoming more difficult for me and the others. The summer resort area and housing were generally not suited to cold weather. My little tourist cabin was an example. It was one small room with a stove, table and bed. There was a small bath with a shower in the corner. The construction consisted of wood siding outside and half-inch cardboard inside. No insulation. The building stood on 18-inch concrete piers and the wind blew underneath. The landlady told me she had to shut off the water when the weather got too cold. She suggested the nearby filling station and did supply a chamber pot. It took a bit of managing to survive in reasonable comfort. But I did.

The stove was a miniature cast-iron woodstove with a cooktop. (Nowadays it would be a valuable collector's item.) This was a lifesaver. I learned a routine that went like this: use flannel sheets in the bed, put my fancy sheepskin coat on top of the bed (I had Doris mail it from Minneapolis). Then, be prepared to build a quick morning fire.

Of course, the stove burned out completely at night. So, I always had a pile of small wood kindling next to the stove for morning. Next, I was sure to have plenty of fire starter. That was a two-pound coffee can, filled with sawdust saturated with kerosene.

Upon waking in the morning, I would jump out of bed into my sheep-lined moccasins and then fill the stove with wood and a big spoonful of starter. After lighting the mixture, I would jump back into bed and watch the action. When the stove pipe would start glowing red hot, I would get up. Soon the room was warm enough, so, I would not see my breath. Dressing was quick and simple. There was no morning shower. The water, if any, would have been frozen. A sponge-bath the night before had to suffice. This was before the days of electric razors, so shaving and tooth-brushing had to wait for a trip to the office lavatory that had heat all night.

One day we got some pleasant news. We were going to move the planning work that had been done in West Yellowstone to Idaho Falls. I was happy to get away from the snow and cold. The snow around my little tourist cabin was about two feet deep.

It has been a great experience and I have learned a lot and it hasn't all been about architecture. A lot of it has been the psychology of human nature. I have had a lot of contact with all of that. A lot of the learning hasn't been pleasant by a long shot, but all has been educational. — **Stan**

CHAPTER 9

Idaho Falls

Looking Back

I remember well the pleasant feeling about driving into Idaho Falls with a friend. It was in the early evening. Buildings were lit and the streetlights were shining. It seemed that this must be the Promised Land. It looked like a metropolis. Again, I found a room to rent and reclaimed my trunk from the railroad station where it had been sitting in storage after being shipped from Great Falls.

The office was in the Armory. It was the custom in those days for most cities of any size to have such a building for use by the National Guard. The one in Idaho Falls was quite impressive and was located near the river. It had a large gymnasium-type drill hall that made a very fine drafting room. When we first saw the place, it seemed like there was a sea of drafting tables and desks.

I found that many of my old friends from Great Falls had moved down and were joined by others from the Twin Cities who had signed up on the project later. Among them were quite a number with families. Some office engineer-types had moved from West Yellowstone as well. There must have been about 150 people.

Life in Idaho Falls was pleasant and the area scenic. Looking to the west from the office, we could see the silhouette of the romantically named Lost Range Mountains. To the east, there were the Foothill Mountains that we found very pleasant to explore with friends. One of these friends was Francis (Frank) Meisch from Minneapolis, who was a very good artist and photographer. On many occasions we stood on the hills looking to the west at sunset and marveled at the beauty of the sky and small mountains on the horizon. I enjoyed his company.

Frank Meisch had some of that special ability that famous photographers like Ansel Adams possessed. With even a simple camera he produced some very fine pictures. Frank had a great eye for natural beauty. In later years, he became a widely acclaimed watercolor artist.

Letter Excerpts from Stanley to Doris from Idaho Falls

Oct. 17, 1941, Friday

(On Hotel Bonneville Idaho Falls Community Hotel Corp. paper)

Sweetie Pie,

We are now in Idaho Falls and it's some place. A town as big as Minot, ND, and a shopping district like Minneapolis. We are stopping at a swell hotel. The people are the smartest dressers here that you can imagine. Great Falls is twice as large but can't compare. The town is full of smart shops for ladies and men. There must be a reason. The place, of course, is booming.

We still haven't settled our pay, so we don't know whether we will like it or not. Van T. threw a fit this p.m. and said he would quit the job and close the office because the army rejected his flat roofs. I'll let you know more tomorrow, Sweet.

Oct. 22, 1941

My Snuggle Bug and Billie,

Tonight, I got your two letters—the one long one you started at the shop and the one you wrote right after you talked to me. Of course, as usual, I have nothing but possibilities to talk about.

October 26, 1941

I got an Idaho residence license for $2 and so I might as well use it. My boots haven't been sent down from W. Yellowstone yet. The maid service is only three times a week between here and there. I'll have to use my old shoes for tramping in the woods and brush.

Last night Menno and I went to see Honkey Tonk with Lana Turner and Clark Gable. It was entertaining and that's about all. Every remark in it could be taken two ways and the audience reaction indicated the wrong way was most popular.

All I do is sit and yawn today. I guess the relaxation is too much for us, so we don't know what to do with ourselves. We have decided not to work nights anymore. Mr. Van doesn't appreciate it and it wears us down.

October 29

My Lil' Sweetheart,

Today is another cold day. It snowed last night, and we could see that the mountains about 50 miles to the west are now covered white. People are on the way to Sun Valley. It won't be long before people will be going skiing up there. It melted off by noon, but it never got pleasant. Now we are all figuring on handling the snow problem at the camp. A winter average snow fall is 153 inches and as much as 50 inches in one month. It really creates a major problem and is a source of worry.

I got your nice thick letter this noon and now have finished the third reading of it. I'm very pleased with the way you have handled our finances. No one could have done as well. I know I couldn't.

✧ **Billie: Throughout the years that Dad was traveling with work, Mother took charge of all the finances; bookkeeping and investing in the "market" (stocks and bonds). She was amazing.**

Since my pay keeps coming, I think I'll continue here. Bill Jones found out just this morning that I had gotten a raise since Great Falls. He expressed his pleasure and of course it made me feel good.

We are trying to earn our pay and in so doing, we really sweat. The two of us have an enormous responsibility and it hasn't been easy to keep track of this vast project. However, if fortune smiles, we'll come out all right.

I really enjoy your accounts of our two-year-old. I can still hear her footsteps on the stair and her calling "I'm coming." The little darling. I miss her so much that I want to leave at a moment's notice for home. She is in a class all by herself and what a class.

All my love to you and my little pumpkin seed.

Stanley

Nov. 3, 1941, 9 p.m.

My Honeybunch,

How the months go rolling by! Soon Thanksgiving, and I'll be home. We've been conferring with a lieutenant, a captain, a colonel, and a major. That's one place where I shine. For some reason, they don't scare me. Menno and I are the only ones who have anything to do with them. (Not even Bill Jones). Our new site plan has been basically approved already. We started this morning. The major is taking it with him tomorrow.

Menno and I can't be fooled. At least we'll be done in two or three weeks. This camp must be definitely done on paper by Dec. 15th or a week sooner. That's orders. Site planning must be done before some of the others. I think that two weeks should be ample.

Nov. 5

Sweetheart,

Today was payday which is not hard to take. I always go down to the bank on these days and get $10 in one-dollar bills just for a novelty.

These silver dollars drive me nuts. Of course, I could stand the inconvenience of a suitcase full, but they don't come that way.

I'm finally letting down my hair to Moorman's office tonight. I don't think there's much chance because of the slash in other offices. But it's worth a try. At least they'll know I'm in the market.

Meisch is all down in the dumps because he is all set for the army, A-1 classification. He could take one of these government jobs in the tropics on a year's contract but those are tough.

I ordered some of the new "minicolor" color prints of my Kodachrome slides here. They are 75 cents each and are 2-1/4" x 3-1/4". I thought it might be fun to take some of Bill and have them printed for some of the family.

I'm going to finish this and send a letter to Moorman's tonight, so will add a bit after that.

PHEW!

That's that, now I've done it. I've finished my letter which got so bulky that I'm sitting on it to flatten it. I think it was pretty good. Now to await developments.

All my love, Tootsie Snoots.

Your puppy, Stanley

Nov. 6, 1941

My Honeybunch,

Another tough day and I'm much nearer to you than ever, Sweetheart. Our work will be soon done. I think that I'll hang in and make as much money as possible. But it will be near the first of the month anyway. Unless of course, I hear favorable news from Moorman (which I don't expect).

Our stenographer at the office says that she is hunting for a job now in Wahoo, Nebraska. However, the wages are lower now than previously.

If I'm to be home for Christmas, I would rather be able to work almost until then so I could afford to maybe loaf a couple of weeks during the holidays, rather than try to find a new job which might start out of town before Christmas. I'm quite sure that I'll be able to find work out of town, but not much in town. Meisch and I have planned on leaving together if things work out right.

Good night my sweet little Snuggle Bug, Your loving Stanley

Nov. 8

Hello Sweetheart,

Many of the boys are applying for jobs advertised in the Employment Column of Pencil Points. You might look in the last issue and see where you would like me to go. It's quite a problem to know what to do these days.

All my love, Squirrelly Stanley

Nov. 12

Sweetheart,

Whatever work comes in soon, I doubt if it will keep me away from home at Christmas. Whatever I land, I hope will not start before Jan 1st. Those of us who have been kept on (The army won't release us until Dec. 15th) are not quite so well lined up for jobs as those who were fired a week ago. There are some fair jobs in the Philippines and Alaska which I'm going to apply for.

If the government will pay my fare one way and a good enough salary, it would be worth the opportunity to see the world.

All my love, Precious, Stanley

Nov. 18

My Darling,

I received your letter today and want to reassure you of many things. You know I love you and Bill more than anything in the entire world. It hasn't been easy for me to remain away from you two so long. The thought of leaving you again so soon makes me very unhappy. I love you so, Hon.

Last night it started to snow. A beautiful feathery snow 10 inches deep. I was so homesick! I remembered the long walks we used to take on Summit Avenue when you went to Macalester. How wet we used to get! All the plans—do you remember? How we would have a nice house with pretty windows and how I would come to see you. We would have a competent maid to keep our house nice and plenty of money. Really, Hon!—It seems as if we have come nearer to realization than I could have ever hoped. It is tragic that I can't be with you.

All my love, Tootsie. Give Bill a big kiss for me. Stanley

November 20, 1941 Thanksgiving

It's a beautiful Thanksgiving morning here. The only thing that is wrong is that you and Billie are not here. We are invited out to St. Anthony which is forty miles north of here. One of the girls at the office is the generous one. She is quite a skier and wants Menno and me to go to Sun Valley with her and a girlfriend one of these weekends. We may go as it would be a wonderful opportunity to get some wonderful snow pictures.

I rented a typewriter for a week to turn out some application letters. (I'm sure this letter is easier to read.) I will be sure to bring my portable if I leave home again.

I don't think much of this applying for jobs by letter, but most of the fellows here were hired in just that manner. I have a lot of places to apply. There will be no scarcity of jobs these days. The only thing is that so many of them are at the far corners of the earth.

Menno just pulled in and found that his starter is stuck. He lives only a couple of blocks from here so we are going to go and fix it if we can.

More later—All my love, Stanley

Nov. 21

Hello Tootsie,

Here I am again with a letter made with the rattlebox (typewriter). It is so noisy it almost rattles my teeth loose, but it is more legible than my longhand, I am sure. I have it setting on a card table that is so rickety the machine jumps all over so that I have a hard time finding the right keys!

I am trying to recuperate from the strenuous day yesterday. We had a fine day and a fine meal. The girls wanted to go skiing after eating, so we took them out to the Sand Dunes. This is a place that has drifting sand dunes just like you see in the movies of Egypt. Some of them are over a hundred feet high. There was a thin coating of snow on them so they looked like immense snow drifts as far as the eye could see. Of course, you know me. I couldn't monkey with a small one.

I managed to climb to the top of the big one and then the fun started—me with my good suit and hat on, and an overcoat, too, of course. I came sailing down the hill like the wind and landed like a ton of bricks. That sand may look soft in pictures, but it is like a pavement. I landed so hard that I have been sitting down very carefully since. Some fun! The girls of course were raised in this country and are quite at home in such surroundings. Menno is nursing a sore ankle after his jaunt down the hillside. I did manage to get some pretty good pictures despite it all.

I hate to close these letters because it is just as if I were talking to you and had to sign off. Do you remember those two-hour telephone calls to Mac? No small wonder the rest of them got so mad. But it was a lot of fun wasn't it? It will be wonderful to see you again. I am getting as excited about it as a kid in anticipation of Christmas. I hope that everything will go as I want it to. Frankly, I can say that I will be glad to get out of the Wild West for a while. It doesn't excite me after so much of it and I want you here to enjoy it with me, anyhow.

Well, goodnight, Sweetheart. I'll write soon. All my love, Stanley

Nov. 23, Sunday

Hello Sweetheart,

It is evening again and, as always, I am thinking of you. Today was such a nice day that I got some more pictures of the spots of interest in town. I got some good close ups of the Mormon temple here which is a "doozie" as our friend Mr. Brandhost would say. It is very much of a modern affair.

What do you call this for making up for lost time? Don't you think that I am doing pretty good for writing so often? That is what you have earned by writing so often yourself. It will be nice when I can see you and tell you all the news and all the stories in person. There are plenty of those, I assure you.

More news when it breaks. All my love, Stanley

Nov. 24

My Little Sweetheart,

Now, I am sure that this letter will be a lot of fun for you, though, it isn't a bit of fun for some of the fellows. Our department finally ran out of work so I will be seeing you around the first of the month, aren't you glad? Then I will spend the month of December at home. The War Department has been squawking about the large payroll at the end of the job and my big wages make me subject to the axe. Despite all Van's promises, he hates to see us getting good pay. He had yelled about it many times to the rest, but, of course, not to me. At any rate, Mr. Shanley has told me on several occasions that he wants Menno and me to stay for the construction work after this thing is underway. However, it is not too certain that this firm will get the supervision as Van has alienated some of the army brass.

I am going to try to find something to keep me busy in the Twin Cities.

Looking Back Continued...

Idaho was famous for its russet potatoes. I was reminded of this fame when I checked in at the Bonneville Hotel. This establishment had matchbook covers that were decorated with a picture of a gold-colored potato. Unfortunately, the potatoes served at the meals I took in the restaurant were not good.

There were several things about Idaho that made it a bit different from other states that I had visited during my travels. One was its preference for silver dollars. After a bit of national legislative effort some years before, the one-dollar bill had replaced the silver dollar and had become the standard currency item. Not so in Idaho. Because the state had a tradition of silver mining, the use of dollar bills was considered disloyal in some circles. As a result, there was not a place for the silver dollars in the newer cash registers in most places of business. The silver dollars were often kept in an empty cigar box by the cashiers' desks.

As time went by, the weather got a bit colder, and because of the snow, our travels were restricted. The bird-hunting season provided some diversion for the outdoor-oriented people. Game birds such as pheasants were plentiful and were a pleasant food source for those of our group who had established households in rented homes and apartments. The nature of our project with its indefinite time span discouraged us from settling in well.

For those of us who had left our families elsewhere, the approach of the Christmas holiday season did not buoy up our spirits. Our options were limited. Jobs for engineers and architects were scarce, in fact, practically non-existent. That was the reason we had left home and had taken work on this project.

Finally, an event occurred that changed the outlook for us in a very dramatic way. Some of the uncertainty about how we would spend the holiday season was eliminated.

A Surprise Announcement

One morning, the first of December, Van T. came into the big drafting room at the Armory and made an announcement. To attract our attention, he used a drafting board brush or some other instrument to hammer on the top of a steel filing cabinet. Unlike his usual practice, the words that he spoke on this occasion were brief and to the point. I recall that all he said was, "I am sorry to announce that this project has been cancelled. You may collect your paychecks at the business office at the end of the day."

No further explanation was given. Obviously, the War Department had made some basic decisions about the kind of war the U.S. might be fighting. There were, of course, rumors passed about as to why this action had been taken. One story that circulated was to the effect that one of the generals who had stayed at the Madison Hotel in West Yellowstone before it had closed for the season, had suffered some sort of a stroke or heart attack due to the high altitude, and had taken a dislike to the project. I think that's a very unlikely reason.

My reaction to this exciting news was swift and simple. I just got on the telephone and called home. Then I picked up my paycheck. Next, I made train reservations for my trip to Minneapolis and then packed my trunk. I discovered that the most direct route from Idaho Falls, Idaho, to Minneapolis was through Omaha, Nebraska. I thought I would be able to see a bit more of the U.S.

I bid good-bye to the middle-age couple that had rented a room to me during my stay and headed for the railroad station. As usual, my trunk was carried on a fold-down rack on the back of a taxicab. I have sometimes wondered what happened to such equipment. Perhaps it just disappeared when people decided they could get along quite well with only a couple of suitcases when they traveled for even long distances.

A few of my friends from the project were at the station when I arrived. Oddly enough, I was the only one headed directly for Minneapolis. Others seemed to have chosen different destinations, so I traveled without any friends or acquaintances to keep me company, and perhaps join me in a card game. The coaches in use on that run to Omaha were not particularly comfortable.

It was a relief when one of the dining car staff came through beating a chime and announcing dinner. Sitting in a dining car chair was preferable to coach seating. It was also nice to be waited on. The standards of food and service in those days were quite high. Linen tablecloths and napkins, along with a multitude of heavy silver-plated service items and good-looking china and glassware made a very attractive setting for dining. Anyway, it had the effect of making the food, which might have been quite mediocre, seem quite outstanding. At the conclusion of the meal, finger bowls appeared as a final touch of class, along with a bill, of course.

After a few hours' layover in Omaha, I boarded a train for the final leg of the trip to Minneapolis. I don't remember much about it other than there was a lot more snow and was farther south. It was obviously much colder too. Trains were not well-heated in those days, since they used steam piped from the locomotives and the systems were not efficient. In the coldest weather there sometimes was insufficient steam to heat the coaches well enough.

Home, Very Sweet Home!

My arrival in Minneapolis was a joyous event. Doris and our baby, Billie (who we sometimes lovingly called Bill), were at the train station, along with a couple of friends. It seemed as if I was returning from a very long journey. After arranging for a taxi to pick up my trunk the next day, we headed for the comforts of hearth and home. The day after my return to my hometown, I checked the mail and found a letter from my draft board that warned me of my vulnerability.

It was Sunday afternoon on the 7th of December, 1941. It was the announcement of the Japanese attack on Pearl Harbor in Hawaii. No ordinary news anchor made that first news announcement. It was FDR. We will always remember President Roosevelt's words.

— Stan

CHAPTER 10

Draft Boards and Shocking News

Looking Back

The draft boards were very diligent in keeping track of the eligible young men in their communities. I don't recall whether I had to notify them when I went out West on the military camp project, however, I probably did. It seemed like I'd been busy for the past year filling out forms from time to time telling about my family and employment situation. I remember making the statements on the form to the effect that I was principal breadwinner in the family and that I had a young child at home.

I'd arrived in Minneapolis from Omaha mid-week. That gave us a bit of time to plan the weekend. We thought it was a good idea to have some family members join us to celebrate my return. One of Doris's brothers, Allan, a dentist living in Montevideo, and his family consisting of a wife and young son were invited to spend the weekend with us. They arrived on Saturday and spent the night and had Sunday dinner with us. After dinner, we sat near the fireplace and I took advantage of an audience to tell about my adventures in Idaho and Montana. People didn't travel long distances very often in those days. Finally, I had exhausted my fund of tales of the West, so we turned on the radio for some diversion.

Radio was an important source of news and entertainment for most people living at home. Some Sunday programs were rather special and developed a loyal and devoted listening audience. It was one of these news programs that we tuned in on that day that made an indelible impression on the memories of us, the nation, and the world.

Billie: Mother kept the Minneapolis Sunday Tribune's anniversary edition (December 6, 1942) with four pages of "hitherto unpublished photos" of the event.

PEARL HARBOR
ATTACK PICTURES
Four Pages of Hitherto Unpublished Photos

Minneapolis Sunday Tribune

MINNEAPOLIS SUNDAY TRIBUNE AND STAR JOURNAL

Naval Station at Pearl Harbor Was Turned Into Blazing Inferno When Japs Struck

Smoke and flames fill the sky, and the wreckage of navy planes lies strewn over the ground at the naval air station at Pearl Harbor. A navy spokesman said that 60 or 70 fighter planes, able to get into the air, could have saved the day. The first objective of the Japanese was the naval air station at Kaneohe bay (about 30 miles from Pearl Harbor). Seconds later enemy torpedo planes and dive-bombers swung in from various sectors to concentrate their attack on the ships and bases. The attack started at 7:55 a.m. and enemy aircraft retired by 9:45 a.m., after temporarily disabling every battleship and most of the aircraft in the Hawaiian area.

19 U. S. Warships Were Damaged or Sunk, But Only One Is a Total Loss

The above caption reads: "Smoke and flames fill the sky, and the wreckage of navy planes lies strewn over the ground at the naval air station at Pearl Harbor. A navy spokesman said that 60 or 70 fighter planes, able to get into the air, could have saved the day. The first objective of the Japanese was a naval air station at Kaneohe Bay (about 30 miles from Pearl Harbor). Seconds later enemy torpedo planes and dive-bombers swung in from various sectors to concentrate their attack on the ships and base. The attack started at 7:55 a.m. and enemy aircraft retired by 9:45 a.m., after temporarily disabling every battleship and most of the aircraft in the Hawaiian area."

MANY AMERICAN PLANES WERE SHOT TO PIECES ON GROUND

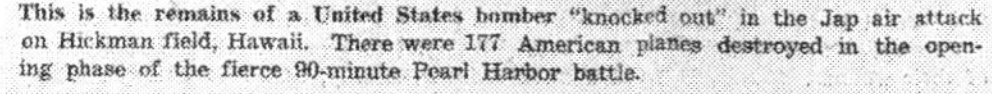

This is the remains of a United States bomber "knocked out" in the Jap air attack on Hickman field, Hawaii. There were 177 American planes destroyed in the opening phase of the fierce 90-minute Pearl Harbor battle.

This United States navy plane, an observation scout seaplane, had its engine ripped from its housing by a Jap bomb. When the attack came, the navy had 202 planes of all types on the island of Oahu and 150 were destroyed.

(left photo caption) "This is the remains of a United States Bomber 'knocked out' in the Jap air attack on Hickman *[sic]* field, Hawaii. There were 177 American planes destroyed in the opening phase of the fierce 90-minute Pearl Harbor battle."

(right photo caption) "This United States Navy plane, an observation scout seaplane, had its engine ripped from its housing by a Jap bomb. When the attack came, the navy had 202 planes of all types on the island of Oahu and 150 were destroyed."

December 14, 1941

Dear Frank, (Meisch, a college friend),

Well, I am home again trying to live a civilized life. Living is all that I am doing. There is not much in the way of defense work here except with the New Brighton affair. That is too temporary, and I am afraid that if I were to accept a job there, I would be unable to leave if I were to find a better one. With the war underway, I am sure that I had better get located in some job that I can hide behind.

Let me know how things are going and if you know of any openings, I'd appreciate a tip. I wrote to Menno the other day but haven't heard how he was making out. I am afraid that this immigrant business may affect his work. (Menno was an immigrant from Holland.) I know that they are checking over all immigrants in this district. Drop me a line when you find the time. In the meantime, good luck!

Yours sincerely,

Stan Moe

PART IV

1942

Wartime Work in the Wide World
(Aboard a Ship to Who Knows Where…)

Our carefree days are gone.
Our little world seems all upset.
I wish we could fix it.
Oh—to be kids again in school.
— Stan

CHAPTER 11

Uncertainties

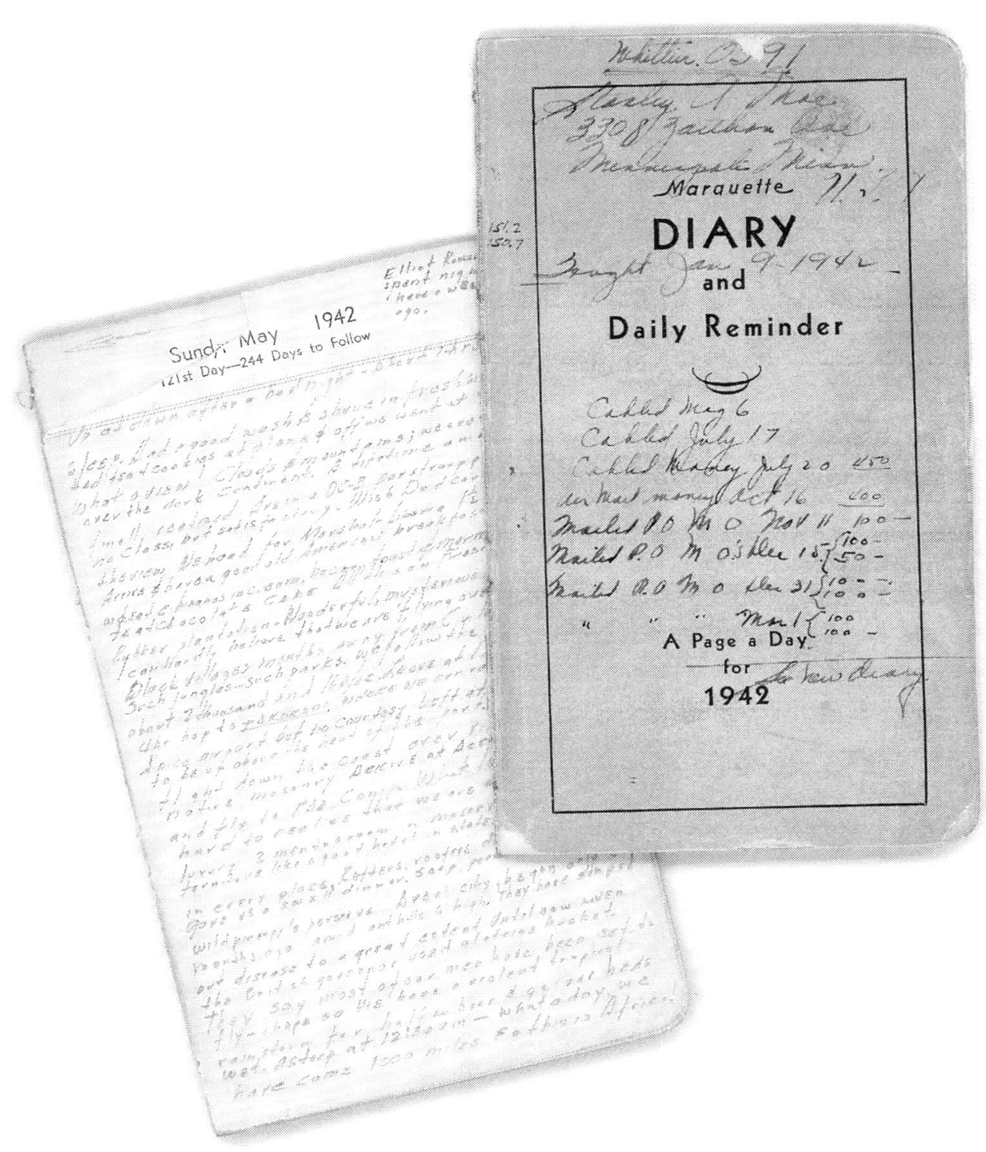

Stan Moe's Diary, January – December 1942

Billie: Dad left Minneapolis with this diary. He kept it in his pocket. He wrote/printed each day he was away. He was able to get this diary home, despite the censors, but his 1943 diary was taken from his trunk on the way home in late 1943. We relied on his letters to Mother, family, friends and his memory in "Looking Back" to get the details of 1943. The actual size of this diary is 5-7/8" by 3-3/8". His writing is very small on the days he had lots to impart.

Diary Entries

January 5, 1942

I made the rounds in St. Paul. My efforts don't produce much hope. Hiring is flat. I stopped in at Ellerbe. They said there was some chance they'd be hiring, but not until after February first.

I was losing hope, but decided to stop in at Johnson, Drake, and Piper.

(J, D & P) This chance meeting with Johnson, Drake & Piper provided an opportunity to do projects to assist the U.S. military in the European Campaign. I readily agreed to take the job and was sent to a physician's office.

I would be leaving for New York on January 10th. From there I would sail to points unknown. I had four days to prepare for a transcontinental journey.

January 6, 1942

I sent a telegram to Fargo, North Dakota, requesting a copy of my birth certificate. It would have to be sent from Bismarck. I received confirmation of my request. The remainder of the day was spent shopping for clothing and going to the doctor's office for the required physical.

Doris was attending a decorator's showcase. I called her from the doctor's office. She dropped everything to meet me in The Radisson Hotel downtown. We quickly decided the opportunity was too good to pass up. After the days and nights of worry and concern about taking the job in Yellowstone, it was incredible, we could agree to this longer and more distant position in less than an hour.

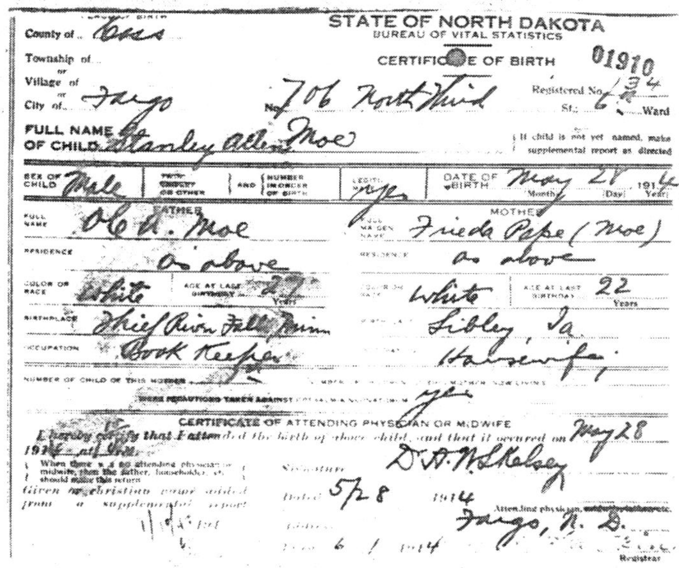

County of Cass
STATE OF NORTH DAKOTA
BUREAU OF VITAL STATISTICS
CERTIFICATE OF BIRTH 01910
Township of
or Village of
or City of Fargo No. 706 North Third St. Registered No. 134, 6 Ward
FULL NAME OF CHILD Stanley Allen Moe
If child is not yet named, make supplemental report as directed
SEX OF CHILD Male | LEGITIMATE yes | DATE OF BIRTH May 28 1914 (Month) (Day) (Year)
FATHER
FULL NAME O.C.A. Moe
RESIDENCE as above
COLOR OR RACE White | AGE AT LAST BIRTHDAY 27 Years
BIRTHPLACE Thief River Falls Minn
OCCUPATION Book Keeper
MOTHER
FULL MAIDEN NAME Frieda Pape (Moe)
RESIDENCE as above
COLOR OR RACE White | AGE AT LAST BIRTHDAY 22 Years
BIRTHPLACE Sibley, Ia
OCCUPATION Housewife
NUMBER OF CHILD OF THIS MOTHER
WERE PRECAUTIONS TAKEN AGAINST OPHTHALMIA NEONATORUM yes
CERTIFICATE OF ATTENDING PHYSICIAN OR MIDWIFE
I hereby certify that I attended the birth of above child, and that it occurred on May 28 1914
Signature D.W.W. Kelsey
Date 5/28 1914
Attending physician
Address Fargo, N.D.
6 / 1 1914
Registrar

Stanley's birth certificate, Fargo, North Dakota

January 7, 1942
A fly in the ointment. I received my draft questionnaire. J, D & P gave me a letter to take to the draft board. The clerk, an unreasonable person, said I had to fill out the draft questionnaire. He indicated the draft board "might" consider a deferment.

January 8, 1942
I take the questionnaire to the draft board. A pleasant fellow is there today. He tells me to call at 3 p.m. I call… they have accepted my deferment. Hurray!!!

The gang congregates for a send-off party. We fry steaks in the fireplace and have a grand time.

January 9, 1942
We met Mae and Burt for cocktails at the Viking Room. I tell them about my draft board deferment that ended in acceptance. Burt may be drafted. Bill Diamond is also having trouble.

Our carefree days are gone. Our little world seems all upset.
I wish we could fix it. Oh—to be kids again in school.

January 9, 1942 - Letter to Frank Meisch
Dear Frank,

How's every little thing? I am to leave tomorrow morning for New York where I will go through the usual monkey business to get out of the country. I got my draft questionnaire on the same day that I got my job so had to go through red tape to get released. I am still waiting for my birth certificate from Bismarck which should arrive in the morning's mail.

Well, I very likely won't see you for a couple of rainy days, so I hope you will continue to keep ahead of the draft board. "We have chosen this profession and must be willing to accept its bad angles too." (Here I'm quoting Van T., the s. of b.)

Yours sincerely, Stan

My letters should be addressed as follows:
Stanley A. Moe
North African Missions Office
c/o Johnson, Drake and Piper, Inc.
Asmara, Africa
For security reasons this must be enclosed in another envelope addressed as follows:
Stanley A. Moe
c/o Home Office
North African Mission
Room 2604, Munitions Bldg.
Washington, D.C.

Diary Entries

January 10, 1942

Up early. Harold Grey and Van drove us to the station. We wait and wait, but finally the Zephyr pulls in. A quick goodbye to Doris and our friends, No time for remorse.

I think of my daughter, Bill. She didn't see me go.
Why do men leave home?

It's a long trip, and I find a few friends on board. Mostly carpenters. I'm out of my field. I changed trains in Chicago and remember that I forgot my rubbers to go over my good shoes and I know it will rain. Must buy another pair. I have dinner on the train and crawl into the upper bunk of the sleeping compartment.

January 11

We pass through the "Industrial East." What a dump. I'll take Minnesota! We arrive in New York at 9:30 a.m.

I took a 'hack' (taxi) to the Holland Hotel. Seems as if we're not going to be leaving soon. I take a walk around Times Square—the gateway district of New York.

January 13
I had my immunization shots this morning. My arms are sore as blazes. Home to rest.

January 14
Rockefeller Center is deserted. Not many tourists in New York City these days.

January 15
Afternoon off work. Window shop along 5th Avenue. Prices are so forbidding I wonder how they have customers.

January 16
I went to the Metropolitan Museum of Art and the American Museum of Natural History. What a sight!

January 21
I had a bad night. My arm is as sore as can be, and I have a fever. I went to breakfast late to find out that I may not go over. The boat is small, and we are too many.

The past couple of weeks are filled with work at the office, shots, and sightseeing. Aymar Embury and Douglas have us doing "research." Anything to keep us busy until we sail.

I've become acquainted with the Automat, an interesting place. You see your food through a small window, put in your money, and the window opens. You take out the food, get your utensils, and sit at a table or counter and eat.

January 22
I made my usual rounds and had frosted Mayflower donuts and Maxwell House Coffee on Times Square. I sure go for them in a big way. It would be nice to have a place like that over in the country of Eritrea, Northeast Africa, where it is rumored we are heading. We will miss such luxuries when we leave the States. Everyone who has been away says the same thing. I wrote my usual letter home. As yet, I have not gotten my Lil' Bill her "black baby."

January 26

I moved to the YMCA. I was assigned a tiny Moab cell.

January 27

Didn't sleep well last night—new place, I guess. Got a letter from Dad today. It was delivered to the office. I was relieved to know he didn't think I was crazy. Maybe I am.

I had dinner at Paddy's Oyster/Clam House tonight. Fine food, but a rough atmosphere.

Good news! I found Billie a black baby in the Village in New York.

✧ **Billie: Greenwich Village, probably.**

February 2, 1942

I went to the Abraham and Strauss Department store in Brooklyn. Tonight, I saw Fred Waring at the Vanderbilt. The hotel is impressive, and the music thrilling.

I've seen some great entertainment. Radio City Music Hall and the Rockettes, Fred Waring and his Orchestra, Francia White, Judy Garland in Babes on Broadway. Saw Gulliver's Travels at the Paramount. Lots of museums.

February 4

Still no word about when we will sail.

I walked to Radio City Music Hall. Ball of Fire was playing. The movie was good. As for the Rockette's … they were wonderful. Such precision.

February 5

Doris and Billie must come with me for a shopping spree in New York. We would all have a lot of fun.

February 9

I went down to the piers and watched the SS Normandie burn.

Photo courtesy of the New Jersey Maritime Museum, Beach Haven, N.J.

From the newyorkhistoryblog.org: On February 9, 1942, crowds gathered at New York City's Pier 88 to witness a spectacle. The largest ocean liner in the world was on fire. Firefighting efforts successfully contained the fire after five and a half hours of effort, but the effort was in vain. Five hours after the flames were out the stricken vessel rolled onto its side and settled on the bottom of the Hudson.

February 11

Maybe, when the war is over and cars are produced again, we can get a Buick from Detroit and drive it home. Doris could pick me up in New York.

February 12, 1942

Went to Macy's tonight to buy a shirt and tie. It's hard to get books, now. No gloves for little Billie either. I'll have to try a specialty child's shop.

February 15

I got up late and had breakfast across the street. For some reason I was very tired, so I went back to the 'Y' and slept until after two p.m. Then I went window shopping up 5th Avenue and Madison to see the Sweetheart Broadcast at 5 o'clock. It was very good.

I had a bite to eat on Times Square, then went to see Judy Garland in Babes on Broadway at the State. Serge Murphy and Robert Montgomery made personal appearances. Finally, back in my room. My feet hurt. I wrote a short note to Doris. I've developed quite an appetite. I could eat a meal every hour. To bed at midnight.

February 16

A damp, quiet day with heavy fog. The first boatload of fellows left today. We may go by plane or by water. Who knows! Five days? Ten days? Fifteen days? All guesswork.

Back to my room early. No letter from home. I write a long one to Doris and had my hair cut. CUT? So short I feel terrible.

It's raining, so I'm glad I'm safe and sound inside my room. I may go down after the late mail and see if I got any more. I feel foolish asking so often.

February 18

I went to Wannamaker Department Store. What a swell place. Saw boots like Doris got me. I bought socks and had to leave before I spent all my money.

Back at the "Y," I watched a travelogue on Persia.

February 19

Today, I went to see the William Randolph Hearst Collection. SOME SHOW. Enjoyable. I saw a robbery while I was there. Someone stole a necklace from a secured case.

February 22

Drove with Art and Marion to Harrison Park and up through West Point to Newburgh. A wonderful drive. West Point is an impressive spot of unequalled beauty.

No wonder our officers are such dreamers!

Chapter 12

In Limbo

February 25, 1942 - New York City

My Darling,

Finally, "It" has come. Art got definite word from the personnel office this p.m. that we would be mailed Special Delivery letters on Friday or Saturday which would ask us to meet with the officers in charge on Monday or Tuesday. By the 5th of March we should be out of here. It is the only definite information we have received on this thing so far. It will be a large boat as there will be about 500 men. Some will be part of other outfits going to Persia.

I'm thinking very seriously of sending my overcoat home in my suitcase. It will only be a worry to me, and as I will likely return during some winter, you can have it for me there. I will get a good waterproof jacket with a wool lining. That will protect me while we are sailing to warmer climates and for cold weather in the mountains. I can get one for around $9.00.

This news of sailing was brought to a head by Art's asking for tomorrow off to take his wife to the doctor. They came out with the news. They wanted to know where to find him in case of sudden news.

We also have heard that the staterooms on the boat have been removed and hammocks are to take the place of bunks. SOME FUN! I never could get used to one of those. It will be like the movies with Abbot and Castello.

They sent out a list of all the available materials to be had at the base. Of course, we can't be sure of sizes. It wouldn't be fun to wear stuff the wrong size.—HA! We will not be permitted parcel post service. The only thing we can get is magazines and newspapers in addition to letters. I'll maybe have you send me a paper or something while I'm there. We won't have much reliable news otherwise.

At dinner tonight, there were several young RAF (Royal Air Force) pilots in the dining room. It's quite a novelty to see them eating. Fork always in the left hand and knife in the right—held like a pencil or pen. They are a handsomely dressed outfit with dark blue-gray uniforms. They have been training down in Florida so are very tan and healthy looking. They seem to prefer pie, fruit, and milk to all other foods. One often sees them making a meal of them. I don't suppose they get much of that kind of food over there.

All my love forever, Stanley. Tell Billie that Daddy loves her.

February 26, 1942

Sweetheart,

Home again and I've just finished reading your letter. I hope you are now in better spirits. Please, don't be blue. It is for our security that I'm doing these things. I don't even dare to think about my being away from you. But the army or WPA (work project administration) would get me if I stayed. Some people work harder for less and we have health. One of the fellows here—a big rough refrigeration engineer left a wife and two and a half-year-old daughter in Syracuse. Already his wife came down here and spent a week. Now, he asked to be allowed to go home and stay until called. He will receive the same money. I don't want to be that way! He would just talk himself into homesickness and chase around with the "babes" down here. The solution seems to be in keeping one's mind occupied with other subjects. My problem is mainly worrying about getting out of here soon so our finances will not be crippled.

I keep thinking about finances. Your allotment is $50.00 a week. You will receive it three weeks after I sail and every week thereafter. After eight weeks the balance of my pay will be deposited to my account at the bank in NYC. I will get some for spending money, and some will be put in war bonds. It sounds confusing, but there will be about $225.00 per month income to you. We are planning for the future—future—future!

Most of the fellows have been spending more than their pay here. I feel lucky to be able to save something for you. But it is a long time since I was bringing or sending home regular checks.

I am at the YMCA and pay only $1.00. I have been going to free broadcasts [radio] and four or five movies which cost around 88 cents total.

You understand, I'm not trying to build up a case on my little money. I'm just talking it over. I wish telephone calls were not so costly. No way out but I hope and pray for a miracle or something. We'll be on easy street if we can only get on the boat. It looks very good now for the 5th of March.

I'm going down to eat and then over to Macy's to look at a Zelan jacket with wool lining. I wish you were along with me. Such a lonesome life we lead. Isn't it awful! Poor us! But we will be together before long. Tell Billie that Daddy loves her.

Goodnight, Sweetie Pie. All my love, Stanley

February 27, 1942

Darling,

I went to Rand McNally and got a map for you of Eritrea and Ethiopia. Now you can follow some of my meanderings.

I am going up to the country with Art again tomorrow. His wife will come in with him in the morning in the car and we will all drive back together. He insists that I come, and they are such informal and hospitable people that I always have a good time.

I heard that Art called the P.O. and that minimum air mail service to Eritrea is 70 cents. It would hardly pay to send a letter each day. One a week or one a month is better. We'll see.

Walked up to Time Square for some Mayflower doughnuts and Maxwell House Coffee. They do a big business—like in Minneapolis.

February 28 - Diary

Went to the famous Hotel St. George. It has a swimming pool.

March 2 - Diary

No sailing word, yet.

Sunday, March 2

Sweetheart,

The weather was very nice today and I walked over on 32nd Street this evening. That is where all the big camera shops are in NYC. All within one block! Bell and Howell cameras and projectors are as scarce as hen's teeth! Some of the places are twice as big as Northern Photo and have only Eastman and cheap Premier Cameras.

It certainly is nice we have such a remarkable child. I can just see her and her spilled powder episode. She is too wonderful for description. I'm glad she has such a marvelous mother to take care of her when I am gone. I'm sure she had a wonderful time at the ice show. It would have been fun to be along so she could tell me her reactions. I'll try to picture her enthusiastic description of the spectacle.

Billie takes stuffed animals for a ride in her sled

March 3, 1942

Darling,

It's late but after I ate dinner tonight, I decided I had to do something to break the monotony, so I went to a show. I went to the Radio City Music Hall and saw Spencer Tracy and Katharine Hepburn in Woman of the Year.

It's extraordinary. I think Hepburn's acting is the most convincing woman "stuff" I've ever seen on the screen. It was a worthwhile evening spent.

It blew something terrible during last night. I thought the whole "Y" would blow over. It was tough on the boys out to sea. Today it poured most of the time and only let up this evening. I hope it doesn't blow too much when we are out on the ocean. I'm not sure of my sea-legs.

How I miss my sweetheart! Half the fun of seeing new places and good entertainment is a loved one enjoying it with you. Thank you for sending the picture of you and your new shoes!

All my love forever and ever, Stanley

Look, new shoes!

March 4 - Diary

Stopped at the Georg Jensen Shop. I got a couple of serving pieces for Doris. Such extravagance! But it is worth the money.

March 4

Sweetie-pie,

I'm again in front of my two-by-four-foot desk and am all washed and shaved. Even my hair is washed. I have a lot of opportunities for hair washing here in the shower. I hope we have good showers abroad.

As I was walking down Fifth Avenue today, I had to stop as I got near the entrance to the Vanderbilt mansion. A hearse was at the curb and a fancy silver (or aluminum) casket was carried into the house. It was covered with a flag. Only a handful of Rolls-Royces, Cadillacs, and Mercedes Benzes were at the curb. Apparently, a shirt-tail member of the family was having a funeral. I guess the millionaires don't fuss much at one another's deaths.

Coming by Rockefeller Center, I stopped to watch them ice-skating at the rink. Proud mammas sat inside the fancy terrace restaurant eating and smoking and watching their buck-toothed and piano-legged offspring enjoy a whirl around the ice at 75 cents a swat. An occasional dimpled darling proved to be quite adept at skating and at the age of no more than five or six.

I had a wonderful walk down Fifth Avenue before dark. It is only about a mile and a half from Rockefeller Center to the Y. The shops are already preparing for Easter and when they do, they really make a job of it. A lot of color and black and white chicks are being shown. The hats have very much of a "Gibson Girls" look and shape to them.

"The Gibson Girl was the personification of the feminine ideal of physical attractiveness as portrayed by the pen-and-ink illustrations of artist Charles Dana Gibson during a 20-year period that spanned the late 19th and early 20th century in the United States and Canada." — Wikipedia

I imagine that the Easter parade here will be much tamer than in previous years. The war is being felt. People talk of nothing else and are quite optimistic. They expect losses, but plan on victory in the end. Of course, none of us would entertain any thought of defeat.

I'm always thinking of you when I'm up town. You would be so thrilled with everything. A marvelous variety. No end to things on all sides. Fifth Avenue even has a Woolworth that is pretentious and tries to look like little "Tiffany's." With all the glitter of cheap plated ornaments, it doesn't do badly. Except, Tiffany's ornaments don't really glitter. Sad to say, its windows usually have one small jewel in each. Just to arouse the curiosity. Cartier's had some nice diamond engagement rings in the windows. Small, like streetcar tokens or sunflower seeds. No "ICE" in their merchandise.

Billie: Mother and Dad always called fake diamonds, "Ice."

It is approaching 11:00 and I am tired. No letter from you today (or yesterday), hope so tomorrow.

All my love, Stanley

Without two-way communication, no cultural improvement is possible. I can see how people who live alone begin talking to themselves. — **Stan**

Chapter 13

Getting to Know NYC

Looking Back

I was given notice to report for duty in New York City. I finally took off with my trunk filled with what the many months of service overseas turned out to be non-essentials. I don't recall if I was excited or just plain docile at this point. I had little knowledge of what I would find in New York. Everything was new—the city, the job, the company—all of it! The train arrived in some rail station that I don't remember. The day was a cool January day with a heavy overcast. The place did not look glamorous. In fact, it looked gloomy and seedy. I found my trunk and a taxi and then headed for the hotel where the company had said we were to stay until we went to Africa.

I appeared at a desk with a JDP sign on it and gave my name to the secretary and clerk. After a few minutes I was called and went over to another desk where a fellow produced a sheet of paper with my name on it. When he determined that he was talking to the right person, he said something in the way of welcome, and congratulated me on my being given a job as a rod and chain man on a survey crew on the Egyptian project.

To put it mildly, this was a bit of a shock. Although Richardson had not told me specifically what my architectural job would be, I could not conceive of any such mix-up in job classifications. A rod and chain man is, perhaps, the lowest classification for anyone working in a construction and technical field. He is the person who holds the other end of the tape used to measure horizontal distances. He also holds the rod, a stick marked with measurements that a survey instrument views to measure vertical distances. Any able-bodied person could do that sort of work. Any high school freshman would be overqualified.

I quickly found someone in charge of personnel processing and told him that something was fouled up. He said I should go across the street and speak to the man in charge of the design of the African project. He recommended that I see Mr. Embury. This I did in a hurry.

I discovered that the project design office was located on the top floor of an office building that housed, on the lower floor, what was then called the Curb Exchange of the US Stock Exchange. It has for many years since been the American Stock Exchange. I didn't have to wait long to see Mr. Embury. On the office directory I noticed that he was listed as Aymar Embury II. Then it dawned on me that this was the well-known and quite famous designer of mansions for the wealthy people of New York. I quickly learned that Embury was a well-connected Democrat and had been chosen for a very important role in the immediate post-December

7th U.S. military construction period. He was the interim chief engineer for the North Atlantic Division of the U.S. Army Corp of Engineers.

Embury greeted me cordially. I was impressed with his genteel appearance. He wore a blue serge suit, a white shirt and a black knit tie. His hair was salt & pepper gray and a bit longer than is common. His manner was a pleasant, gracious one. He listened to my tale of woe and smiled. He soon put my mind to rest by saying he was generally aware of the problems JDP was having dealing with professionals and that he would see that I was given a job appropriate for one of my education and experience.

I was given an assignment that was not any challenge, but one that should keep me busy for a few days until I sailed for Africa. I met some pleasant people in this department of the office and marveled on how they could do such menial work. Our work was simply the computation of shipping cubage requirements. In other words, we reviewed the plans being prepared in the office to determine what materials would have to be shipped from the US and how much space aboard the ship would be required.

There were several people in this little department doing the same sort of low-level technical work such as estimating shipping space. Most were in their 40s and 50s and had come from other government or institutional employments. They were beyond draft age, but for some reason their jobs had been fouled up by December 7th. The only other fellow who was vulnerable to the draft was a young fellow by the name of Art Paulson. We were to become good friends.

After a week or so, it became obvious that we would not be departing for Africa very soon. With the U.S. declaration of war after December 7th, Atlantic Ocean travel became very hazardous. The German Navy had stepped up submarine operations off the eastern shores of the U.S. Early in January, U.S. ships were being attacked off the New Jersey coast. The beaches were covered with ship fuel-oil and other debris from the sunken ships. Neither we, nor the people who were to ship us, were eager to sail anywhere.

As the weeks wore on, the uncertainty of a departure date was very frustrating. Life at my hotel was not very pleasant. I did not have a congenial relationship with my assigned roommate. Moreover, the hotel was filled with many hard-drinking rowdy construction workers who created an unpleasant environment. I decided to move elsewhere and managed to make arrangements with the personnel office of JDP for a cash allowance in lieu of the room at the hotel.

My new residence was the Sloane House YMCA on 34th Street. This was a couple of blocks west of the Empire State Building in a pleasant neighborhood. Someone had recommended this place to me. The name sounded fine, but it was a YMCA. The person who had put up most of the funds for its construction was Alford P. Sloane. The name Sloane had a very important touch of class, since Sloane was a major executive of General Motors and a well-known philanthropist.

Sloane House had a very interesting program. It catered to the needs of single young men. The public and recreational areas were very nicely decorated and equipped. The meals were served in a rather austere environment but were wholesome and inexpensive. Radio was the main source of entertainment in those days and some stations had rather impressive programs devoted to music and drama. These usually occurred on Saturday and Sunday evenings. At Sloane House, there were large rooms set up like lounges or theaters where the residents could listen to their programs. Nicely dressed elderly men would pass out programs for the visitors when they came to the broadcast. Everything was very proper.

The rooms were very small, but clean and well-maintained, the furnishings minimal. There were no telephones or even a lounge chair, as I recall. Everything in the establishment was neat and orderly. There were no loud drunks yelling in the halls in the evening as was the case of the hotel that I had just left.

March 5

Darling,

Mark Hayes asked the assistant architect here about our probable sailing. Now it's rumored for the 15th. Another heard we would leave from Miami. I'll know we are sailing when we're in mid-ocean. So much monkey business tires me.

Lately, I've been very busy at the office. Clerical and estimating work, but I don't mind at $65.00 a week.

I'm managing to keep up my diary since I came down. It is quite a job to remember it and find stuff for it. It seems old after I've written it to you a few minutes before. A friend of Art Paulson's on the first boat said that he has kept a journal of 3,000 words a day since he left. He is quite a writer and should have quite a book when he gets there. He had been keeping it up for a month when he wrote about it. He also sent back coins from all the countries he visited. A good idea.

✧ **Billie: Dad had cans filled with coins from all over the world.**

The people here put so much importance on letters from the boys. Women carry them around in their purses and everyone reads them. Most travelers do not realize how important letters are to those who remain behind. I think that I will have to do a good job of reporting for those who are back home. Of course, the worst thing for the writer to say is, "Am having a wonderful time." People who stay behind want to know what they see, hear, and do. What the people look like and say. Seems strange, but that is what seems to put spirit in a letter. A letter really ought to contain elements of a diary.

I just went downstairs and found I had a letter from you. WONDERFUL!

I'm glad that Billie is having such a time. I'm sorry I couldn't have been the one to take her to her first circus, but I'm losing a lot of things and I'll lose plenty more before I'm through.

You had better not try to call me except in an emergency, because I'm out most of the time and the floor phones where we get incoming calls are very poor and one had to shout to hear at all. More tomorrow. I will give you a full report on the St. James Hotel when I examine it this weekend. I intend to keep you posted on these places.

All my love, Tootsie, Stanley

March 6

Darling,

Here I am again, still here despite all to the contrary. We have heard again today that it will be next week, but we take it with a grain of salt. Again—I'll have to be gone before I'll believe it.

I just finished the next-to-last installment of a continual story in the Collier's magazine and now I hope I can read the end before we go. I've been reading the Collier's quite religiously since I came down here. I'd probably go "bugs" if I didn't read.

March 6 - Diary

No letter waiting for me when I got back to the "Y" tonight. Can't get one every day when Doris only writes two or three times a week.

Without two-way communication, no cultural improvement is possible. I can see how people who live alone begin talking to themselves.

March 8

Darling,

Today was a beautiful, warm, sun-shining day. And believe it or not, I went out to Coney Island. Of course, the concessions are not operating, but the boardwalk was crowded. They have a wonderful boardwalk extending for two or three miles along the shore. I walked the whole length. It offered a good view of the ocean out toward Sandy Head. There was a 30-40 ft schooner and a yawl of about the same size moving offshore and I got quite a thrill out of that. New York yachtsmen go out anytime if it isn't a hurricane.

People here love the sun. They were sitting in deck chairs absorbing the sun at the rate of 10 cents per hour chair rental.

Last night was warm and pleasant so I walked down 34th to the Savoy Theatre across from Macy's near Broadway. H. M. Pulham, Esq was playing, and Tarzan was the second feature. I went in and had a pleasant evening. I thought the world must be full of H.M. Pulham.

March 9

Sweetheart,

At last, the seemingly impossible thing has happened. I received notice by special delivery tonight that we are to meet and leave next Sunday. (This is confidential, and I don't mean maybe.) It would be easy for someone to "Blitz" us if we let out too much. We are to carry only a small handbag and the rest will be checked at Pennsylvania Station. Either we go by bus or plane, and I'm quite sure we go to Florida. At least now you will know what to expect. You very likely will get no more than a card from me there—if even that. I feel better that we have something definite in view. You should feel better, too, now that that much is settled. I sure do!

I may scratch off a note this evening to Mom and Dad and set their minds at ease. It will be much better, of course, to leave by some southern route as we have too many sinking ships off New Jersey.

It's been two months since I left you. I can hardly believe it. I'm missing you and Bill more than I can say but, I know it is much too early in the game to let it get me down. I really don't dare—it would be SO easy!

Now to go downstairs and mail this before getting a bite to eat. Be a good girl and don't worry. I'll be as fit as a fiddle and better for my experiences. I've already got enough stories stored up to fill about every evening by the fire for the next few years. When I return, I should be able to give some pretty blood-curdling tales. (Without preying on my imaginary powers). Tell Billie if she is a good girl, Daddy will send her something nice from Cape Town. (Of course, I would anyway.)

All my love, Tootsie, Stanley

March 10 - Diary

Doris finally received the maps and Georg Jensen pieces I sent. I'm so pleased she liked them.

March 10

Honey Darling,

I see the Birth of the Blues is up at a small theater a couple of blocks from here so I can kill a little time. It may be months before we see another movie.

Aren't the newspapers tiresome? You can imagine it here. This town is always twice as war crazy as any inland town. The war looks gloomy. I'm sort of glad to be near the source of activity. It makes me so mad! If I were single, I'd be in the army and no mistake. We may see some action yet. It doesn't worry me, either.

Remember everything is hunky-dory. I will be seeing you before you know it.

All my love and hugs,

Stanley

March 11 - Diary

I bought a coat at John David on 42nd Street. A swell deal, but it wasn't cheap. Then went to Macy's to get pants. Now, I should be well equipped.

Went with Art Paulson to see his wife, Marion, and the new baby. They look great. The nurse let Art hold the baby. That is not something usually permitted at the hospital.

March 12 - Diary

I went back to the hospital with Art to see Marion and the baby. Art held his boy again! Swell nurse.

March 13 - Diary

I called Doris and she was excited to receive the phone call. It was like really being home. The expense was worth it. A pity Atlantic Telephone is so expensive.

✧ **Billie: Right after Daddy left for Africa, Mother took in a lady named Estelle. She cared for me, the house, cooking, and for that she got room and board and some spending money.**

March 13

Darling,

I just got upstairs and really feel better having talked to you. It was wonderful. I could hear Estelle say that New York was calling and your excited squeal. Also, when Billie ran to the phone, I could hear her feet clatter on the floor and everything. As a matter of fact, the connection was much better than I sometimes get when calling from uptown Minneapolis.

Say, I'm sorry I forgot to get the addresses of the gang so I can send them cards from the far corners of the earth. Maybe you can send them when they arrive. I'm going to turn over a new leaf on letter writing and card writing. People are going to know where I am this time.

I'm filling out a regular blank Will Form with some short, all-inclusive statements. It will give you executive powers and will say that you are to have everything, all real and personal property and all moneys and credits. It should cover everything. Insurance provisions are well-established already.

That will cost only about 50 cents instead of $5 - $50.

I'm sorry to leave you in such a broke stage, but we have our intermittent famine and plenty.

I received a letter from Dad today and Don has gotten into the Air Force and is being trained for an instructor. Beats the Army and he will be stationed at Minot airport.

Such a business! I wonder if the good old days will ever come back. It doesn't seem possible that we have gotten into such a mess. I do hope we will get out. It will require a super-human effort to do so.

Hon, I could just visualize the whole set-up at home this evening and felt as if I were right in the dining room. It did me almost as much good as a trip home might do. Two months of separation and now I'm to start off again from here. Wonderful thing the telephone!

All my love, Snooks, Stanley

March 15, 1942 - Letter to Frank Meisch

Dear Frank,

I'm not sure whether I have a letter from you to answer or whether it is the other way around. At any rate, it is time I sit down and give you some of the latest dope.

We are on about the last of our work. It's been a grind, and it is nice to see the end come into sight. We are hoping that it has done some good for our war effort. As far as I'm concerned, though, I'm sick of corrugated iron and Masonite push wood. It will be a great day when I can again design a good masonry building with some real detail.

I'm not sure just when I'll be leaving, but at any rate I'll be in the last group. The cleanup work will be some of my problem this time. Then, too, I don't mind staying longer here as I have nothing in sight at home. I'm sure the Army will take care of any threat of unemployment that I may have.

Saw the pictures of you and the "big shots" which appeared in the Minneapolis paper. You're doing all right by yourself. It's all the better these days to have work in private set-ups.

We were quite sure of going into the Army Engineer's Corps here, but we now have run into some difficulties. It is much easier to get a commission in the States than one when near the battle zone.

Give my regards to Elaine. May see you all soon - I hope.

Regards,

Stan

***The people here put so much importance on letters from the boys. Women carry them around in their purses and everyone reads them. Most travelers do not realize how important letters are to those who remain behind. I think that I will have to do a good job of reporting for those who are back home. Of course, the worst thing for the writer to say is, "Am having a wonderful time." People who stay behind want to know what they see, hear, and do. What the people look like and say. Seems strange, but that is what seems to put spirit in a letter. A letter really ought to contain elements of a diary.* — Stan**

Chapter 14

From City to Sea, at Last

March 15, 1942 - Diary

We begin our travels.

Woke up early to go to the Pennsylvania Hotel. They told us we were going to meet at 9:00, but we sat around until 11:20 before leaving for the station. They marched us back and forth in the station for about two and a half hours. Everyone was starved. We climbed aboard Pullman cars and headed south. We had a nice view. The train traveled all night and part of the next day. Then they shipped us to a warehouse on a pier. We sat and waited all afternoon. There was NO FOOD. A local church came through with bottles of milk, Ritz crackers, and candy bars. Not so hot. We cleaned rubbish and later were moved to the end of the pier. The Army fed us a meal. About 11 p.m., we got aboard our ship after a hasty customs exam. It's a real 'stinko' boat. We (Hayes, Jyring and I) have a cabin to share that's 5' x 6'6".

March 16 - Diary

Our ship has a history like Captain Bligh. There are 20 French nurses on board, a Portuguese or Puerto Rican crew, and a lousy mess. It is dirty and overcrowded. Some men are sixty to a room. Hayes, Jyring and I enjoy comfort of a sort.

Some men didn't get in until about 4:30 a.m. and slept on deck benches. It's a real mess. During the night a fight started among the crew. No one took charge. Such a hoot.

There's a mixture of college graduates and laborers. The college boys have white shirts, but the others have heavy yellow-unbleached muslin. The "white shirts" got the tiny rooms, but the laborers were in hammocks in a huge area with about 70 people. Then the army came aboard and some of the hammock guys found they lost even those hammocks to the army guys. Not fair, I know.

There was so much noise all night, no one could sleep. There are two fellows in sick bay with D.T.'s.

✧ **Billie: Dad doesn't mention the name of the ship and I wonder if he was banned from writing it down. Also, notice, especially in the next letter, but in general, that Dad would give a more positive slant on things in the letters to my mother, whereas the diary entries provided "the rest of the story."**

March 16, 1942, Monday

Sweetheart,

We are en route so will take this time to send you some extra dough. It isn't much: $20.00. We were paid just before we left so I will have $50.00 for the trip and you will have $20. There is considerable effort to conceal our travels and this will be mailed from New York by an employee of the company. A natural protector.

We have a congenial group and are traveling in good style. The food is good, and the uppers and lowers are OK.

Billie: Dad is referring to upper and lower berths.

I'm up and Art is down. Had a good night's sleep, too.

I may have to tear up my letters from home as all written matter carried is confiscated by customs. They are very particular about all documents we might carry. We are instructed to keep very close together and our mouths shut. There are so many, it is like handling a herd of cattle. We all have metal identification tags on leather cords around our necks, like dog licenses. A large green tag is fastened to our lapels giving our name, classification, and group letter.

Love, Stanley

March 17 - Diary

We woke up bright and early for breakfast and found there was a line-up by 'position.' Scrambled eggs in grease, hardtack, boiled potatoes and saltpeter coffee. There was also dry breakfast food if we preferred. Some fellows didn't get breakfast until 1 p.m. Others weren't served dinner until 9 p.m. I was lucky. Good being in "C" group. Dinner was boiled potatoes, boiled beef, bread, bread pudding, coffee and an apple.

There was a lot of trouble because the canteen only opens about ten minutes a day. This is a hell of a system.

Soldiers had dispossessed about 60 men from their bunks. Those guys now have no place to sleep.

We moved up and down the rim (of the coast) all day. Finally went up for refueling. A slow business. The ship was moored offshore all day. We watched the city. Still so far away.

March 18 - Diary

What a night! I woke up at 2 a.m. to find the room filled with a terrible smell. I dressed and went on deck to find out we are back where we started from and are near a paper mill. On the deck I see how badly some of the other boys are faring. I am lucky.

It was raining hard. One fellow had gone nuts and was taken into a warehouse on shore and was screaming crazy stuff. Later I saw a fellow taken off on a stretcher and found out he was the third one to go. (One with appendicitis and two were crazy.) No wonder… it is a small boat that has about 1500 on board and space for only 1100.

The navy hasn't okayed our ship. We are installing a lot of new guns and loading 50 caliber ammunitions, depth bombs as well. I return to bed and sleep until 10:30 in time to eat. What a breakfast. Hard-boiled eggs, coffee, cereal, real cream and moldy bread. I spent some time on deck getting some sun. The 20 nurses on board seem to be as much "on the make" as the boys. What a bunch.

We have started a campaign to improve the quarters of "Hayes, Jyring and Moe!" Not much use but we try our best.

Then we heard a load of men will go off the ship and more are coming on. We must watch our "state rooms." We can take NO chances.

There is a rumor that we may embark by midnight.

✧ **Billie: There were five groups aboard. They were: The Foley group, The Douglas group, the Johnson, Drake, and Piper group, the army, and the construction workers.**

A fellow from the Foley Group is truly driven. He has a large state room. He came out and washed his hands in a drinking fountain while Hayes and the rest were waiting for breakfast.

We now have two meals a day. Ate breakfast at 10:30 a.m. and dinner at 6:30 p.m. What lousy meals.

Behind our ship, the SS Brazil has been loading all day. Thousands of troops who are now loading, are cheering at the top of their voices. It is 7:25 p.m. I hear thumping in the engine room. We must be about to embark. What a tub. Not one toilet in ten is in working order. We went stealing buckets today so we could store water up for washing.

Some fellows are throwing down coins to Negro porters and freight men. The captain threatens to shoot them.

✧ **Billie: "them" meaning the fellows throwing the coins, I think.**

March 18, 1942 -
Letter from Frank Moorman, A Moorman and Company, Minneapolis, MN

Dear Stan,

Thanks very much for your recent letters. Please know that we are very much interested in hearing from you and in learning of your experiences.

We just received a letter from Martin Behrens, who is now stationed with the Naval Air Base in Pensacola, and he is having quite an interesting time down there.

Because we are naturally interested in your doings, and, also because we would like to continue to keep in touch with you after this war is over, we hope that you will continue to write us.

With kind regards, I remain
Sincerely yours,
Frank Moorman… (And three others from this office)

March 19 - Diary

Left port at 8:30 this morning. A second day with a lousy breakfast. I felt a twinge of sea sickness all day, so ate NO dinner.

It sure is a swell ocean—beautiful, with a lot of white caps. Our boat really vibrates and rolls. I hope the weather continues fair so we will not get seasick. Art and others can't eat.

I spent the whole afternoon on deck dozing in the sun. The wind is cold. We always must wear life preservers. Mine is a relic. The lifeboat drills are a farce. I hope we don't have to rely on them.

A bomber flew over us in the morning. We didn't know what caused the excitement. Found out later they saw a submarine near-by.

Our group is large, and we are having a hard time getting into the ship's canteen. Such prices. Candy is 2/15¢, cigarettes are 15¢ a pack, cola is 10¢ a bottle. Some crew members are selling individual cigarettes for 50¢ each. Dirty swine.

We hear there are 12 men in the brig. Some stuff. We are under military law. It is noisy, but efficient. The current captain is a mule skinner.

✧ **Billie: Someone who might skin or outsmart a mule.**

We had a beautiful sunset tonight—a wonderful movie camera opportunity.

Hope I can sleep okay. I'm not seasick at all. Hope it holds. I sat on the deck tonight watching the phosphorescent sparks—a glow emitted by bioluminescent plankton, I'm told. New experience for me.

March 20 - Diary

I took a cold salt-water shower when I woke this morning. Really refreshing. I had to wash some of it off. We now are obliged to make our own lunches. If I get home food again, I'll stay home. No more roaming for me!

We are making fair time in spite of a lot of zig-zagging. I am trying to figure out our approximate position. Salt spray is tiresome when you have it everywhere.

We now have blue bulbs in all our lights. So, no more reading at night.

March 21 - Diary

Calisthenics was at 6:40 this morning. Afterwards, I ate a lousy breakfast, sat on deck and went to sleep. When I woke up, I checked the time and noticed I had a hole in my watch pocket. I lost $45.00. A terrible thing when I think about what I might have bought, or what it might have done for the home bills. It makes me sick. Many of the boys offered to lend me money. I may accept from a lot of them. I still want to send stamps and stuff home.

I may have lost it last night. Who knows? A grave error on my part, but I didn't want to leave money in an unlocked room. No use crying over spilt milk, I guess.

One of my friends insisted on loaning me $10.00. Not necessary but handy. We won't be let off the ship anyway, so no use for money. Would like some stamps.

Art came in and now I'm in crew mess. Art put up the dough for me. Swell guy.

March 22 - Diary

I am reconciled to the loss of my money.

Up at 5:30 a.m. A beautiful Caribbean sunrise!

What a pity we can't have cameras.

We were told we sank three subs since leaving the U.S.

Saw a ship on the horizon at noon today. First time.

I was assigned to garbage duty this morning. I never handled anything but had a lot of fun in a cold room eating delicacies. Eating mess with the crew was swell for breakfast and lunch. I almost got in K.P. for the voyage, but no luck.

San Juan, Puerto Rico, came into sight this afternoon. It is beautiful. It looked like a fairy city on the Caribbean as we entered the harbor.

Louis Rosenberg and I finished our garbage detail, then came up to look at the city before we went to bed.

March 23 - Diary

There was no blackout last night. It was a nice night except for the fights. Liquor came on board. So, some of the fellows had a wild time. No one can go ashore.

The harbor is landlocked. Hills to the south are beautifully wooded with mahogany and orchids. There is a national park with a fresh-water pool—a true honeymoon spot. I'm going to bring Doris and Billie here for sure.

✧ **Billie: And he did take the family!**

We watched native boys diving for coins alongside the boat. They are really good. When oil comes to the surface, they push it aside. Some other native boys were shot at while swimming to the boat.

Two of the boys from the Foley Group were sent back to the U.S. by plane. One had jaundice.

We left at noon and sailed to St. Thomas.

We watched four Barbados negroes diving for coins alongside. They are fine physical specimens. Negresses walk with piles of wood on their heads. Looks funny. There are many palms and live oak trees. Oh, Boy! No one can imagine the beauties of the Lesser Antilles.

Doris and Bill must come down here with me.

Billie: My parents' ashes were spread here in the waters of St. Thomas, Thanksgiving 2012. The family took a cruise and visited many of the islands Dad's ship anchored at during his trip to Africa in 1942.

The US Destroyer Cole tied up to us tonight. Boys from the Cole tell us that two subs have been sunk since they escorted us here. Tough for the U-Boats.

March 24 - Diary

We have a lot of trouble with one of the captains. Some of the boys tell him off. How he has changed.

I spent the evening on deck with Hayes and Jyring. It is nice to know such swell fellows. We listened to the singing. There are some good voices on board.

March 25 - Diary

Did my laundry and wished for home. My sunburn is turning brown.
I spent all the afternoon reading Nana on deck. What a book!
Have been thinking of home today, which is bad.

What fools we men are—never knowing when we are well off.

March 26 - Diary

Several people are suffering from exhaustion, sun poisoning, and other kindred ailments.

My throat was very sore last night. I had my throat painted this morning. I'm taking sulfathiazole for tonsillitis.

The canteen is finally open. We can get soap, tokens, cigarettes, and peanuts. That helps some. They will stay open until they sell out. No clothing, however. We're getting low on fresh water. We have to use saltwater to wash and bathe.

Our trip has only just begun. There will be such a long time to follow. I'll be happy to get to work.

One's mind stagnates here.

We are still not across the equator. Everyone is wondering our possible destination. We are told by the captain that ten days remain on this leg of the voyage. Hard to believe.

We are nearly out of water.

March 27 - Diary

We've been told there is no more fresh water even for washing. So, they commanded us again—we must use saltwater.

I was up at dawn and, as usual, did not have a good night's sleep. I was able to doze a bit on deck, but the sun was too warm.

Because the boat is so large and has over 1,000 passengers. I don't see my friends often. We have few diversions. Someone broke the rowing machine the first day it was out. There is some work being done to set up the ship's library.

We've heard that the cruisers out ahead of us got a sub last night. Rumor has it that we are bound for St. Helena. If so, I had better send a lot of letters to friends. They would appreciate the post mark.

Tonight, there was a lot of singing on deck by a bunch of fellows. It is a pleasant diversion.

We all still reminisce about home. What a lot of foreign languages are spoken on this boat. Cosmopolitan!

March 28 - Diary

Today is our 14th day at sea. Four weeks to go. An endless period. There were several bad fights last night.

We are now a small convoy. Some say we have one destroyer in our convoy, but I don't see it.

Even though we are near the equator, it was cool last night. My throat is cured. Sulfathiazole is a wonderful remedy.

The library opened today. We have a lot of stuff to read.

✧ **Billie: Literature, music, movies—in fact, all the arts—was mother's milk to my dad.**

I have started to read The Letters of Gertrude Bell (Arabian Diaries—Travel Narrative—by Gertrude Bell, 1927.) I am enjoying the book. I will read short stories for a while.

The W's eat first today, so we had a long wait. It will take hours to get to the C's. The boys are singing again. It is strange how music brings all of us together.

We traveled east all day today, as usual. We are close to the equator. Sticky heat and no fresh water for washing. Who knows when we'll have clean clothes again.

March 29 - Palm Sunday

Army Captain White will do the Palm Sunday service at dusk today.

We crossed another time zone. Clocks are set ahead one hour. We awake in the dark. I was so tired, I sat on deck wrapped in a blanket and dozed.

Early morning chill and wind is no fun. How can the wind be so strong? Today was a gloomy and dark Sunday. I didn't attend services. They were crowded and the sea was rough. The afterdeck pitches considerably. I spent the afternoon reading and sleeping. Not much else to do.

Spent some time bragging to my friends about Doris and Bill. Who wouldn't!

Art has been figuring our position. We crossed the 45th meridian yesterday, and we should cross the equator tomorrow. Should be easy to find our position!

March 30 - Diary

Today is the turning point. We will know if we are headed for South America, Ascension Island, or St. Helena—a volcanic tropical-island in the South Atlantic Ocean. Last night we supposedly made a detour of 90 miles north to avoid a hurricane. The seas were plenty rough, but the hurricane never materialized. Some of the boys were seasick. I went back to bed this morning to get more sleep. Rest is a big problem with the heat and noise.

There was a big riot down in the after-hold last night involving about 100 fellows. The infirmary was full this morning.

One of the planes took a backflip trying to land on the carrier in high winds.

The cruiser was trying out its anti-aircraft guns today. Nice show.

We can now see the Southern Cross in the evening. It reminds me of old sea stories.

March 31 - Diary

Now we are out of fruit, and the commissary is all out of tidbits. Too bad.
We changed course 90° at dusk. Perhaps to fool any subs?
Washed my clothes in saltwater. Lousy deal!

April 1 - Diary

Saw a school of porpoises to our port. Hundreds! Jumping through the water. Quite a sight! Some fellows saw a whale this morning. Supposedly our next port is a black town, at least fellows who have been there say so.

We live on rumors.

April 2 - Diary

Rumor has it that we will land tonight. I hope so.

Al Edwards gave me the dope on dengue fever. I wouldn't want to get it. I wonder how explorers do so well on rough jungle excursions. What I wouldn't give for a good freshwater bath!

We heard $28,000 and about $2,800 of commissary goods were left on the dock in Barbados.

April 3, Good Friday - Diary

How I miss Good Friday service at Westminster in Minneapolis. I'm sure I will appreciate them more when I get back. We never know how much they mean until we are away. Services were stopped at 2:15 p.m.

We are two miles from Freetown in West Africa on the Atlantic coast—a yellow beach, few palms, and a hell of a hot sun in the haze. There are low hills in the background with a few small white buildings perched thereon.

CHAPTER 15

The Black Continent

We had to destroy all correspondence when coming aboard
— Stan

April 3 - Diary (continued)
There will be no shore leave. Cholera, typhus, and dysentery in town. Blacks were chased away from the ship. We are out of luck.

The fire alarm went off at 10 p.m. There was a fire in Number Two Hold—a couple of bunks were destroyed. Luckily no baggage was lost.

How will this ship ever reach its destination? Such a mix-up!

April 4 - Diary
Everyone is perspiring in the heat. What a life!

Home was never like this. I slept in and had a splendid breakfast.

There is NO saltwater fit to use. Bad!

There are dozens of ships in the harbor. Also, many feluccas with funny sails...and, cayugas. Today is hot and misty. The natives pull many cayugas alongside. The crew shoots at them, then turn the hoses on them.

Malaria is rampant. Sweat mosquitos!

✧ **Billie: Cayugas and feluccas are small sailing vessels.**

April 5, Easter Sunday - Diary
We had Easter Service from the afterdeck. A chaplain from a ship SS Brazil gave the talk. The balance of the service was conducted by a Mississippi Presbyterian minister. Handel sounded strange on deck under a blazing sun. The rumor is that we will have baked ham. We'll see.

We had tough chicken. I made a chicken sandwich to take away for the evening. We saw some drunk French sailors in a sailboat.

I don't think I'll ever leave home again. This is NOT like home.

April 6 - Diary
What a night. I finished Drums Along the Mohawk. I hope we don't stay here much longer. There are lots of rumors about our lousy ship. Two British convoys came in. Twenty ships each and an incredibly large liner loaded with troops. Also, a few full-size battle wagons.

It rained all afternoon. The boys spread canvas on "A" deck and took rainwater showers. Dinner was bad, as usual: pork, kidney beans, sauerkraut, potatoes, and chocolate pudding. The bread was sour. I have indigestion.

Ah! To be home again and away from all this!

April 7 - Diary

We've been told all our eggs are case eggs (eggs in crates that are cracked each day as needed.) I can't see how they spoil them so!

There was a bad fight in the kitchen tonight between the black boys and the Puerto Ricans. One was stabbed through the thigh several times.

We spend a lot of time sitting around and talking about home. Especially about our favorite foods. Fruit soup was the main topic tonight.

I'm thinking more about home. I hope Doris isn't worried too much. She will become accustomed to slow mail. If we could only reach Cape Town.

April 8 - Diary

We are still in port. The boredom is intense. Several rumors have been circulated that we are about to leave. Yet, we are still here. There was a near riot at mess this morning. Grapefruit was secured for us that we otherwise would not have received, since we were last in line.

Everyone is very tired of staring at the shoreline and hills. The mechanics are still working on the engine. Another small convoy left today, and we remain. We may be here for good.

Tonight's dinner was not bad, except for conditions. Tough beef, pasta, pudding, rice soup, succotash. The bread was better today.

I talked to Clint Cessna quite a bit. He has had considerable success. An engineer says he has never seen such a foul outfit and he was a sailor! I'm really losing weight where it does the most good. My muscle building is okay, too.

April 9 - Diary

Same weather. The temperature must be over 100 in the sun and the humidity is very high and it's only spring here.

Today was like all previous days except it was better.

Edwards smuggled a steak to me with some good French-fried potatoes for dinner.

One hundred men will be allowed to go swimming and washing on the beach. We are 1500 on a ship that can accommodate 1100. We won't be here that long, I'm afraid.

More convoys left today. The harbor is less crowded. There must still be about 100 boats.

There must be a native festival across the bay. Dozens of dhows (small sailing boats) were crossing.

I took a good shower at high tide and feel better.

The officers told us they called New York. Our families will be notified that all is well.

We are to go swimming on the beach on the 20th of April.

I hope we're not here that long!

April 10 - Diary

We now have about 50 cases of yellow jaundice on board.

We've been in Freetown a week. Last night we had a near hurricane and the water was phosphorescent. It made quite a show.

Air was cooler, so I slept well.

There is talk today about sending people ashore to buy curios and stuff for the men.

Someone saw a French seaplane sink near their ship. The wreck was raised later in the day. A large French hospital ship moved out today. One hundred of our fellows had a fine time on shore, swimming and trading with the natives.

Today we received the news of an unsuccessful evacuation of 36,000 US soldiers from Bataan in the Philippines.

Perhaps we're being held here because there is fighting in the Indian Ocean.

A jazz band has been organized. They entertained us this evening with old favorites. Not bad.

April 11 - Diary

It's been two months since I left home. Seems like we have been gone a year, and we haven't gotten to our destination, yet. Nine months to go for this contract.

Lt. Dillon shot at a native boat over our stern. The four natives jumped out and one was drowned. Two white men from our ship and one soldier jumped into the sea to save him, but the tide was too strong. Our deck officer didn't want to launch a boat to save the would-be rescuers.

I posted an airmail letter on the island earlier today. It cost $1.00, but I was relieved to send something.

April 12 - Diary

Four weeks since we left New York for our trip. My health is excellent. I've been losing weight, steadily. However, exercises have built up my physique.

April 13 - Diary

One fellow threw his food in the garbage yesterday and got in trouble. However, he got out okay. There was a near riot at the mess over the bad corned beef and cabbage they served. Also had rotten meat loaf in the later mess. A petition was circulated protesting the food.

Tons of beef were put on board during the night from another ship when the other ship's refrigeration plant had broken down.

What a mess!

April 14 - Diary

We had a good roast pork dinner today. I ate my fill.

I'm finishing Pride and Prejudice.

April 15 - Diary

A Johnson, Drake and Piper carpenter was taken off the ship today because of a letter he gave to a native to post. It contained damaging evidence of some sort. The censurer had just read it. I hope my letter goes out without trouble.

Fellows have been using our veal stew to catch fish. They made spinners from the lining of cigarette cases. Some Pepsi Cola was brought up from the hold. It was hot and sold for 15¢ a bottle. I was able to bring a sandwich away from mess today. I won't be hungry tonight. No food from 3 p.m. to 7 a.m. is a long time.

April 16 - Diary

Breakfast was a nice surprise. We had fried eggs and ham. Then we had steak for dinner. Wonders never cease.

When our boys go ashore, they are being fooled by the natives. The natives are much better traders than we are. Our ship is now full of baskets and coconuts.

Pan American finally delivered the equipment needed to repair our ship. We should be able to leave in a week.

Our last sheets and towels were delivered today. There won't be any more until the laundry is done in Cape Town. It will be good to feel clean again!

I finally drank my Pepsi Cola from St. Thomas. Artie cooled it in the ice box. How I miss the good old "Coke" from Minneapolis.

April 17 - Diary

Word came down that we are to leave Freetown and fly to either Cairo or Asmara in East Africa directly. I'd prefer Cairo, if possible. Better than Cape Town. Asmara is south of Egypt and the capital of Eritrea.

Here's the order in which we will depart: first the army, then the Foley group, the Douglas group, Johnson, Drake & Piper, and the construction workers. Then, the word was we were to fly in small groups to Asmara. We were all elated. Later in the evening, the captain said that in ten days we would go by army transport along the planned route. The news was a great disappointment and made us all depressed. Pan American Airlines flew the army men out tonight.

April 18 - Diary

This is a sad ship today. The disappointment of yesterday is deeply felt. There were many fights on board last night. One fellow had a cracked skull from being slugged with a piece of handrail pipe. Food is again at a low ebb. Stews and hash. Soggy cake. I haven't even been up on deck today.

The USS Fairfax just dropped anchor on the way back from the job. I wonder if any fellows on board are sick of it all. They are workers and families returning to the States from Lagos, Nigeria. I'd like to talk to them!

There was lots of excitement tonight. A sergeant was taken off on a stretcher for internal hemorrhaging. One fellow broke his back when he fell down the stairs. More jaundice and other illnesses are coming up all the time.

There was a new riot by the Foley officer to get more medical care for his team. The SS Combs is on the way here from Trinidad. It's a troop transport ship which is supposed to be empty and is being loaded with provisions at Trinidad. It's due to arrive in one week.

April 19 - Diary

Life goes on much as before. We had a bad breakfast and my group is now last in line for meals. All our troops are gone and so are the doctors. Only a broken-down ship's doc remains. More jaundice and other ills are coming up all the time. A new riot by the Foley group broke out—to get more medical care. Mail now to go back on the Fairfax. Three cents, so it will be mailed in New York. We hope we can be sure the letters will reach the destination without mishap.

We are having a hell of a time. The Foley group is rioting in the forward.

Many men will be going back on the Fairfax. Hard to accomplish, it takes politics to swing it.

April 20 - Diary

What a night! At least a dozen fights broke out in the lobby and no one could stop it. At least a dozen fights occurred in the mess line also. Everyone is trying to get off the ship. Bud Milbank is coming down with jaundice. One of our ship's "horse" doctors left. Hayes and Jyring are both sick, too.

We just got word that the last planeload of soldiers crashed a mile and a half from the airport. Twenty-one soldiers and two pilots were killed. No one could be identified. They are all are buried in a common grave. We will remember what fine men they were.

Had mania on deck tonight. It's the wild west as usual. Some beer that was stolen by the Foley's crowd from the steward's store was the issue.

April 21 - Diary

Memorial services are to be held for soldiers on deck today. Three faiths.

Boys have had good fishing. They caught a couple of four-to-six-foot long sharks. I'll take black bass for sport. I was starved for the evening meal. Ate like a horse.

We had a Crime Club movie on deck tonight. It didn't amount to much because there is no sound. A poor Eastman projector.

Artie and I had a good bull session. He's okay. The hold is full of fellows drunk on warm beer.

April 22 - Diary

Everyone was drunk last night. Breaking down doors and stealing cigarettes. Some fellows on night crew baked a forty-pound fish with French fried potatoes. We were also able to buy a batch of apple and cherry pies at $2.00 each.

Cheese and crackers were in almost every room. Even ginger ale was flowing freely. Surprising what food is on hand when one looks for it.

We have had a lot of excitement today, as usual, with everyone recuperating from a drunk.

No one is in authority.

Foley threatens to throw the steward overboard.

Artie and the fellows had filet mignon and French fries with apple pie and lemonade at 2 a.m. Lucky. They are the biggest arrangers I've ever seen. A lot of fellows were swimming alongside today in the sewage-strewn water. It's plenty dirty. I'm sure I wouldn't care for swimming in it.

Movie again last night. A Crime Club mystery. No sound.

Letters Home to Doris

April 22, 1942

(stamp, 3d, a three pence-British stamp) Sierra Leone
Darling,

This will be the last letter (I hope) from this port as we are expecting a new ship to take us the rest of the way. Conditions will very likely be much improved, so we are in better spirits. Perhaps we will be less crowded and have better eating conditions. At any rate, we will have a lot less trouble with our ship. It will be newer and should proceed without further mishaps and breakdowns.

I'm having time to catch up on my reading and have been doing a lot of studying. They are engineering studies which will equip me for my registration exam as soon as I get home. I'm going to spread my own wings when I get back and we should profit by it for sure.

It is no harder to find a robust career than to find a job.

April 23, 1942

Sweetheart,

We have a nice group of fellows who gather every evening on a rope locker on the top deck: Louis Conrad Rosenberg (the great etcher), Mark Hays (from Jim Hills' office in Minneapolis), Bud/Jerry Jyring (from Hibbing, Minnesota), two structural engineers and myself. We have a lot in common and have a good time. While we have been stranded in harbor here, we have had movies every night. So, when we tire of chatter, we gather at the afterdeck and see outdoor movies. Supposedly 16 mm sound, but there is no sound. They have a new Eastman sound projector and it sure is lousy compared to the B&H 16 mm sound apparatus. The first time it was used, the sound went on the blink, so we have had silent pictures since. A lot of Wild West and Crime Club movies. The latter aren't so bad. It breaks up the monotony of the trip.

If all had gone well, we would have been at our destination now, but, of course, it didn't. We were in on old tub that had boiler trouble all the way across. Not able to repair it either. So, we have been waiting all these weeks for a substitute ship. We have been getting our mail by hit and miss. Some mail was given to soldiers leaving for Egypt, 21 of whom, plus two pilots, and they were killed in a plane crash the next day. Some of the mail was given to British soldiers to post in town, and some mail was sent on cruise ships bound for the U.S. And this, finally, is to be posted on shore through regular channels. I will be glad when we arrive at our job and can send regular mail. I don't like to feel that every one of my letters has less than a fifty-fifty chance of going through. This one is my number six letter so you can check it with its predecessors or those to follow.

We've bought the whole town out of their supply of pith helmets. At first, they cost $2.00 and now they are $5.00. I hope to have a better situation at Cape Town. After all, that is supposed to be quite a metropolis. I will certainly welcome the pavements of Minneapolis when I get back. Strange, I haven't seen any place since, which I think can equal it for shopping facilities and opportunities for a full life.

I suppose you have all been wondering how long it would be before we would write and say that we had arrived. I wish we knew. We should be there by the time you get this. But we can't be too sure. There always are delays coming up. So far, there has been little excitement. The boys have caught several four-foot to six-foot sharks over the side since we arrived here. But give me a Lake Lida black bass for a real fight. The fellows had the night catch of a 40 lb. fish that looked like tarpon. They had quite a feed. It cost them about $20 in bribery to get the meal prepared. It takes a lot of bribery to get anything in the way of favors. Everyone seems to have his price. Plenty of corruption. These New Yorkers are past masters of the art of "fixing." They are always figuring out some way of "organizing" a racket. Some of the cooks are busy baking pies after hours with company materials and charging $2.00 a piece *for them. A good steak would bring about $5.00 now. And I imagine they sell plenty of them at that rate.*

Some of the boys have been busy sending postcards home. But most of the cards from here have naked Negroes on them and of course the U.S. postal authorities will not let them through. So, a lot of them will be surprised when they are held up. There is a pretty loose-marshaled settlement on shore here. All the men and women of the black group run around with only a little clothing around the hips. The free and easy life! Not a very wholesome looking lot either with every imaginable physical defect/disease. British have done wonders to improve conditions, but it is not an easy task.

About stamps—they are hard to obtain. Ben Hallberg and Areal are a couple I would like to get some for. Save all the envelopes for postmark as well as the stamps, okay? Maybe Ben will be interested in them. It is my intention to send out a lot of cards at Cape Town if we can get ashore. All the ships are under quite rigid supervision on the matter of shore leave and we haven't done too well so far. Maybe better later. They are afraid some of the boys might get into mischief. They really would, too. Some of the fellows represent some lower groups of mankind. We have all classification of labor and professions abroad. And some of them are rough.

I hope you can read my regular line of chatter. One thing leads to another. I always write as I think and that is an ever-changing lingo of many subjects. But so many things come up, so, down they go on paper. You can look at them and laugh. I usually find I would laugh, too, if I should read them myself.

We are only about one day's run from the equator. Despite that, it really is not too hot. It is not nearly as uncomfortable on shipboard as it was in Minneapolis in the summer of 1936. It is now the peak of the summer here, too, with the sun directly overhead at noon. On shore it is quite hot and, though it hasn't rained since we came here four weeks ago, it is quite humid. There is a lot of heavy jungle growth on the mountains overlooking the harbor. Many of the trees seem as green as any I've ever seen. I believe that there is a great deal of mahogany here. A few palms are to be seen along the white sand beach. They should be just about stripped of coconuts after a long time spent here. They are quite small coconuts, but a welcome treat.

My usual scrawl is made much worse by the fact that since leaving New York, I've been using a scratch pad on my knees as a writing table. And usually, I write in a hurry to meet some deadline on mail. Today, for a change, I can write a bit more leisurely.

I'm looking forward very much to arriving at our destination, so I get some mail from you. I wasn't even able to take any of your letters to me along with me to reread.

We had to destroy all correspondence when coming aboard.

For safety sake, in case we were captured, we were told. So, I have only yours and Bill's pictures to look at.

When you write, please be sure to put in as much detail as possible and answer all my multitudinous questions.

I'd give plenty for a couple of Scotch and sodas in the Viking Room with the Gang. And a big steak dinner at Harry's or Charlie's afterward. We will really have a celebration when I get back. Right now, that is what most of us are thinking about—me, particularly. I never knew what I was missing before. We are really forced to leave home before we appreciate it fully. Most of us will be much better for the experience. Most people will not believe us if we tell the stories of what happened. Well, goodbye until next time, Sweetheart. I'm feeling fine and love you and Bill more than ever before.

All my love, Stanley

April 23 - Diary

Fellows were tossing a drunk in the hall last night and he collapsed—a degrading affair.

They say they now will accept mail to be censored here on the ship. I'm tired of all the monkey business and am hoping we will soon be on the SS Coamo (American Steam Passenger Ship—1925–42).

We will have no shore leave when we reach Cape Town by convoy. Such a mess.

Now they are selling postcards at 16¢ each.

Artie and the rest had a feast last night. Lamb chops, cottage fried potatoes, blackberry pie, lemonade, salad.

Word just received—The SS Coamo was given up for lost. So, we will likely return to Trinidad (in the Caribbean) or go to Cape Town, Africa for repairs. They are now inventorying supplies. We may be rationed.

A lot of men are now on ship's payroll. No more details. Bought five pounds of cheese, so now we have cheese sandwiches. No more pie—they had been bootlegging. Louis and I tried to buy one for $2.00.

Tonight, we had another good movie, Something to Sing About. No sound as usual.

Bull session until 12:00.

April 24 - Diary

We have a new K.P. and dish crew. All get paid $82.50 per month. Not a bad deal if one needs some extra dough. No one will get paid until they arrive at Massawa, Eritrea.

As usual, we have little to do during the day.

I took a little trip around the boat to get exercise and diversion.

April 25 - Diary

We were up at 7 a.m. We are first to eat before our trip ashore.

We had a pleasant trip to shore. Then we were able to see our boat as others see it. What a tub.

Saw native troops and nice British soldiers.

The beach was white and beautiful. Had a wonderful swim and wished Doris were here. She would be thrilled with the waves.

Billie: Mother was a swimmer, a lifeguard and first-aid swimmer. In several places where there were beaches, even if they didn't go ashore on this route, he would comment on how Mother would love to see these beaches and these waves.

The natives do a thriving bazaar business and are real bargainers. We never get value for our stuff.

A water boat has been alongside our ship all afternoon. I think we are filling up for departure on Monday.

They are trying to arrange for mail and money in Cape Town. Maybe? Now they have moved the player piano upstairs. So, we have plenty of din. We were all to be interviewed tonight for a Mechanical Draftsman position. Now, we find it is dirty politics.

April 26 - Diary

Okay—for a Sunday at home! Feel sort of down-in-the mouth today—we are so unsettled and have little hope for better.

April 27 - Diary

We hear the rumor that we will go to Trinidad because of its dry dock facilities. We are sure uncertain of our future. Anyone's guess is good.

We are ordering a case of chocolate bars from shore…$3.00 for thirty-six pieces. A high price, but candy is precious. Had our usual bull session and lunch in our room. Cheese and peach sauce juice. We really ought to have a quart of ice-cream and a piece of cake (at $2.00 each). We are all chafing at the bit and raring to go.

April 28 - Diary

We had a beautiful night last night. There was a full moon and a good pianist at the piano. I was up on deck enjoying a lot of memories brought on by old favorites. It's enough to make one homesick.

Flour, salt, and sugar are being loaded now. A lot of green bananas were put on too. News is that we will now eat the same food as the captain eats. Things may improve. We finally got only five of our candy bars.

April 29 - Diary

I am to get first clean towels in three weeks! No sheets though. About 20 large ships came in a convoy—large liners with perhaps 4000 men each.

Mostly Canadian ships, so we can expect a large offensive convoy. Now I'm trying to draw $5.00 from the commissary as well as $10.00 when we reach Cape Town. I hope we have shore leave.

The dining room is being reorganized. I think we may be rationed soon.

April 30 - Diary

Today we had a good breakfast because of the new system. Lt. Dillon stayed in the dining room to enforce it. He did a good job. We shall eat better from now on. There were a lot of comments for and against.

Heavy rain brought everyone up on deck for a shower. We acted like small boys in the summer.

I hear someone is looking for Bud. I told Bud, that before long someone will call for Moe. When I got to the office, I was asked to be ready to fly in two hours.

I halted my dinnertime and was soon packed with Artie's help.

We are truly over the black continent — a lifetime ambition finally realized! This is my first time on a plane — it's a DC-3 paratrooper. **— Stan**

PART V

1942: Africa

Louis Rosenberg made this Christmas card for Stan who sent it to Doris for Christmas, 1942

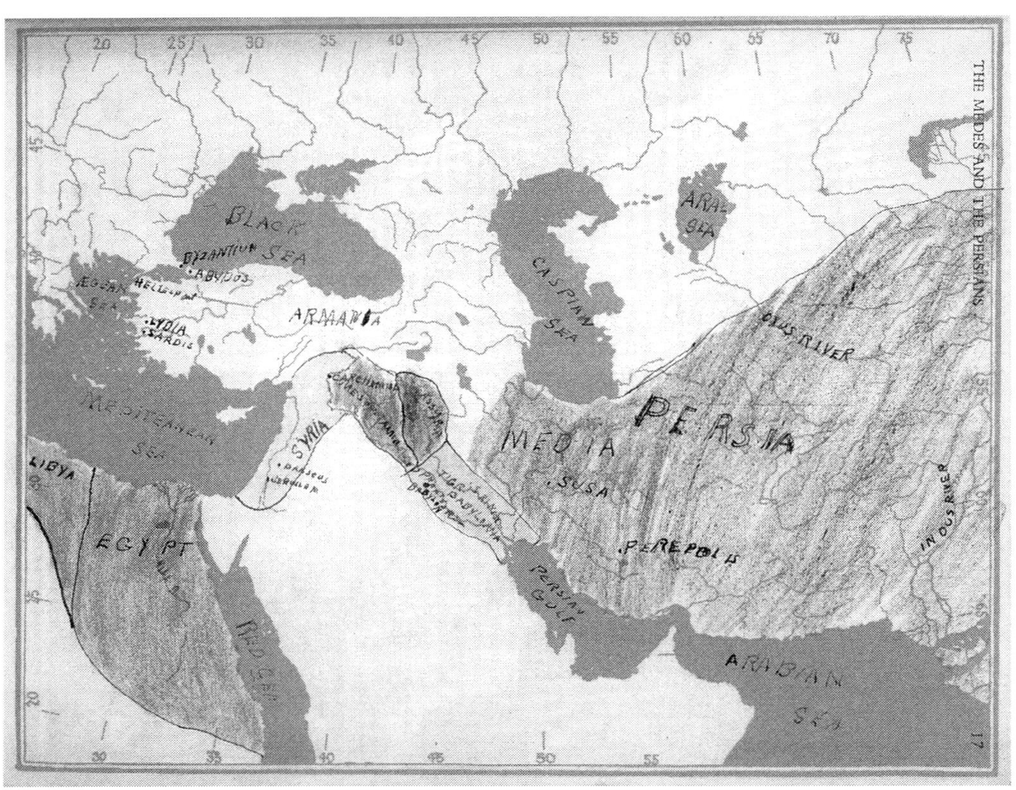

Stanley's map drawn in 6th grade world history class

CHAPTER 16

Flying Over the Dark Continent

April 30 - Diary (continued)

A tug soon took us to Freetown. What a place! It's more exciting-looking in person than in the movies!

After a breakneck truck ride to Hastings Airport, we arrived at dawn. A beautiful winding road. Many blossoming trees and bushes.

May 1 - Diary

The plane took off at 9 a.m. What a view! Clouds and mountains. We are truly over the Dark Continent—a lifetime ambition finally realized! This is my first time on a plane—it's a DC-3 paratrooper.

Wish Dad could see the view.

We head for Marshall, Liberia (90 minutes away). Arrive and have a good old American breakfast: shredded wheat and bananas in cream, bacon, toast and marmalade, tea, and chocolate cake. We're on a Firestone Rubber Plantation. Wonderful, mysterious Africa!

I can hardly believe we are flying over real Black Villages, months away from civilization. Such jungles—such parks. We follow the beach at about 2000' and 160 mph. Leave at 1 p.m. for the four-hour hop to Takoradi where we arrive at 4:05. A nice airport, but no courtesy.

We left at 4:25. It's nice to be up above the heat of the port. A pleasant flight down the coast over villages of native masonry. We arrived at Accra (Ghana) at 5:05 and were flown to a luxurious camp. It is hard to realize that we are at war.

We were weighed and assigned to tents. Then to the center to buy Scotch and beer. The Royal Air Force took us to dinner which was swell. Tea in enormous cups. Corned beef, lettuce, mashed potatoes, and fruit for dessert.

I had a bad night trying to sleep on springs with no mattress. I also started on quinine tonight and slept under netting because mosquitos give no warning. Gnats are a force to be reckoned with. This is Negro country and their way of life is strange to behold. What a night under the moon. I got about one hour's sleep.

Billie: When Dad got settled later in the day, this is where we continue the travel to Eritrea, eventually.

Two men to a room in masonry barracks. Furniture like a good hotel in the United States. We see mahogany in every place; rafters, roofers, doors… black, too!

They gave us a swell dinner. Soup, pork chops, fruit, wild pineapple preserve. A real city began only five months ago, sits amid ant hills six feet high. They have stamped out disease to a great extent. Until now, even the British governor used a latrine bucket. They say most of our men have been sent to fly. I hope so. We had a violent tropical rainstorm for half an hour. Our beds get wet. Asleep at 12:30 a.m. What a day. We have come 1000 miles.

So, this is Africa! One third of the year is gone!

May 2 - Diary

I was awake at 5:30 a.m. Luckily, I sleep like an alarm clock. I washed and went to mess. A good breakfast… grapefruit, pineapple preserves and toast, scrambled eggs, and good U.S. coffee. Set off at about 7:30.

A lot of interesting things to see. We saw the "slave" market where native help is hired. Looked like The Sun is My Undoing. We passed over a lot of tiny farms with palm groves. A lot of rice paddies, too.

Our plane was stifling hot inside and my mosquito bites itch. I hope quinine is good. Arrived at Accra at 9:10 a.m. and had a nice rest and orange juice. Wish all stops were as pleasant. Would like to send a letter home but none of the facilities are open to civilians. I set my watch ahead one hour. We pulled off at 10:58 a.m.

Accra is a nice-looking city from above. We crossed a loop of the Niger at 12:20 p.m.

I discovered I lost my Parker fountain pen—after 12 years. And finally reached Kano after an hour of bumpy air. Kano is the head market of the caravan routes of the Sahara. The temperature stays at 120°.

We were taken to the Royal Air Force station for wonderful curry. Vultures and lizards abound like cats and dogs.

We got back in a stifling hot plane at 3:30 p.m. The last lap of our trip was tough. Violent motion. I got sick. When we landed at Maiduguri, I was relieved.

We could see a bad sandstorm approaching. It struck two minutes after we landed. We were lucky!

A small rain shower got all our beds wet, so we slept on old cots. Dinner was wild goose, goat, and steak, followed with fine pineapple pie.

Some of the boys have nice horses—I wonder how much one would cost.

May 3 - Diary

Our plane took off at 6:08 in the morning. I sat up front. The flight was a bit smoother. Several rocky pinnacles can be seen through drifted sand, brush, and a few Arab camps.

At 11:30 a.m. we landed at Germania, the Anglo-Egyptian Sudan. It's 105° in the shade.

Boys were busy trading knives; they don't seem to mind the filth. Such drought, like Death Valley.

We get to relax at the Royal Air Force base. A lot of wrecked planes. We hear that a sandstorm has struck El Fasher, in Northeast Africa, our next stop. So, we may stay overnight. I really hope so. We were served goat meat sandwiches. Not too good for me now.

Boys came back with a beauty of a spear. I picked up a plain one. It's not so good, but it's something.

There is a sandstorm at Khartoum that is so bad our plane will stay here until tomorrow morning.

For the first time in seven or eight weeks we can listen to the radio. Seems strange.

I see my first camels. They look rather sick. Who wouldn't be with so much heat?

Despite the heat, this camel is smiling at me!

We're shown our quarters. They look like a set from Beau Geste. Egyptian beds, a shower with one quart of water. We slept through a sandstorm until it was time for tea. (4 p.m.) We sat under a gas lamp and drank good hot tea. Dinner was tomato soup, asparagus, potatoes and hash, and canned beans. We had Turkish coffee in the lounge. We listened to the radio. I heard Lord Haw Haw (radio show) for the first time.

Got back to our rope beds and tried to sleep. The banging shutters and the heat didn't help.

May 4 - Diary

Up at dawn after a hot night. A bad breakfast. I would give a lot for some ice water.

We stowed our spears and other paraphernalia and took off at 6:08 a.m. We could see the village where our spears were made. At 6:45 a.m. we approached our first range of mountains. We were up high. Up here the temperature is cool and nice. At 7:20 a.m., we are on the other side of the first range. A few mud villages and an area of large open plain. At 7:35 a.m., we flew over El Fasher the town where we originally planned to go. It is a large village with many clay walls on the edge of a real sand desert. At 10:50 a.m., we could see the Nile.

We arrived at Khartoum Agricultural College Airport at 11 a.m. We were taken to the college buildings. We were served limeade from water coolers. All the buildings are yellow brick with soft reddish tile roofs and pea-green shutters.

Our plane took off for Asmara this evening. We should be located tonight. The trip over the mountains was uneventful. We were surprised at the tilled fields. Asmara looked like a good place to us despite all the bombing it has endured.

No one expected us in Asmara. We had to wait in the airport for a bus to take us at a wild pace, down the mountain to Gura. Many of our old friends were there to greet us. Good food and wonderful quarters.

CHAPTER 17

Eritrea, East Africa, 1942

This is the Africa I have always imagined! — Stan

Billie: I selected excerpts from certain letters I thought Dad would like to share with the reader. That is why there are "missing" numbers.

May 4 - Diary (later in the day)

We were taken for a sightseeing trip around Gura. It is unbelievable. Tough for the Italians to lose all this. Miles of construction. The extent of the city is unbelievable. Old Italian forts look down on us from the hills.

The terrain looks like Nevada or Idaho. We took the station wagon to Asmara for an inspection tour and a session with the bosses! Asmara is very decadent, but full of modern Italian architecture—Beautiful villas.

JD&P has the classiest hotel and a villa.

We wonder about our salaries. Embury's letter should help us to meet the $125 per week minimum.

The native market in Asmara was very picturesque, but dirty. A lot of craftwork is in evidence. Good shops, however, are sold out and one must patronize the side-street shops.

Italian people are good looking, but poor. They have small Fiat cars and pony carts for travel. A sad downfall for an industrious people. It is surprising to see walls enclose fine trees and gardens when all around is desert.

The fields and roads are filled with goats, sheep, donkeys, and small Brahma cattle. The natives are the poorest we have seen. They work hard to earn 22¢ (American) per day.

Billie: Letter from Stanley dated May 5, 1942, received by Doris, July 13th: Parts of the letter have been cut out. I cannot determine places because all the place names have been deleted by US censors. Stan and his group have finally arrived in Africa around the end of April, beginning of May. Dad put specific details in his diary, but the letters to family were censored and sometimes several sentences were "sliced" out with a razor blade.

May 7 - Diary

We moved into the Asmara Hamasien Hotel. Our room is about 22' square with 14' ceilings and a quarry tile floor.

May 8

Honey,

My first position is Job Captain (Squad Chief). My crew consists of Brown (American), Youseff (Egyptian), Amadini (Italian), Cassio (Italian), and Sleiter (Italian). Gura is my responsibility. (About 30 buildings.)

I've gotten to the point where I don't pay any attention to these foreign languages. Some fellows got homesick from not hearing enough English. When I think of the brand of English I heard in New York, I don't miss it. The dialects here are strange and numerous. But, when it comes to a business transaction, there seems to be some means of contact.

Money talks as loudly here as anywhere else!

May 9

Honey,

There are many churches in town and each noon and evening we hear a regular chorus of bells. It hardly seems we are so far from the states. There are many different religions, and they can worship as much as they please without being molested.

Missionaries are not much in evidence, as most are Christians here. The Catholic faith is perhaps the strongest.

May 13 - Diary

I received letter #8 from Doris.

Today was good, except we couldn't get money. Our wage advances aren't here yet. Had to borrow 40 shillings. ($8.00—a fine thing!)

It is the rainy season. The terrain almost looks like Montana, except with a lot of Muslims.

May 14 - Diary

Today was a good day—but a hard one. We have a lot of things to accomplish in a short period of time. I'm swamped with work. We put in another three hours of overtime. That's $9.90 for me. At this rate I should be able to live for a while. I would like to begin collecting souvenirs while there are a few available.

Finally got home at 9:45 p.m. Had a good night's sleep… but my stomach is still bad. Too much good food?

May 15 - Letter #5

My Darling,

Eternal sunshine can get tiresome. I don't ever look out at the beach anymore. Nothing changes day to day, so we would even welcome a rainstorm.

Doubtless, war will greatly change our standard of living. Let us hope that we do not lose out too much. We lived rather well up until now and I'd like to continue. With any luck we should improve it a lot.

I shall profit by this experience in maturity, if not professionally.

It will be good advertising and that seems an important element in all this architectural stuff. If things are anywhere near favorable, I shall certainly establish my own office upon my return. That is one's only salvation in these times.

May 16 - Diary

I went for a walk with Art this evening. He said Marinelli thought my work was too much for me to handle. I'd better show them! As I wrote before, I shall profit by this experience in maturity if not professionally. It will be good.

May 17 - Letter #9

Sweetheart,

We drove around town today sitting on a plank across the rear end of a Chevrolet pickup. A good "rubberneck" bus. We find the place very beautiful, for the most part. The native quarter continues to astonish me with its filth and misery. All cities must have their slums, I suppose. The U.S. has plenty.

May 18 - Diary

I'm re-organizing my work to include more control. I hope I'm successful.

May 19 - Diary

Three and half hours over time. My laundry finally was brought in. Like seeing a long-lost friend.

We are often short of essentials.

But in many ways, this is a soft life and I have little trouble enjoying it. We work long hours.

May 20 - Diary

We watched the movie, <u>In Person</u>, a real old-timer. The clothing was vintage, 1934. Surprising how "corny" the movie was.

May 21 - Diary

A fellow had his head blown off in Gura. A land-mine. He had six children.

We can't complain about the hazards of our indoor work.

Caaran was leaving for Cairo in the morning, so he took us to the Croce del Sud. Jerry and I had a beer. What stuff! We could hardly drink it! Everyone else had brandy.

A single cigarette is well-received as a tip.

May 22 - Diary

Almost everyone was out in the field today, so our office was quiet. Our Mrs. Guanti, office worker, was home sick, too. She and I have a good time gossiping.

Mark was down in Giado and said it was SO HOT and the place is full of asps, adders, and cobras.

We are too lazy tonight, so I am going to see about my Scarpa hiking boots. They cost a lot of money, but I need them, badly. Payday today was welcome.

Now we are shooting the breeze about income tax. The Egyptians and British pay 8% here. The English are only able to send £10 home. Their main problem is family subsistence.

I've made enough overtime to make up for the money I lost on the ship.

May 23 - Letter #10

Honey,

Some of us wanted to buy some Arab ponies. One of our stops along the way was a great breeding center for them. The Americans stationed at those points would buy a pony and a new saddle for about ten pounds ($40). A boy would feed and groom the animals for eight shillings a week ($1.60). And, what animals! Beauties, though small and as spirited as a bronco. You ought to see them travel in the sand. A cow pony from America wouldn't be able to stand the rough life. I'd like to have taken a couple home with me. As for the saddles, they are beauties—silver mounted and covered with dyed Moroccan leather.

Curfew is early and soldiers and Americans are around at night. One wanting a date with a local girl must obtain a permit from the police to keep her out until 1 a.m. There is an abundance of beauteous white girls. Nice families, too, many being quite wealthy.

May 24 - Diary

I saw two new Leica Lenses, a Summer (£50) and Summary (£60). I was tempted... but not enough. (The Leica Summarit camera costs 3-4000 £ now and the lens costs 180£.)

May 27 - Diary

I ran around like a wild man all day. Now, I feel better about my job.

I must learn to not take things too seriously. One wonders why we were worried.

May 28 - Diary

Today is my 28th birthday. I wonder what Doris is doing.

The Dionne Quintuplets are eight years-old today.

May 29 - Diary

I bought a bracelet for $1.10 and a ring. Hope Doris likes them. I'm going to get some ivory and ebony ones too.

May 30 - Diary

I've quit smoking…Again.

May 31 - Letter #11

Angel Pie and Bill,

We are not learning the Arabic language very fast, much to the dismay of our teacher who gives us three lessons a week. But we are most in need of knowledge such as: "How much?—Too much!" (We use this a lot!) or "Be quiet" (This is for the beggars), and "Good day." It is not a difficult language but is spoken very fast, so it is hard to understand.

June 1 - Diary

I had a good, busy day with things clearing up, again. Then, at noon I developed a bad stomach-ache from eating oxtail stew. I went home and didn't eat, but still spent all night throwing up and running. It's the worst I've ever had.

June 3 - Diary

Letter # 12 has arrived from Doris.

I was in bed all day. Doctors came up to visit me twice during the afternoon. They doped me with pills and a quart and a half of orange juice. That's been my only food since yesterday at noon.

June 4 - Diary

I am still not up to going to work. I spent the morning in bed. At noon I bathed and shaved. I feel somewhat better, but I am very weak. I had a little broth and meat. Not a good decision. The doctors can't seem to agree what my diet should be. Liquid? Solid? A fellow could starve, and none would be the wiser. I've been lying around all evening. I don't have much pep. They call it "Gippy tummy" or "Egyptian stomach." This is really a hell of a place to get sick. No one cares much or is about to do much.

I hope I'm on the way to recovery tomorrow.

June 5 - Diary

I went back to work. My knees were weak but held out all day. I'm now eating a normal diet.

We got word that the carpenter arrested for sending classified material in a letter from Freetown in April, was shot.

I felt well enough to put in some overtime. Mark and I ran up against a tree outside the office. I "barked" my forehead. I look tough.

Mark was given a presentation dagger. It's quite an item.

June 6 - Diary

I went to work today but felt very woozy. I had to leave at 11 a.m. and stayed in bed all day. I had a session with the doc. He said I should only drink boiled water. At supper I could only eat the peaches and potato soup.

I've learned to relax at all costs.

All the boys are going out for champagne.

NUTS!

June 7, 1942 - Letter #13

Sweetheart,

Many of the fellows went out to a battlefield near here where the decisive battle for this area was fought. Picturesque though it may be, I didn't relish a lot of gruesome scenes just now when my stomach is not up to par. It is said to be left in much the same condition as when the battle was over. One sees enough gruesome sights here without looking for them. It seems that in a country or climate like this, in addition to very lush vegetation, every disease and physical deformity also flourishes. Even the insects are bigger. Beetles two inches long, grasshoppers three inches. Every little germ has twice as good a chance of doing harm as in a temperate climate. We people from Minnesota believe that, as a state, it has the best climate in the world. Most invigorating, anyway. And the seasons are nice.

Here, there are only two seasons: the dry and the rainy season. And the rainfall is so slight up here, one can hardly tell the difference. We are supposed to have gone through a little rainy spell now and none of us can seem to remember it. The heavy rains are yet to come.

Today a lot of horse and camel races are going to be held out of town. I would like to be there, but not this time, I guess. Some good movie material. Some of these camels can really travel! One wonders how they keep from coming apart. The rider really takes a beating as well.

June 9 - Diary

The impossible has happened—two letters from home. One is a card from Billie, which I read immediately. The long thick letter I held until noon. Sixteen-pages from Doris.

It is as if new worlds were opened.

My fears were unfounded. She is well and happy, and so is Bill. A few tears did trickle down these sun-kissed cheeks. Oh, what an undeserving human I am to have such a lovely and loving wife and child.

I put my money on this one to win the race!

June 10 - Diary

I continue to read the large letter so as not to miss a bit of it.

After work, I bought a pair of ebony elephants with white tusks. They're the best I've seen. Now to write a letter home. Letter 15. It will be a long one. I should answer most of Doris' questions.

June 11 - Diary

DiRiengo came around and told me they would try to get me $135 a week. I would be a $7,020 a-year man. I hope and pray it goes through.

June 13 - Diary

I ordered a box to be made for my stuff. A little Syrian carpenter who is an expert at box making is doing it for $5.

June 14 - Diary

I was up early after a good night's sleep and went to church with Millbank. The service was pleasant, but different—a good difference.

June 16 - Diary

I got my box today, but only after a lot of argument. For $5.00 I did okay. Shins, spears, and shields should fill it.

June 18 - Letter #15

Angel Pie and Bill, Honey,

You don't have any idea how the letter struck me. My love for you was so beautifully echoed in your letter that a tear or two trickled down my cheeks. I could never have expressed my love for you and Bill. It is so wonderful to be sure. Isn't it?

I can't think of much more to say except that as soon as the war is over and my term is up. I'm dashing home to stay. Money or no money, I don't have to go away from you and Bill ever again. This time I really mean it. The war was my last reason and that will soon be over. Nothing is nicer than living a normal life with you and Bill in our own home and circle of friends. Trips to the lake, new cars, new shoes, and new movies just back from the processor. Here's to their early resumption!

June 19 - Diary

A lot of Douglas men and women have arrived. The Star of Oregon picked them up in Bombay. Their ship, the Monterrey, was laid up for repairs.

Christian was sent back to the States as an oiler. He'll be making $600 a month.

June 21 - Diary

I attended church again. It was a long service with a very sincere preacher. Reminded me of home.

We attended a movie at the Asmara, then went to the Odeon. What a place! It reminds me of the play Nana. So many floozies around.

June 26 - Diary

An eventful day. We left for Ghinda and Nefasit with Mark and Marinelli. First, we went to Nefasit. What a wonderful experience. Saw a beauty of a baboon. Would have liked a color camera very much. What a fool I was not to have taken it with me. Marinelli told some good stories about the country.

No word yet about the new contracts.

June 27 #17

Sweetheart,

I had a very nice day yesterday. We drove down the mountain about 3,000 feet and had a change of scenery. It was much warmer and more humid. We had a Chevrolet sedan like Dad's, so it was a comfortable drive. There were a lot of baboons out. We saw one old fellow who sat about four feet high. He had a beautiful grey mane, which hung around him like a shawl. They live on the cactus. The cactus was brought in years ago, but since the baboons have taken to eating it and spitting the seeds, the whole country is covered with it.

I've arranged with the army officers to use a "goat-car" tomorrow to visit a battlefield. It will be an interesting trip and should take us into game country. There are supposed to be rhinoceros and lions in the place where we are headed. Not many but some. In fact, they have seen several giraffes there lately. I hope we are going to be fortunate enough to see some, too.

June 28 - Diary

Up at dawn. Had an early breakfast, then we got our Chevy station wagon. Bud, Jerry, and I go to Cherin. What a drive. The battlefield was quite a sight. It reminded me of the Missouri River Bottoms I saw in The National Geographic.

✧ **Billie: My dad's world and knowledge of geography before he left the United States was largely based on the world of National Geographic.**

Wish Dad were here.
This is the Africa I have always imagined!

July 4 - Diary

Busy all day. More shopping and saw another movie, Cain and Mabel, with Clark Gable. A corny bit. The rains have started.

July 8 - Letter from Doris to Stanley

We had the sunfish Estelle caught yesterday for dinner tonight and they were excellent.

Billie is well-acquainted with all the neighbors now and bats around asking for cookies here and there. She usually gets them, too! She pulled a good one the other day—a dragon fly was sitting on Mom's arm and she looked at it for some time trying to think what to call it then said, "There is somebody sitting on your arm, Grandma."

My cousin asked her where her Daddy was? She told her "in Africa" and she hasn't forgotten the black baby either. She said with great confidence that she had already gotten her black baby from NY. Smart little girl you've got, Honey, and worth anything in the world—but both she and I will be glad when you are back here, and we can live a happy, normal life again.

I can so appreciate the effort you have to put forth and I can understand, at least in part (from what I can put together), what it must be like there. But I'm thankful for your safe arrival. I sometimes get panicky, but I always talk or think myself into a good frame of mind.

Friday we'll be going out home, so again sending you all my love and hoping you get some of these letters. -

Your loving, Doris and Billie

"My Black Baby," by Billie Crouse

Apparently, Daddy, knowing that he was going to Africa, promised to send me a "Black Baby-doll" before he left the USA. (I was 2-1/2 when he left Minneapolis.) Many of his letters and diary entries, while he was in NYC, mentioned his efforts and frustrations with "finding Bill a Black Baby."

But Daddy did find her, one day in Greenwich Village. She arrived safely and much to my delight. Black Baby, which has always been her name, lives with me and stays with Judy (another doll my parents gave me Christmas 1941). I keep them both in the antique "candy display case" from an old apothecary shop in Chicago, which is in the living room of the house that Dad designed for Dean and me. While she is over 79 years-old (at this writing) she is still a baby and very vibrant!

My adorable Black Baby

July 12 - Diary

Doris is 28 today. Next year we will really celebrate.

Today was damp and cold. Nothing to do but try to keep warm. At noon, I began a letter home lamenting my lack of mail. I went for a short walk this evening. As I was going into dinner, I noticed three letters for me in the box. Hooray! A card from Mom and Dad and a card and letter from Doris. Thank God everything is okay. Doris is busy.

✧ ***Billie: Dad bought the following card for mother in New York City in anticipation of sending it to her in July for her birthday. Planning ahead!***

This is the front of a birthday card Stan sent Doris for her birthday

The inside of the birthday card Stan sent Doris

July 15 - Diary

Three hours overtime. I called the warehouse about my trunk. They said it would come by Thursday. However, I found it when I arrived home at five o'clock. What a picnic! It was like Christmas. Last time I looked in the trunk was January ninth. Everything was there. The trunk is badly scarred, and the small drawer is broken, but everything can be repaired.

The fellows came in after work for a review. We had Scotch and I opened a can of peanuts. It was a 'housewarming' of sorts.

July 19 - Diary

We are planning a weekend excursion next Sunday and we ought to see some good country. There are many herds of very nice camels I'd like to photograph. They aren't quite as mangy looking as those we see in the circus.

I'm trying to buy some baby leopard skins for Billie, but they are hard to get. They are very soft and have small spots on them. I can buy dozens of large ones, but they are so coarse.

July 25 - Diary

I was married five years ago today. It seems like yesterday. Sundays are the only days we don't have to rush around. I reread my letters frequently. Either my letters are going somewhere else or none are being written. Art found a letter from May 11th that was for me…then I found three more letters. Plenty of letters are missing.

July 25 - Letter from Doris

My Honey,

Tomorrow, it will be five years. Boy, I wish you were here. But really, we're celebrating together. They have been the best five years of my life and the most eventful —little did we dream when we were married all these things would happen—Billie, the house and least of all the traveling you must do! We are certainly having adventures and I say "we" because I'm with you every minute. When you get back, I hope every one of our friends will be in their right places so we can continue from where we left off. Everyone will have had so much adventure—maybe our jaunts can be even that much more interesting for all of us…if only it settles back.

Hon, I don't think I ought to risk sending film unless I can send it to you with someone. It was swell of Frank Moorman to write to you. The last few pages are sorta like Rosenbaum's, "Thoughts While Shaving" column.

✧ **This column was written in the forties and fifties in the old San Francisco News by the columnist, Jack Rosenbaum, known as "A Nice Guy in a Tough World."**

I wish you would get my letters as quickly as I have been getting yours. I have had NINE in the last three weeks. I told you about the two I received before leaving for the lake and the one from Freetown dated April 23, that I got at the lake.

Sunday, your folks and the kids stopped at Stanley to have some of my birthday cake and ice cream. Your mom brought me a celery and pickle (combination) dish. Mom gave me a nightgown. I haven't bought anything except necessities since you left, and I guess I was practically falling out of my nightie. I'll want to stock up like a bride when you come back!

Your dad got a job in the Federal Land Bank and is to start Aug. 1. Your mom seemed a bit upset that she would have to manage the harvest, but I told her a lot of women were doing things they hadn't had to do before now. I'm sure she is capable. I suppose they will move permanently after the grain is in. They have been looking for a house.

I need Billie so much to fill time and for loving and she is the sweetest thing—a bit spunky at times but mostly good as gold. She told me to tell you she would like a little tiny letter just to her and to send you a kiss and a big hug from her. She has her definite place just like you have that can't be filled by anyone or anything else, but she is so much comfort now.

Congrats on the raise, Honey! When I receive what you intend to send me, I will bank it and we will have the fun of getting something together.

You said you hoped you would have a reply to your statements on contract renewal. Do you want to know what I think you should do? I can't really say, Honey.—It all depends on you, your health, and living conditions. It sounds not too bad from this end—despite how much I would like to have you home. I'd say if you think you should extend the contract, take it up. You wouldn't be home long, anyway. If other options are to be considered, unless your service would be considered adequate for you to leave, which I doubt. If they need you bad enough, extend. You aren't on the front lines, anyway, and if you came home you might not be at this end either—but you never know. If this mess is cleaned up before the contract ends and it's possible and you aren't released, Bill and I will come running to where you are.

Billie said the other day that when she got big enough, she was going to school.

Estelle asked, "Where, Billie?"

Billie said, "Africa."

I laughed and said she may not be too wrong.

Estelle asked, "Where will I be then?"

Billie said, "I'll leave you off in New York."

Billie says she will take a "couple of magazines" with her to Africa!

We don't know what will happen—but I know God will make it turn out the way it should. In the meantime, nothing is so bad but what it could be much worse.

Gee, honey, it's 10 minutes to 1 a.m., so, now it is our anniversary and it's about 9 a.m. there, so, I'm sure you are thinking about it, too. After five years, I love you more than ever and it just seems to grow more all the time. It's very wonderful, isn't it?

Now, I'm off to bed to have sweet dreams of you.

As always, Billie and I send you all our love.

Your Doris

P. S. Billie recognized you immediately in the picture you sent on the horse cart. She was so excited. The fellows standing around, she told me, are "black babies' Daddies!"

"Oh, those are the black babies' daddies!"
Billie said.

July 26

Good morning, Hon,

I woke up in time for breakfast without rushing for a change. We went for a drive in three horse carts. We investigated the photographic possibilities of the native quarter. Then, examined the Coptic Church.

Rallie got four letters. That startled me, for I got none.

We watched Give Me Your Heart *with Kay Francis and George Brent. We all related to the adopted son. Not a good movie for homesick people.*

My darlings, you may receive this before hunting season starts, so I want you to go out as usual. I like to think of you as tramping through the woods and fields. Also, I like to think of you as using my gun. No one else can use it, but you.

July 27 #22

Sweetheart,

I received a bunch of letters from you. I hadn't received them before because the mailman thought I was at the South Tip. Hearing that Billie is growing up, and I'm not there to see that, saddens me. I have felt I had to make money, though. I didn't think it would be fair to sit at home getting no income while I waited for my draft notice.

July 31 - Diary

Worked three and a half hours overtime. Little Bill is three years-old today. Wish I was there to give her a hug, the little darling. Rain storms every day. More movies, shopping, and a lot of work. Sundays we tour as much of the surroundings as possible. Still an irregularity with my mail. They don't come in on a regular basis, or even in chronological order.

We have started trapshooting.

August 2 #23

Honey Darling,

Louis Rosenberg said he would like to go "down below" for some sketching as he had seen some very interesting subjects. He asked me to go. I was delighted, having not made the trip before. I went in the Chevrolet station wagon and took my roommate and Jerry Jyring.

We left at seven and drove a long time. The temperature was good and comfortable. Like home in September—cool. When we finally got "down below" it was HOT. Within twenty minutes after we arrived, we were steaming with sweat. It ran off our noses, ears, and elbows. Helmet, shorts, and lightest shirts possible were all we had. Louis sketched while we sat in the shade. Does this sound like a story from a travel book by an imaginative writer yet?

We had a fine time. I took three rolls of film and the subject matter was swell. Saw some swell camels and many Arabs and their mosques. (Many houses have a fancy second story with close latticework behind which the "big shots" and their many wives might look out on the street without being seen.) The buildings are made of coral stone and have high-beamed ceilings. They are relatively cool inside (maybe 90 degrees or more).

We have a very handsome little black boy named Waldo who goes with us on our tours. Louis is a born shopper—he will walk miles every night on such excursions. He has spent a good share of his life in Europe and has excellent taste and experience.

Tomorrow night we are going in search of leather. His wife has a hobby binding books. There is some leather available.

August 5 #24

Honey,

Artie is getting ready for an excursion which will last six months or so. He should be a regular T. E. Lawrence when he returns. He will be hundreds of miles from nowhere. Ali Baba and the 40 Thieves will have nothing on him. While it will be hot, it will be adventurous, and I sort of wish I were going too. Life is growing dull here.

I was glad to hear the Lake level has come up as in former years. There may be some hope for that part of the country after all. It makes me want to build another nice new sailboat.

Billie: He and Doris built one when they first got married.

You see, I'm a fresh-water sailor now. I've had enough of the salt-water sort!

Also, I've got some ambitious plans for what I will do when I return. One of the fellows here is an 8mm movie bug like I am, and so we are "doping out" some good ideas for sound addition to projection. He is Herb Fragen from

Minneapolis and is an electrician by trade. One has plenty of time to build castles about the future. It makes the time pass more swiftly.

I'm glad you are taking plenty of pictures. The little children here are very pretty and when I see little girls Billie's age, it makes me homesick. But I don't let on. Some fellows here, even the 50-year-olds, burst into tears and can't work when they see kids. Not me.

✧ **Billie: The following photo traveled with Dad wherever he was working—and was front and center on his desk**

Billie's third birthday; July 31, 1942

August 6 - Diary

I took a bath and was all decent for the banquet at the Strand. They fed us goat, as usual. It wasn't bad.

I miss my Honey and Bill a lot. Damn this war.

August 7 - Diary

When I get home, we're going to go for a nice leisurely trip through the states. It will be a second honeymoon—no less.

We all feel that the U.S. is ten times better than the whole rest of the world and want to obey the saying, "See America first." Nothing quite compares.

August 10 - Letter from Frank Moorman, A Moorman and Company, Minneapolis, Minnesota

Dear Stan,

We were all very happy to receive your most welcome letter of July 23rd. It arrived in our office last Saturday, August 8th. Really, we obtained very good service in the delivery of the letter.

Each one of us, I believe, has read it through several times and it is surely filled with interesting news and comments. Mrs. Whiting left Saturday for a week's trip up to her cabin on the North Shore and I am sure that she joins us in sending you our best wishes.

Please continue to write us, Stan, as we are always happy and eager to receive your letters. We don't know how long this war will last but I do hope that sometime when it is over and we can continue our work at a normal pace, that we can again have you with us.

Charley and Pete are also sending their comments on the bottom of this letter and again may we wish you success in your new work.

Sincerely,

Frank Moorman

August 11 - Diary

Ahh… for the days I went home for family nights.

August 19 - Diary

Jerry and I talked about a trip to Abyssinia.

✧ **Billie: Abyssinia was the foreigner's name for the Ethiopian Empire.**

Marinelli agreed to arrange for the transportation. We went to the consulate and to Personnel. We'd like to have some assurance our trip will go okay. We've been told Abyssinians are taking pot shots at some of the cars. It is still "open season" on white men.

August 21 - Diary

I spent the morning trying to obtain a passport and an identity card. After all the chasing around we found out we must have a special letter of release from Marinelli. Of course, we can't get one.

The trip to Abyssinia will be risky. They won't give consent. However, they will "overlook" the trip if we go across the border without the letter of release.

Clancy and his gang had a brawl in the canteen until the wee hours of the morning. Now this place is full of soldiers who are noisy and rough.

August 22 - Diary
We chased around to find food and supplies for the trip. We are sick of begging and scheming for cars, passes, and visas.

August 23 - Diary
We were up at 3:30 this morning and at 4:30 were on the road. We saw fine prehistoric ruins. There were beggars and lepers in abundance. On the trip back, we encountered a camel caravan. What stubborn, ornery beasts they are.

August 24 - Diary
Today was great. I got two letters from Doris with three pictures of her and Billie. This is a very welcome addition to my collection.

August 26 - Diary
Heard our raises went through without a hitch. Thank God.

August 27 - Diary
We had a busy day and were told we would have to move again.

August 30 - Diary
What a pompous bunch the Italians are.

August 31 - Diary
Jerry and I walked to the native village to do some shopping. We saw a heartbreaking leper who'd already lost fingers and toes. What a place!

September 1 - Diary
At long last we signed our new contract. I will be paid $135/week. My contract started on August 30th instead of August 23rd because of my over time. We may buy savings bonds while we're here instead of sending our money home.

September 2 - Diary
Got a big paycheck today. It will be my last big one since I am now a contract employee. No extra for overtime. I'll be able to send money home soon.

Paul Germain (our engineering head) wants me to take charge of the office. He said I would be able to hold the men in line. I've been told that things are much improved with me here.

Billie: During the month-long contract Dad was given more and more responsibility. At mid-point he was responsible for projects in four cities. He filled his spare time with hunting, shooting, and a favorite pastime, photography. On September 30th, a member of his team invited him to join the American Volunteer Guard. Dad refers to drills, marches, uniforms, identity cards. Sounds like the unit was not well-disciplined. Dad quit after someone slung a rifle and chipped one of his teeth.

September 13 #31

Dear Honey,

Today we had another outing. At first, we ate some locally made ice cream that was like sherbet. That is, we did, until we found out it was made from native camel milk. No thanks—no more for me! Just mention of an ice cream soda or sundae will make any of us go on talking about home food for hours.

I'm going boar hunting.

September 20 #33

Darling,

Thursday, I went out of town with Jerry to inspect one of four bases. On the way back we found that our chauffeur had delivered back issues of Vogue magazines to a couple of nurses here. We had a busy hour refreshing our memories on how American women look. You'd have gotten a chuckle out of the two of us dressed in shorts and helmets, riding in a new Chevrolet sedan, reading Vogue and riding through the wild-thorn-overgrown country!

Cover of *Vogue*, July 1942

We have at least three different American movies a week to see, so we have plenty of that kind of entertainment.

Every once in a while, I must stop and take stock of things. It hardly seems possible that we are apart and across the world from each other. It serves to demonstrate that people can do many things if they really must. We won't do this again from choice.

It is particularly hard on those who did not need to come here for a job. Many bitterly reject it and are homesick. Conditions are good, though, and much better than I expected. Things like ice cream, candy bars, and chewing gum are all in the dim, distant past and would bring their weight in gold (almost) if they were available. One really craves such things when they can't be had. A stock remark is: "To think that I've ever turned down a candy bar or ice-cream soda!"

September 23 - Letter from Frank Moorman

Dear Stan:

Your charming wife was in the office yesterday and she showed us several photographs recently taken. They were interesting and absorbing. Apparently, you are in a beautiful country—wherever that is—and your work, together with the interesting natives and scenery much be satisfying.

Please continue to write us from time to time as we are always happy to hear from you about your experiences.

With best wishes, we remain,

Sincerely yours, Frank Moorman

October 10 - Diary

It is sort of a surprise to me that the white man has had so little sense as to attempt to acclimate to such places. The black men seem to be able to stand it, but they have a different philosophy of life. They do little work during the heat of the day. Even the sidewalk bazaars and shops are closed. As the sun sets, one sees the awnings stretched again and the coffee pots going.

October 13 #40

Dear Honey,

Our last Sunday's trip was successful. We reached our city while the Mohammedans were celebrating the end of their fast of Ramadan. Every Arab was dressed in gay colors. All the men and boys wore long snow-white gowns. Over those they wore vests of silk in some of the most exotic colors—candy stripes in red and white, green and white, pink and white and so on. The women looked like rainbows in beautiful silk shawls and scarves. One wonders how they manage to keep the stuff so clean.

We got some good shots and will send you some when they are finished.

It was a hot day being about 105 in the shade, but not as humid as usual. We had a beautiful ride through a cool, starry evening. Made Jerry and I homesick for a North Shore drive.

October 19 #42

Sweetheart,

Thomas' place sounds very nice.

✧ **Billie: Thomas was one of the people Mother worked for.**

I would like more room and some trees next time I build.

I would really like some "ground" and have a distinctive enough place so people wouldn't have to look at the house number to be sure.

✧ **Billie: Years later, Dad wanted people to know any home he designed and built was a recognizable MOE house.**

Who knows—we may have such a place before long?

October 24 - Diary

We hear and see little change in the war from day to day. Heavens, what we do hear from home is not exactly encouraging. It seems that, knowing Americans as we do, that they won't worry and strive to win until it is almost too late. I will write Doris tonight. It will be #43.

October 28 - Diary

I am considering taking the seven-month extension that comes with a raise. A lot of the fellows are taking it.

October 31 #45

Sweetheart,

We hear a lot of war news here, but we hardly know what to believe. It doesn't seem as if things are going well.

Heavens, we have hopes of it ending soon, so we can go home.

If they give us a seven-month renewal it will take us up to about the 3rd of next September. But they may only give us four or five months so our contracts will end the same time that the boys who just signed their extension contract this week.

I would much rather go home than re-sign if there was anything to do for me except the army.

But we will see, time will tell. I think that when I do get home, I'll spend weeks just talking to you for the sheer joy of it. One can make friends and see places, but no one can replace that one person.

You really are important, even more than you think. It is more evident each day that I need you and Billie with me in order to make life worthwhile. This is just existing.

November 10 - Letter from Frank Moorman

Dear Stan:

We were all glad to hear from you and to learn of your experiences.

We are still quite busy although, of course, we don't know how long it will last and, in the meantime, we have obtained several other men who might be with us only temporarily.

It is hard to give any exact information, but I do know that we will all be glad to see you when you arrive in town and can then discuss future possibilities. We are still going after various prospective jobs and around the first of the month there may be other jobs coming in.

In the meantime, we want to send you our best wishes and look forward to seeing you.

Sincerely yours, Frank Moorman

November 11 - Letter from Frank Moorman

Dear Stan:

Your last letter of October 27th was tremendously interesting to all of us. We have reread the content thereof quite a few times. The work you have been doing somewhere in northeastern Africa must have been very helpful in assisting the allied forces on their recent drive in Egypt and at present at Libya.

At this writing it appears that Rommel is heading for the "trackless wastes of Libya" and, in addition, the Anglo-American force is now taking over much of the northwestern Africa. By the time you have read this letter, I presume the situation in all northern Africa will have crystalized.

We just heard from Norman Widen stating that he is in England with the flying fortresses and Martin Behrens, now commissioned as an aviator of the navy, is stationed near Seattle and is doing air patrol work through Puget Sound and the Straits into the ocean.

In a week or two I will know whether I will receive a commission or whether I will be in the army as a private. It looks as though we are all in this war for keeps and will be in it until the issues are decided in our favor.

Please write us again when you have time and know that we are very much interested in hearing of your achievements and experiences.

With kind regards, we remain

Sincerely yours,

Frank Moorman

✧ **Billie: Two other people wrote additional personal notes.**

December 5 - Diary

I got the notice of my promotion. My pay will go from $135.00/ week to $150.00. Also, I now have the title of "Chief Draftsman."

December 6, 1942

Billie: Dad took the following pictures this day and commented on the back of each photo.

"These little boys followed me for two or three hours, just looking! I aimed the camera on them and they stopped, smiled and ran away." — Stan

African schoolboy with slate

Schoolboys in Eritrea

"A little boy coming home from school. Notice the wooden slate on which he has been writing his lessons. Notice the writing isn't in Swedish! He is joined by two other school friends. The lady in the background is carrying a heavy load." — Stan

Teacher and students and student teacher at the far right

December 29 - Letter to Frank Meisch

Dear Frank,

It's about time I sit down to answer my pre-Christmas mail. It will be some days before that will come about. The one desk we have here is overworked.

Thanks for all the news. I now have a fair idea what has happened to some of the boys. This war has spread them out thinly over the entire globe. Minnesota boys don't do badly. You seem to have made a wonderful contact. Here's hoping it will be a permanent, post-war connection. My work is interesting and somewhat hectic. We have some strange experiences. Here's our setup: Adobe walls, teak-wood rafters and palm thatch. How's that for a combination of luxury and poverty material? I'd like to empty my trunk and fill it with teak 2 x 5's. We use what we can get and where we can find it. Often it is camels, instead of trucks, to haul material at our out-lying spots.

This war will do a lot of harm, but in general, it will give many young men an enlarged perspective. It will arouse some interest in the rest of the world. But as for me, the good old U.S.A. is unexcelled. It is surprising how the rest of the world looks up to us for leadership in almost any line of endeavor.

I can't get home soon enough. When the war is over, I'll do some fast chasing to get home early. No more customs, no more censors, no more flies! What a day it will be!

We have much to photograph over here, but film is hard to get. Local photo finishers ruin the negatives and have print paper that must be ten years old. Many fellows here have Leicas, Contax, and Retinas, but the results aren't as good as a box-camera shot, developed at the corner drug store.

When I think of the consistent good results you got, it makes me very sore. One gets over here once in a lifetime and has such luck!

Doris keeps me well informed on local doings. It seems as if she is saving our "stuff." We will really have a good "binge" evening when I get back. Except for an occasional bottle of Scotch, which I'm able to chisel off some unwary Brit, I'm as parched as the desert sands. Let me tell you—one swig up here really hits one. It must be the geographical location. Most of our casualties are from too much cork smelling.

I understood you two are fixing up quite a place. It's some job and, as you see, we aren't done yet. Doris has, however, been able to make some real showing since I left.

Keep up the good work. Let's hope we don't have to bat-around-the-world much longer. You airline fellows have really done things. We saw them all the way down and around.

Give my best regards to Elaine and to you both, my best wishes for a successful 1943.

As per usual,
Stan

Counting the days. And 34 = 55 days to end

I was assigned to rehabilitate port facilities in Massawa. The town of Massawa was four or five miles away from the port itself and was only a few feet above sea level. — **Stan**

Chapter 18

My First Exposure to Eritrea

Looking Back

This is a quick summary of my first exposure to the country of Eritrea in Northeast Africa. My recollections cover: the history of the country; the conditions we experienced; and some observations about the Eritrean people.

Eritrea was a colony of the Italians, who enjoyed access to it by sea, traveling down the Mediterranean, through the Suez Canal, into the Red Sea and into the port of Massawa. (That port is at about the mid-point of Eritrea as it is today and towards the southern end of the red Sea.) Italians are great boat builders, by reputation, but they also quickly built a road up to the mountains to the colorful area near Asmara when they first arrived.

The city of Asmara became the colonial capital of Eritrea in 1897. When the Italians came, Asmara became an Italian hill town with traditional curvy streets and tall houses with red tile roofs. It looked very much like some Italian towns.

The war in Africa really heated up and the British were determined to drive the Italians out of Africa. They concentrated on Eritrea and Ethiopia. Ethiopia had never come under strong control by the Italians, but Eritrea was a bit different. The British were successful in defeating the Italian troops in the Battle of Keren in the spring of 1941. So, by the time we arrived there in May of 1942, the administration was totally British, and the place was well maintained, and well organized. After World War II, Eritrea was annexed to Ethiopia.

The first goal of the U.S. programs that had been established in the fall of 1941, was to strengthen the harbor of Massawa so it could accommodate British and Allied ships and to establish air bases and hospital facilities in support of the British. If Cairo would fall to Rommel, we would be moving east very aggressively across the northern desert.

I was assigned to rehabilitate port facilities in Massawa. The town of Massawa was four or five miles away from the port itself and was only a few feet above sea level.

Our living conditions were difficult. What was particularly difficult was the fact that the weather was terrible and that Massawa was not even a city, but simply a collection of small huts and buildings related to port operations. The Italians had attempted to make the port completely unusable by anybody else by sinking the dry docks. They sank the remainder of the battalion of Italian military vessels at the dry docks.

This brought up two areas of expertise needed from the U.S. They brought in a prominent navy commander named Edward Ellsberg. He had written a book about the sunken dry docks entitled, Under the Red Sea Sun. Our admirals had developed all the techniques for re-floating dry docks. The professional divers welded and closed openings in the hull of the dry docks while underwater. These divers received outrageous salaries for their services.

Further inland, there was a port. Next to the port was Ghinda, and I was assigned to develop a hospital base there. They expected to have all kinds of wounded that had to be taken care of.

The area was extremely rocky and some of the rocks were huge like those you find around Chatsworth, California. Some planner decided that you can't build eight buildings in a row if you're building a hospital. You must scatter them around like helter-skelter so that if a bomb fell in there, you wouldn't be out a whole row. It was a very strange concept. I decided I wasn't interested in that kind of project. I didn't know much about hospitals, anyway. So, I chose a site a little farther up the mountain at about 500 feet called Gura. It had been a small fighter field area for the Italians.

This project kept me busy. I ended up in charge of about 15 or 20 young architectural draftsmen plus structural engineers. And we worked hard for months and months, building all kinds of facilities. We even found a stack of buildings that had been built by the Italians. They were steel-frame buildings that came in packages. The resultant buildings were about 20 feet wide, 30 or 40 feet long, and 10 feet high. These buildings were down by the shipyards near Mogadishu. We went down there and confiscated the "stuff" and moved it up to higher ground. It was quite an interesting project.

During this project, we became so curious we looked all around the area outside Asmara. On the weekends, we took all kinds of excursions. I found one good way was to get around using local taxicabs. There were a surprising variety of cabs in Asmara, all American sedan automobiles—that had been converted to burning charcoal! I never really understood the process, but instead of having a carburetor where you're dealing with gasoline as fuel, you'd set up a tank on the back of the car that you'd fill with charcoal. It was slow and burning the charcoal would be under fire. Usually there'd be a water tank, but there would be an area in the base there where the charcoal would be burning and giving off terrible fumes that people discovered when they tried to heat their houses with charcoal. Methane gas would poison and even kill them. They had to be careful.

In the case of the cabs, the methane gas would be sent by a flexible metal tube into the carburetor. One would start the car by cranking the electric starter to get it going. They weren't very powerful. The taxis always had a big bag of charcoal up on the roof, so sometimes they had to feed it into a tank-like device on the side.

On one occasion we went down mountain roads to the area of Keren toward the Sudan to the west. It was amazing how fine most of those road builders were. We found signs of a battle. We saw graves along the side of the road. There were bottles with pieces of paper in them. On the paper was written the name of the person who was buried at that point. Then the military was supposed to come in later and reclaim the body to take it to an appropriate cemetery.

This trip made us sad and unhappy. We realized that our work took us into the rough business of war; of having to take responsibility for what we've done to other human beings on a battlefield, and how we have to be part of cleaning up after a battle and getting rid of the bodies. We found evidence that British colonial troops had been fighting with Italian troops. We discovered parts of Scottish tartans worn by the soldiers hanging on barbed wire, cacti, and stuck to bushes. Once we found part of a leg that was still in the boot—a horrifying sight. You can only imagine what a tremendous task that would have been to clean up after a battle. Just how well they were able to record the names of the bodies anywhere, I don't know, but it was in Keren, and we were seeing this now, a year later, in the spring of 1942.

Looking Back (recorded on another day)
Eritrea had been an easy conquest for the Italians. However, there was no love lost between the Italians and Ethiopians. They turned on one another with considerable hatred. When the British took over Eritrea, they tried to get the Italians to treat the Eritreans better. Before the British were in control of Eritrea, if you were driving and you knocked down a pedestrian, it was thought to be better to drive back over them and kill them. In that scenario, you only had to pay a "death duty." But if you just injured a pedestrian, you had to account for the medical and other care until they were well. The British said that this was no longer *proper!*

Yes, those were rough times. (After about a year there, I moved up to Cairo.)

Despite the negatives, I had some rich memories of my time in Eritrea. We had very likeable fellows in our office and we got along well with them. I want to tell you about two of these young men in the office.

One was Waldo, who was good-looking, had dark skin and nice features. He fancied himself to be somewhat of an artist. If you look at Ethiopian art, you'll find that paintings of people look like mannequins. They seemed flat because they don't have a third dimension. His were like that.

One of the men in our group was a wonderful artist. His name was Louis C. Rosenberg. (Several of his drawings are included in *Middle East War Projects of Johnson, Drake & Piper, Inc. for the Corps of Engineers, US Army 1942-43*)

Work by Louis Conrad Rosenberg that was prized by our family

A portion of the print showing detail

Louis wanted Waldo to take more pride in the artwork that he did. So, one day Louis said, "Now I have an original Waldo!" He had gotten one of Waldo's works and framed it that night. Waldo's grin was ear to ear, he was so pleased.

There was another young guy in the office that didn't have the artistic talent, but he had personality and a big smile. These two young men were our favorites.

We discovered that they didn't like to eat meat. We were going on a trip as a group and took along sandwiches that had been made at the hotel. These guys wouldn't touch the meat that had been put in the sandwiches, so picked out the meat and just ate the bread!

In Eritrea, there was a place called Axum [now called Aksum]. In this town were some of the early Coptic Christian buildings. I found that I could get a company station wagon on the weekend. Because Louis Rosenberg was doing some illustrations for a Johnson, Drake & and Piper book, Axum was a great destination for an outing. I suggested we go down to the area of the town station and take pictures and make sketches.

So, on one occasion, we went there and looked at the pillars at the temple.

I was so impressed with the regalia. People were walking around with crowns and paraphernalia of the old Coptic Christians and put on quite a show for us. I photographed everything.

Coptic Church possibly in Eritrea

I believe we were highly respected (as travelers). We had put a five dollar can of gasoline in the back of the station wagon plus a couple of extra tires in case we needed them. Louis and I had a wonderful outing. On another occasion, Jerry Jyring (from Minnesota) was also on the project. He became quite fond of Louis, too.

Stan, Jerry Jyring & Louis Rosenberg

PART VI

1943: Africa

This war will do a lot of harm, but in general, it will give many young men an enlarged perspective. It will arouse some interest in the rest of the world. But as for me, the good old U.S.A. is unexcelled. It is surprising how the rest of the world looks up to us for leadership in almost any line of endeavor. — Stan

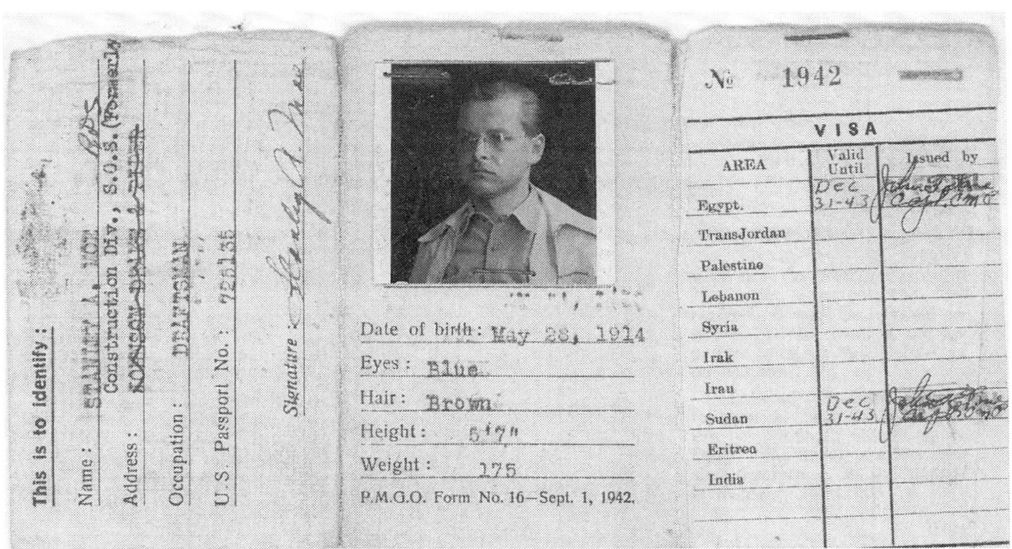
This is to identify :
Name :
Construction Div., S.O.S. (Formerly
Address :
Occupation : DRAFTSMAN
U.S. Passport No. : 725135
Signature :

Date of birth : May 28, 1914
Eyes : Blue
Hair : Brown
Height : 5'7"
Weight : 175
P.M.G.O. Form No. 16—Sept. 1, 1942.

№ 1942

VISA		
AREA	Valid Until	Issued by
Egypt.	DEC 31-43	
TransJordan		
Palestine		
Lebanon		
Syria		
Irak		
Iran		
Sudan	DEC 31-43	
Eritrea		
India		

I.D. issued 1942 to be good through 1943

***The thousands of camels and donkeys would make the average human rejoice—that is, if he's a camel and donkey fan.* — Stan**

Chapter 19

Letters from Eritrea, Sudan, and Egypt

Envelope for the card Hakim sent from Cairo

Greeting from S. Hakim (aka Hakim)

Excerpts of Letters

✧ **Billie: There are no Diary entries in 1943, as his 1943 diary was confiscated from his trunk by Customs when he arrived in this country. Remember, I selected excerpts from certain letters I thought Dad would like to share with the reader.**

January 5, 1943 #65

Sweetheart,

Darn it, I sure do miss you and Billie these days. It is so lonely without you. When things slacken up, I get more and more conscious of my separation. It seems so interminable. One never knows if it is one more month, one more year, or what. It has been a long time. I can still see you on the platform with your new tan coat. You were brave then, as always. We didn't realize what a long time it would be. It is fortunate that we didn't know. It would be harder to stand if we had to look forward to such a long time all at once.

Since Christmas and New Years are in the background, we can look forward to Easter. It will only be another day. One realizes more and more that no holiday means anything if one is away from home and friends.

January 8 #66

Sweetheart,

Billie was certainly a good sport for not raising her suspicions about Santa being a hoax in front of elders!

January 16 #69

I fully intend to go out tomorrow for a color shot of the mosque from across the plaza by the fountain. I've been waiting for the clouds to sit just right. Then I'll send it off. You should see them before many weeks. The boys do threaten to write you about my sour puss when I've had my picture taken!

January 17 #70

Honey Darling,

My roommate and I went out at 8 a.m. with two other engineers who had some work to do. We traveled by an old road which hasn't been used for years. In five hours, we saw only one other car. A short way out, we came over to a ridge and saw a sea of clouds. A few peaks sticking up here and there were all we could see. Our road disappeared into this. A most breath-taking scene like one sees in movies such as Lost Horizons. I got two good color shots of it. Our road, which was hardly wider than a cow patch, wound around the peaks down into the mist.

All at once the view changed. Through holes in the clouds, we could see cultivated fields and little plantations nestled among the peaks. Fields were so precariously located that should an ox fall while plowing, he might find himself a 1000 or more feet down a sheer bluff. It really was a scene, indescribably beautiful. Long lanes of dew-dripping eucalyptus trees and coffee groves. Spanish moss on the trees. Dense woods on all sides of our tiny trail. None of us ever realized that such a place existed. The woods were full of brightly plumed birds, which sang beautifully when everything else was silent. We saw many such scenes during the three hours before we hit the plain. Yours, Stanley

February 3 #75

My Darling,

Mail service is only fair. It seems like a long time since we got mail every day. Even when you write every day, I only get mail once a week. I received your letter #50 and #48 the week before, #49 is still to come.

My new contract goes into effect tomorrow. I shall be able to reap a golden harvest. This will be my one chance to build up a fund which will take care of my planned post-war extravagances. My 20 percent increase will be paid in a lump sum when I arrive in N.Y. or just before sailing. I won't be able to spend it until I get home.

Also, we can pay our five percent Victory Tax on the amount we earn while we're here. That means, if I'm in Africa for all of 1943, I will only have to pay five percent on the amount I've earned.

By now you should have received my color pictures. How did you like them? This is such a long-distance proposition. I forget my questions before you answer them!

Sunday, we went for a drive. Bob Romans, Newsom (my roommate), and myself in his little Fiat Topolino roadster. We stopped at a native village where there was a native wedding in progress. The groom, a shy good-looking boy of about 20, sat astride a white mule, waiting for things to start. He was dressed in white and carried a white umbrella. The umbrella is a very important part of it all.

Two priests were also on mules and were an escort of honor. Now this is strictly a man's business, and the women could be seen only peeping from half-closed doors. There were perhaps 50 young fellows dancing about; wearing spears, scimitars and shields. They were all very happy and were dressed in ceremonial trappings which were embroidered with many scenes in local history. A couple of elderly chaps were blowing on long six-foot trumpets. The shaft is wood, and the bell is brass with one small ornament. They play only one note which sounds like the bawl of a sick cow!

Then this whole procession started down the way for the bride's house in another village. She had been selected by the boy's father and the couple had been "keeping company" for about 8 months. Now, they have a civil ceremony and live together for 6 months.

At the end of this trial period, the boy may send her home if she has proven unsatisfactory. If all is okay, they have a church service, and all is final. This is how it was explained to us by Waldo, our office boy.

We got some good color shots of the proceedings.

This is all for tonight. Goodnight, my sweethearts.

All my love, Stanley

February 10 #76

Darling,

Here are my earnings from January 11th to March 15th while I waited in New York last year. I received $64.35/week for nine weeks. Since I've been out of the country for nine months, that money is tax exempt.

I'm accumulating money and now have about $300.00. I was going to use it to purchase some goods if I'm transferred to a place that has a good shopping area. But, I'm not sure that transfer will happen. I'll send the money home. No use having it accumulate here. At home, in the form of War Bonds, it might possibly earn some interest. Every dollar will count one of these days. And it may be sooner than we think. We will know soon.

The cold at home must be intense. This is the cold season here, too. I don't remember Minneapolis getting to 31 below zero. I do remember 40 below zero in Grand Falls when I was a schoolboy.

February 12 #77

My Darling,

The pictures you sent in the letter I received today were very good. They bring memories of home. It took this letter 33 days to get to me. Billie has certainly grown. That is the hardest part. I miss you both to no end. I'm afraid Billie will be in kindergarten before I see her again.

We are the last outfit not under the army. Two days ago, they announced we have the choice of army or home. If it is army, I will be in a special service organization. The pay is supposed to be higher, and I would have my same relative rank, but with a military title. My job should be good for at least a second lieutenant. And, at long last, a person with a college education will receive more recognition. In time, I might earn $200 a week.

Since you told me to make my decision to stay if possible, I'm working along those lines.

Your Stanley

February 18 #78

Honeybunch,

I don't know what trick fellows like Elwood used to evade the draft. Perhaps Broch was able to secure a deferment for him.

By May, I will either be on my way home, or be inducted into the military.

There are a lot of unpleasant angles associated with going home. The government was very tough with the last home-going bunch. They take all diaries, stamps, pictures (if they indicate locality) souvenirs, and what have you. That would represent some loss and annoyance. I'm having my negatives censored here and forwarded through Washington. It may take time, but I won't lose them.

I've put in an application to work with the army which pays very well. They probably won't contact you, but I'm letting you know just in case you've heard any rumors. I was afraid you'd be concerned and worried if you heard any rumors and wondered about it.

If I come home, I'll be there for harvest. That may offer some work. I'm doubtful about other choices for work.

✧ **Billie: One of the letters from Dad mentioned Grandpa putting in a crop in Ross this spring. It seems the government is paying a generous acreage bonus for just "attempting" to grow flax, so the country must need it. It became part of the "soil bank," so Grandpa was paid for not growing wheat. Flax is for cattle feed.**

February 22 #79

Sweetie-pie,

I'm sure we will experience a good share of the war, if not all of it settled by next year at this time. If I am assigned as an architect/engineer to a camp in the states, I probably wouldn't be inducted into the armed services—but

My dad (Billie's grandfather) in front of his field and car

my income would be somewhat reduced. I wonder what this war has in store for us. After the war, it is likely to be no bed of roses for those of our profession.

I just had injections for typhus, cholera, and tetanus. I should be immune to anything now. I have an inoculation schedule a foot long. The army gives us no choice about getting the shots. It is wonderful insurance. I often wonder how many times I've been exposed to the various diseases.

February 28 #80

Sweetheart,

Things here are the same. I should be home for Billie's birthday, July 31st, with luck. None of the other opportunities look as if they will materialize.

Mark and I were discussing it the other day, and to us it seemed better if we had no choice but home. Why prolong the agony of separation? On the other hand, it seems strange to be sorry to leave. But, being here has been a form of security for all of us. You are getting your checks each week. That makes the immediate future secure. For a couple more months my pay will continue. The crossing by ship will take that long. As soon as I get back home, our lives will become insecure again. In any case, the homecoming will be a glorious thrill.

The only way you will know that I'm on my way home is when you stop receiving mail. Then you can "kill the fatted calf" for my return!

I bought three very good books from our library. I chose thick ones to read on the long voyage home.

March 1 #81

Sweetheart,

I'm enclosing two $100 money orders. That leaves me a bit over $200 in the bank which I will maintain for my trip home.

I bundled up all my negatives and had them censored and sent home by first class mail. The package is sealed and stamped "censored." I hope the U.S. Customs treats them nicely. They are all quite innocent.

March 12 #84

✧ **Billie: Mother took me to the dentist when I was 3 and a half. My dentist was my mother's brother, my uncle Allan (Dr. Anderson).**

Sweetie Pie,

I'm glad Billie liked going to Doctor Anderson. I well remember the fuss I raised when I was five. Even promises of a tricycle made no impression. Talk of Mom and Dad about their tooth troubles frightened me, I suppose.

I don't want Billie to be afraid of the dark, people, responsibility, or anything else. I've been timid most of my life and it is a very great handicap.

It is well for Billie to become accustomed to going to the dentist.

Regarding whether to sell the lime green rug, rugs may be next to impossible to get by the time the war is over. I want you to do what you think is best.

I sometimes feel, as you do, that my future destinies are not tied up in Minneapolis.

The world is full of opportunity and an architect's future may be far rosier away from a city full of architects as is true in the Twin Cities.

I most certainly want to be more than a draftsman. The very name is distasteful. The world has a low opinion of draftsmen as a rule.

One really notices that attitude in the East.

I'm going to register as an architect as soon as possible and then I will try to conquer the world.

March 14 #85

My darling,

Our future is so uncertain that I find little satisfaction in discussing it. The present isn't very interesting, so I've reached the end of my rope.

Apparently, the army position I mentioned a few letters ago, seems unlikely now. We are hearing very little about it, except for rumors and gossip through the grapevine.

We are going to be sent back to the states in four groups when our work here is done. I will be in the last, and smallest, group. That's okay with me. I'll be getting paid for all the time I'm here, and the crossing will be more comfortable.

March 20 #87

Sweetie Pie,

I've been told there are open positions for civil service work. The pay can potentially be $5,000 a year. I will apply for a position. It will only be a six-month contract.

I feel bad about writing to you about so many "possibilities." Maybe I should only write about realities. But, if I let you know all the pros and cons of each job, I feel as if we're making decisions together, even though I must make the final decision by myself. I will have the job before you get the letter.

April 2, 1943 #88

Darling,

Well, I'm still out in the sand and it is getting much hotter, to make things more pleasant. Haha! The temperature hovers around the maximum for Minneapolis during any hot summer. And this, is only the beginning.

All in all, the experience is interesting enough. I've had some real shopping excursions since arriving.

The other day, Jerry and I had a real orgy of buying. I spent about a hundred dollars in one big splurge.

There are some real shops and the craftsmanship of the workers is the best that I have seen over here. It is nothing like India, from what I hear, but nevertheless, typical of the country. I managed to fill some of your orders for trinkets. For example, I've bought: the silver bracelet for Shirley; ivory salt and pepper shakers for Estelle; leather handbags and desk pads for anyone; and heavy beaten silver ankle bracelets (which were made for small girls but can be worn on an adult's wrist). I've also obtained heavy ivory elephants, rhinoceros, hippopotami, gazelles, and other strange animals. How's that for a collection? Now, I can catch my breath and tell you some of my other purchases. Snakeskin slippers and other native slippers are included in my plunder. It was a lot of fun, and I kept thinking of how delighted you and Bill will be when you open the boxes some months from now.

There are so many things to see. Life here is so unspoiled by modern "improvements." That is, it is unspoiled in many places. Of course, in other places the natives use five-gallon gasoline cans on the ropes of their irrigation water wheels instead of earthenware pots, but still, it is pretty much the real thing. The thousands of camels and donkeys would make the average human rejoice, that is, if he's a camel and donkey fan.

So far, I've written only to you and the folks since coming here. I've been so busy that the days have gone one after the other and by night my weariness is too great for me to sit down and scratch off a few lines. There is so much to write about that I hardly know where to start.

The evenings are so nice that if it weren't for the flies, one could ask for nothing better. The air is so balmy and still that the sky takes on the appearance of a velvet coverlet dotted with very white stars. There is perhaps no more romantic spot in the universe, that is, if one is to believe all the references to this in the histories. Someday, you and I will come here at just this season of the year and it will be a great excursion.

There is always an abundance of primitive river craft to be seen. Most of the commerce is still on the water, much as it has been for the last two thousand years. The boats are just as clumsy as ever.

April 10 #89

My darling,

My trip this week was with Jerry and it was a good one. We left on Tuesday morning and travelled for twenty-six hours by train and came back last night after a similar time in route. We travelled in typical European compartments like one sees in the movies. It was a lot of fun even though it was a good bit more tedious than necessary. We had berths made up at night so slept very well despite the rough roadbed. The food was served in a tiny dining car and was very good, though very British. Fish (or some sort of fish cakes) were served before each main course.

One of the novelties of the trip was the route which took us through some real desert, complete in many places with sand dunes. The sun is so intense that the windows are glazed with smoked glass and one always sees the out-of-doors as being a bit dull and cloudy. We would stop at nearly every village, as the rear dozen cars on the train were filled with people packed in like so many sheep. Some of the country was very wild and we saw much that was foreign to us. While we were eating breakfast yesterday morning, we frightened a bunch of ostriches which had been feeding near the tracks. There were two cocks and about five or six hens. The males have much darker feathers and are a bit bigger than the others.

The round-trip cost about sixty dollars apiece and we of course are reimbursed for any cash outlay. The round-trip mileage was over fifteen hundred miles. It was nice to see the sea again and the air was cool after the desert heat. The temperature is always around a hundred in the shade, lately. Lucky it was cool there, for I sprained my ankle quite badly the second day out in the field and I am still limping. The coral rocks are hard to walk on and Jerry and I were doing our own field surveying.

April 23, 1943 - Letter to Frank Meisch

Dear Frank,

Your letter arrived last Wednesday, so I had better answer it now while the news is hot. All news here is of the rumor variety and is usually very wrong. This time, however, I have something definite.

I signed up with the U.S.E.D. (U.S. Engineering Department) for another six months. The future didn't look too prosperous at home, so I took a bird in the hand for the two in the bush. While the work may not last for the full six months, it is, at least, that much nearer the end of hostilities. We had all tried to get into the Army here, but the red tape was too much, and so far, no one of us has succeeded. I'll be able to tell you some good stuff about it when I see you.

You have a nice set-up there with NWA—Northwest Airlines—and I hope that the draft won't get you. You must have a good-sized department there. I worked with both Gordon Johnson and Magnusson at Rydell's. Both are nice, easy-going fellows. I suppose that the draft will get most of your fellows if they have fewer than six children or more than one leg. I expect an invitation from Uncle Sam soon after I return.

Perhaps you have heard of or seen my Kodachromes which Doris said she received around the end of March. It was a great relief to hear that they had arrived safely. It was such a tussle to get them. I made a deal with an ex-roommate of mine who went north, that if he would take the surplus of color film that I had and get pictures up there, I would get duplicates of all the transparencies. That was a good bargain for I just heard that he had spent about a hundred and fifty dollars for transportation in the several days he spent taking pictures of the various temples and tombs that we studied in school. He has a very nice Leica with all the attachments except gas and running water, so he should be able to do justice to the scenes. I used that camera for the last three rolls of color I sent Doris. The pictures will be about the only thing that I can take home with me, except for a few tall stories which no one will believe anyway.

*From what I hear, the rationing must be cutting into one's lifestyle these days. I daresay, they must still have a lot of beer and liquor. The accounts of nightlife in New York, which we devour in the gossip magazines that the ferry pilots bring over, is as gay as ever. The supply of beefsteak must be somewhat reduced. The supply of Bully-Beef over here is still beyond any danger of depletion. Today was the last day we are to get American cigarettes. From now on it will be a form of seaweed (I think that is what it is) wrapped in paper. They are called V*cigarettes. I don't know if that is what we are fighting for or what we are fighting to get rid of. Anyway, I don't let it bother me because I quit smoking about six weeks ago.*

That is about all that is new. Give my regards to Elaine. May be seeing you all before winter.

Best regards,
Stan

April 28 #93

Honey,

I just realized that yesterday was Easter Sunday. It is strange how holidays mean nothing to me, unless I am with you and Billie.

It is a big holiday for the local Catholics. The shop windows were filled with candy eggs and animals. Children are pretty much the same the world over. They all get a thrill out of the same things. I still laugh when I think of the time you shared that Billie had with the little chicken she received for Easter when she was two years old.

The Snow Girl is Waving at Daddy!
Easter Time in Minnesota

African girls at around Easter!
Definite contrast of climate, right?

I hope that the war won't prevent me from spending next Easter with you.

The JDP crew has mostly left. The army soldiers, and other civilians under contract with the army, have filled the hotel.

They are moving in and the rest of the staff will be housed in another hotel.

May 2, 1943 #98

Dearest,

This country is more suited to taking movies than any other type of photography. It is so full of action. The people don't like their pictures taken, however. You can only get a shot when they're on the run, so to speak.

Movies can really capture some of the resulting action.

Someday, I would very much like to take a trip, and capture some of this country with a movie camera and a lot of color film.

May 3 #99

Tootsie-Snoots,

I have signed on for an extension. Mark will be heading back to Minneapolis. I am glad you have become friends with his wife, Vivian.

Your purchases of clothing sounded so much like you. I can just see your excitement over the selections. I wish I could have been there with you… better still, I will see them when I get back. Six months isn't such a long time. Don't wear them out before I get there. You really needed the things too, I am sure.

May 11 #101

Dearest,

Saturday evening Bob Romans and another fellow and I went out of town for a weekend trip. The town was southeast and on a road we hadn't traveled before. The trip was enjoyable, as I hadn't been out of town for several weeks.

Most of the trip to the town was in the dark. We had a great time with the little Fiat. We had to make repairs every few miles. The Fiat is so small, we had a devil of a time finding room for ourselves and the baggage.

Much of the route was at a high altitude. The scenery on the way back was wonderful.

May 15 #102

My Darling,

Roman has been building a ritzy estate in Brazil. I've been working on the plans with him. I enjoy helping him with this project. I'm gaining experience that will translate to work I hope to do after the war is over.

I am considering getting an Exakta camera instead of the IIIB Leica. The Exakta is just as nice as the Leica, and it is cheaper. A fellow who had a good camera had been fortunate enough to pick a very big telephoto lens for it for the ridiculous sum of $20. The lens gives him a magnification of 10 times. It is possible to see a fly with it on a wall across the street. I wish I had something like that when I took pictures of the camera-shy natives in the marketplace.

May 19 #103 (part of this letter was cut out by the censors.)

Honey,

About the insurance—much has changed. I will tell you about it when I see you. I don't want too many holes in my letters.

The sewing machine must be very nice. I know you always wanted to have a portable because they were cute. You will have a real project with Billie's doll clothes. I'll have to build a real doll house for her.

May 26 - #106, 18 Weeks to go

Sweetheart,

Bob Romans and I went out for a "pete's" pie tonight and just returned. They are an Italian dish made from a sort of flat bread dough with tomatoes, cheese, fish, and spices on them. They are baked on the bricks of an open oven after the fire has been pushed aside. They aren't very digestible but are quite tasty. I've sampled a lot of odd dishes here.

I'm working on some sketches for a new house for you and me to build when I land a good job which seems to be somewhat permanent. I want a bigger place to take care of our new furniture acquisitions.

✧ **Billie: Mother was buying some nice quality pieces which she would sketch on her letters and send to Dad.**

We get furniture to fill our house and soon need more house to fit the furniture. I'd like a larger living and dining room set up. Perhaps all on one floor, this time. We need some elbow room.

Particularly so, with an active, growing daughter. Next time it won't be so compact. I hope this will all come to pass within a couple of years or so after the war.

Billie age three

CHAPTER 20

Work in Africa Winding down

In a couple of days, they found space for me on a plane hauling machine parts, cable, etc. It was the usual DC-3 aircraft. The plane had no insulation or other lining. The seats were a series of metal pans attached to the sidewalls. They really were intended for passengers with parachutes attached. — **Stan**

Looking Back

In the spring of 1943, the work in Asmara was winding down. There was much conversation about closing all JDP design and construction operations in the area. The U.S. Army Corps of Engineers was getting ready to take over the management of the projects and transfer all administration to Cairo. The few Corps officers in Eritrea had little knowledge of the actual construction underway or completed. That presented a bit of a problem for JDP since they were operating under a cost-plus contract and it was a bit difficult to prepare a final report of what work had actually been accomplished during the 18 months of activity.

There was talk about opportunities for work directly for the Corps after JDP left. I thought that that might be a good move for me as it would mean that I would be transferred to Cairo. There were also a few of my friends who were interested in the new operation. Bob Romans and a few others working in Asmara also decided to transfer to the Corps payroll. I heard that my good friend Jerry Jyring, now in Khartoum, Sudan, was also interested. I don't recall the sign-up process. It was informal.

The Corps and JDP had a rather fuzzy record on the status of completion of certain projects in the Sudan. They needed a hands-on survey of some of them so they could complete their reports and get reimbursed. I was assigned the task and headed for Khartoum. This was not a simple effort. We had to plan for a flight by military aircraft that operated on an on-call basis. This was to be the last of several trips to Khartoum.

Fortunately, I didn't have to wait long for a flight. In a couple of days, they found space for me on a plane hauling machine parts, cable, etc. It was the usual DC-3 aircraft. The plane had no insulation or other lining. The seats were a series of metal pans attached to the sidewalls. They really were intended for passengers with parachutes attached. Of course, there was no air conditioning. The only ventilation was in the form of a two-inch plastic plug fitted in the center of the small plastic window. Each plug was attached to a piece of flexible braided metal wire that was attached to the window frame. These plugs were always popping out when the pressure changed with the altitude. Quite primitive but this seemed like a good system.

The flight itself was not pleasant. The pilot chose to fly at a rather low altitude and there was a lot of bumping up and down. This was no good for a queasy stomach. My flight companion, a young Egyptian engineer, and I had an unpleasant time. However, the few hundred miles separating Asmara and Khartoum did not take long to traverse.

After being chauffeured to the Grand Hotel in a pickup truck we settled in with our local friends and compared notes on the change in administration of the project. The president of JDP, Robert Bayard, was on hand. He had flown down from Cairo. I relayed to him the lengthy oral instructions I had been given by the construction managers in Asmara on how they proposed to get the JDP people out of the Sudan, so they could get the ship out of Masawa that was due to leave in a few weeks. He didn't like it. I don't recall what scheme they finally adopted. I and my friend Jerry had work to do that didn't involve Bayard.

After a few days in Khartoum we decided that we had to make an on-site field survey of the work JDP had done in Port Sudan. There were some petroleum storage tanks and pipelines that had never been properly inventoried for reimbursement. This seemed like an interesting assignment. I had never been to that part of the Sudan.

Port Sudan is on the Red Sea and the easiest way to get there was by train. The route was along the Nile River from Khartoum to Atbara. Then, there was a branch line to the Red seaport of Suakin. Port Sudan was located a few miles north of there.

The train was not very comfortable even though Jerry and I did have a compartment for ourselves. The windows were tinted a deep mauve color to cut down on the heat transmission. In addition, there were folding shutters with louvered slats as an alternative way to cut off the sun. The route along the Nile was quite historic. The railroad, itself, had been built by Lord Kitchener in the 19th century to transport British troops to Khartoum to rescue General Gordon who was being held captive by the rebellious Sudanese.

✧ From Port Sudan, Dad went to Cairo, from where he wrote letters without being allowed to disclose his location.

One of the biggest challenges facing military in the Middle East was moving supplies long distances by rail across desert areas (for example, between Cairo and Lebanon). The roads were poor and not too secure for the civilian shipping of goods. The small rail system had been constructed over the years by British military and others so that there was a sort of link between the major business and living centers. But the system was not as good as the U.S. forces would have liked.

It was out of the question to build new lines, so every effort was being directed to making the existing system more efficient and reliable. A Corps of Engineers officer from the Los Angeles District Office was recruited to direct the effort. We heard about some of his activities and could only be sympathetic over the difficulties he was experiencing in his problem-solving program. He had some real obstacles to overcome.

The rail line from Cairo to Tel Aviv was single track for most of the mileage. There were some sidings so meeting trains could pass. In the daytime, approaching trains could see one another and the courtesy system in effect required the train nearest a siding to pull into or back into, thereby allowing the other train to continue on the main line. They had no radios in use so they couldn't discuss the matter. But, in difficult situations they might send out runners who would confer, negotiate and/or take messages back to their engineers. It was a time-consuming exercise and was wasteful of both fuel and water. Most of the trains were pulled by coal-fired steam locomotives.

The Corps of Engineers officer struggled with this inefficient operation and seemed to be making some slow progress in improving matters. A new difficulty came to light when the Army discovered a major problem with rail shipments by night. It was a matter of security. Many of the shipments to Tel Aviv were of rather important commodities such as medical supplies and other sensitive material. Such material would be carefully packed, inventoried and loaded onto box cars called "wagons to the British," that would, in turn, be a part of a train sent north. The problem that surfaced was that, though the train might arrive in Lebanon in good order, some of the cars might be missing.

The honesty and integrity of the train crews and other related labor was probably not too outstanding. After getting very poor explanations on how the cars could have disappeared, the Army sent out some investigation in trucks to scout along the rail route. They checked every siding and spur but found nothing. They put a lot of heat on those who were responsible for loading the cars but got nowhere.

After a few weeks had passed during which there were some very windy days, part of the mystery was solved. One day the crew of an Army patrol truck noticed something sticking out of the sand along the track out in the desert. It looked like the corner of a large box. A bit of digging revealed an entire rail box car. Apparently, it had been uncoupled by crew members during the night when two approaching trains had to adjust their positions and one had to go to a siding. One can only imagine the size of the crew necessary to uncouple, roll off the rails, and then bury a box car after looting its contents. Of course, they had only four wheels and were quite small compared to the ones in the U.S.

Obviously, the train crew must have been cooperating with the looter. Maybe the car was the last one on the train and could have been uncoupled while on a siding without the train's engineer knowing about it when he pulled forward off the siding onto the main line. Anyway, I heard that The Corps of Engineers officer gave up his program and returned to Los Angeles.

***We have been invited out to some of the local homes. In one we had one of those famous twelve-course dinners. I've never seen such food! The nation prides itself on its eating habits.* — Stan**

Chapter 21

Letters from Cairo

June 5 #109

Sweetheart,

Jerry is a big husky rancher type fellow from Colorado—Greely to be exact—a college-trained engineer, too. Might be well to have him and Fragen and Hayes for dinner. Then you could see the pictures that Fragen has. He could bring the movies. Herb is a good fellow—a bit uncouth—but a good friend of mine. I sure have a lot of good friends from over here. I didn't work at cultivating them either. Our room was always sort of the headquarters. Incidentally, Jerry is the biggest eater I ever saw—a three helping man—I don't know what that will do to your rations.

June 8, 1943 #88 letter from Doris to Stanley

Hi Honey,

Boy, have I been showered with letters. Yesterday p.m.'s letter was #106, dated May 6, and today's letter is #107, dated May 29. I just can't get over it. Your whole tone is waiting for the end of your contract. So am I, Honey—I miss you so much and it seems as if recently Billie is in great need of you. You have a delicate job of discipline in that young daughter of ours. I think she gets her brains from you (she's way ahead of me) so I'm afraid you'll have to deal with her. She has unbuttoned Dickie's pants twice and I think I have finally stumbled on the reason. (I know it's <u>not</u> morbid), but she has found that when he has his pants unbuttoned or off—especially with her—he gets a good spanking and she admits she likes to get him in a jam—Isn't that <u>lousy</u>? The time has been inopportune for me to spank her and Estelle has spent more time getting the full truth out of her. She just smirked today.

✧ **Dickie was the little boy next door.**

I'll be glad when I'm home all the time and I'll try, if possible, to keep a constant eye on her. I feel so alone on deals like this. This is silly stuff to write about and by the time you get the letter it will probably be all taken care of—but I so feel the need of your advice or discipline or both. I'm really counting on your coming home this fall—I hope neither of us will be disappointed.

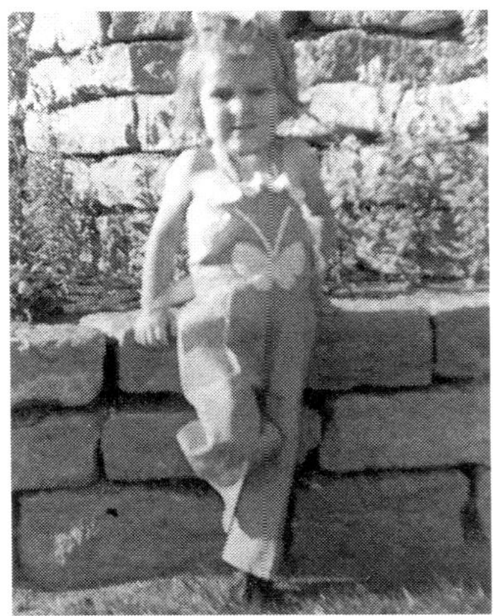

Billie's innocent "smirk"

I just finished making this suit

June 17, 1943 - Letter to Frank Meisch

Dear Frank,

I received your May 12th letter just the same day I flew up here. Now I'm up and at it again. It is much better seeing this country (Egypt) than having our Prof Mann tell about it, if you know what I mean.

This is a land of plenty. While there are a couple of meatless days a week, we do have good fish on those days. We go up to the nice hotels in town for a splurge a couple times a week. You know which one too—that is, if you read Life Magazine.

All in all, it is a bit of improvement over my last location. My living accommodations aren't good but there is plenty to do. My problem now is to spend money and still have some left. We have so many theaters and taxi cabs to take our few piasters.

Billie: Piasters are coins used in Middle Eastern Countries, including Egypt.

Most of the outlying architectural wonders are a day's journey by train. So far, we haven't moved around much. We have four big ones outside of town, though, which I'm going to see Sunday. I'll arrange for the rest when work gets dull. That will be soon.

Billie: I believe he's referring to the pyramids.

You may remember some of the stories about the iniquity of the town. Some may be true. At least, there is a certain laxness of morals, hereabouts. You ought to see the "belly-dancers" in the cafes. Shades of the Arabian Nights! Wonderful city for back-alley shimming. We have friends who have lived here all their lives and who worked with us before. They serve as good guides.

We have been invited out to some of the local homes. In one we had one of those famous 12 course dinners. I've never seen such food! They serve wonderful food in the good homes. The nation prides itself on its eating habits. No wonder all the gals are as broad hipped as boats by the time they are 18!

You talked about laundry. Boy, you don't appreciate your good luck. When I see my white shirts being beaten with paddles on a stone it makes me ill. When the laundry man irons clothes, he sprays the sprinkling water on them from his mouth. He takes a mouthful of water and shapes his lips like an atomizer and lets it go! Not bad—but not very sanitary. I've had to revise my standards on sanitation. I don't think I'll fuss much about flies when I get home. I'm being educated downwards.

So, Hayes has finally reported home. He should have plenty of tall stories to tell. I have a few myself, which I don't expect anyone to believe. If Hayes can land a job at home, he will be lucky. I wouldn't mind one there myself just now. I sort of feel I've done my overseas duty for a while.

My desk, which is a suitcase on my knees, is beginning to wobble so will end this.

My regards to Elaine.

Yours,

Stan

Note my new A.P.O. (army post office)

June 19 #111

Honeybunch,

Sunday evening, we went to Hakim's for dinner. Hakim, his brother, my roommate, Jim, Paul Germain (our engineering head), and I were there.

Sharif Hakim's uptown apartment is large, has balconies, and all the trimmings.

✧ **Sharif Hakim, often referred to as Hakim, was from Cairo and became a life-long friend.**

Our menu… in the order it was served:

Steamed brown rice with meat sauce
Breaded lamb chops
French-fried potatoes and French-fried cucumbers
Okra (like little cucumbers) stuffed with meat and rice, then baked
Radishes and pickles soaked in salt water
Native bread
Real old wine
Roast young hen turkey, served on a large platter of green beans
A large plate of the seedless heart of sliced watermelon cut in chunks
Bowls of fresh sugared strawberries
Bowls of stewed whole apples with oriental spices

We ate for a couple of hours, then sat on the balcony to watch the lights come on over the city. The "dim-out" (AKA black-out during WW2) cancels most of it.

The meal was served by black fellows in white gowns, bare feet, and red fezzes.

Quite a thing.

North African Marketplace

June 23 #112

Sweetheart,

I went out shopping with Bob Romans. The last place we struck was a perfume shop. We came out smelling like cosmetics. The proprietor insisted upon our having samples on our shirts. I had Christmas Night, Chanel #5, Musk, Alter of Roses, Jasmine, Violet, and I don't know how many others; all over me. Flowers grow in profusion—(roses are delivered in bundles like wheat)—and much oriental and flower perfumes are distilled here. It is possible to buy one ounce of the pure essence for less than five dollars. It is so strong that it is intended to be diluted with 1 to 10 parts alcohol; normal commercial strength. Let me know what you want, and I'll bring you some. The flower scents are the best and purest as they originate here. It is all very confusing to me. I was more mixed up with each scent I smelled. It is quite a show—this buying perfume. You sit on low divans around a low inlaid ebony table while the salesman chatters and you drink nice Persian tea—which is good—served in little glasses. I'm always thinking how much fun it would be if only you were along. Enclosed you'll find a copy of the list of scents from one place. I get a kick out of the names of some of the blends.

July 4, 1943 #114

Sweetheart,

In these days of instability, home stands out in front of me like a goal. It isn't because I'm feeling low (as I was for a few days), but because I've never put it into words before. I love cleanliness and comfort. Damn it all—I haven't really seen either since January 9, 1942.

Your mention of Billie is a bit surprising; I was not prepared for such mischief as you describe.

You might remember little Jerry in Ross and some of his unaccountable acts. It is difficult to know what to do about it. Somehow, I feel it should be stopped at once. Particularly that very forward and defiant attitude. "Spare the rod and spoil the child." I never remember such before. Yes—I'll take her in hand when I return, but you must convince her of the error of her ways now. Perhaps a child psychologist could do something in the way of advising you on discipline.

✧ **Billie: When Estelle started, it was thought that she would only be there a year. However, the summer of 1943 she got a job with Honeywell in Minneapolis while continuing to rent a room from Mother until Daddy returned home. I'm sure having Mother be the primary caretaker and Daddy being away, led to some of my "mischief." Mother would go to Estelle to ask her how to handle me!**

Mother didn't mention this in her letter of June 8th; I would roll into balls the stiffly starched dresses that Estelle had so carefully ironed because I did not want them to be so "scratchy." I clearly remember Estelle's reprimand and was told to go outside with her, choose a thin branch from a bush in the yard. She would cut it for me, and I would have to peel the bark and the leaves from the branch. Estelle would then switch my ankle-high leather shoes, never touching my skin. Then,

I would have to tell her what I had done wrong that resulted in this switch.

It must have worked because it acted as a deterrent after the second time! Mother shared that she (Mother) had gone so far as to tie a rope around my waist and attach it to a tree in the yard to keep me out of mischief while she sat in the yard and wrote a letter to Daddy.

July 14 #117

Sweetheart,

Someday I want an office or a position where I feel my life's work lies, and then I'm going to become established and never move anymore. I want to settle down as a substantial citizen and enjoy life. Make some money of course, and live well, but the main thing is to be rooted somewhere. The sooner the better. I would like it to be a nice town.

Give Billie a hug and a kiss, if she has been a good girl. If not—tell her I said she shouldn't have any. I hope you have managed to control her monkeyshines.

July 18 #119

✧ **Billie: This was written from the hospital where Dad had been for 8-10 days with an intestinal issue**

Honey,

I understand your frustrations with our being apart. Everyone has his day and we shall have ours. Two years deserve some compensation, and I mean to compensate. Don't hesitate to give vent to your feelings because it sometimes helps to yell.

I should be out of this JOINT in a couple of days. You should see my svelte figure—I am 138 pounds, like I was in college. I don't advise this method of dieting, but it is effective and doesn't leave one with a big appetite.

Hon, I'm so glad that my return means so much to you. It makes one feel so important to be wanted. Things will be wonderful, won't they? Rationing and such like will mean nothing. We can live on happiness, if nothing else. I think that I shall never grumble again.

July 21 #121

My Honey,

I read your letter describing Billie's bad behavior. She's only three-years-old. Perhaps she's just being a little kid.

It's only ten weeks until I leave. I'm really looking forward to being home. I haven't been able to leave my place for the past eight days. I've been sick.

✧ **I must have gotten the independent thinking and adventurous spirit from Dad. My mother must have been very frustrated, wanting some immediate feedback regarding my behavior/misbehavior, but because of the time lag between letters and long delays of letters being sent, the frustration must have mounted. She would write a letter about what was on her mind that needed his advice and viewpoint, and it might take a week to ten days or sometimes two to three weeks to get to Dad. And his response came with similar time issues.**

With today's Email, Skype, FaceTime, Facebook, and other means of communication even between opposite sides of the world, parents can discuss issues, and the children can have face-to-face conversations with the parent who is away.

July 24 #122

My darling,

I finally recovered. It took me ten days, but I'm back at work. Most of the fellows are leaving. Bob Romans will be going to the Caribbean.

July 25, 1943

Billie: My parents' anniversary is today. Dad had seen a pencil artist in Cairo that he thought was talented. He decided to sit for a drawing to send home to mother.

I had this Pencil drawing done in Cairo for Doris

July 26 #123

Sweetheart,

Yesterday was our wedding anniversary. Last night, when I returned to my room from a long day's excursion, your letter #95, was waiting for me. It made the day even more pleasant.

We got up early and were uptown shortly before breakfast. Bob, Jim and I met Hakim and two other fellows. We set out by taxi for a Coptic church in the old city. Services were underway when we got there, so we were able to watch the ritual.

The church is very old. It was built over the ruins of a Roman fort. Seven-hundred-year-old paintings graced the walls as well as many examples of marble columns and carvings. There were fine cedar screens, inlaid with ebony and ivory. They were also very old and very beautiful. The ancient barrel-shaped wooden roof was assembled with wooden pegs. And, the floor was covered with timeworn hand-woven carpets. All in all, it was a beautiful place.

Later, we went to a Roman Church and saw the crypts beneath the church. We were told that the church dates back to the time of Christ. Because of the climate, the church weathers the same in 100 years as it does in 500. It is hard to determine if the stories are true or not.

We examined a Roman aqueduct as well. There's no doubt it was the "real thing." It had wonderful brick and stonework.

Later, we had lunch in town. Artisan beer, at $1.00 a quart can was a good find since we had worked up a ravenous appetite.

After lunch, we went to the citadel and examined a mosque. It is enormous and is a copy of St. Sophia in Istanbul.

Billie: Hagia Sophia, Istanbul, is the former Greek Orthodox Christian patriarchal cathedral, which later became an Ottoman imperial mosque. This Istanbul structure was a favorite of Dads and the whole family visited it.

The mosque in Asmara has a European character. Strange and unusual for Eritrea. The carpets were in sections and very old. They covered the entire floor—perhaps two acres in extent. The entire building was made of marble inside and out. It has an outer cover of colonnades made of alabaster.

By the end of the day, we were exhausted.

July 31 #124

Sweetie-pie,

One morning, about three weeks ago, when I was ill, I carelessly shaved off one half of my mustache. When I realized what I had done, in order to keep accounts straight, I shaved off the other half. I felt naked for a time. A few days ago, I started to grow it back again. The boys said I look better with the mustache. They said I looked five to eight years younger without my mustache. I don't want to look like a high-school boy again!

Sweetie-pie, you will notice by the date that I know that Billie is 4 today. It hardly seems that long. As it should be on the anniversary of her birthday—it is hot and sticky. We are having Minnesota-July weather.

The war news is very encouraging and while it may be a bit optimistic, many of our gang feel that it will be over with Hitler by January! I hope so but am a bit more pessimistic. Then, it will be up to the rest to pitch in and lick the Japs. That won't be too easy, I'm afraid.

August 1 #125

Sweetheart,

Last night was a big evening, so I want to tell you all about it. Six of us—Geo Brewer, Tom Motter, Ralph Torluemke, Bob Romans, Jim Farrell, and I went to the town's most famous hotel and celebrated. You wouldn't know it, but we were celebrating Billie's 4th birthday. Her anniversary was well taken care of.

We had drinks in all the hotel's three bars and finally ended up for a dinner of filet mignon in the dining room. If you read Life Magazine, you will know how the place looked. The meal was wonderful—being the first real steak I've had since I left the states. The evening was costly, but very pleasant. Billie, someday, might get a kick out of how her birthday was observed. She was toasted eloquently and often, and we had a good time. Maybe she will even see it sometime.

Billie's 4th birthday with Doris

✧ **Billie: The U.S. censors did not allow the people to write where they were or any details about the area. However, my sister Myra and I, figured it out. We knew he was in Cairo and that the hotel had a great view of the city's art (the pyramids). The Mena House (now the Marriot Mena House) has been in existence since 1869 and was written up in Life Magazine.**

I did see the hotel in 1965, but I did not know the story of my birthday celebration until I read his letters after he passed. Here's a quote about a historical event that took place in that hotel. "This is the place where history was written. In November 1943, the Prime Minister of the United Kingdom, Winston Churchill, the President of the USA, Delano Roosevelt, and Chinese general Chiang Kai-Shek have met to decide about the positions of allies towards Japan. In the older part of the hotel, hall walls are embellished with historic pictures which commemorate the meeting from 1943." (copied from the hotel web site, 2020)

Aug 6, 1943 - Letter to Frank Meisch

Dear Frank,

I was glad to get your most welcome letter a couple of days ago and to hear that you were still in circulation. You must have what it takes. Old Uncle Sam must come very near to tapping you on the shoulder. Here's to your continued good luck!

We are busy as the devil and are working somewhat in your field. Anyway, it will soon be over and then it will be time for seeking something else. Less than two months remain on my contract and then I head for home. It will probably be November 1st before I hit home, if then. I think that my twenty months out of the old U.S. are enough for this trip. We have plenty of opportunity to tie up with other outfits, but now I'm interested in home first before I listen to any preparations.

A very good friend of mine is looking into the new program of European post-war reconstruction. It might provide some interesting experience—if one didn't mind moving about a bit. However, I don't think Europe would appeal to me in its present state. I wouldn't mind a job right at home for a change. Hotels, barracks, rooming houses and even tents have lost their fascination for me. Anyway, time will tell. It may work out that the only good jobs are those which require travel and frequent changes of residence.

I'm having a whale of a big time here. It is the most fascinating city in the world—for my money.

This city is a wonderful spot for a photographer—color, texture, pattern (and filth) at every side. One can shoot a roll every ten minutes on a Sunday's walk and still feel that he hasn't covered it at all. As for architecture—it's all here; Roman, Moorish, Crusader, Arab, Indian, Persian and all the various European styles of Gothic, Tudor, Italian, French, and so on. This year is said to be the thousandth anniversary of the founding of the city.

That will give you an idea of what history has passed here. We have several engineer friends who are of the pure races (such as the Egyptian race or Sudanese race etc.) and are full of stories about the country. They have been wonderful guides on our excursions about the countryside and city. All the crafts are practiced here. All the metal workers, weavers, spinners, coopers, potters and the rest ply their trades in much the same fashion as was common hundreds of years ago. All good picture material.

Some swanky hotels and restaurants are to be found, too. Food prices are fixed. All dinners everywhere are 30 piasters or 20 piasters or 80 cents. Nevertheless, we go down to the swanky hotel on Saturday night and bend the elbow before downing their special tenderloin steak dinner. The only steak in town and it tastes almost American! Most all cooking is French—greasy!

Conversation among the boys lately is turning to plans of a celebration in N.Y. when we return. That will be a real splurge. Most of our fellows are New Yorkers and of course pine away for want of bright lights. I wouldn't mind a few myself, about now. About the lights here—well, I'll have to tell you about them over a couple of snorts at Charlie's or something. Some very strange customs!

I've covered all fact and supposition, so I'll give up for now.

So darn little that can be said while keeping the censor's knife at rest. It will provide conversation material for some time to come.

My best regards to you and Elaine

Stan

Hope by now you are registered—I must take care of that myself when I return.

Aug 15, 1943 - Letter to Frank Meisch

Dear Frank,

Excuse the tracing paper stationery but airmail paper is becoming very scarce. Most common items are very hard to get. If available, they cost too much. A bottle of American fountain pen ink, for example, sells for sixty cents a bottle.

Things here are much the same as ever. That is to say, hot and sticky. I've seen much hotter places here, where one got prickly heat after one day, but for long weeks of sun and humidity this place is a close second. Now and then a cool breeze comes along in the evening, scented with odors of garbage and worse. It hasn't rained here since about December. Not a sprinkle. Things are kept green and alive by constant irrigation and resulting heavy dew, but it all adds to the humidity. Practically all money above 4 cent and 8 cent pieces, one piaster and two piasters respectively, is of paper. If one isn't careful these small bills of poor paper will disintegrate in one's pocket. One always seems to have a handful of five, ten and twenty-five piaster notes which appear to have been printed on toilet paper. The pound ($4.14) notes are *larger and on good paper. Oh, for the good old American dollar bill or even Idaho silver slugs!*

We are still busy as the devil, but before long I'll be pounding pavements at home looking for a new job. Maybe I'll end up on another foreign job as some of my returning friends have done. I would rather stay at home next time.

I hear from Mark occasionally and he seems well set in the role of family man. It is not hard to enjoy home and comfort, I'm sure. That is, if Uncle Sam is willing and that's doubtful.

Film, in the popular 120 and 620 sizes, is now almost nonexistent. Since local finishing is poor anyway, I've lost interest in much picture-taking. Aside from using up my Kodachrome soon, I don't think I'll be doing much. What a place this is for color, but one can't record the smells and that's a pity. No place quite like it, defying description.

Jack Benny, Anna Lee, and Minnie Shaw are in town and they caused quite a lot of excitement here. Soldiers' entertainments, you know. They happened in on us last week one night while we were celebrating a friend's birthday in a garden restaurant of the most famous hotel in town. I never even recognized them at first except that they looked like Americans but that is not a novelty here. The city is lousy with them. As Benny put it when describing his fast trip across: "Breakfast in ----, lunch in -------, and departing here, all in one day!" That's about right. Only he is lucky to have not had the dysentery.

The war news sounds good, but I'm not as optimistic as some. I doubt if the Germans will be licked in '43. They have a long way to fall back. Hopes sure ran high when Benito fell off his pedestal. Still, I don't trust the Italians. They are opportunists.

Time for lunch, so I'll get this off.

Give my regards to Elaine.

Stan

August 15 #128

Sweetheart,

You are certainly becoming domestic with all your canning and other activities. It will be a real treat to eat home-canned vegetables and fruit. Don't worry, I'll be able to eat my share.

So, Billie is a slow eater? I can remember the extensive spankings I received at about the age of five or six over my perverse actions at the table. I didn't like the food—or some such excuse. What I didn't know about food! I think the idea of having her leave the table with you is a good one. But watch her weight, so she gets enough. Maybe a hot weather problem, don't you think?

September 3 #133

Sweetie pie,

Jerry Jyring and I are going on a trip Sunday. You'd get a bang out of the car we are going to use. It is a 1929 Model A Ford with a charcoal burner on the back. Every few hours the driver must stop and stoke the fire.

We went out to see Judy Garland in Little Nellie Kelly this evening. It was very cute. She's cute like you are and made me think of you all the while.

I'm glad Bill can't realize the evil of war. I would hate to have her little mind cluttered up with war and such. She can go on living in her happy little world without any fears. God is kind to allow us to provide so well for her. When it is all over, you may be sure we three will have great times together. She will have a lot of fun. We will sail boats and build a doll house for her with electric lights and running water.

September 6 #134

Bob Romans has decided not to go back to Minneapolis. He has taken a fifty-two-week assignment in Brazil. I promise I will not do anything that foolish.

September 9 #136

Sweetheart,

You will remember what Dad once told me. That is—that I had never spent that bachelor period (unattached) after leaving college. Chasing around with the "fellows" and all. Well, this past twenty months has offered me just that opportunity. No women figured in any of our skylarking (playing around). None of our gang seem to be "that way inclined." Then too, we have had one of the busiest oriental cities in the world to do our skylarking in. It's been a whale of a lot of fun and except for my bellyache, my stay here has been interesting. It will be an awful lot of fun looking back on it from afar. You know how I was for sitting around like a "bump on the log" and letting other people have fun. I've been up with them neck and neck so far. It seems that I got in with a gang of my own background and temperament. They would fit in with our home crowd very well.

The days are sure getting short here. Now it is exactly 8 p.m. and it is jet black outside. A couple of weeks ago it was so light that it was hard to see the outdoor movies when they began at 8. Fall is here.

Being Thursday night, I hear them tuning up the orchestra across the street. They have a dance on Thursdays and Sundays on the terrace. It is popular with American Civilians and British and American military. A few of the local younger gentry are to be seen staging their version of the American jitterbug. They are an awful bunch. The local young people are hell raisers. Even the ones from good families.

September 12 #137
Only 18 days to go. ………… I have your Chanel #5. …. All my love, Stanley

Sept 16, 1943 - Sunday, Letter to Frank Meisch
Dear Frank,

Your letter came in yesterday's mail, so I'll get off an answer at once. Things are usually in such an uproar here that I soon forget to answer my letters if I don't do it at once.

My gang is all gone. Some to the U.S., some to places I don't know, and others to Persia and South America. I hope that I'll be able to depart soon. I'm to have my first physical exam next week so it must mean that our departure is imminent. They tell us extraordinarily little about such things here. I spent one morning last week trying to get sent home by plane at once when my contract was up. No luck. But it looks like we will leave soon anyway.

Congratulations on your registration!

✧ **Billie: I believe he is referring to registering either as an engineer or as an architect or both.**

I will need to work on that myself when I get back and have been settled for a while. Since my last job here was as a structural engineer, I have been able to pick up many of the loose ends of my mechanics, but I shall have a sweet time going over some of the other things. You're wise to think of national registration now as it really is valuable. It doesn't pay to delay too long.

I'm glad that you and Elaine had an opportunity to see my slides. I'm quite curious as you can really imagine, to see them myself. There are two more rolls in the mail of more familiar scenery—that is, to you and me. I'm hoping that they turn out well, too. That is the tough part. If one doesn't get a good shot the first time, there is no coming back again for a retake. Jyring had the shots on his last roll—only to throw it in the waste basket later, thinking it was an empty spare. He had half the staff in the hotel looking for it, but it was never found. A roll of color film is practically worth its weight in gold here. Someday—there is always that "someday"—I want to come back with a hundred rolls of color movie film. Most camera subjects are in motion here—and I do mean motion. No one here, except for street urchins, wants his picture taken. They are particularly opposed to it.

Thanks a lot for your efforts in finding a position for me in your outfit. I hope you are successful. There are plenty of jobs like mine now—out of the U.S.A. I'm anxious to get home, however, and stay there for as long as they will let me.

They have been after me to sign up for a few more months here—for $500-a week, but not again, I thought, and turned them down. When I made up my mind on going home Oct. 1st, I meant just that. Some of the boys here *seem quite content to spend several years here, but I can't become accustomed to all the flies. So, this time, it is home and snow for me.*

While the gang of fellows was intact, we made all the spots of interest and had a whale of a time. If one wants a "big" time, this is the place. Every known form of entertainment is here, (and some which must remain unknown). Then too, the war has had an effect on the city and its pleasures. They are just as numerous, but they cost a good deal more. I'll give you some stories on them over a tall drink sometime. This place will have a lot of memories for me.

While I can't know just what will happen in the next few days, I still may see home shores before you receive this. That will be only if things work out perfectly. See you soon.

Regards, Stan

September 19 #139

Darling,

Vic has asked me if I am going to stay after my contract is up. I assure you I will not do that. Paul Germain told me that he would make sure I am not pressured into staying here. Many of the other men have been.

✧ **Billie: Again, though the letters couldn't say, he was still in Cairo at this time.**

Yesterday our trunks came in—finally. Bob and I spent last night packing and unpacking. The trunk must have had a hell of a trip for it shows marks—even though heavily crated. A bottle of white shoe cleaner and a bottle of shaving lotion had exploded in the top drawer due to exposure to terrific heat. You can imagine the condition of the interior of that drawer. Luckily the trunk was upside down when it happened for it didn't spoil anything else.

Yesterday, I will be leaving for home in a little less than three weeks.

All my love to my darlings,

Stanley

September 22 #140

I am looking forward to returning home. Right now, it seems I will be sent home by boat. I'm ready to be back in Minneapolis.

September 25 #141

I spoke to Vic about my journey home. He was not very encouraging. Seems as if the officers and the ones with pull get to leave first.

It will be so good to see you in New York. We will have a grand time.

September 30 #142

Most of us continue to work even though our contract is up. Those that decided to not work after the contract was over aren't getting paid.

October 5 #143

I will have to stay here until January 1st if I want to get out of paying income tax. I haven't had any luck joining an early group to go back to the States.

One of the men here went out to celebrate on the last day of his contract. He was killed in a Jeep crash that night.

October 7 #144

I've had no luck getting transportation home.

Chapter 22

My Departure from Africa

Looking Back

When I finally wound up with the Corps of Engineers, I had managed to get extensions on my contract. I stayed WEEKS over my contract and didn't sign the one-year contract. I signed the six-month contract with Corps of Engineers under Johnson, Drake & Piper and in Asmara.

I went by train one night (77 miles) on the "Cairo to Suez." It was in Suez I would board a ship to the U.S.

When I arrived, I was told the following. They gave me a mess kit and a blanket and told me they'd find me a place to stay. All I had was in my duffel bag and what I had carried on the train. Now I had a mess kit and a blanket in the Egyptian desert. I found a tent that wasn't occupied, but there was NO BED. Am I going to lie on the sandy ground with a blanket? Yes, that's what I did. During the night I had to find the toilet. They had dug pit latrines. They had planks across—and you had to stand on a plank. It was primitive.

I saw a little truck going by with some nice-looking people on it and they said, "Would you like a ride?"

"SURE!"

They looked like Americans. We went down the road a mile or two.

We stopped at a Red Cross place and there were American ladies, missionaries, who had cooked up little meals for us. They identified us as being with the American military. It was SO NICE.

I finally heard, after two nights in that place, that there was going to be a ship out of Suez. A truck came and hauled us "boys" with our duffel bags. Sometime later, while going through my duffel bag, I found out that somebody got into my toilet kit and stole a ring I had had made by a nice jeweler with an Ethiopian symbol on it. Oddly, that was the only thing missing.

At last a pretty good-sized ship arose out there at Suez and we saw a bunch of trunks. I could see my trunk there. I had not seen it since I left NYC (except for a brief connection in Cairo). Big rope slings were used to get the trunks to the deck of the ship. Then one of the slings opened and dumped all the trunks in the water. I didn't know until I got to New York two weeks later that my trunk was one of the ones that didn't fall in. Thank God.

I got on board the ship called the <u>RMMV Stirling Castles</u>. It was a British cruise ship that used to go from England down to East Africa, down to Durban on the east side, back when that part of Africa was an English Colony. During WW2 the <u>Stirling Castles</u> was used as a "troopship."

Lo and behold, one of the men in the group was a Corps of Engineers civilian from Los Angeles. He was a very pleasant fellow and we had a cabin together. No outside ventilation, but it was clean. It was kind of interesting, because, we went through the Suez Canal, to the sea-coast town of Port Said which is an Egyptian port. It is quite an attractive area. That's where all the yachtsmen were for weekend sailing. So that scene was very colorful; sailing ships coming out in a big community at the north end of the canal. I have always loved sailing boats. The harbor was full of yachtsmen in fancy boats.

This was during the war but not everybody was fighting. After all, it was "somebody else's war."

Then the ship headed off across the Mediterranean. Suddenly, we ended up in Italy. Next thing I found I was taken out of my cabin. I, along with some other people, was assigned another space that took up a large open area at the tip of the ship. I think it was the tearoom or lounge. This open area had been filled with bunks made of two-by-fours, rope slings and old mattresses thrown on top. The West African troops had been housed here. Some of them had complained about bedbugs to guys in our group and someone shouted "bedbugs!" So, alright, now what do I do about the bedbugs?

I zipped up my duffle bag. Better that no bedbugs got into my duffle bag. I had a process of dressing every day to avoid the bugs, and I was lucky in that regard. The food, however, was not good.

In Italy, we weren't aware of anything that was going on. We found out that the ship was going to take back a bunch of the U.S. troops who had fought in terrible battles in Italy. There was a famous battle at the time, and we were taking back soldiers who had been wounded. There wasn't much sign of physical damage; they were wounded where it does not show on the outside. I remember these people coming up the gangplank and I met a couple of them. One young fellow couldn't have been more than nineteen. I couldn't see his wounds except in his eyes, he was so, so, sad. He had a little American flag on a stick in his shirt pocket. I thought, maybe, somehow, that had kept him going. But, that boy… this war is something else.

✧ **Billie: I believe the battle Dad referred to was code-named "Operation Husky." Wikipedia writes: "The Allied invasion of Sicily, codenamed Operation Husky, was a major campaign of World War 2, in which the Allies took the island of Sicily from the Axis powers (Fascist Italy and Nazi Germany).**

"It began with a large amphibious and airborne operation, followed by a six-week land campaign, and initiated the Italian Campaign. Husky began on the night of July 9, 1943 and ended on 17 August, 1943.

"Strategically, Husky achieved the goals set out for it by Allied planners; the Allies drove Axis air, land and naval forces from the island and the Mediterranean sea lanes were opened for Allied merchant ships for the first time since 1941."

After we left Sicily and headed for Gibraltar, the Germans were shooting at us quite often at night. There were aircraft guns mounted on ships alongside as part of our convoy. They would shoot up the German planes overhead.

We finally got to Algiers. Things quieted down when we saw the city on the hillside. Little did I realize that when I was seventy-one years of age, I would have a project in Algiers. We moved on farther out and we finally got to Gibraltar. We didn't go ashore. The troops left us, and we were back in cabins with no bugs!

We headed across the Atlantic for home.

We hadn't been out of the port more than about a day when WOW! A tremendous storm came up. The ship was lightly loaded because the fuel was low. There was no cargo other than two hundred passengers. We were moving with the storm. The ship would go up and down every so often and the bow or the stern would come out of the water. BIG waves there. Finally, the captain announced that we were doing serious damage to the engine from the fact that the bow was not constantly in the water and so we were going to have to roll with it.

We just hung on. I came down with a terrible head cold at that time. It was a British ship, so the British medics aboard helped us with our ailments. The treatment for a head cold was, you got something that looked like a jug. It was a jug with hot water in it and a drop or two of menthol or something. I can't remember quite how it worked, but there were two spouts on one side to the top of the jug and you put your mouth over a spout and inhaled. You got the fumes. That would get rid of a head cold.

And the ship rolled and pitched up and down. You'd hear the doors and stuff all going bang-bang-bang. Doors and drawers popping open…unnatural motion. Oh, it was something.

We finally got to New York and sailed up to a pier. And, I found my trunk! I hadn't seen it for quite a while. I had finally seen it in Cairo, but I had to open it so it could be inspected by Customs. You can't have any documents that tell where you've been or what you've seen. No photographs. No this, no that. Whatever they decided would be confiscated. A friend of mine had quite a rifle—an Italian-Military type, but an innocent little thing. He thought he might like that thing at home. But he said that they would probably confiscate it.

He asked me, "Why don't you take the block and I'll take the rest?" They confiscated the rifle, but the little block that I had from the rifle went unnoticed in my trunk.

I'M HOME, AMERICA!

First order of business, of course, was to find a place to stay. One of the people I had gotten to know on the trip said one of his favorite hotels was right off 5th Avenue on 55th called Gotham—a very elegant and nice hotel. The man that had told me this was a very elegant guy himself—a New Yorker.

I got a taxi. In those days the taxis had a fold-down rack on the back for trunks. Many people would have trunks. I had my trunk on the back, and I got out in front of the Gotham Hotel.

I went into the desk and they laughed and said, "We're full up." (I suspect I didn't look like one of the people they welcomed having been on a "troop-ship" for two weeks and having slept in tents before the ship.)

Okay. I thought, I'll go down to the New Yorker hotel down in Midtown Manhattan where I had stayed the last three or four days before I had taken off for Africa a year and a half before. I got checked in.

I found my 1942 diary that I had put in the lining of my suitcase with many of the notes for my memoirs; my book, my diary, and my appointment book.

My 1943 diary was lost, but Doris kept all the letters I wrote-even those that had parts cut out by the sensors, so many of the stories in my memoirs that concern 1943 are from the letters.

✧ ***I believe it was shortly after Dad settled in that Mom arrived to be with him. What a reunion that must have been!***

Nov. 13, 1943 Letter to Frank Moorman from NYC

Dear Frank,

Well, I finally made it! It hardly seems possible that I'm here and that Doris is with me here in New York. In no time at all I think that I will be quite civilized again.

It is surprising what clothes and good food can do for one! We are trying to see as many people and places as possible. The city is practically the same as before.

I've sent the application form in and will be available for an interview Monday the 22nd. Thanks for your help.

This will be all for now. I hope to see you and your family soon.

Best regards,

Stan

PART VII

1944–1952:

Duluth, Minnesota, and Van Nuys, California

Big Moves: Home and Career

It is no harder to find a robust career than to find a job. — Stan

Stan Moe, back from Africa and raring to go!

SEASONS
GREETINGS

DORIS AND STAN

A linoleum print carved by Doris and Stan

Chapter 23

Billie's Memories of Exciting Family Events!

When Daddy came back from Africa in 1943, my parents decided to sell our house and move to Duluth sometime in 1944 when it warmed up. My dad must have enjoyed his freedom as a young kid so much that he bestowed that freedom on me. When we moved to Duluth in 1944, I was four and a half years old. We rented a house with a large backyard that sloped down to a creek.

At the end of the block was a big Catholic church. Next to the church was the house that the priest lived in with his housekeeper. I discovered very quickly that the housekeeper made fresh cookies every day. There seemed to be no restrictions on my going where I wished and so I went down the block to have cookies and milk that the housekeeper seemed happy to provide. If my family ever worried about my whereabouts, I never knew about it.

I also went door to door when we first moved to Duluth to see who had kids. I'd knock on the door and ask if they had any kids and if I could play with them. I was allowed these freedoms; perhaps because it was a different time. In any case, the perception was that our environment was not dangerous but completely safe. My father had lived a similarly unrestricted early childhood.

Mother got pregnant with Myra in the late summer of 1944.

In November, I was diagnosed with Scarlet Fever. They put me in the hospital for several weeks until Christmas Eve day. Before I was discharged, the nurse took me to visit polio patients in iron lungs who were about my age. There were 6–8 iron lungs in a room. She lifted me up to look through the little round windows. Their heads were sticking out, but I could look through the windows to see their arms and legs. I talked to these kids and wished them Merry Christmas.

In addition, the little boy in the room next door shared a wall with me. Because he was a TB carrier, we couldn't visit with each other. We "talked" to each other by knocking on the wall between us and must have figured out a code. Before I left, the nurse let me see into his room and I could see him in his crib on the other side of the room and we waved and said hello to each other. I was sad he could not go home for Christmas and felt lucky that I could.

Feb. 6, 1945 Letter to Frank Meisch from Doris - Duluth, Minnesota

Dear Elaine and Frank,

I have owed you a letter for so long. I finally can send one.

We were in Minneapolis as of Tuesday last week but were so rushed we didn't call anyone. The purpose of our trip was to say goodbye to my brother, Allan, who is being sent overseas, so our time was spent with him.

Besides being snowed in up here, I'm not so anxious to gad around. Come April we are expecting "Charlie," that brother Billie has talked about for years. Which means, too, that we would love to buy back the crib, if you can get something for your little guy. And by the way—how is he? Is his hair still red?

Billie had Scarlet Fever before Christmas. She was released from the hospital Christmas Eve, so that made our Christmas a genuinely nice one. She missed quite a lot of school, but I guess that isn't too serious at her age (five). Her case was very light, and she has no after-effects.

We're having a good old-fashioned blizzard today. Not very cold, but plenty of snow whirling around.

Time to get dinner. Stan is going to study tonight, and he wanted to eat early. He is taking his registration exams.

Let's hear from you!

Love,

Doris

In April of 1945, Myra was born. We stayed in Duluth until 1948. Dad worked for a man named Harold Starin in Duluth and for a couple of other companies.

I have my new baby! I told the kids at school that there was a new supply of babies at the hospital. If they wanted a baby, they should have their parents go get one!

Easter 1947 — Myra and I dyeing eggs in our kitchen on Vermillion Road, Duluth (Notice: Myra's shoe on wrong foot)

Still in Duluth

Sometime in 1947, Dad teamed up with a couple of his friends. One was an engineer by the name of Bjarni Larsen who was also Scandinavian. The other friend was Norman Fugelso. So, there was Larsen, Moe and Fugelso and they decided to set out for Southern California, which they heard was growing, and set up an office together. Moe and Fugelso were architects and Larsen, an engineer. The name of their company was Larsen, Moe and Fugelso.

We moved to Van Nuys in 1948 and I went into the third grade. Myra was three and I was eight. At first the three partners found an office in LA, then moved and set up business in Van Nuys. Larsen had a boy and a girl, Dad had two girls, and Fugelso had two boys. I was the oldest of the six kids. We played together and were delighted when our dads bought a horse for us kids to ride.

Mother taking a picture of Myra and me shortly after moving to Van Nuys

I am 10, Myra is 4: Dad caught our reflections in a round beveled mirror (Matching dresses made by Mom)

All three families found places to live, of course. Fugelso lived in an apartment in Sherman Oaks, Larsen rented a house with a lot of property at Nordhoff and Van Nuys Boulevard. Mom and Dad bought a tract house designed and built by Trousdale (whose first big job before he became famous was 99 tract houses). Our house looked the same as everyone else's in this lower-middle class neighborhood of Van Nuys.

Myra, mother and I in our new back yard

I believe these were the first tract houses in Southern California. Later, Trousdale went on to do other fancy, houses in Beverly Hills and his name became well known.

To buy the house, Dad and Mother borrowed $16,000 from my Grandpa Anderson. The house they bought cost $10,000 and was on a half-acre. Dad wasted no time making it his own. First, he built a breakfast room to make the kitchen bigger. Then, between his travels, he added a large master bedroom and bath next to the swimming pool. I can't remember how many square feet he added to the house.

Dad and the other partners designed the Presbyterian Church in Van Nuys. They designed the Safeway grocery stores and the Bank of America banks. They got contracts on residential homes too. They started doing commercial property and those L-shaped strip malls that became "a thing."

Dad got involved with many business organizations in San Fernando and Los Angeles. He knew how to network, a skill that became a life-long asset. When we moved to Van Nuys in 1948, Dad was a member of the Architects of the San Fernando Valley. He received a Junior Chamber Distinguished Service Award in 1949. Junior Chamber of Commerce in 1950, named him "Man of the Year," And then he became president.

In 1952 Dad was hired by Daniel, Mann, Johnson, and Mendenhall (DMJM) who offered him a position in Japan. Though he worked abroad for DMJM, he continued his interest in his company, Moe and Larsen. We lived in Van Nuys until Myra and I were out of school.

PART VIII

1952: Japan

Photo by Stan Moe from Japanese temple

✧ Billie: "After Japan surrendered in 1945, ending World War 2, Allied forces led by the United States occupied the nation, bringing drastic changes. Japan was disarmed, its empire dissolved, its form of government changed to a democracy, and its economy and education system reorganized and rebuilt. Years of reconstruction were required to recover from thousands of air raids, including the atomic bombings of Hiroshima and Nagasaki. By the 1950s, a former enemy became a Western ally, parts of American culture became part of the Japanese landscape—and Japan began to find its economic footing as a manufacturer of consumer devices and electronics." From, The Atlantic, March 12, 2014.

Hayama is a beautiful spot and very clean. The water was perfect with little rollers. The Emperor came into the bay or cove (less than a mile wide) in his small yacht and visited a prince who has a place on the shore. — **Stan**

CHAPTER 24

Never a Dull Moment in Remarkable Japan

Feb 13, 1952 #1
(This was written on blue Pan American World Airways Air Gram)
Dear Hon and Kids—

We had a nice sleep last night with very clean berths.

Bigger than a train suite. About one hour before dawn, we landed on Wake Island which is a tiny coral island. We had breakfast in a Quonset hut and waited around until the sun came up for refueling and so on. The views were interesting, so I took a few shots.

✧ **Billie: At that time, airlines had sleeping berths. It was a wonderful time to fly.**

Feb 14 #2
Dear Hon and kids,

I've just finished my first day in Tokyo, Japan, so will bring you up to date. There's a lot to tell and I will have to do it by stages as no one letter can handle it. Nothing is as I expected it. That is a good start and I can go on from there.

We landed at the airport and stayed for about an hour for clearance in the dingiest airport terminal in the world. Then, we went by the PAA (Pan American Airlines) taxi to the Meiji Building across from the Imperial Palace. The moat comes right up to the street. The building is about the same size and type as the NW Bank Bldg. in Minneapolis.

The trip uptown was through many miles of dreary wood buildings. No one ever paints anything here. The city in winter, I've been told, is almost always gloomy and dreary. No sun for weeks, they say. And since they burn soft coal, everything is sooty. The people dress in dark, dreary clothing and only a few of the women wear kimonos and clogs. Most wear western clothes.

Typical Japanese wood-sided buildings, unpainted

I'm staying in Army Hall which is a large hotel—all majors and colonels or civilians of equal rank. I had a better room in Asmara but hope to make a change. I am alone in a room 18'x 40' with three beds.

All the people in the office are very cordial—many have been here ever since 1945 (civilians at that). For several blocks around our building, one sees nine civilian or military Americans to one Japanese.

My big problem right now is money. It takes a bit more than I thought. Membership in the Union Club is $2.50 a month or $7.50 a quarter. For civilians only. A small and equally ritzy version of the Jonathon Club (a private Los Angeles social club founded in 1895) stands about 6 stories high. We eat lunches there. (Meals range from 40 cents to 70 cents.)

Feb. 15 #3

Dear Hon and Kids,

Today I walked down to the Ginza, the Main shopping street in Tokyo. At one side of it is a park which parallels the river and is now occupied by the Ginzakan Mart. The shops once were little stalls in the street selling everything from nylons to fishing rods and suitcases. They are now housed in neat-clean stalls as of Jan 1st. I picked up a fountain pen for 30 yen or about $1.17. It writes well and looks exactly like a Parker "51." In fact, not one person in a hundred could tell the difference. Clever people—these Japanese.

Feb 18 #6

Ho hum! Another day and another $47.00! First, my minimum requirements:

Food: breakfast, 40 cents, lunch, 50 cents or so, dinner, 55 cents or around $1.60 including coffee or about $12.00 a week

Laundry: about $1.00 a week

Cleaning: about $1.00 a week

Stationery and stamps: $1.00 a week

Miscellaneous: shows, taxi, magazines: $5.00

Total: $20.00 per week

An architect-Engineer firm doing work for FEAF (Far East Air Force) is called Pacific Associates. The big boss and some of his helpers were in today.

It was Antonin Raymond who spent 35 years in Japan before the war and who collaborated with F.L. Wright on the Imperial Hotel. The plans I saw were lousy. I wonder who drew them?

Feb 24 #8

Hello Hon,

The new room I have is in a part of the building where only field-grade officers live—Majors and Lt. Colonels. Full Colonels live in the Imperial. Our toilet and shower set up is unique. All the fixtures are in color (a nice green) and small size like one might find in a boys' school. You see, these Japanese are small in stature. It is a rare one who is over 5' in height. That is particularly true of the ruling classes. Our end of the building was formerly Japanese officer's quarters.

Modesty is a queer thing around here. It seems that every morning when I am at the urinal, I find a gal washing the one next to me. They are wonderful cleaners. All young; 16-20—nice looking girls. They don't pay a bit of attention to us there. However, in our room, it is different. I was writing a letter here the other day, completely dressed and in came two girls. They were embarrassed and tittered and giggled like a bunch of schoolgirls. Things seem in reverse.

I am learning my way around including the Meiji Bldg., Marunouchi Bldg., the waterfront, The Ginza, The Takashimaya Store, and the Mitsukoshi Dept. Store. There are free army buses that run all over town. It is a problem to know where they make connections and to determine their schedules.

As much as possible, I'm traveling alone. That way I can concentrate on what interests me. And it all interests me. If I'm with someone else my schedule is always upset. Much of the time I have no schedule. That way I end up in such fascinating places. You have me with my 180-degree vision. I see an awful lot of stuff without turning my head. Most of the people completely ignore strangers and Americans in particular. At least we are no novelty.

I will have been gone two weeks tomorrow. Aside from a current shortage of cash and lack of letters from you, I do okay and am really very happy. It appeals to my inquiring mind. I can spend a year here and only scratch the surface of what is going on. Eretria was so very simple. I'm going to try to make friends with good educated Japanese who will be interested in giving me a guided tour.

The city is so vast that it is almost impossible to find one's way around. It is not as densely populated as New York and is therefore more spread out. There are few multi-story buildings in the residential class. Consider the size of a city and you will see how spread out it must be. And public transportation is not good.

The duty is now 60% on American imports. Part of our Japanese recovery deals. I was hoping to find a good friend and buy an MG together. They are ideal for narrow roads in the country.

I wish I had a typewriter (Royal Portables cost $160.00 in Jap shops. I don't like to write letters, but I like to pass on what I see and hear. Tokyo lays flat except for the mound at the Palace and has some of the same mud and *dust problems Van Nuys had after the flood. So, it is always dusty. Also, they are always digging up the sidewalk to get at water pipes and cable for power and telephones. I'll be happy when spring comes in earnest. There are still small patches of snow in shady parts of the parks.*

I bought a book on Japanese yesterday so am now engaged in learning the language.

It is curious—this is sort of a lonely life, but when I analyze it, I seem to have been just about as lonely all my life even when I am at home and among friends.

That is why I can keep my wits about me when I'm away from home. Three or four of the fellows in our gang here are dealing with loneliness in the same way. They have been travelling like this for years. All are swell fellows. Like the best of JD&P—all prefer single rooms, too.

Feb 25 #9

Dear Hon,

I went to the Mitsukoshi Department Store yesterday afternoon and had a gay time. The top two floors were given over to an exhibit of antique Japanese Art. It was very good—and crowded. I meandered all through the store. They had one whole floor of kimono silks. All in rolls 13" wide and enough in each roll for a kimono. You buy the whole bolt. Some very beautiful. I wish you could see them. They would put a rainbow to shame.

I must wash my hair and study my new book; Learn Japanese in 30 hours.

Lots of love, Stan.

Feb 26 #10

I wrote my first A&E [architecture & engineering] contract today for a job where the architectural fee will be about 3.5 % of 8 million dollars. There are lots of restrictions and complications with people who have worked for DMJM other places in the world.

March 4, 1952 #11

Hon,

This past Sunday, Henry Hesse and I went to Kamakura. We left at noon and arrived here at about 7:45.

Kamakura is certainly colorful and will be more so when the cherry blossoms are in bloom during the month of April. The train going down there, on 2nd class, which is very good, is 180 yen or $.50. Bus trips around town are 10 yen each. The buses are clean too. We are hoping to go down there for an entire day next time. The Japanese are just as nuts on sight-seeing and picture taking as we are and outnumbered us many times on this trip.

Henry is a very nice sort and had his own office near Pomona. We have much in common and get along fine.

March 19 #20

Dear Hon,

We went on a wonderful trip to Atami, which is on a peninsula 65 miles south of Tokyo. Henry and I went down on an early train on Sunday to spend the day. The weather was nice and spring-like. The country is lovely, and the train went along the seacoast through numerous tunnels, past pretty villages, and terraced fields. We arrived at 11:30 and walked up to the hotel, which was supposedly the best in town, and had lunch.

After lunch, we strolled around down the hill and took a lot of pictures. Atami is called the Riviera of Japan and I can see why! There are countless small hotels, inns, and shops for the vacationing Japanese. We had a good time. We got pictures of very choice octopus and squid dangling on strings in the shops amid fancy delicatessen supplies. We have some swell shots.

Japanese resort towns are strange. The Japanese, when they arrive, (most wearing western clothing) go to an inn or hotel, remove shoes in the lobby, walk to their rooms and remove their clothes. They then dress in a kimono furnished by the hotel and wear this until they leave. The kimonos are of nice silk but dark in color (as my photos will show). Each hotel has its own kind of kimono. Women's kimonos are a bit lighter in color than the men's kimonos. Then the people go shopping, strolling in the streets, etc., and always wear these kimonos and wood clogs. Quite a custom. Some of the Americans did the same, early in "the occupation." I may try it before I leave, but I might feel like a fool. I couldn't pass for a Japanese and would no doubt attract attention.

Most Japanese men who patronize hotels at the beach or resorts do not take their wives. They bathe, eat, stroll, sleep, and so on with geisha girls and have themselves a nice dignified "time." About four years ago a large part of Atami burned up. Most of this has been built up with commercial and residential structures of a nice type; with fine, delicate Japanese detail with some of the most delightful workmanship you have ever seen.

One can look into the entrance areas of the little geisha houses and see beautiful flower arrangements. All the geisha houses are immaculate. In most Japanese cities, the geisha districts are the cleanest and the prettiest with the best architecture. All geisha houses are not "bad." In most houses, only those girls with extremely long kimono sleeves are "available."

Everyone seems amazed that Henry and I grab Japanese trains and go everywhere. One the majors in the office wants to go with us next time. He has been here a year and only seen the inside of the Tokyo bars and clubs! After Egypt and Eritrea, I don't mind jumping on a train to see where I will end up.

Billie: I always did this when my husband and I traveled. Though sometimes nervous, we enjoyed the adventures.

March 21 #21

Sweetie pie,

I got a good deal of razzing over showing up with a Royal Stetson Hat on the first day of Spring! It was warm today. I had been walking around here in the snow and rain ever since my arrival. Today was the Vernal Equinox Day which is a Japanese National holiday. All Japanese go to the cemeteries to worship their ancestors. It is sort of a Memorial Day or Decoration Day.

April 5, 1952 #29

The delicatessen department in the Takashimaya is very interesting. Boiled octopus, eel livers, etc. Some stuff is so strong smelling from soy sauce, which they have as thick as molasses, that I had to hold my nose! At the delicatessen—what should I see but a display of candied, dried snakes! Nicely displayed too, all coiled with the head sticking up! They grind them for the customers, using a small version of the old grocery store coffee mill. Can you imagine? About that time, I felt a little green. These people out-do the Arabs!

Geisha Houses

This is the lowdown on geisha houses. You see, the Japanese man is traditionally the boss of the family and he is supposed to have all the consideration. After a hard day or morning at the office, he would go with some of his friends to a geisha house, which is tastefully furnished, and they don a kimono and sit quietly and sip sake and then have a lunch or dinner. The geisha girls sit around, beautifully dressed and with fancy hairdos, and entertain the diner with songs and soft music on a sort of mandolin. They are also trained to make light, polite conversation to take the man's mind off his troubles; such as his wife, home, and kids as well as his work. Wives are generally at home busy raising kids. He probably had had nothing to say about whom his parents selected for his wife, anyway. The geisha house was like a nice club. Of course, there are some red-light district spots, but they are separate from the traditional geisha houses.

When the Americans arrived on the scene, however, they had a notion that all geisha houses were brothels. The Japanese, eager to please—and to make a "buck"—decided that they would give the Americans what they thought they wanted and asked for. So, the brothels got fancier and much more numerous and were called geisha houses to satisfy Americans. Americans, in true smart aleck form, would rather say they had been to a geisha house and smirk than say they had been to a brothel. The head of the Japanese equivalent of the General Electric Co. is a "friend of a friend" and will set up a traditional "geisha event" for us. The "proper kind"—so don't worry. I'm getting too old anyway!

April 7 #30

Sweetie-Pie,

The wind is whistling outside my window and it sounds for all the world like the San Fernando Valley. It is not cold today, however, and it is the first time I've gone to work without my topcoat since arriving. I think that spring has come. All our cherry blossoms are due to pop anytime this week. Ah—to see Japan in the spring! That is how the travel folders sound, don't they?

April 8 #31

The cherry blossoms popped all around today and Army Hall is surrounded. I'll get some pictures of the sights. The people here are nuts about cherry blossoms—more so than Americans. The stores have been filled with paper cherry blossom decorations for the past month.

I sure do love you and wish I were with you to snuggle instead of having to go to bed all by myself.

April 10 #33

Today was windy and warm. The cherry blossoms are out all over and I'm going to take appropriate pictures on Saturday and Sunday. The wind blew so hard today that the canals and streams were covered with petals. What a sight!

April 13, Easter Sunday #34

Sweetheart,

Got up early this morning and went up to the Shrine to get some cherry blossom pictures. We have had wind and rain which speeded up the dropping of petals. Today they blew around like snow.

After breakfast I rode down to the Meiji Bldg. to look for mail and found your pencil note in a small envelope as well as a letter from Billie. I will say that Billie is somewhat illiterate for a seventh grader. However, it was nice of her to write and good practice if she keeps it up.

✧ **In the early years, Mother and Grandma Andrine were the ones who oversaw my "learning problems," but the schools did not have the formalized testing for learning disabilities. When my 5th grade teacher had given me many unsatisfactory grades, Mother insisted they give me an IQ (intelligance quotient) test and my results were in the gifted range. I would think she shared this information with Daddy, but in those years, IQ and reading and writing abilities were likely not connected.**

Friday noon, Hopkins took Hesse and me out to the Ueno Park where there are pagodas, shrines, and blossoms. They are pretty, but it was very cloudy. Friday night, Jones, Hesse, and I went up to the north side of town to a park where people go to celebrate cherry blossom season. It is quite a season of finality. One classic way to enjoy it—is to sit under a tree loaded with blossoms, "contemplate" the blossoms, sip a little sake, and when well "primed," dash off an ode or poem to the blossoms.

Today, being Easter, I went to church at the G.H.Q. (General Headquarters) chapel. It was the evening service and the choir of about 125 Japanese voices sang the Hallelujah Chorus by Handel with wonderfully sweet voices and very good Japanese direction. All in English, of course. I'm sending a program under separate cover. I will try to make church a regular Sunday event hereafter, as I felt much better afterward. 140 yen by taxi each way. A lot of Japanese were there too. Some Nisei of course, and G.I.'s with Japanese wives and girlfriends. Most people around here seem to be backsliders when it comes to church.

The services today were attended by about 2500 people and, of course, there are other chapels near the housing centers. There were sure a lot of American women in fancy clothes—a strong showing of oriental materials, brocades and satins.

I go wild when I get into the textile departments for the big stores. I wish you could see the materials. They make luxurious in Minneapolis look pale and dull. Such brocades! Cloth of gold, etc. Anything one could ever want. I could spend all day just looking at the stuff. An amazing thing is that silks are inexpensive. I wish you would send me your yardage requirements for dresses, cocktail dresses, jackets, etc., so I can send you a piece now and then.

April 23 #39

This past Sunday, Henry and I took a trip to a place called Odawara. We went 3/4s of the way by train, then, an hour more by switch-back trolley up the mountainside through country that rivals Yosemite. After that we took a cable car up and up until we were in the clouds. Before we took the cable car, we stopped at a fancy hotel, called The Gohra Hotel. Modern and swank, it overlooked a beautiful mountain valley covered with trees and believe it or not, cherry trees among the pines. From a mile or so distance, they looked like splashes of paint on the forest.

At the top of the cable run, it was COLD and wet. We finally convinced the people where we wanted to go. We ended up traveling by bus for one hour around Lake Hakone and on the north side in Fuji. We saw neither as we were in the rain and clouds. It was the roughest and narrowest road you have ever seen and all along the brink of some awful drops without guard rails. We changed buses and travelled for another hour down the mountain and finally out of the rain and fog. I always wondered what kind of people the Japanese were to produce such as the "kamikaze" or suicide pilots. I know now—it was easy—they merely recruited them from the run-of-the-mill bus drivers. We finally arrived at the bottom of the mountain where it was warm and dry. Next time we will check our weather a bit sooner and plan on a warm, sunny day.

April 28 #41

Sunday dawned bright and clear and we decided to take a trip by train (changed 3 times) and after 3 hours ended up in a fishing village way down the east side of the Chiba Peninsula. Very interesting. The trip was beautiful and the train not too dirty or crowded. The town, if you have a map, is called Kominato. They build large wooden fishing boats there and it is all very picturesque and surprisingly clean.

As James, Hesse, and I walked around the bay we became more and more impressed with the scenery and finally missed the 5 o'clock train back to Tokyo. Since we had more time we walked some more and chanced upon a Buddhist temple in a shady valley which had some of the most exquisite detail I've ever seen. It was tremendous in size and completely devoid of paint. We figured that we had really stumbled upon something off the "tourist track." At sunset it was tremendously impressive. I shot at least a dozen shots in color as the sun set.

Today we found that it is one of the oldest and unrestored Buddhist temples in Japan. 800 years old! All out of wood. As we left the temple grounds the sun was setting and as we were a bit tired and thirsty, we spotted a tea house out over the water and went in for tea. We finally got across what we wanted and had tea and biscuits. About 4 pots of tea and a half dozen cookies cost only 30 YEN or 8 cents for all of us.

They don't know much about Americans here. We sat on the floor by a little table out on a roofed terrace overlooking the bay. It was a small bay like a mountain lake and very beautiful as the stars came out. The fishing boats started to come in with a twinkling of light and soon the wood smoke began to fill all the low spots around the bay as the evening cooking fires were started. The smell of oriental wood smoke is very different. It reminded me of Eritrea. We headed down the trail for the station and it got chilly.

By the time the train arrived at 7:20, we were really freezing. We tried to buy second class tickets and we thought that the ticket agent couldn't understand us when we ended up with 3rd class. When we saw the train, we knew why. This train was all 3rd class (or lower). The cars were dirty and cold and busy. Such activity!

At Oritzu, Katsuura, Hara, and finally Chojamachi the country women began to come aboard with their loads. The "payoff" was when a robust little gal about 5 foot-tall tossed a couple of empty bags and a basket onto a seat and then shoved a large wooden box down the aisle and sat across from me. She carefully dusted off one of the cushions (they have wood backs) and "plunked" a basket on the seat. I wondered why she was fussy, because she wore baggy pants and seaman's rubber boots.

She ripped off the lid of the wooden box and began to extract live lobsters! At least 50 lbs. of them—all sandy and lively. And they were really kicking up a fuss with their golden, beady eyes glowing in the dim light. I'll bet they hadn't been out of the ocean 2 hours. She put the big ones in the bucket and the small ones in a knap sack. Of course, all this was entertainment for all the country folk in the car. After exchanging greetings with all her friends out of the window at the various stops, she finally leaned over on the box and went to sleep. Oh, yes, she divided up some pieces of dried squid with some of her neighbors and they stripped it down like stick licorice and chewed it before dozing off.

Not being dressed for it, we were really cold, and these characters were always opening windows. Since there are no passable roads and practically no cars in this area everyone travels by train and they know everyone along the way. What a gay time!

After 5 train changes, we arrived in Tokyo at 11:00 p.m., half frozen. These Japanese are still wearing their woolen underwear! Really. Many don't notice the cold. This is NOT first-class travel and you can see why.

Our train fare from Kominato to Tokyo was 370 YEN for 3 people = $1.02. Next week we go again. It is cheaper to travel (this way, that is) than stay in Tokyo on weekends.

Oh, I forgot, we arrived at this place at noon and found no place to eat that looked appropriate. There were only two places in the main part of town, and at the cleanest looking of the two, we were unable to convince the girls in charge there, that we wanted to eat. They had so much fun laughing at our poor Japanese that we gave up. We ate in another place and only because the proprietress was carrying an egg in her hand and we told her we want THAT. THAT and rice which is easy to say… sounds like go-hawn. We got a bowl of abalone soup, and a bowl of rice with a half-fried egg on top together with onion and chopped seaweed. Tasted like they just picked it up off the beach! However, after liberally sprinkling the mixture with soy sauce (they had no salt), I ate most of the rice. Including 2 quarts of beer and 4 pots of tea, the meal cost us $1.75 for three of us. So far, I have not had any stomach aches, so I suppose it wasn't as poisonous as it looked.

✧ **Billie: In the next section, Dad is buying traditional Japanese sandals and the vendor is suggesting which ones to buy. According to Google search: "Historically, geta sandals were worn as part of a traditional style Japanese outfit, styled with a kimono in the cooler weather and a yukata during summer. Sneaker-wearers will know how quickly white footwear picks up the dirt of the street, which is why geta are elevated so high from the ground on their wooden teeth. Zori are flat and thonged Japanese sandals made of rice straw or cloth, lacquered wood, leather, rubber, or, most commonly, synthetic materials. Similar in form, modern flip-flops became popular in the United States when soldiers returning from World War 2 brought Japanese zori with them."**

"These geta for Miss Myra-San. These geta for Miss Billie-San and these zori for Miss Doris-San." (San is an honorific name for Mr. Mrs. & Miss.) He was enjoying himself immensely and enjoyed saying the names. He said his English was a bit rusty because he didn't remember too much of it from

primary school 40 years before! Some of these people are awfully nice. Since this fellow does such a swell job, I thought I might buy some for Don's and Helen's kids. I'll have Mom get their foot outlines.

Today is the last day of the occupation. History is unfolding and from now on the Japanese are their own bosses. Today the streets were full of new Japanese flags on fancy poles with gold colored balls on top. I hope they don't get carried away. The commies are working up the students pretty bad. Maybe we will have some "episodes." We'll see.

May 1st is the big May Day celebration which is a Labor Day with a lot of hot-headed labor demonstrations. They are prepared for plenty of unpleasantness. They have allotted about 28 thousand police in Tokyo alone. The Reds will be at work stirring things up.

May 3, 1952 #43

We had a lot of excitement on May 1, the day of the big labor demonstration. The park in front of the palace and in front of the Meiji Bldg. was full of demonstrators. It ended with a riot, where they burned a bunch of American cars and smashed windows in others. Thousands of police were trying to keep order but had a tough time. I got pictures of the activities from the safety of the roof of our building. Some business! Mostly Communist inspired. It has been a bit quieter since. Today they had another gathering in front of the palace with the Emperor speaking. No American cars or buses were permitted near Headquarters. Thousands of police covered it, so all went off smoothly. That is a bit more like it. I wouldn't want to see many more days like May 1st. The scene from the roof of a real battle below was like looking down on a football game—it would have made some wonderful movies.

June 22 #64

Hi Hon,

We got a bit tired of our food here, so we decided to go someplace else for a change. We went to a tempura restaurant, which was founded in 1885. Since there are only eight seats in it, and we didn't have reservations, we wondered if we might get in. We did—found two seats. I don't know how to describe it but will take flash equipment with me next time. It is typically Japanese in that you remove your shoes and walk around in your stocking feet on woven mats (tatami mats). The room is maybe 14' square. You sit on the mats with your feet hanging down in front of you under the table. (Much better than folding them under.)

They use little screens on feet like fireplace screens to separate your party from the rest. One girl is assigned to each customer and she squats in back and pours sake and brings new napkins. Before food is brought, they bring in little bamboo baskets with hot wet clothes (o-shibori) for washing hands and face. An Excellent idea, by the way. The sake is in tiny cups and served hot from little china bottles. Very good.

We asked for some 'go-hawn,' which is rice. So, they brought us a little wooden tub of beautifully steamed rice and the girls ladled out a bowl for each. They showed us how to eat the whole works together. I guess they think we are dumb.

After dinner, we walked around the corner to the Kabuki Theater—the largest in Tokyo. It is a beautiful, traditional structure with lacquered round columns 3 stories high in the lobby. The Kabuki plays are traditional plays and are world famous. Since they last 3-1/2 hours and it was late, we arrived during intermission. No seats were left, and all ticket booths were closed. They invited us in anyway and we stood near the door to watch a few scenes. Imagine an invitation like that in the U.S! The sets are beautiful and the acting and costumes exceptional.

✧ **Billie—Dad and I went to an afternoon of Kabuki when I worked in Tokyo in 1961. I was fascinated by males playing the roles of females and did much research and gave speeches on Kabuki while I was in college. Mother and Dad collected Kabuki woodblock prints from the 1800s, and now they hang on my walls with the prints that my husband, Dean, and I collected.**

July 24 #82

We took a train to the beach at Hayama. That is a few miles out of Kamakura. It is a beautiful spot and very clean. The water was perfect with little rollers. The Emperor came into the bay or cove (less than a mile wide) in his small yacht and visited a prince who has a place on the shore. As a matter of fact, we swim in what once was his private beach. I got some pictures. He was a little man in a white shirt and a felt hat. Looked like a little farmer.

August 16, 1952 #91

Sweetheart,

I went with Herb Jones to Katakai, which is on the eastern side of the Chiba peninsula and about 2-1/2 hours' drive from Tokyo. I had heard about the place which is not accessible by rail and so has few visitors. It is at least 40 miles of unbroken beach without a sewer or a concession. So hard is the sand that we could drive on it at the water's edge. The place is a center for fishing, small fish like sardines. There are clusters of fishing boats every mile or so. They go out in the morning and lay a mile or so of net and then spend the rest of the day pulling it in. All by hand and what a performance. It is a community venture as no single family could afford a net. It takes hours to pull in a net and dozens of men and women work at it—singing a tune to match the tugs on the net lines.

Most of the heavy work is done by the women, who are a tanned, healthy, happy-looking lot, who wear a big cooling hat and a short shirt like a bathing suit without a halter. The men wear a "g" string or nothing except a string around the foreskin to keep the salt water off. Can you imagine? Anyway, in the beautiful sunshine we got a flock of pictures—in color. Between times we went swimming and "planed" in on the rollers. The beach was magnificent. My skin now looks and feels like a piece of old saddle leather. First time in years it feels and looks good.

August 26 #98

My Darling,

We are having a real racket outside. They are having a bon festival in the parking lot. It is under U.S. and Japanese sponsorship. It is a typical Japanese folk-dance festival. A raised platform in the center, about 12' high, holds lanterns and dance leaders. Hundreds of men, women, and children are dressed in Kimonos. Some kids are only a year or so old. Cute as can be.

This is the Japanese equivalent of square dancing. All the dancers are quite graceful. The music is on a P.A. system with one fellow beating a drum with a funny skip-beat. All this is taking place a hundred feet from my window. Some Americans join in but are a little shy. Wish the kids could be here and could learn it. It is very graceful. I'd do it myself if I weren't so hot. Real oriental music. I'll get some records of it. Would be good for cocktail parties.

Aug. 28 #99

Sweetheart,

You sure do sound lonesome in your letters. I'm happy that you love me and need me so much, but I worry too about how you are getting along. I don't feel that money is necessarily that important. You and your welfare are to me the most important things in life and I want you to be happy.

CHAPTER 25

Japan — A Perfect Trip and Other Stories

September 3, 1952 #100

Hon,

This week Jones and I returned from one of the "best trips ever." Jones is not too adventurous, and on Friday morning he had cooled on the idea of a trip to Skudai as he knew nothing about where to stay. I talked to a civilian employee of FEAF (Far East Air Force) who has been here for about 7 years and got a suggestion on another place to go. He was with military government and had traveled all over the island. He suggested Sado Shima Island and I convinced Jones we should take off. I ran down to the station at noon and got sleeper tickets to Niigata over on the west coast. We had a good lunch and got the two last lower berths. Since it is off the beaten path, few Americans go there.

There are about 12 second-class berths on a train (1/2 coach) so we were fortunate. We got on at 10 p.m. and traveled all night and arrived in the rain in Niigata at 6:30 am. We knew that some American officers were in town, so we went to a small house where they lived. What a dump! Like the Wilson Hotel in Stanley, ND. We grabbed breakfast only and walked around town until the boat was scheduled to leave for Sado at 9 a.m.

This area is quite different from the Tokyo area. Many people in straw coolie hats, straw raincoats, and sandals. Quite primitive—though the town had some nice buildings. By the time the boat left, it had cleared up and was nice. We got cabin tickets, first class for 800 yen each. A nice little white cabin (one of 3 on the boat). Only a small boat, but the sea was nice and the water in the Japan Sea is an intense blue.

When we approached, the bamboo forest covered the isle and the peaks of the hills were in the clouds. A very pretty sight. We were underway 3 hours because they had to repair the engine twice. Each time the captain would apologize in Japanese and say, "so sorry." Sounded amusing.

The island was shaped like a dumbbell with low land between.

When we got off the boat, we were "on our own." We could speak no Japanese and they no English. We finally found a nice-looking fellow standing by a bus, which was in fair shape and we indicated that we would like a good Japanese hotel on the other side of the island. He whipped out some fancy literature with some pictures of a good hotel and all the text in Japanese. We got on the bus.

It was now noon and we were hungry—not having eaten since 6:30. Finally, they collected 800 yens from each and handed us tickets, which looked like fancy post cards. Then we found that it would take 4-1/2 hours to get to the hotel and we had bought a bus tour ticket that would take the better part of two days. Since all the others on the bus were Japanese tourists, we decided to see what would happen if we just "did as the Romans do in Rome."

Often stopping at every stone and stump on the way across the island and listening to a hundred spiels (all in Japanese) we arrived at the hotel, which was new and the caliber of the Lynlan Lake Lodge in the Black Hills. We found out that the fellow at the dock had taken a short cut and was all ready for us and was the manager. We had a fine suite—all Japanese style—on the second floor overlooking the ocean to the west. The place was immaculate. At the door, we left our shoes (which were hidden away until we left) and given slippers. At our room vestibule, we shed our slippers and walked in stocking feet around the room on tatami mats and polished wood floors like furniture tops.

The place was beautiful. Sliding paper panels, etc. Our little maid, who was to wait on us hand and foot until we left, helped us undress and helped us into Yukatas furnished by the hotel. Then, she led us to the bath. We dipped hot water from a large tile pool in the middle of the room and poured it over us and soaped and rinsed. When we were all clean, we got into a big pool and sat, soaked and steamed for a while. Then, went up to our room.

The manager came and asked what we wanted for dinner and seemed a bit upset because we had missed lunch. We suggested a few possibilities. However, we were unprepared for what we had: a plate of beef steak, coleslaw, and sliced tomatoes, a plate of pork shops, cucumber, and French fries, a plate of shrimp and relish, a platter of tempura (fish and vegetable), a plate of sliced beef, cold and warm potato salad, and a wooden tub of rice.

When she came with a plate of Sukiyaki and a plate of raw fish, we had to say STOP. Each time it was an individual serving for each of us. All good, but we felt that there must be some mistake. After dinner, we got getas at the lobby and strolled through the little pine forest on the hill around the hotel. We were about to go to bed when our maid came up and motioned to us to come downstairs to the main dining room. We found all the Japanese guests sitting in Yukatas like ours. We were given fancy programs (all in Japanese) and were treated to a ceremonial dance on a little stage with velvet curtains and all the fancy theatrical trappings. It was very good.

When we got up to our room, we found that the place had been cleaned for sleeping—on the floor. First cushions 4" thick. Over them, a sheet with boxed canvas to keep the cushions together. Then a futon—a heavy silk covered quilt. Then a terry cloth sheet! The pillow was a red Satin roll 12" long and 6" diameter covered with a little linen slipcover which was open at both ends. The pillow had tassels at both ends and was hard being filled with rice hulls. A comforter with sheet basted on it was folded at the foot. A little lacquer and rice paper night lamp was on the floor beside all of this. Some Deal! We slept well.

We enjoyed a good breakfast the next morning and paid our bill, 1500 yen each, (or approximately $4. 06 each) for lodging and food! In Tokyo, just one dinner would have cost us $10 each.

We boarded the bus at 8:30 a.m. with all the Japanese who were now all fixed up, but since men carry no razors and no extra clothes, they all had beards, though their clothes were clean. They must have washed them at night. All the kids were clean and "starched" too. Never a whisper or a fuss from those kids.

Billie: I was surprised in 1961 how quiet and polite the children were. Their little shoes were taken off and placed on the floor so they could have their feet up on the upholstered seats of public transportation. All this had changed when I traveled in Japan in the 1990s and early 2000s.

We toured for 6-1/2 hours and finally ended up at the place where we had started. We stayed at another hotel Sunday night. Had steak for dinner, eggs for breakfast, and pretty much a repetition of the night before. We spent late afternoon on Sunday swimming in the breakwater—in our shorts—to the amusement of all the kids who only wear underclothes.

Monday morning, we paid our bill (1400 yen) and grabbed the boat back. The gals in kimonos and getas carried our bags 6 blocks over uneven streets and then stood at the dock holding paper streamer rolls on their fingers while we held the other ends on the boat. Ah—quite festive—while the loudspeaker played "Auld Lang Syne!" The ocean was like a lake and we got to Niigata at noon. We walked all over town on Monday p.m. window-shopping and then went to a Japanese theater. Lawrence Oliver in Hamilton Women!

We stopped for coffee and cake and then, at dusk, found a wonderful shop. It was the first I have seen for bronze work. I got some wonderful craft articles, which we found were made in Sado. I have a lacquer box for us to give to Harold and Libby instead of the tray or in addition to. So, hold the tray until you get this. I also got one of the smartest tea kettles I've seen. All in fine wood boxes. I'll send all, this week; first class. I'm having a fellow check into lamp bases too. They will be terrific.

Got home 6:30 Tuesday morning and got to work at 7:30, so, I am exhausted. It was the best trip I've ever taken. A perfect trip and it cost me $20 for 3 days—all first class! How I wished you had been along.

Sept. 14, 1952 #106

Sweetheart,

It is almost 8 p.m. and I have just finished dinner. We got in by train at 7:20. So we have been on the go. Our weekend was nice, but we had a hard time getting a room. We found one overlooking a mountain stream where all the gals and women were bathing in the nude. Quite a shock to my delicate sensibilities!

More details later, on this week's trip. I will mark it on a map together with my other trips so you will see how extensively I have traveled. So far, I've "tatted up" a few thousand miles. Could write a book on it, but there are too many already.

All my love, Stan

Sept. 17, 1952

Sweetie-Pie,

It is 10 p.m. and just got home from a pleasant evening with Mr. and Mrs. Ito. He is a Japanese Engineer with a French wife. They took me to a Kabuki play—5 hours of it. We went out for dinner—in the theater—between acts. Mrs. Ito, who speaks excellent English, with a German Accent, explained each story as it went along. Each act is a different story, so one sees 4 or 5. The costumes are wonderfully colorful and the stories interesting.

When I think about you while writing, I wish I could give you a big hug and feel your warmth and sweetness nearby. You are so wonderful. No one has ever been as lucky as I have been in having such a nice wife.

All my love, Stan

Sept. 20 #107

Sweetheart,

Since a typhoon flattened Wake Island the early part of the week, there has been no mail. There's talk of a major extension in Japan… a total of 510 days. Stanley is resistant…

Sept. 21 Sunday #108

Sweetheart,

I too wonder if the additional months are worth it. It is too hard to predict what business will be like in the next few months. I think that it can't be too good in the states or Jack Lipman would not have come over here to run the Okinawa job for DMJM. He is deep in AIA work, (American Institute of Architects), has been treasurer and secretary recently, and has had some nice work too. He is an aggressive and nice fellow. You see, DMJM may have other work out here besides the service contract we are working on here in headquarters.

I bought a bottle (Old Forester, $2.70!) at the Officer's Club and went out to see the Hesse's in their house yesterday afternoon. I couldn't find the place and since they have no phone, I had no chance to call them for further directions. That is the second time that I had had that type of trouble last week. First time was on Thursday when I went out to the home of Ed Shay, the AE [architect/engineer] with whom F. Hopkins is working now, and even *though I had a map and the address and telephone number, I couldn't find the place.*

The addresses are given in a funny way. The ward or precinct name is given, then the name of the block and then the number of the house. The number indicates the order in which the house was built. The first one has the number ONE, and so on. So, it is possible to find the numbers scattered all around the block. Shay's house was number seven. This is a lucky number and I found that no less than four houses have been given this number in a block where the perimeter was sufficient to accommodate about a hundred houses. I found it by elimination.

Sept. 22 #109

Sweetheart,

We are all very sad about Nixon's misstep [1952]. Innocent, no doubt, but a very untimely happening. The papers and Armed Forces' Radio are full of it. May do irreparable damage no matter how it is explained away.

Sept. 24 #110

Hi Hon,

When I hear from Dad, I feel sort of sad. They have a gloomy outlook. Wouldn't it be wonderful if they struck oil? So, then they could really enjoy themselves.

✧ **Billie: After the Moe grandparents died, the mineral rights on the farm were kept by the family and the family benefitted from the oil boom in North Dakota.**

I suppose Billie's dog really gets a lot of attention

✧ **Billie: I got Teeny for my 12th birthday, we always had other animals but not dogs.**

It is nice that she has a pet like that. All children need pets. It sure helps develop character. Myra doubtless gets a big bang out of it too.

The Nixon stuff is enough to make us all sick. The Japanese papers are all on his side for his frankness. I hope that he sticks and that enough stuff can be dug out on the Democrats to offset it. Awful jolt for a young fellow. Could ruin his career.

I'm getting a little cross-eyed from all the writing, so will say goodnight. We do make a good couple, don't we? We are very fortunate. Practically grew up together.

Sept. 28, 1952 (Letter written to a friend)

Dear Ferd,

Now that it is fall here and the people of Japan have an election to take care of as we do in the states, I'll offer a few comments on my observations. The parallel is striking.

Japanese candidates are touring the country in a "whistle stop" campaign which they might have copied from the presidential candidates in the U.S. Since the area to be covered is very small, much of the speech-making is done from trucks equipped with public address systems.

The candidates are so numerous that the air is filled with the racket from dawn to dusk in some city areas. Some of the activity is very amusing. The other day, I came upon a campaign truck with a loudspeaker blaring out the martial strains of "Marching Through Georgia!"

I guess they were only interested in the melody. The advertising people are doing a big business in leasing large balloons which hover over the cities by the dozen carrying campaign slogans on the tether cable.

The labor movement here seems plenty hot-headed and Sohyo (General Council of Trade Unions) instructed its 4 million members to vote for left wing candidates. That makes it tough for those candidates who are more moderate in their aims. The members of communist candidates for public office represent a rather sizable percentage of the total. The country is ripe for communist control, or at least it seems, an administration which is sympathetic toward the Reds. Conditions here are not too stable politically.

As in Europe, the top American "experts" have decided that each occupied country must now try to build up its own defenses against aggressions from the outside. This ties into the present austerity program in Washington, as far as military expenditures are concerned. A nucleus for a defense force in Japan has been provided by the Japan National Police Reserve.

This is being built up without too much fanfare and is perhaps comparable to our National Guard before the war. The radicals have raised a great cry against this operation.

The Reds would be very happy to see Japan completely helpless when and if the U.S. forces pull out.

The Red organizers are getting wonderful support from the little people who, of course, look upon all this rearmament with great alarm. The women are unhappy about the possibility of more fathers, husbands, and sons being involved in war. Men in Japan are few enough as it is, they think. The students in the numerous universities are eager followers of the Red propaganda line which opposes conscription. At least once every two weeks, students and police engage in pitched battle on some campus. The authorities are always opposed to the so-called "peace demonstrations." They almost always end in bloodshed.

Tokyo has been the scene of several wild struggles this summer. The May Day episode took place in front of the Meiji Building while I was there. For sheer excitement and teamwork, it beat any football game I have ever seen. During July, large areas of the city were declared "out of bounds" to American Military and civilian personnel because of demonstration.

Yesterday, 3000 Reds put on another show down the street from the office and for several hours no one could get in or out. There was little violence since 800 policemen were on duty together with dozens of plainclothes men in the crowd. Since Americans are always a target from the frenzied demonstrators, it is a good idea for all of us to stay out of sight. The Japanese government is still paying claims for burned American automobiles from the May affair.

It appears to me that Japan's political problems are an outgrowth of its economic problems. If the economy could be rebuilt, things would be much simpler. In my work, I have traveled thousands of miles through the country. I was amazed to see how highly industrialized the country had been.

There are thousands of factories along the railroads, even the small branch line up into remote areas, and most of them are as large or larger than our Chevrolet plant in Van Nuys. Most of these are idle now and rice paddies have been developed right up to the buildings. The former highly skilled factory workers are back cultivating land by stone-age methods.

Lack of capital and lack of markets have been responsible for the slow recovery of Japan's industry. The U.S. has done a poor public relations job in its encouragement of tuna fishing here and its tariff barrier against shipment of Japanese tuna into the U.S. Japanese newspapers devote more space to trade problems than do American papers. Business is a popular subject for conversation.

The Korean War and the restraint of Japanese trade with China was a great blow. China has long been a big market and source of raw materials for Japan. The Japanese feel as the British do toward Hong Kong. What does it matter what the politics of your customers may be, if you make a profit?

The Japanese don't like the Koreans. Whenever there is a communist demonstration, the newspapers lash out against "these Koreans and students." There are many Koreans here, and while I can't distinguish them from the natives, the Japanese can. They consider them quite inferior and I doubt if any Japanese military forces would be sent to save Korea if the Japanese had anything to say about it. From what our military people say about Korea and its people, it seems that the Japanese are not too far wrong in their opinions. Most of our operations people in headquarters make regular trips each month over to Korea and keep the rest of us posted.

On the lighter side—this is Japan's fall festival season. The rice harvest is on and the crop is good. September and October are wedding months and the sake flows freely. While people in Southern California have all sorts of celebrations recalling the "Days of the Golden West," the Japanese have all sorts of festivals which tie into history, religion, and the glory of the Emperor. Instead of 10-gallon hats and western clothes, these people dig out ancient armor and weapons and put on some very colorful spectacles. Devout Buddhist pilgrims arrive by the hundreds to take part or watch. This country has a very mobile population which seems to be continually traveling. It is not unusual to find groups of a hundred or more school children around the age of 10, five hundred miles from home on tour of the country's shrines. That is one way to develop nationalism.

There is much to write about. The country may not be large, but it is interesting. The manners and customs are not in the least uniform. No one can say with any certainty that he understands the Japanese. The life of even the most enlightened city dweller is guided by strange customs and ancient superstitions.

You may find some of this interesting. I will send along some comments on the amusing local customs in future letters,

Sincerely, Stanley

Sept. 30 #112

Sweetheart, Sweetie pie,

You haven't been writing very much lately.

I haven't had a day off since I arrived and have accumulated so much overtime that they are all worried. I have been briefing Joe on work and so I can take off a week easily enough when I get the notion. So, I'm leaving Friday night by train for Asaka, and from there go by boat through the Inland Sea along Shikoku to Beppu in Kyushu. Then we take the train through Hiroshima to Kyoto and back to Tokyo. That will cost me some money, too, but I want to see that country before the snow flies and that will be soon. Then I will have covered Southern or Western Japan well.

Oct. 8 1952 #113

Sweetheart,

We left Tokyo on Friday night for Kobe. After taking ferrys, horseback and trains we arrived in Takamatsu by the next evening just before sunset. I visited the most beautiful Japanese garden I've ever seen.

Checked into the best Japanese hotel in town for a Japanese bath and dinner before grabbing the night steamer for Kyushu. We arrived at Beppu in the rain on Monday noon. Visited the hot springs (like Yellowstone) and then stayed at the hotel (where the Emperor stays) which was the best in town.

Because we think we do as well on our own, we procured a Japan travel bureau map for our trip as far as Hiroshima. They made reservations for Kumamoto which we reached by train last night. Swell little hotel—1st class. Each time we leave one of these top-notch hotels, we feel like we've acquired a family of friends—such personal service.

We had the most marvelous Sukiyaki at Kumamoto. This morning we toured some castles and parks after which at Shimabara we spent the afternoon prowling the shipyards where they make wooden ships. We took a

4:30 bus up to Unzen Spa where we are now. It is built around a bunch of hot springs like Yellowstone. WHAT A SMELL—sulfur!

We leave tomorrow for Nagasaki where we will be for a day and a half.

Haven't slept or sat on anything but the floor since we left, and my hips are sore from sitting cross legged. The food has been excellent and the weather swell. We caused quite a furor among the schoolgirls. Americans are scarce here, and the girls wanted our autographs!

We just got back from a walk around town in quilted silk kimonos and getas in the brisk fall mountain air. Quite Pleasant. High here.

I will mail this in Nagasaki tomorrow when we find a military PO.

I love you and wish so much you could be with me. I have "staked out" some good spots if you come.

Stan

Oct. 9 Nagasaki Kanko Hotel, Nagasaki

Sweetheart,

We arrived at 4:30 after a 3-1/2 hour bus ride along the south coast of Kyushu. It is a beautiful area. Really the best so far in Japan as far as scenery goes. The bus stopped for nothing, of course, and we got no pictures on the way. That is natural—these are not sightseeing buses.

Due to the slip with Japan Travel Bureau, we ended up in a "western style" hotel. Nice room for 1500 yen each. Had a 7-course dinner with steak, lobster, etc. for 700 yen.

We were a little late on our schedule. Today was the last day of a 3-day annual festival. As one Japanese in Beppu said—"the people in Nagasaki celebrate like crazy." They do too! We saw one evidence of this on the way in. Beautiful children's parades, etc.

We saw no signs of atomic bomb destruction. The area is built up—every square foot and mostly two-story buildings like all of Japan. But—it has a shopping center of tiny streets which is a labyrinth! Strange, that they would rebuild as before. I went nuts and have an armful of stuff to show for it. Mostly Christmas Gifts. But I have the parts for a Halloween costume for Myra. Now she can look just like a little Japanese girl in Nagasaki at festival time. I'll send it air mail from Tokyo and hope it arrives in time—if not this year—then for next.

We went down the street photographing the parades of geishas, etc. What a riot of color! Got some dragon dances before dark too. The place is oriental like the story books. Not metropolitan like Tokyo. More kimonos in evidence too. Place looks prosperous.

We need to make a hotel reservation for Hiroshima where we arrive tomorrow night at 12:00. We will spend most of tomorrow at an island out of Hiroshima where the shrines are all built out over the water. A famous spot and quite unique.

I must stop for a minute.

A bunch of small boys were going by dressed up in silk brocades as Samurai knights carrying swords.

They are accompanied by music and dozens of people carrying paper lanterns on sticks. They are given refreshments at various spots—like 'tricks or treats.'

Will be back in Tokyo Sunday night and should find a lot of mail from you.

I hear someone playing "Auld Lang Syne" so it must be time for bed.

October 13 #114

Sweetheart,

The trip was outstanding and will be perhaps remembered for the rest of my life. For sheer beauty and interest, it would be hard to beat Japan. Nagasaki and Hiroshima were very interesting from the bomb standpoint and were outstanding shopping areas. I'll answer your letters in detail tomorrow, Sweet.

All my love, Stan

Oct. 14 #115

I'm glad Mom and Dad are not too sad. Dad says he netted $1000.00 for a year's farming. Not good. They are unhappy about all the OIL people. Hope they find oil to compensate for it!

Oct. 24 #119

Sweetheart,

My trip to Nagoya was a mad whirl, to say the least. In the morning after we arrived, we went over to Japan Air Defense Headquarters to see the big shots. I got a very nice reception. There were three of us; George Yamashiro, who has a degree in City Planning from MIT, Frank, who has a master's degree from Harvard and me. More like the old Cairo days. Nice traveling companions. The town is like Minneapolis in some respects and somewhat cozier than Tokyo. The nightclubs are more like Cairo. Also, George, who is a Hawaiian-born (American Japanese) was able to handle contacts like Sharif Hakim.

Tuesday, Wednesday, and Thursday were spent at hard work getting some plans together. I was representing FEAF and Frank the A-E. A funny switch!

We got more done than we could have accomplished in 3 months by means of correspondence.

Yesterday afternoon, we had a 16-man conference with General Spiney—who is maybe #4 in Japan. He was very nice and approved our plan. This morning we went out to see an old bombed-out arsenal which we hope to rebuild for a new headquarters. Like the old Eritrea days.

I would like to get out on a trip, but we were plenty tired when we rolled in an hour ago after a 7-hour ride. The train was loaded with Korean War

American GIs. Some on their way home, some leaving rest camps on the way to Korea and some returning from the hospital. (Also, a couple of Powers' Models who are still here after a show last month.) All the boys were 6' husky farm boys who were very quiet. They have seen a lot. A big fat boy who was an MP had two court martialed soldiers in his custody.

I felt so sorry for them. Hand-cuffed together and so forlorn. 19-20 and clean-cut kids. Some minor infraction, no doubt, with no more seriousness than to earn a $5.00 fine and scolding from a judge in the states. In the Army they will get the works and a "dishonorable discharge" which would mark them for life. Probably got drunk and forgot to return to camp for a few days. Can't blame them, either.

I was away a couple of days longer than I expected and am going to devote this weekend to completing sketches for the Bakersfield bank.

✧ **Billie: Dad was doing this California work for his business, Moe & Larsen, in Van Nuys.**

The new movie camera and stuff arrived Monday morning, so it went with me to Nagoya. The shipment really came through fast. My telephoto is the envy of all my friends. It is really a deal. I will get some good representative shots of Japan before I leave. I'll even plan a script for shooting.

Also, I drool when I think of the photographs I should be able to get of junks in Hong Kong Harbor, the dancing girls in Bangkok, the sacred cows in Calcutta and Bombay, and last, but not least, street scenes in Cairo and Port Said.

Oct. 28 #120

Sweetheart,

It seems that FEAF (Far East Air Force) wants me to stay. They have about 4 or 5 others, too, whom they can use. As it now stands, they don't go for the idea of a short extension, because I would leave about the time the next budget session starts and they might want me for 6 months to break in a new man. I told Doug Russell that I didn't want to be stuck for two years away from home. It would mean my family ties were poor or, I was a bum!

Nov. 4 #122

Sweetheart,

My hunting trip (with borrowed clothes and guns) was different and a bit strenuous. Since I was Frank Hopkins' guest for business, it only cost me about $10.00. We left at midnight Friday and drove up in the rain. Arrived at the farmhouse in the rain about 2:30. Dismal. About 30 hunters were around and were mostly from Yokohama, a city south of Tokyo. They were men and some members of staff of European organizations. A real collection of late model big American cars. And such big fellows. Most were from Texas; 6' and over and all had fancy automatic shotguns. Crazy get-ups too; straw hats *and heavy clothes. I don't see how some could raise a gun! The farmer had hired about 30 local fishermen with small boats to act as guides. He was busy "briefing" them on the trip.*

After an hour, we set off down a muddy trail to the boats which were 20' flat bottom deals. By now, it had stopped raining but was pitch dark. What a racket! Small bamboo baskets held his decoys in several boats, and they are noisy.

We were pulled along rivers and creeks for about an hour until we reached marsh. While it was still black—so I could see nothing, everyone started to shoot. Looked and sounded like fireworks. The muzzle blast from a Japanese shotgun is about a 4' flame with burning wads up like roman candles. My boat boy got lost and put me up on a bank in the reeds 8' high instead of in a blind, of which there were dozens.

When it got light enough to see, I shot 3 ducks with my first 4 shots. Then my gun began to fall apart. It was a new Montgomery Ward 12 gage I had borrowed from Frank. I had to shoot it single shot from then on. My boy would have made a poor caddy. I had to spot and find my own ducks. I only found one—a teal.

At dawn I saw, about 100 miles south, Mount Fuji rise out of the mist with its white top of rosy red. It looked as if it were right in the marsh! A beautiful sight and alone worth the trip. I heard rumors that there were 2,000 hunters in this big marsh. Could be—shot fell like rain around me for 4 hours. Around noon, I decided to go in, so we pulled back.

Frank's wife had packed sandwiches, so we had those and loafed all afternoon and told tall stories to the Japanese hunters. The Americans all went home. Frank and I wanted to eat dinner, too, so we ate with the farmer. Japanese farms are really something. We had eel cooked in soy sauce. Good. Candied octopus and little fish 1" long—not so good. And we had carp and bean curd soup, which was good, and big bowls of rice with soft boiled egg over it. Japs eat the eggs raw. And lots of beer. Then we went to a gunsmith to have our guns checked.

When we returned at about 9:30, everyone was in bed. The sliding partitions had been removed and left a room about 20' x 30' and the floor was covered with futons on the mats with big quilts. We found two unoccupied ones and went to sleep. About 3 a.m., we were awakened, and it was COLD! I had slept in most of my clothes. The futon next to me stirred and a head popped up. It was the farmer's 16-year-old daughter. You never know what you'll find. She had slept in all her clothes including a smock type apron. Good material for a story.

The next day I nearly froze but didn't like to admit it. I had on light trousers, summer underwear, wool shirt, sweater, windbreaker jacket, raincoat, a muffler, and gloves. By the time the boat reached the blind, I was like ice. I wished I'd had a charcoal burning hibachi with me like some

Japanese. I stayed out until 10 and decided I had enough. Also, the sun was now warm, and I was sleepy. I sat in the boat and dozed all the way back. We drove into Tokyo at 3 in the afternoon. Quite an experience. Not like state-side duck hunting. All my love, Stan

Nov. 5 1952 #123

Sweetheart,

What a day! We got it over the radio at 3:45 p.m. that Stevenson had conceded. Wonderful news!

I'm going to cable congratulations to Nixon. I think it would be nice—and sort of political.

✧ **Billie: Dad had met Nixon and worked for/with Nixon when he ran for President.**

Nov. 11 #126

Sweetheart,

Just got out of the shower and feel better now. Returned a short time ago from our trip to Sendai and Matsushinia. It was a 4-day trip, but we only spent 2 days up there.

We left on Saturday morning and arrived about 4 p.m. It was a cold, bleak town. The hotel where we stayed was a Japanese version of a "western" hotel, except that the radiators were ornamental. The maid—dressed in a smart blue wool suit—brought in a pair of large, hot charcoal pieces for the hibachis! You could see your breath anywhere in the hotel except in the Japanese bath. We went shopping for antiques and then decided that Sendai had no more to offer. It is about the size of Minneapolis, but it had been badly bombed and is only slowly being rebuilt.

An hour's train ride on Sunday morning took us to Matsushinia, a bay filled with beautiful mounded islands. We stayed in a "spic-and-span" old Victorian-style hotel in the middle of a park by the water. The vistas for picture taking seemed to be limitless. The woods were filled with real maples which donned beautiful autumn colors. Sunday and Monday were like reasonable copies of a perfect Minnesota "Indian Summer."

Had a very pleasant time. We were the only guests in the Park Hotel! They mustered a crew of five every time we had a meal. The food was top notch too!

It was a wonderful getaway.

Nov. 16 #130

Sweetheart,

We left yesterday morning (Saturday) about 10 and drove slowly down the coast to Odawara and then up the mountain toward Fuji. We reached a nice Japanese hotel at sunset. We checked in and then drove up to a pass to get some sunset shots of the peak. It was lucky we did because it was overcast this morning.

The hotel was a rambling affair. All up and down the mountain side with waterfalls and parks all over it. Not heated, of course, so the temperature was 48 degrees F.

Before dinner we got into Yukatas and padded silk robes and went to the bath. A sulfur pool and was it HOT! WOW! I hadn't enough nerve myself to try it, but a Japanese fellow was sitting in it and was alive, so I figured I could too. After I got out, I looked like a boiled lobster. But I stored up enough heat to last until bedtime.

When we returned to the room, there were 2 hibachis going and the chill was leaving.

Those sliding paper doors are good insulation. Dinner was served by a nice-looking young lady in a kimono who was studying design in Odawara and only worked here weekends. We had broiled trout, filet of sole, sardine soup, rice, dough balls, cauliflower, meatballs stuffed with spinach, half a lobster, Waldorf salad, tea, and miscellaneous items like ginger. All wonderfully prepared. We took some flash pictures and then went down to a billiard room to play some 3-cushion billiards. When we returned to the room, the floor was covered with futons and we "hit the hay" at 9 p.m.

Breakfast was just as fancy—except they had ham and eggs instead of so much fish. Both meals were typically Japanese. When we checked out at noon, our bill was 1500 yen each or $4.15. Not bad. I sure wish you had been along.

We drove up over the mountain pass and down into the valley by Fuji, but it was all in clouds.

It seems more like old times to hear about the get-togethers with some of the old gang. I miss them, even though I'm always very busy. I am somewhat older and don't always enjoy the company of younger people who are unmarried or at least unattached.

Maybe that is my trouble. I do a lot of thinking about how much I want to see.

Japan has a fatal fascination for me. That outweighs my homesickness—which has never gotten the better of me. I will always be interested in my surroundings even when I'm too old for anything else. Very few people react that way. That's why we have so much discontent among our people here. Many people let themselves get bored. I have found time passes very rapidly when I'm interested and engaged—which is most of the time.

All my love—forever

Stan

Nov. 18 #131

The encyclopedia is a good thing because the kids need it. Nothing like something to read instead of television. We may have an illiterate race soon with the lack of interest in reading.

✧ **Billie: We were one of the last on our block to get TV—probably not until 1952.**

Nov. 23 #132

Sweetheart,

Our stenographer got a new typewriter, so I am really equipped with writing material, if I haven't forgotten how to type. It is an Underwood and I have never been able to figure out just how they are supposed to work.

I'll tell you about my trip first and then comment on the letters afterword. I went down to Itazuke with Hopkins and Yamashiro; they went with me to the Nagoya meeting as well. We took a Wednesday afternoon courier flight leaving at 2 p.m. and arrived at 1:30 in the morning! We must have stopped at every base in southern Japan. It was a rough, cold, and uncomfortable ride. The worst part of it was the business of wearing a Mae West (life vest stuffed with material that will float) and parachute and having to take them off at every stop and run into the operations building to warm up. Then, the business of putting the vests on again and getting underway.

The plane had a little gasoline operated blower and heater combination which was not working right and was spilling exhaust fumes into the cabin. All in all, it was a rough trip, but I didn't get sick. Frank, who was a fighter pilot in North Africa, was also uncomfortable. The accommodations we had at Itazuke made up for it, however. The V.I.P. quarters were about one hundred feet from the Officer's Club and about 300 feet from the headquarters building. It was the best quarters I have occupied since leaving home. What soft beds! We had scheduled our meetings for 1 p.m. Thursday and Friday, so we had plenty of time to sleep in the mornings.

It was beautiful fall weather down there, with plenty of warm sunshine. We went into Fukuoka on Thursday evening to see the sights and had a nice dinner. The colonel from Nagoya who was with us was a good companion. He always looked to me as if he might be a schoolteacher, but he wasn't. I believe that he had a fund of at least a hundred stories, and he was able to tell them. The town didn't amount to much and Frank and I went in yesterday morning to see what it had to offer. Had lunch at the officers' club in town and walked around. Didn't find much of interest.

We arranged for a good courier flight coming back. We had hoped to get the general's plane which was due down from Nagoya. We could then have flown up to Komaki (outside Nagoya) in style and then hopped a night train to Tokyo. But, as it so often happens, the plane never arrived because of a change of plans. We took the 3 p.m. flight and arrived at Tachikawa (out of

Tokyo) at 6:30. A great improvement over the flight down. We travelled on a C-119, which is the infamous "flying boxcar" used to haul trucks and equipment for airdrops over Korea. Being a V.I.P., I rode up front for part of the time and part of the time in the pilots' compartment. I spent the first hour and a half taking movies and color shots from a nice window and should have some good stuff on Japan from the air.

Am running out of paper again so will call it quits. Am going down to Takashimya to get an armful of Tabis for you, for gifts.

All my love,

One big reason that I am set on NOT signing for another full year, trip home or not, is that I enjoy it here and it could get to be a habit.

Dec. 1, 1952 #136

Sweetheart,

Monday again—got in this morning on a sleeper at 6:40 a.m. and managed to get up to Army Hall to shave and wash just before going to work at 7:20. Just made it.

We hit Kyoto at 6:30 am Saturday and had two delightful days there. Perfect cool and sunny weather. I imagine I saw about 1/100 of the spot. Managed to see some of the finest places, however. I can see Allan's enthusiasm for Kyoto as it was untouched by war and is much like what was old Japan's best.

✧ **Billie: Allan was Mother's brother (the dentist) who was there during the war**

Every craft is developed to the nth degree. Wood carvers, cloth weavers and buyers, fans, and temple-goods makers everywhere. They dye about 100 million dollars' worth of material a year. One fifth by hand and washed in the rivers—a colorful site. I should have some wonderful shots. Both movie and still. I will visit the shop on another trip. I didn't want to waste the sunshine this trip.

Mail sure is scarce! Only one letter since the 23rd—and that came on Nov. 28. Are you mad at me?

Dec. 14 #145

Sweetheart,

I spent a rather lonesome day today. Went down for mail at around 10 and then went by taxi up to Ueno (pronounced "way-know") Park to see the exhibit of bonsai trees and plants. All the famous growers in the area were there with exhibits.

It is a little startling to see an orange tree with fruit the size of currants. The Japanese know how to dwarf trees, and how to keep them that way. I took a lot of pictures and am enclosing a few postcard-size pictures I bought there. The trip was well worthwhile.

I took a taxi from the park to a busy shopping area call Asakusa. The place is very colorful and busy, so I got some movies. Then I walked for a couple of miles along 22nd St. where things are very interesting. Hundreds of shops selling Buddhist Temple goods.

From there I went to the Takashimaya where I found some colorful groups of people. The place is as swank as Dayton's (Minneapolis) and jam packed. Christmas shopping full tilt. While they celebrate New Year's by buying lots of gifts and so on, Christmas fits in so they get into the spirit of things. Christmas carols and "Silent Night" on the public address system and Santa Clauses all over. A revealing display of children's mannequins on the first floor, modelling western style dresses with angel wings! The stores are wonderful and out-strip our finest stores with colorful and tastefully displayed merchandise.

Dec. 16 #147

Sweetie-pie,

It is rainy and gloomy today but not cold. We have really had decent weather so far so we shouldn't complain. I'll take one or two rainy days per week but NO MORE. Then I get depressed.

Even though you sent Christmas cards, I sent a few to people who should have my personal attention in addition to our joint venture. The Japanese wood block print cards are very beautiful. I'm going to bring home a collection for fun.

I had plenty of invitations for Christmas. Christmas Eve at Hopkins' with eggnog and turkey and to help trim the tree. I will go to the Goldsby's for Christmas day buffet dinner and trimmings. I certainly miss a home in which to do the entertaining necessary to repay some of these courteous invites.

There is a lot of sweat around here with the people who are trying to get home for Christmas. Many fellows got a release early this month but because Korean veterans have a priority, they have a real big time watching their names go up and down on a list which is revised hourly.

December 23 #148

Sweetie pie,

My hands are so numb from the cold, I have a hard time writing when I write you; I don't seem to be able to get the words "off my pen." I can talk so much faster than I write that I perhaps get a bit tongue-tied on paper.

To put it mildly—I love you more than anything in the world. My being away is perhaps a bit like being in the position of "hitting myself on the head because it feels so good when I quit." Perhaps the homecoming and 3rd or 4th honeymoons are worth it. We should appreciate each other more once we are together again. Possibly, I'm not well organized enough to be away from home. That sounds flighty doesn't it? I'm just a bit sentimental.

The other day, going down to Oki, I had a strange experience. The lower deck of the plane had a stack of plywood boxes tied down onto the floor. I suppose there were 12 or 14. I asked the pilot's "load checker" about them. There were two on each deck. He said these were the personal effects of the fellows shot down up north in a B-29 by the "Reds" while on patrol duty. A hell of a Christmas present for their families. It was then that I decided to be more of a homebody and not ramble so much.

Dec. 23 #149

Sweetheart,

Tomorrow night is Christmas Eve. It seems like time has really caught up with me. I'm faced with a terrible problem—or at least I was before I sat down—whether to write to you or not. At least your Christmas will not be without mail as mine is. But I decided that even if you were a stinker for not writing, I didn't need to be—so here goes…

Dec. 25 #150

Sweetheart,

It is now 12 noon on Christmas Day. I didn't feel I could "stand the gaff" of being alone around too many people today. I finally got up at 10:00. I was too lonesome to stay in bed. Everyone seems to be gone. Since I have the car today, I drove down to the mail and, of course, found nothing. All the mail that arrived this week was a card and a nice note from Irene Brezina.

✧ **Billie: Irene was our dear neighbor from Van Nuys who died in 2019 at age 99.**

We had a Christmas party in our office yesterday. Since we have the biggest open room it would handle all the people in various installations. They had exchanged names by rooms so everyone had a gift. The Japanese employees participated, and everyone had eggnog and fruit cake. It was very nice with a tree and decorations. I got a little woolly toy dog from someone. It was a very safe and sane party. No heavy drinking as is done in the states. The club bars do not even have Christmas decorations. That would be too sad and make the fellows too homesick.

Dec. 26 #151

Sweetheart,

Arrived at Himeji this morning and got some swell shots of the castle. This afternoon was spent at the business of shopping in Kobe. We arrived here at the hotel at 5:30 p.m.

This once was an "occupation hotel"—when I came last year. All changed now. This will be my second "western style" hotel in Japan. Steam heat has its points in cold weather, particularly after walking around in the cold all day.

We will browse around town this evening and tomorrow morning and then head for Nara and up to Kyoto in the afternoon. Sunday sightseeing and shopping in Kyoto and home by train Sunday night. We couldn't get sleepers on the night train so will sit up in reclining chairs.

11:00 p.m.

We just finished a walk through the shopping area. FABULOUS! Beats anything so far, it's so colorful and bright, with exquisite shops. Prices are lower than Tokyo. This is called the Venice of Japan. Many nice canals with floating restaurants and such. Like a fairy land. I'm sorry I didn't come here sooner. It will be a MUST trip for you and me someday. Since New Year's is near, everything has a carnival spirit with all the decorations that go with it.

PART IX

1953: Japan

NOTICE TO THE HOLDER OF THIS CERTIFICATE

1. If you change your normal place of residence from the one last recorded in this certificate you must report the change to the Police within 72 hours of your arrival at your new address.
2. A TEMPORARY absence of less than 2 months from your registered address need *not* be reported, but if you are away for more than two months and are still in the United Kingdom you must report *to the Police of the district in which you are registered* your address at that time. any subsequent changes of address and your return home.
This may be done by letter.
3. You need not report to the Police on your return from a temporary absence abroad unless fresh conditions have been imposed on your stay by the Immigration Officer. If you have been away for more than 2 months you must report your return but *this may be done by letter.*
4. You must report within 72 hours to the Police of the district in which you are registered any change in the particulars recorded in this certificate other than those mentioned in the preceding notes. This includes any change in your place of business or employment, or in the conditions attached to your stay.
5. If you stay at an hotel, lodging house, boarding house or any other place where lodging is provided for payment, you must write your name and nationality in the register on arrival and complete a statement in the form provided.
6. If your children are living with you in this country and they are not British, they must have separate Certificates when they reach the age of 16.

Failure to comply with any of the above requirements,
making any false statement to a person carrying out registration duties,
altering this certificate in any way,
failure to produce the certificate when required to do so by an Immigration or Police Officer,
having in possession or using without lawful authority for the purpose of the Aliens Order any forged, altered, or irregular certificate, passport, or other document,
will render the offender liable to be detained in custody, and to a fine of £100 or six months' imprisonment.

A 606361

Aliens Order, ~~[illegible]~~ 1953.

CERTIFICATE OF REGISTRATION

You must produce this certificate if required to do so by any Police Officer, Immigration Officer, ~~or member of Her Majesty's forces acting in the course of his duty.~~

I feel that my destiny will be in big work around the world for some time to come. I might just as well apply my talents to big work as to small work at a reduced fee. — **Stan**

Chapter 26

Silk, Geishas, Cherry Blossoms and Pearls
More Letters from Fascinating Japan

January 1, 1953 #152

Sweetheart,

It is now a quarter to five and dinner won't be served for a while yet. So here goes. I think it is over a year now since I decided to go to Japan!

Today was predicted to be cold and wet. It was clear, warm, and dry. I'm happy that it was. Jan. 1 is a very important day in Japan. All businesses close. Many days before, everyone cleans house and gets ready for the big day. In the morning everyone takes a bath and dresses in clean NEW clothes and visits the shrines. It is really like an Easter parade, and what a parade!

Women and girls

Man on horseback in Japanese parade

All who have hair long enough, wear it in the traditional styles. And Kimonos! I took two rolls of movies and one of 35mm. Now people will loaf for 4 days and enjoy life. Not a bad idea.

We work tomorrow but have 2 more holidays afterward. I will probably cover a few of the Tokyo scenic spots for pictures. I am going over my pictures and find a few gaps in my Japan "travelogue." Not many, though.

We had a nice turkey dinner here in Army Hall tonight. I think they do well since it all came from the States and it has been in cold storage. No mail, of course. Your Dec. 19 letter was lost. Maybe tomorrow.

All my love, Stan

Jan. 2, 1953 #153

Sweetheart,

I'm glad you liked the pearls. What kind of strings do you like? The Mikimoto are the best and run from $35 to $175 for a tapered average size string. Color and luster variations make the difference. I would say it will cost about $100.00 if they are unstrung—on thread only and clasp loose—and the duty is 25%. If strung complete with clasp, it is 33 1/3 % duty.

I'm always worried when I hear your letters say, "I don't write because you will be home soon." Maybe you have your dates mixed up. I will show you again how it works. Sure complicated, apparently—but actually simple.

Love, Stan

Billie: Dad went through the specifics of the dates at least into March. He continues to be frustrated with her lack of letters when he writes and mails so many. However, Mom must have suffered some frustration from continual extensions in his time away and delays in his coming home.

Jan. 9 #157

Dear Hon,

Billie is becoming quite a social butterfly! Nice that she is not shy and feels enthusiastic about her social life. She is starting much sooner than I. It is good training.

Love, Stan

Billie: Our mother was quite strict with me. I, being the oldest child, was the one who taught her how to be a mother, as most first children do. She was critical with me. Dad was my go-to parent. He ran interference for me my whole life. My sister, Myra, was very close to Mother. I was Daddy's girl and Myra was Mommy's girl.

Around this time, Dad still had interest in his architectural office in Van Nuys, California, at the same time he was working under contract with DMJM. Mother had opened her interior decorating shop in Van Nuys, and they wanted to put money aside for Myra's and my college funds.

Money was tight and Dad's office at home was not making money. What would he do when the Japan/DMJM contract was over? He mentioned several options in letters to Mother. They were firms he had worked for in Japan: such as John W. King, Co.; Adrian Wilson; Skidmore, Owings, and Merrill, and others. Our parents were always practical and did not feel comfortable when they had debts. I often heard it said, "You shouldn't buy it if you don't have the money in the bank to pay for it."

January 27, 1953

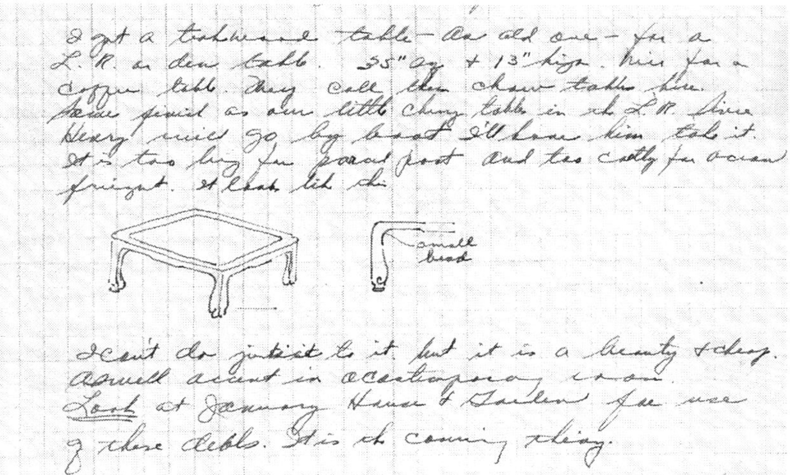
I got a teakwood table — an old one — for a L.R. or den table. 35" sq + 13" high. Nice for a coffee table. They call them charm tables here. Same finish as our little cherry table in the L.R. Since Henry will go by boat I'll have him take it. It is too big for parcel post and too costly for ocean freight. It looks like this

small bead

I can't do justice to it but it is a beauty & cheap. A swell accent in a contemporary room. Look at January House & Garden for use of these tables. It is the coming thing.

Billie: In one of Dad's letters to Mother, I found this drawing from his first year in Japan. It was a feat to ship the table home. The table lived in Van Nuys, California, and is now in Sandia Park, New Mexico. Dad often sketched things he wanted to explain to mother.

Jan. 29 #165

Sweetheart,

Am all set to go out and present a job to a building committee of the American School for John W. King, Co. A little practice for when I get back home. This is largely promotional. He doesn't have the contract yet. But John King is on the board, so it looks good.

I almost shed a tear, too, when I read that the kids were disappointed at my not coming home. They are sweet and must be fond of me. I wish you could send me some pictures of the kids. Here I sit with three cameras (4 with movie) and don't even have one at home. I don't use the Reflex anymore. I'll send it home and you can get some snapshots with it. Japan has gone Reflex crazy and there are about 30 makes on the market made here. I wouldn't get anything for mine. Movies are different.

I can't imagine how Billie must be. From what you say she must be quite a young lady. So, she is now a teenager!

Stan

Billie: When Mom was raising me as a teenager (or trying to), she would say, "I had four brothers. I know the way boys talk about girls after a date. Whether or not anything happened, they have to tell a good story so you have to be sure you don't do anything that would raise a story!"

Feb. 1 #166

Sweetheart,

It's Sunday morning and I am sitting in my room for a change. It is rare for me to be here on Sunday as you know. I travelled enough yesterday to keep my travel quota filled for the week.

The Hesses haa the car yesterday and asked me to join them in a trip to Fuji. Good old Fuji; we try to get a good picture any time we can. We drove to Odawara in the morning and reached the Fujiya Hotel at noon for lunch. It is a Special Services hctel at Miyanoshita open to military and civilians attached to the military. We had very nice service and a wonderful lunch for 80 cents. It is a very plush old place.

We drove up through the foothills over icy roads to Lake Hakone, then south of the lake to Atami. It was a wonderful view of the Pacific on one side and the bay on the west. Poor old Fuji had a cloud on its top and even after waiting for an hour it didn't move. The toll road from Hakone to Atami was very nice but terrible roads were the only thing we had from Atomi to Odawara. From Hakone to Yokahama—a distance of 50 miles—we found it took 3 hours. This country is no place for cars except in large towns.

Love, Stan

Believe it or not, I am writing a second letter today. I feel so near to you that I just had to talk to you a bit. When I sit here and think of how we are going to feel when we are together again, I could just bust!

Boy, I sure do love you! I feel so confident as to your ability and support in my planning. We can always be sure of what the other thinks. It is so easy to do a good job here when I know I can count on you. It is surprising how many fellows here worry over the activities of their wives. They worry they throw away their money, run around, or cry and fuss. People are surely not very stable, are they?

Sometimes when I get down in the dumps, I wonder how good I am at being calm and collected. I've only been down for a couple days at a time and only a half dozen times this past year.

Feb. 6 #169

Sweetheart,

Times are difficult as the contract with DMJM is just about up and special friends are scheduled to go home. Wish I was coming home right now.

All my love, Stan

Feb. 8 Sunday #170

(written on 'The Far East Society of Architects' Tokyo stationery)

Sweetheart,

Well, we are just about over with the contract. 1/2 day tomorrow and I am through. It was a long pull. This first part was slow and the last part fast. Wonder how the next few months will go.

There was a big party at the Grant Height Officers' Club for Lt. Cols. Panlick, Burdick, and Toler. All nice men. They had a joint farewell. They are all staying in the Air force and are being assigned to various posts in the states.

Except for rubbish, I have about everything packed now so will have an easy time moving. I will be staying in less expensive quarters so will save some money. I'll give you ample warning of my new address, so we won't miss mail. It will be some days yet.

All my love, Stan

February 12

Sweetheart,

I think I will stay at the Shiba Park Hotel as it is only a couple minutes' walk from the King Office. They have also bought a two-story office bldg. across the street from the hotel. That is going to be most convenient.

Oh, that boat-like thing with a wheel is a Japanese carpenters' chalk box. They use a lamp black paste in the bowl and fish line on the wheel. It runs through the holes and they use it for snapping lines. I found it in a carpenters' tool shop in Takamatsu over in Shikoku in October. It is the finest I've ever seen. The carved turtle on top is wonderful. I got it as an ornament. Nice?

A Carpenter's chalk-box tool

Billie: This was always on display in the folks' home and is now in my home. The carpenter's tool with the little turtle and the crane on the top is called Sumitsubo—an ink-chalk-line device for carpenters to mark straight lines on the floor, on the walls etc. They go way back, but many carpenters still use them. In Japan, many are ornately carved.

I've been working myself to a frazzle at King's. It is a relief, though, and I can produce when I must. I'm designing from scratch a $400,000 building for personnel procuring for FEAF. Must be complete in 17 days.

All my love, Stan

Feb. 13, Friday

Sweetie pie,

Just one year ago today I arrived here in Japan! It was on a Wednesday, though. Times sure does fly. Sometimes it seems like 10 years and sometimes it seems like nothing at all.

✧ **Billie: The change from DMJM to King came with some money issues. The salary from King was partially in yen and not dollars. Exchange was complicated. Dad was also having to figure taxes and duty on items he was bringing home.**

Lou Purcell of Thomas Baurne, Co. (A&E) saw me the other day and wanted me to go see them for a job. He was sorry I had made a commitment to King. They can furnish logistical support and all pay is in dollars.

You are awfully sweet, and I do miss you so very much. It will certainly be a second honeymoon when we see each other again. Hope for mail tomorrow. All my love, Stan

Feb. 16

Sweetie-Pie,

It is awfully nice to know that you would be excited to see Hawaii if you met me there. We can take an excursion some time before too long. Fair chance that I will be part of an international architectural practice soon. I look forward to a bit of trekking back and forth across the Pacific to take care of my "interests." Would be fun.

All my love, Stan

Feb. 18

Sweetheart,

10 p.m.

I'm really putting in the time. 10 hours a day. They have such a sweat getting work out to meet the deadline that everyone is on edge. It is like "old times" in our own office. The Military boys are not easy clients. Indecision is maddening.

Feb. 21

George Yamashira, the Hawaiian born man I wrote you about who has a city planning degree from MIT, has been giving us a lot of laughs lately. George talks like an American and has lived most of his life in Hawaii or the States, but sometimes behaves like a Japanese man.

For the past two years he has been giving English lessons to a young girl who is a Mitsui. The Mitsui family is comparable to the Rockefellers in the states. I met the girl and she is very nice and refined and quite westernized. Her father is not too wealthy because his funds are tied up as a result of War. George likes the girl and has hoped to ask her to marry him but never dared breathe a word about it to her or anyone in the family.

Last week the girl's brother-in-law came to George and asked him if he would like to marry her and if it was agreeable to George, he would ask the father and daughter. Then he came back later and said it was okay with them too. Now George must make a formal call on father and daughter next week to ask them.

FACE is so very important here. One never embarrasses anyone by a direct question. If George had asked the girl before, it would have been embarrassing if she had said "no." Also, if he had asked the father and he had said "no," George would have not wished to embarrass them by going to their house again. This way if the brother-in-law had run into any opposition as a go-between, it would not have altered George's relationship with the family, and he could have gone on visiting and giving lessons as before.

This is Japan. We get a great kick out of the details. No "mooning" or passionate love here in a formal marriage. At least we have relaxed conventions enough to permit the fellow to ask the girl herself. Even so, George knows the answer.

I still like the American system! Love, Stan

P.S. I am so grateful for the wonderful friends I have here; not only for socializing, but also for working together. They are; Ed Shay, Eileen and Henry Hesse, Ed Lind and his wife, Jones, Irene and Al Price, Jack Lipman, Barbara and Joe Goldsby.

March 7, 1953

Sweetheart,

Saturday night and I'm happy that this week is over. I made about $125.00 in overtime alone—so you see I have been busy.

I'm leaving for Sendai on the 25th. My work will be much more pleasant. I will be only an hour from Matsushima Bay, a very special cherry blossom spot in April. I'll be happy. It is a perfect place to stroll among the hills.

March 10, 1953

Sweetheart,

Last night after working late, Ed and I went down to the Imperial Hotel and ran into some officials of Thomas Baurne Company, together with Baurne himself, his wife and eighteen-year-old daughter. They did not mind telling Ed to his face, that they had wanted me and would have hired me if I had seen them first. They had James and Hesse. Baurne said he had heard so much about me, he wanted me too. Nice to be wanted. He is big time. He always has 20 million or so on the "boards" in each office. He has a main office in Wash. DC. Big staff in Alaska too.

I leave for the north on an inspection trip on the 20th. Then I will be in Nagoya on another trip. Better send my mail to me at the John W King office. I'll continue to write you via APO as I will live on Army posts.

Frank Lloyd Wright designed The Imperial Hotel

✧ **Billie: Dad was always an admirer of Frank Lloyd Wright and while he was living in Tokyo, he had accommodations in the Imperial Hotel designed by Wright. Dad's room was over the laundry and in the days of no AC, that room was always steamy and warm. But he loved being there because the hotel was right next to the Imperial Palace.**

March 19

Sweetie Pie,

I've been sitting here organizing my work as much as possible before going up north tonight. I've worked myself into a spot where I have a little time.

I'll be at Shiba Park for about one week and then to Sendai.

Sendai was completely flattened by the war. Since it was rather thinly rebuilt, with broad unpaved boulevards with few good buildings on them, the town has a barren look. Since it is only one hour by electric train from Matsushima, I will spend my weekends there. Matsushima is one of the "Three Wonders of Japan." (The others are Miyajima Island out of Hiroshima, where I've been; the other is a place out of Kyoto where if one looks between his legs at the view, the bridge is supposed to appear as if it ascends to Heaven. This one I haven't seen.) The Matsushima Bay is a National Park. Filled with pine and birch covered islands, it is nice. A couple of nice hotels there, too. One Japanese and one Victorian western style.

All my love, Stan

March 27, 1953

Sweetie Pie,

As I said before, get all the Arrowhead stock you can. It looks like a great investment. I have some more nice woodblock prints and will send them soon.

Billie: Mother was the primary investor and bookkeeper. She had recommended this investment in an earlier letter. Dad began a collection of woodblock prints (1800s)—Kabuki theme. My husband and I too began collecting the prints.

I have five by Toyokuni from the 1800s—very choice. He was/is one of the top two such artists in Japan. I will have fun seeing them when I get back. They should have a special place like the old maps.

All my love. It will be three and a half months left when you receive this. Boy—will I be happy to be home!

Stan

Sunday, April 5, 1953 Easter Sunday

Sweetheart,

Today is a beautiful day with warm sun and blue skies. According to the paper, the cherry blossoms are in full bloom at the Yazakuni Shrine back of Army Hall. So, I'll get myself over to the Hesses and see if they want to go "snapping" with me. I will finish a roll of movie film which has been in the camera.

It occurs to me that this is Easter Sunday. I'll go over to the Chapel Center today/tonight to attend their musical program like last year. I don't want to be a complete heathen. I've been poor about attendance to church over here. The chaplains I have seen are very low caliber too—which doesn't make for much enthusiasm.

I'll be leaving again this Wednesday night for about two weeks. My mail will be forwarded up from King's office with only a short delay.

All my love again, Stan

April 6, 1953

Hon,

I stepped out of the room for a minute and when I came back it smelled like a rabbit hutch. I guess I should stop smoking. I have been planning on quitting again soon. Hope I make it O.K.

Billie: Myra and I had pet rabbits. Dad had built the hutch for them. We also had cats, a dog, bantam chickens, a duck, a parakeet, and a hamster on our half acre in the San Fernando Valley.

As I said in yesterday's letter, cherry blossoms were out. I went to the parks and shrines and took pictures. Ueno Park was loaded with picnics. Families sitting under the trees drinking sake, singing, and dancing. I got some good shots.

April 11, 1953

Sweetheart,

I went into Tokyo at 10 a.m. after an all-night session in a "reclining" chair car. Transportation is really a tough item now up north. We were unable to contact any sleepers or reserved seats until Monday night, so we will lose a day on our schedule. May have a chance to rest up a bit, though.

I'm getting accustomed to living out of a suitcase, but my laundry is getting a bit "grey." I'll be happy when I can set up an office at Sendai without coming down here anymore. Since I'm living in Army Billets or on trains, I gave up my room at Shiba Park. I hadn't intended to come down this weekend, but since a proposal was required for a contract increase, I found myself here without a room. I finally have a room for tomorrow night and tonight at the Matsudaira Hotel.

I'm surprised at the high duty on silk. About 30%. I found that they now have some nice nubby raw silk in mixed colors and will be nice for kids' skirts. Will send some small amounts, and duties seem to vary. $3.00 is not bad, though. I got another lens for the movie camera. A1.9 focusing mount, NIKKOR. Finest made for $19.00. Not bad! Oh, and I had a suit made from a wonderful wool tweed for $20. The hotel had a custom tailor do it.

I'm awfully tired… so goodnight. All my love, Stan

April 18, 1953

Hon,

A beautiful cool, bright Saturday morning. Camp Sendai is located on a wooded hill covered with large Japanese cedars—some like small redwoods. Since this is a headquarters, the place is quite residential in character. A sleepy place where no one works very fast. Since the boys are back in Tokyo for the weekend, I'm enjoying its peace and quiet. The climate is cooler up here and cherry blossoms are just coming out. I hope they stay all week because they do transform the view.

I just returned from a ten-minute walk up the hill where I had breakfast at the officers' club. It is a very nice, small "mess" and quite different from the Air Force mess. I have a nice room in a guest house on the post. It is clean and comfortable and will be headquarters for the duration of the contract. Our Japanese helpers are housed in town and enjoy being there more anyway since they can stay in Japanese hotels with familiar equipment. I get a big kick out of how much these Japanese engineers enjoyed getting a ride in a Pullman. It is very beyond their means ordinarily.

Besides just loafing this morning, I will be able to take a few pictures of blossoms on Japanese tulip trees (magnolias) which are now fully opened. I'm going to have a lot of fun this weekend with a second chance on the blossoms and festivities. I have the new lens on the movie camera, and it seems to be a honey. I hope the pictures are as impressive as its appearance.

I went over to Matsushima today to have a nice stroll around—the blossoms were very beautiful. The sunny days have been unusual—four in a row.

Time is passing swiftly, but, as you say—not fast enough. I'm going to "make as much hay while the sun shines" as I can. Then we will be together again. When I think of all the things we can sit and talk about, I can hardly wait. It seems like such a long time.

When I sit down and think about it, I can't make it come out as being worth it from the emotional standpoint. From the financial it does have certain merits.

All my love, Stan

May 1, 1953

Sweetie Pie,

Today is May Day. How well I remember making little paper baskets when I was a kid and filling them with jellybeans and little wilted crocuses! I suppose kids don't do that anymore.

I will be very happy to be home and I think that things will work out well.

I feel that my destiny will be in big work around the world for some time to come. I might just as well apply my talents to big work as to small work at a reduced fee.

The problem will be how to work the firm in. I can see much work in Korea.

Monday and Tuesday are holidays. Monday is Boys' Day and what a fuss people make over it. Such a lot of FISH FLAGS flying over houses. Some beautiful displays of dolls too.

All my love, Stan.

May 14, 1953

Sweetheart,

Leaving for the North Country again on the weekend. Will try to hit Nikko on the Sunday morning so I can get movies of the big parade at the shrines.

All my love, Stan.

May 19, 1953

Hon,

Up in Haugen again trying to get some work done. It is quite a job working this distance from the home office. Fortunately, we have a hard-working group of Japanese surveyors, so we have been making good progress. One problem is trying to get a day's work completed while relying upon Army transportation. The Army seems to keep "banker's" hours: 7:30 to 4:30. The driver gets started 15 minutes late and pulls in the motor pool a half hour early. Some way to run an Army.

The weather is beautiful. We have the green hills to the west and the blue Pacific to the east. Still snow on the peaks to the west, too. The wild azaleas have perfect blossoms now. Some bushes about 4' high and solid color, like splashes of paint on the hillsides. When I think how we struggled to grow our puny ones! These run from dark pink to light red with some blossoms 3" across. The country couldn't be more beautiful than it is here this time of year.

Our survey work will take longer now than we had planned, but we should finish our other work in a couple of days—then to Sendai. Makes for quite a tour. Since the weather is cool, I don't mind. It is better to do this field work now rather than later during the heat of summer.

Will get this in the mail so we can get back to work. Hope I will find some mail when I get back to Tokyo.

Love, Stan

May 21

Sweetheart -

A beautiful day with gentle breezes blowing and blue skies with white clouds. Really a pleasure to work up here. I'll hate to get back to the dust and dirt of Tokyo. Unfortunately, our work is not breaking at a rate which permits the establishment of a branch office here. It is still a bit scattered and each job is too small to warrant my being full time anywhere.

Mark Fjilstad, who has been DMJM's man on Okinawa is very good and has said he will be very interested and will come up and see us about it soon. He should be free before July 1st and I would like him to take over the northern work and free me so I can go home. If he does—and there is always an "if," I would be home by our anniversary. I don't see how I could do any better. Also, it would be a very tight "squeak" to make it by July 12—your B-day—I wouldn't want to leave them in too much of a sweat. Also, it would not be allowing enough leeway on 510 days. (Tax issues based on how long out of U.S.A. are very strict.)

I'm planning on going back to Tokyo on tomorrow night's train. Will probably be up in Sendai during the early part of the week. I'm hoping to get my work crews broken down into several good working units. So, I won't have to sit over them all the time. I find it a little tiring to play nursemaid to a bunch of adults. These people—Americans included—don't have too much initiative and must be told what to do, how to do it, and when to do it. If they encounter a problem slightly unusual, they will sit on their fannies doing nothing.

Hope that Myra's ear trouble is cleared up by now. It will be quite a problem if anymore sicknesses occur when you are there alone. I should be there with you. You will have the added problem of the kids having too much time on their hands during the summer months. We will try to keep them busy when I return. Maybe some trips or summer camps, or both.

I had quite a rat race Sunday. I took the morning train (7 am) to Nikko and photographed the parade with movies. Got it coming down the hill at 11 a.m. and going up the hill at 12:30 p.m. The Hesse's had a nice spot up on a wall, so, I joined them at noon. They had several packages of sandwiches and a quart of Martinis. It was very nice since I had had no breakfast.

I waited until 2 p.m. for an archery exhibition on horseback—very good. In the early evening I got a train back to Sendai.

Will get this into the noon mail tomorrow.

All my love, Stan.

May 26, 1953

Sweetheart,

We have been having a gay old time here. I don't believe that I told you about the house party I went to on Sunday night. It was quite a deal. McCarthy was guest of honor and very nice. Very much like Bill Diamond in looks and manner. The fellow leads a busy life. He had returned from a week in Korea and urged us to "get on the ball." The set up will be wide open for someone with my talent. I'm the only one who has done post-war reconstruction. We will be able to get a lot of work. I see that we are likely to get the reconstruction of a University first. Plans will be like with JD&P, only a few weeks ahead of the construction. Plan as we go.

I'm going to try for a relation between King's outfit and Moe & Larsen, my company in Van Nuys, California, like I had with Harold Starin in Duluth. Remember, we had a 40-60 split on profits in addition to a 40-60 split on proportion of salaries? He put up all the money too and took the most risk in exchange for my talent. It will be harder to sell these boys because they don't understand the problem fully. A new company will have to be formed with a joint-venture structure. It sounds very complicated.

We would have to maintain an office, say in Pusan (also known as Busan), Korea, and work on the site. Getting dimensions, and drawing architectural plans there using Korean architects who have staffs. We would "farm out" the mechanical and electrical stuff to the Tokyo office. That way we would require good architectural and structural people in the field. I would like to be the project manager for the entire Korean set up. Much would have to be worked out. This is under UNKRA (United Nations Korean Rehabilitation—or Reconstruction—Administration) which is a going institution and, I believe, largely U.S. financed.

While Ed Shay must rush over next week to Pusan to see how things go, he still has no idea how this thing is to operate. I will have to be the one who works out the proposal. So far, I've had no help and it is a "lonely road!"

All my Love, Stan.

Chapter 27

Last Trips in Japan. Sayonara!

June 2, 1953 Tuesday

Sweetheart,

I'm leaving for up north this evening and will return on the Thursday night train so will be in Tokyo on Friday. It has been so humid here that I hope to have a few cool, dry days. We have been having some heavy rain, even though our "rainy season" is not supposed to start until June 30 or July 4. I'll be happy to get back to dry California.

I received a letter from Phil Daniel the other day—after I had written him about my old, expired ticket. I've been trying to get it settled now so that I will have everything set for a sudden departure. These boys here are so vague and confused that it is hard for me to impress upon them the fact that I'm leaving soon for the States. They don't easily accept the "facts of life." Some day they will wake up and find that I have "flown the coop." It will be as soon after the 510 days that I can possibly make it.

All my love, Stan

✧ **Billie: At that time, one had to be out of the country for 510 days in order that their out-of-country income not be taxed.**

June 6, 1953 Saturday morning

Sweetheart,

I served notice on the firm of my leaving on July 15 at the latest. I made up my mind on Thursday night while I was up north that I was now "fed up." Shay is in Pusan and is heading for Seoul today. However, with all the peace talks, he said when he talked to me on the radio phone yesterday, that things are very much up in the air and things are not moving as fast as originally reported.

My reason for going home is two-fold. First, I want to see you all and to look at the Moe & Larsen business. Second, I want to have a chance to view all this stuff here, from afar. It is possible to consider more than one set up—if I should want to return. That is always a possibility.

All my love, Stan

June 7, 1953 Sunday

Sweetheart,

I had intended to go up to Nikko this morning and get some flash shots all by myself of the intricacies of some temples. Had the operator call me at 6, but when I looked out the window, I decided that it was a poor day so went back to bed. You know—sometimes the "ideal climate" is in bed. Remember? Today is such a day. I slept until 9 and was too late for breakfast.

Ed Shay is still in Pusan. I talked to him by radio phone Friday and he was hoping to leave for Seoul this weekend. The peace business is now hot, and the Korean government is now getting annoyed with all things American—including reconstruction. Ed says the work is not as rush-rush as he thought from talking with the "powers that be" when they were over here. That is usually the way.

I think the next few weeks will go by quite rapidly. And before we know it, this will be only a memory. It still will be a minimum of 6 weeks from today that I could arrive—or 5 weeks from when you receive this. I still want to swing by way of Hong Kong and certainly spend a couple of days in Hawaii. Two hours by plane layover is too short.

It sure is wet outside. I'm listening to a portable radio George Yamashiro left here. Church services and watching the rain. I wish it wasn't so often wet. Rain depresses me. I can see why I didn't like Duluth weather. I guess I do like California after all.

I love you, Stan

June 11 (written on paper from The Miyako Hotel, Kyoto, Japan)

Sweetheart,

I'm sitting here on a sun deck (no sun) and enjoying a view of Kyoto. I still think that it is one of the most beautiful cities I've ever seen. Someday, I want you to sit here with me and we will enjoy it together. I found that business was a bit dull and since I wanted to come here again, I decided to make a four-day trip out of it. All by my lonesome, too. It happened rather fast.

It is now about 9:25 and I am working out my itinerary for the next few days. Since today is cloudy, I will stay on my inside work—weaving shops, wood carvers, ana potters. Then when the sun comes out—which it MUST—I will cover the rest. It would take a year of weekends to even scratch the surface here. It is so vast and filled with true oriental beauty.

This hotel is strictly first class and believe it or not a single room with bath is $4.17. It is more convenient to stay here than a Japanese hotel since one doesn't have to spend half the day drinking tea and waiting for meals which are all served special.

All my love forever, Stan

June 14, 1953

Sweetheart,

Today is my last day here in Kyoto. It has been an interesting stay and I've been able to do many of the things I didn't find time for on my other trips. Even so, I wore myself down to a nub while doing it. It has been a lot of fun, though lonesome.

One of the fellows from our office has been ailing somewhat about a visit from his mother. He is an only child and momma really overdoes it in the "doting" mother role. They came into Kyoto last night and I ran into them at breakfast. She really ruined my breakfast—quite a character, incessant talker. She "knows" everything about everything "cultured" and sees to it that everyone else gets a liberal education. What a bore! I'm happy that I'm leaving on that score.

The country is full of GIs on R&R (Rest & Recuperation) from Korea. Some are poor specimens of American culture. They all have girls living with them who are rough. I find it quite offensive. It seems to be sanctioned by the big shots here in Japan. I'm happy to say that I haven't found out yet why it seems so necessary. Since these fellows have no hobby, they are not able to think of any other way to spend time.

Hope I find a letter when I get home tomorrow.

All my love, Stan

June 24

Sweetie-Pie,

I'm quite overcome! Your June 19th letter came yesterday and your June 20th letter this afternoon. Really wonderful service and two letters in close succession. Very, very nice.

I laughed when I read about Billie's "worlds to conquer" at Robert Fulton Junior High and Van Nuys High. She must be quite a young lady. I won't know her, I'm afraid. I keep looking at the pictures I have with me and can't quite realize that she is no longer a little girl.

✧ **Billie: I was born in 1939 and when Daddy left in '52, I was 12 and when he came home in '53, I was a couple weeks short of 14 and was dating Pat Gillick, a fifteen year-old amazing baseball player who became a life-long friend.**

Myra's artwork was very good too. It seems, she too, likes animals, as Billie does. What a gang of pet fanciers we have. I don't hear much about the livestock. How are they all making out?

✧ **Billie: Myra majored in art at USC in Los Angeles. She has done many things, but most are centered around art.**

Oh, say, I finally got a foreign exchange back here from the customs. It allows me to buy optical goods without 30% tax. Since I would like a telephoto lens and some "trinkets" for 1/3 stateside price, please-pretty please send *me a bank draft for $150 so I can use it to deposit in the bank to "buy yen." Will you do it soon? What a HUNK OF GLASS a Nikon telephoto is! My last extravagance. I may need some money en route through Hawaii. Maybe you can mail me some U.S. bills before I leave. We will see. I will let you know.*

All my love, Stan

June 26, 1953

Sweetheart,

It's a warm evening without a breath of air. A little dry heat will be a welcome relief for me after Tokyo. Guess I'll go to the beach on Sunday.

My work is picking up again and will continue to be hectic until the minute I leave. A good way to make time pass—now that I'm planning on leaving of course it makes me a bit sad, but since I have something so wonderful to go to, it isn't so bad.

I plan to throw a party and invite all who have been so nice to me. I have some good friends here. Jack Lipman and the McClement's, the Hesse's, the Jones, the Goldsby's, Lt. Colonel Borielbis and Major Moses.

July 3 Friday p.m.

Hon,

Got in this morning from up north. I'm worn out. My last trip to Haugen. Things are winding up now.

No—I won't linger. In fact, I went down to PAA (Pan American Airways) this noon and got a reservation for 1:30 p.m. July 16th. Will arrive 1:45 p.m. July 16 Honolulu. (Some speed!—date line, you know.) I leave Honolulu Saturday noon July 18 and arrive direct to LA at 6:30 a.m. July 19th!

How do you like them apples? They assured me it will be daylight. With the daylight savings time, and all. So, you will see me in a short time… and I will see you, too.

July 8, 1953 Wednesday

Sweetheart,

Another warm day. A little rain and a little sun and a lot of humidity. I'm sitting in my room here with the fan going full blast. Will be nice to leave all this.

I found a call from Lipman at the hotel when I got home at 6:30 tonight. He may have some dope on my ticket. Since I don't have his phone # here I can't call and find out. I think he also just returned from Korea.

This is sure some hotel! I always get a kick out of sitting in the lobby in the evening and listening to all the languages. Last night a bunch of French and Swedes. Night before Indians, Chinese, Norwegians. Tonight, it is Danes. Ah—quite cosmopolitan. I'll miss it. Must be fun to hear and understand what other people are talking about.

My dinner party is all set even to flowers. Wish you could be here. I'll take pictures of it. Nice memory. My flash is now quite dependable.

I'm giving away my worn clothing to the Flood Relief at the Red Cross. Will do some real good.

Seems funny (and wonderful) to have reached the point where i am now so close to going home that mail will arrive almost as soon as I will. Nice.

Sure, will be mighty nice to get away from the mildew. What a smelly business. Everywhere there is upholstered material, it smells that way. My bed does not this year for some reason. It did at Army Halls. More later. Will mail at Ernie Pyle Theatre.

All my love. See you soon (doesn't that sound nice!) Stan

July 16, 1953 (written on Pan Am "Clipper" mailgram and mailed from Wake Island on the 17th)

Dear Doris, Billie, & Myra,

Well, I'm finally under way and it is, as before, a beautiful flight. I had almost forgotten the luxury of Clipper travel.

It was hard to say goodbye and more than one tear was shed. Some people in the office didn't realize that I was leaving until 10 min. before I left.

Eileen (Hesse) and I had lunch at the Union Club and met Henry's sister who had come in on a boat at Yokohama this morning. Eileen will be very lonesome for my shining face. Henry was down south. So, I didn't see him.

The Hopkins had a party for me last night and Joe and Barbara Goldsby were there too. Very nice. It ended early and Joe and Barbara drove me home.

It seems like I will be back again. It didn't really seem like goodbye, because I like Japan so much that I can't imagine not returning. Ed Shay was on the point of tears too. Funny guy.

Will see you Sunday morning with all my paraphernalia. I was told I had exactly 66 pounds besides what I hand-carried!

All my love, Stan

…I will always be interested in my surroundings even when I'm too old for anything else. Very few people react that way. That's why we have so much discontent…many people let themselves get bored. I have found time passes very rapidly when I'm interested and engaged—which is most of the time. **— Stan**

PART X

DMJM Grows!

Daniel, Mann, Johnson & Mendenhall

CHAPTER 28

Daniel, Mann, Johnson & Mendenhall, Moe & Russell

Arthur E. Mann

Philip J. Daniel

S. Kenneth Johnson

Teamwork of These Six Men Established Thriving Architecture And Engineering Firm

Irvan F. Mendenhall

Douglas A. Russell

Stanley A. Moe

(The text copy has been removed from the above for clarity)
This collage of photos courtesy of Southwest Builder and Contractor, Issue of September 27, 1957

DMJM'S Code of Partnership Ethics

1. Acceptance by each member of the management of this firm of his pro rata share of responsibility for the getting of the business and the handling of it.
2. Willingness on the part of each member of the management to assist each of the other members in the discharge of his responsibilities.
3. Desire on the part of each member to build up and extend the influence of the other members.
4. Unwillingness on the part of all members ever to speak disparagingly of another member to anyone.
5. Unwillingness on the part of any member to profit at the expense or embarrassment of any of the other members.
6. Willingness on the part of all members to face all firm problems objectively and dispassionately.
7. Unwillingness of all members ever to take an arbitrary position about anything.
8. Avoidance of destructive criticism.
9. Substitution of constructive suggestion.
10. Willingness on the part of each member, either to sell his ideas or to accede to the judgement of the other members of this management.
11. Acceptance by each Partner of his responsibility to protect the interests of other Partners when delegated the authority and responsibility to act for the other Partners.

(Ethics Code courtesy of *Engineering News-Record*, Feb 11, 1960)

For detailed information on the growth and production of DMJM, please see appendix three.

CHAPTER 29

My First DMJM "Boss" — Phil Daniel

Looking Back

Phil Daniel was the first founding partner of Daniel, Mann, Johnson and Mendenhall (DMJM) and he recruited me to do my first job for DMJM. That led, within a few years, to my becoming a partner in 1956.

Before that happened, from 1952 to 1953, I was self-employed in Van Nuys, but Phil was my supervisor in Tokyo, Japan, and Okinawa. From 1952 to 1960, Phil was my contract supervisor in The Netherlands, Denmark, Norway, Thailand, Hong Kong, Japan, Philippine Islands, Jerusalem, Switzerland, Tokyo, Okinawa, England, France, Belgium, Portugal, West Germany, Italy, Egypt, Turkey, and Vietnam.

To say Phil was an important and key person in my career is an understatement. Phil was a beloved friend. In this section, I reflect upon Phil, his gifts, and his personality.

I was just reading in the paper this morning about people in foreign countries inventing things and getting things done faster than in the United States and it reminded me of an incident in Europe.

In January 1954, after I had set up the London Office, I was often in touch with Phil. Phil had a gift for making contacts with interesting people about noteworthy projects. He knew that I was running the London Office and although he knew I was extremely busy, he still wanted me to do some exploration of business opportunities that he had uncovered. I did this for him over the years. Sometimes a project would materialize, sometimes not.

Phil was one who met all kinds of interesting people.

Phil liked to use me to round out the details on how bright ideas might be passed onto other people. It was one of these conversations with someone, that prompted Phil to put together a proposal (along with Irv Mendenhall and others who had had experience with large civil engineering projects) for bringing services to the Aswan Dam Commission in Egypt.

I made plane reservations to go to Cairo. I was told by Pan American Airways that I didn't need a Visa. I arrived in the middle of the night and I was held up and kept in a room of the terminal building which I had designed ten years prior. I HAD needed a Visa. It took a bit of time, but I did what Phil sent me there to do and came home.

On another occasion, Phil was guest at a fancy cocktail party at someone's apartment in New York City. It seems that the hostess was a collector of fine art, and she had invited a famous artist who was in the process of making his art available to the public.

And Phil said, "I'd like to help you!" It wasn't long before a big carton came to the Los Angeles office and, because Phil Daniel had decided to help this man launch his career as an artist, he sent invitations to all sorts of art collectors in the Los Angeles Area. In order to help the cause a little bit, Phil put some pictures on consignment—in other words, he put up money on these things and hoped he would be able to sell them. Well, we got out from under that, mostly. I think we were burdened with a few thousand dollars' worth of 'stuff,' some of the lesser work of this individual. We did find a few of our clients who had a lot of real estate projects, who were interested in and purchased some of the pieces.

Phil spent so much time away from Los Angeles that he had difficulty keeping a secretary. He'd been gone for weeks at a time and here was the poor secretary who had nothing to do and so she would be reassigned to another part of the company. Out of consideration for Phil's needs when he returned, another would be hired to fill in. On one occasion, Phil had developed a close relationship with a client back in Washington, DC. The client was a part of a very important agency, but Phil became quite frustrated with the person in that agency who was obstructive, non-cooperative.

So, one day when Phil came back from a trip, he sat down and dictated to his secretary a letter directed to that gentleman who was the cause of his annoyance. It was a pretty frank letter about what ought to be changed in the way this person was handling their job. The letter was never sent because Phil dashed off to do something else again. The letter was typed up in draft form and put in a pending basket where secretaries stored these things. Lo and behold, one day, another girl had been brought in to take care of Phil's concerns when he got back. She found this unsent letter! And she said, "Oh my goodness, the date is a while ago. I'm sure that they intended to get this sent." So, she types it up and mails it to the person to whom it was addressed. Well! Phil never intended this at all. I can't remember the outcome of that one, but it was exciting! Fortunately, I was out of town on a trip at the time. So, I heard the details of the fireworks from the firm's client who had been upset by Phil's frank, unintended letter.

Phil was a genius in finding all kinds of projects for DMJM. As a matter of fact, he found the project in London for the Third Air Force. He was the reason for my going to London and taking my leave from my firm Moe & Larsen in Van Nuys in the Fall of 1953. When I arrived in London, I was greeted by a civil engineer,

Fredrick Snow, who had just received an OBE from the Queen. There he was knighted. Phil had a business relationship with him at his firm.

Sir Fredrick Snow had introduced Phil Daniel to London club life in an interesting way. Phil knew nothing about the very exclusive men's clubs in England. Several were on St. James Street between Piccadilly and St James Palace. Another one was down on Pall Mall Street. I recall the story he told about the first venture into one of those clubs as a guest of a member.

Phil had been invited to lunch at a club by Sir Frederick Snow and Phil was sitting in a big lounge room by a big fireplace before lunch. He found it an awfully cold, drafty place. Phil probably never weighed more than 110 pounds (I exaggerate) and couldn't tolerate the cold well and was sitting there shivering when Sir Frederick went out to the men's room. When he got back, Sir Frederick found that Phil had moved to a nice cozy chair right next to the fireplace.

Sir Frederick said, "Oh, no, Phil, you can't sit there!"

Phil said, "Why not?"

"Well," Frederick said, "That's Lord So and So's chair!"

"Well," Phil said, "He's not here?"

"That's true, he's been dead for years, but nobody ever sits in his chair."

The years passed and Sir Frederick and I became fast friends.

There were other occasions where Phil made some good friends. One time, he had been invited to a nice party in New York City. While there, he met a lot of fascinating people. Among these was a gentleman; an outgoing, crazy type of character who owned property down in the Caribbean.

✧ **Billie: This was probably Colin Tennant—see the documentary about Colin Tennant, *The Man Who Bought Mustique*.**

As a matter of fact, this gentleman owned an entire island, just about twenty-five miles south of St. Vincent. It's a very prominent and well-known island—a favorite of yachtsmen. During the conversation with the owner of Mustique, Phil was able to tell about DMJM and some of the services they rendered. This gentleman was fascinated and said that he was planning some expansion on his estate there and wanted to improve the air service to get in and out of the area. There were very limited port facilities except for a harbor that would take care of yachts.

Phil said, "We're going to do a study for you—an economic and engineering study."

I can't remember how they decided on the cost of services, but lo and behold, DMJM got the assignment to do the study.

Well, years had gone by and I was told that the owner of the island had run up a sizable bill with DMJM and hadn't paid it. So, I wanted to do something about that.

Doris and I were on vacation in the Caribbean and during our travels, I said, "I might as well check into this thing in Mustique."

Doris stayed in Barbados with some of her friends, vacationing.

I talked to a taxi driver and asked, "If I were going to Mustique, how would I get there?"

He said, "That's no problem I'll give you the name of someone and you tell them I sent you. They have a little charter airplane and they'll fly you down there.

So, through a maze of contacts, I was able to set up an appointment with Colin Tennant and arranged for the charter flight over.

The little charter airline, a lovely little plane, landed in a meadow. Not far from the little grass landing field with no pavement, there was a house, a couple of colonial houses with a porch running all the way around it. Very informal. And out of almost nowhere a very nice-looking young lady walked up wearing a uniform, a business suit.

She said, "Oh, you're Mr. Moe. We've been expecting you. I'll take you up to the house." She had a clipboard and showed me most of the house. There was a fellow sitting on the porch. He had a small desk out there. The roof went out over the whole porch so if there were rain, the porch would be dry. It was a nice breezy place.

The fellow came over to me. I noticed that his shirt was tied in a knot in front of him and he was wearing shorts and sandals. He was Colin Tennant. He appeared to be about forty or forty-five years of age, and slender. I wouldn't call him a hippie type, but I remember that he was very informal. He said, "I've been expecting you."

"Well," he said, "Do you really want the project?"

I said, "I'm here to talk about the study we already did for you."

And he said, "Have you seen it?"

"No." And then I looked at the title on the outside of the report. I knew the person who did the study, I remembered hiring him five years before.

He said, "Maybe you'd like to see it." I grabbed a stool and sat down. I asked a few questions about the report and suspected that the report was unrealistic.

He said, "Let me show you around." He got one of these little cars—like a little dune buggy or a golf cart, but real fun and nice. Anyway, as we drove he said, "I've got to show you some stuff. See, according to the report your company did, you saw what was recommended. As I show you around, I'd like your opinion as to how appropriate that development might be for this area."

It seems this guy had inherited the island from his family and decided to set it up as a place where things would be designed for quality—houses and vacation-type places—and that would be nicely maintained. But there were different types of communities. Some communities would be more formal than others and so on. He added, "We do all our own construction here. We have our own architects."

We drove around and then he began to describe the owners. "That plot is owned by so-and-so. There were lots of big names. There were three families from Virginia. I think the Mellon family was one.

"The wealthy people inherited these properties, but probably the most casual of all the tenants that you might know about would be Princess Margaret from England. She was a bit of a rich, difficult person. Not like her sister at all, who was so dignified."

And he said, "I'd like you to see the recommendation for airport development." He took me to the bay. They felt that they ought to have the airstrip built into the bay. They did that in Hong Kong.

"Well, I'll take you over to my beach club and have lunch. What time is your plane going to pick you up?" I told him the time that the charter was going to come back to pick me up. And he said, "Well, I tell you what. You can do me a wonderful favor. One of my men was injured here this morning. He was chopping wood or something and cut his foot with an axe. I've got to get him over to St. Vincent to the hospital so he can be properly treated, would you take him?" I said that I would be happy to.

Anyway, I had lunch all by myself. It was an open-air area. It had a diving board right by the water, one could drive right down into the ocean there. He had shown me the whole thing and he said, "You have viewed the situation here. Oh, incidentally, a ship had sunk; a big ocean-going ship, had sunk off that bay. Well, they are recommending an airstrip. I don't know what the timeline was on it one way or another."

I said, "I'll write a report back to the office." And I thanked him for the hospitality and the lunch (that he never did have with me) and went home.

I called Jim and said, "I think that our person who wrote the report and the people in the office weren't dealing with the real world when they went down and made recommendations like that to Mr. Tennant.

Phil said, "No worries, the bid was only for about thirty-five-thousand, anyway." Phil always knew there was an abundance of leads for work, so it didn't bother him to waste a few in the pursuit of finding jobs that were right for DMJM.

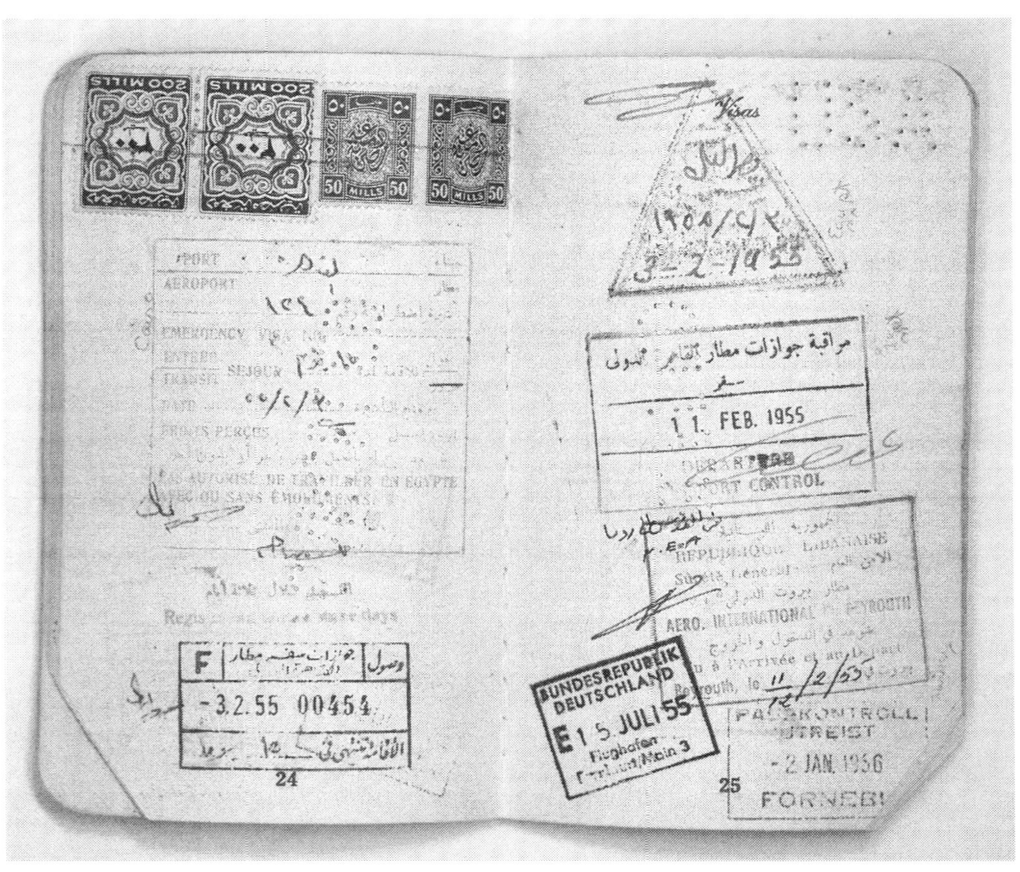
200 MILLS
50 MILLS 50
مراقبة جوازات مطار القاهرة الدولى
11 FEB. 1955
REPUBLIQUE LIBANAISE
AERO. INTERNATIONAL
BUNDESREPUBLIK DEUTSCHLAND
E 15. JULI 55
Flughafen
Frankfurt/Main 3
-3.2.55 00454
24
25
- 2 JAN. 1956
FORNEBU

Chapter 30

Early DMJM — Lots of Work!

Looking Back

Let me tell you about the story of how Doug Russell came to the firm. Daniel, Mann, Johnson & Mendenhall were just starting out and weren't making any money. Finally, Ken Johnson's wife, Kathy, said, "This is awful. We've got four kids, a big house, and no income. We never know when the money is coming in. The company's so busy, so, how come?"

Someone had told Ken about a consultant who would come in and survey the situation and decide what they ought to do about it. He said they'd give him the name of a company – called Booz Allen Hamilton.

I got one of the Booz Allen Hamilton executives on the phone and described the problem and they said, "Well, we'll assign somebody to you to take a survey of the operation and make some recommendations." And, who should appear on the scene other than Doug Russell. He was a new employee of Booz Allen Hamilton and had just graduated from Harvard Business School.

Doug went through the process of evaluating the firm.

He said, "One thing is apparent, you know nothing about how to conduct a business. You've got a lot of money flowing into this place, but you don't know where you're making money or losing money. You don't know whether a job is successful or unsuccessful." Then he said, "You need a general manager."

We ask, "What would it cost?"

"You ought to pay figures of at least twenty or twenty-five thousand dollars, per year, at least."

That was an exorbitant amount of money back in 1958, so the partners said, "Well, that's just too much money."

The partners didn't know how to find anybody qualified to be the general manager. So, Doug Russell said to the partners, "Well, I might be available."

"If so, what would you want?"

"I need to make twenty-five thousand dollars."

"As we said, we can't afford that. The money that we take home is only about ten-thousand dollars ourselves right now."

Doug said, "I'll tell you what I'll do. You pay me ten thousand and then give me a percentage of the profit you make in that first year. I'll work on that basis."

At the end of the first year, for the first time, we had accounts in order, and we had made money. I think on that percentage basis we found that Doug was entitled to about fifty-thousand dollars. Well. Gee, whiz! We figured our own equity in the firm, our share of the capital, or something like that, and with a modest sum, DMJM made him a partner!

They said, "We really can't make you partner, because you're not an architect or an engineer." Doug became a partner anyway. Now he had bought his way in so that he had an equal amount of interest in the company. And he was given a Dodge Sedan car that became company property.

Two and a half years later Doug left the firm and I took over as general manager. What happened was this:

I was working for DMJM in England and received from Phil the following telegram:

FINISH WHAT YOU'RE DOING RIGHT NOW OVER THERE AND COME BACK AND BE A PARTNER!

So, in late 1956, I returned to L.A. from England, where I was assigned a general management responsibility. As general manager of DMJM, I was responsible for the coordination and direction of all day-to-day activities of the firm, including the planning of the firm's long-range policies and the direction of the firm's widespread domestic and international operations. During this period, 1956 to 1971, we all became successful in our areas. I was in the technical area; successful in the areas of military and business. With good people on our staff, it became obvious we would keep making money like everything.

The firm grew from approximately two hundred employees to one thousand. The operations increased from one domestic office to nine, and the international overseas offices grew from three to sixteen in fourteen different countries. The firm's volume of work, as reported in *Engineering News-Record* during those years, placed it in the top ten of the five hundred largest U.S. design firms.

And what happened to Doug Russell? He set up his own consulting firm to do what he did for us, with other companies. One of the companies that he had was *Peterson Publishing Company.* They own an automobile museum, and they had a whole slew of magazines, *Road and Track* among others.

PART XI

1954–1956: England

Registration Certificate No. A 606361
Issued at Piccadilly Place
on 26. 1. 54
Name (*Surname first in Roman Capitals*) MOE. Stanley Allan
Alias
Left Thumb Print (*if unable to sign name in English Characters*).
PHOTOGRAPH
29 JAN 1954
Signature of Holder Stanley A. Moe

ALIENS REGISTRATION OFFICE METROPOLITAN POLICE PICCADILLY PLACE W.1

Nationality U.S. Citizen
Born on 28.5.14 *in* Fargo. N. Dak.
Previous Nationality (if any) Nil
Profession or Occupation Architect
Single or Married Married
Address of Residence Washington Hotel Curzon St. W.1.
Arrival in United Kingdom on 20.1.54
Address of last Residence outside U.K. 14668 Vincennes St, Van Nuys Calif
Government Service Nil
Passport or other papers as to Nationality and Identity. American Passport No 548022 issued Washington 30.1.52

Chapter 31

Billie's and Myra's Memories — Living in England

Billie's Memories

In January of 1954, Dad was living in England. Mother, Myra, and I were living in our home in Van Nuys, California. To set the scene a bit, I had gone skiing over Christmas and injured my right ankle, so was on crutches.

My school district had been re-zoned and while I had attended Birmingham High School first semester, I was told I had to register at Van Nuys High School for the second semester. Because I was on crutches, Mother went with me to register. The school counselor told mother that, in no uncertain terms, based on my test scores, I needed to fill my schedule with as many home economic and shop classes as possible because I was probably not "college material." After a polite thank you, Mother propelled me out of that school as fast as my crutches would carry me.

Along with the disconcerting opinion from the school counselor, the fact that many of my wild girlfriends were pregnant or in trouble because of the crowds they ran with, increased my mother's resolve that we get on the move as soon as possible. Within a matter of weeks, Mother, Myra, and I were on a plane headed for England to live with Dad.

There, I was tutored in math, language arts, and history by the Gerrards Cross Vicar's wife and French from the French wife of a US military man who lived in the same house that we lived in. Myra was enrolled in a private Catholic school that was attended by the Ellis children whose house we rented in Gerrards Cross, Buckinghamshire, England, (Bucks). Both Myra and I kept in touch with the Ellis children well into adulthood.

The next school year, September of 1955, the family had moved to a rental house in Farnham Royal, Bucks, near Windsor, and I was enrolled as a junior at Bushy Park, Central High School (an American Dependent School) in London area. This was a wonderful experience and I met some lifelong friends. During this school year, October to March, Mother had to return to California, because her interior design shop in Van Nuys was not going as well as she had hoped in her absence. She took Myra with her and I stayed in school in England and continued living with Dad.

In England, while I was there with him, Dad/DMJM had an office in Uxbridge. The office was on the second story above where the farmers' market had been. The office was then moved to "the base"—Ruislip—an RAF base that also had an American base adjoining it. The PX was at Ruislip.

This was a special time for Dad and me. Though he had been away many years of my life, 1941 through 1943 and 1952 through 1954, and many extended trips around the world in between, we had always enjoyed a special bond. In England, we kept house together and stoked a coal burning furnace that heated our two-story brick house. The sink in my bathroom dripped and it was so cold, that by morning, a little icicle hung from the faucet. The builder of the house, an American military person, had put central heating in the house, but the pipes were on the outside of the walls on the backside of the house where they could be accessed when it got really cold. (The usual way was to put water pipes in the wall, but they could freeze.) So, Dad and I would have to warm up those water pipes on the outside of the house. Dad would sing, "I loaded 16 tons..." while he was shoveling coal into the stoker and I would climb up a two-story ladder with a pot of boiling water and pour that onto the outside frozen pipes to get the water flowing again.

I liked keeping house for my dad; shopping and cooking and working together on all the activities of daily living shared under the same roof.

Dad hosted several parties for the DMJM staff and the Air Force personnel that he was working with. Hank, the office manager arranged these parties and I got to be the hostess when mother was away.

I hosted Dad's 40th birthday party at The Bull Hotel in Gerrards Cross

One party I remember, was close to Christmas. The staff had arranged with Hank to give Dad a Christmas present of a stainless-steel Rolex watch; the kind you had to wind up. Dad would set that watch every time we went to London. "The Science Museum of London," Dad said, "had the most accurate clock in the world."

Dad loved to go to movies. When Dad and I lived together in England, we'd go to see movies—especially, Dean Martin and Jerry Lewis movies. He would giggle and giggle and giggle. Dad wasn't the type to giggle and this was especially fun to watch.

The great grandkids remember Dad as very serious, but they didn't see the lighter side of their grandpa that I experienced when he was younger. For example, if there was a movie, it seems he never missed it. He would tell me how, on the ship going over to Africa in 1942, they had movies five nights out of seven. There were both dramas and musicals, all in black and white with no soundtracks, because there was no sound equipment on the ship. But he attended them and figured out the plots and would give his opinion on the films and their stories.

In his diaries and letters of 1942, he'd write about being on the ship with all these assorted men that often got drunk, fought, sometimes threw each other off the ship and even killed each other. But there were people like Dad who got their entertainment from movies and music. Later, when they arrived in Africa, they went to the local hotels that showed Hollywood movies.

And then there was traveling together. I especially savored the trip to Norway for the Christmas of 1955 to see Dad's ancestral farms and meet two of the elder relatives. This proved exciting, surprising and even a bit shocking to us both. Dad's stories of his travels in general incited in me a love of travel which evolved into a life-long pursuit.

Simply being together was an experience that Dad and I talked about many times in our lives. Mother and Myra returned to England and as a family, we moved into a large estate in Penn, Bucks, England. The house, with the title of "The Danes" was on 72-1/2 acres and had a small pool.

This was "The Danes" 1956
Note: Not shown are fishpond, swimming pool, and tennis courts

But this pool was not like a Southern California kidney shaped turquoise pool. It was about 15 feet by 20 and was filled by a hose and had a plug, that when pulled, would empty the pool to the pasture where the bullocks grazed! The estate also had a tennis court, and two "keeper's" (caretaker's) cottages at each of the two entrances. As I remember this story, the playhouse, was large enough for Sir Charles and Lady

Colston and their children to live in during WW2 when they turned their big house over to the British military.

There were gifts from the Queen scattered about the salon, music room, and dining room. The home had a thatch roof, which I thought looked like a house from a fairy tale. One of the guest bathrooms was big enough for dancing to my 45 rpm records when Shari and other girlfriends came to sleep over. The maid's quarters had three bedrooms, and there was a valet bedroom across from the master suite. When my boyfriend came out to Penn from London, he got to sleep there. His dad worked for the U.S. Ambassador down in London. Sometimes I would go to London for the weekend and stay with his family.

In contrast to all this grandeur, there were Gypsies living nearby. One day, my friend Shari and I, on a curiosity outing, jumped from the wall into the meadow where the bullocks grazed, up the hill, through the woods into some farmland where the Gypsy encampment was located. There was a rundown barn and old Gypsy wagons. The Gypsies themselves had perhaps gone into town to sell their wares. So, we felt free to poke around. We looked into the barn and saw hundreds of rats; all sizes running over and around bales of hay. There were a lot of pigs in a pig sty.

We investigated one the wagons and saw a mattress on the floor with a blanket wadded up on top of it. The blanket moved and a cat leapt out of it and bolted out the door, past Shari and me. We let out a short yelp and decided to make for home immediately. We found out later from a person in town that the Gypsies were raising rats for testing at medical facilities.

Gypsy Wagons seen alongside highways outside London

At the Danes, a Rolls Royce was parked in the garage and the husband of the housekeeper would sometimes drive me in the Rolls Royce to the nearby village where I would catch the bus to school (about one hour in good weather). As I recall, this wonderful estate, the house with all the finery, only cost Mom and Dad $600 a month! In addition to warm family experiences and a happy time in school, every Sunday afternoon, there was a meeting at the "American Teenage Club" which met at the American Embassy in London. I went almost every week on the train to keep my social life thriving as well.

In my mind, England equaled expansion and new vistas.

Myra's Memories

I have many memories of the time Mom, Billie and I went over to England to live with Dad in early 1955. We lived in three different locations, one of which had kids; the Ellis children, who became life-long friends of mine.

Me (Myra) and my friend Sarah Ellis with a large black bird!

At one point, Mom and I had to come back to Van Nuys to sell her business. But when we returned to England, one of the most interesting places we lived in was Sir Charles and Lady Colstons' house, called "The Danes," on 72-1/2 acres of land. Sir Charles had been the executive of the Hoover plant of the United Kingdom. (By the way, in England you don't vacuum a floor, you Hoover it!)

I found out later, in order to rent out the estate, my parents had to be interviewed by the homeowners, the Colstons. Mom and Dad met them at their flat in a lovely section of London. Our parents obviously "passed muster," because we moved in The Danes right away! The Colstons owned several residences in the British Isles.

At the Danes, there were interesting things I'd never seen before. For example, there was a crater in the forty acres where the cattle grazed and where a bomb had hit during WW2. I found if I ran fast, I could run around inside the edge of the crater without falling down to the bottom. I used to go and collect mushrooms in the fields from under the trees where the cattle were much of the time. Billie would scare the bullocks away while I gathered the mushrooms, but I, for one, never ate them. The maid would peel the wild mushrooms.

There was a small swimming pool, which my mother painted blue and filled with water. It had a huge plug, about six inches in diameter. You pulled it to let the water out and the water went out into the pastures. The property also had a tennis court. Somebody that lived there had stilts, so I learned how to walk on stilts.

Mother and I on the back side of The Danes

The bullocks grazed the land and could walk up to that wall where I am sitting and put their chins on it. They could look at the house but couldn't come up into the yard.

We heard there was a Gypsy encampment nearby. I wasn't allowed to go there, but the maid's kids and I were allowed down into a quarry. That was fun, but it takes a lot more work to get back up than you think, because you are always sliding backwards. You learn basic gravity at a time like that!

The maid had found a bat that was just a little tiny thing. My parents put it in a vase in another room. It got out of the vase somehow and it walked along the floor and came up between a guest's two feet from under the sofa. The whole thing wasn't 2 inches long; maybe 2 inches by 1-1/2 inches. I called it my little baby bat.

I'm holding my "little baby bat!"

When we were in England, if it rained, we went to museums on the weekend. If it didn't rain, we went and viewed old houses. In Britain, there are beautiful mansions where certain parts of the houses are open to the public. I remember old paintings; probably from the 1700s or earlier.

I loved the outings to museums, especially the science museums. And doing space projects—I got my love of astronomy from that. Years later, I used to lie in the back yard in Van Nuys and watch as Sputnik went over. You could see it, when the sun reflected off it, it was shiny. All the other stars were standing still and this one was moving slowly.

Chapter 32

Stan's Memories — England and Norway

Looking Back

Doris and the girls and I lived in England for a few years in the 1950s. Recently, I found a letter I wrote to my Mom and Dad that nicely summarizes some of my experiences living with Billie during the time Doris and Myra were back in California for a time.

January 14, 1956 (Stan's letter to his parents)

Dear Mom and Dad,

Billie and I have just finished dinner and the dishes. While she is doing the ironing, I'll take advantage of the opportunity to get off a note. We have worked out a good routine and things are working smoothly. It takes me about half an hour to drive from my office and it takes Bill a bit over an hour to get home from school by bus, so we have to work things out quite systematically or we should soon find ourselves in a bind. Housekeeping is done twice a week by a lady who worked for us when we lived in Gerrards Cross.

It hardly seems that we have been back from Norway and France for almost two weeks. We found that there was so much to take care of that the time has really rushed by. I am glad that we took advantage of the slack season to take the trip. We might not have gotten away if we had waited.

I'll send you some maps of Norway and some other stuff I acquired on the trip. We got a lot of pictures and will send you some color prints of them. It was sort of strange to visit a country which is so different from the preconceived ideas I had of it. I suppose that we all sort of think that things stay the same. Almost all the world has made great progress during the last fifty years. I mean, the people have become more "westernized" and enjoy the same sort of opportunities that we do in the states. During my trip to the Middle East last year, I noticed that the people of Egypt were just about the same as they were fifteen years ago.

Norway is gaining the reputation of a model country. They are extremely proud of the strides they have made in improving the lot of the ordinary person. Oslo, for example, has nothing in the way of slums. The general architecture and appearance of the city reminds me of Minneapolis or Saint Paul, but without poor dwellings. They have systematically torn down everything that is sub-standard, and they don't have anything which appears to be more than seventy-five years old. That is true of the farming country too. Carl said that most of the houses in his area have been built in the period since World War I.

People are well dressed and seem prosperous and busy. When one compares the healthy, tall and good-looking Norwegians with the poorly dressed and pasty-faced, generally unattractive British, Norway looks very good. I would like to spend a lot more time there.

The advantages of development are offset by loss of a picturesque character. They have had to build "folk museums" in some of the major towns to preserve the houses, clothing and household articles from complete loss. They have built some big villages in these museums and have moved houses hundreds of miles to these sites where they have reassembled them. Even the Norwegians go to these museums to see what a spinning wheel or krumkake[2] *iron looked like. I'll bet there are more of these household articles, showing the old craft work, in Minnesota than there are in Norway. It is hard to find such things as lefse, in fact, it is hard to find people who know what it is. In Oslo, anyway.*

We did much better in Lillehammer on that score. The manager of the hotel up there took delight in trying to get me to try all the old dishes. I did okay, but I found that gommelost[3] *and fermented raw trout brought tears to my eyes and I can't say that I am a convert. Bill got tired of seeing a smorgasbord for every breakfast and lunch where the main thing was ten kinds of fish and as many kinds of cheese. I tried them all and sort of settled on "brisling" as the nicest fish.*

Speaking of fish, one finds it hard to get away from it at any time. They use fish oil in making soap that they use for scrubbing floors. Even very nice department stores have wood floors and the atmosphere is clean but a bit fragrant. They are extremely clean, and the farmhouses are better kept than in North Dakota, as I remember the farms.

Back in England, we had six inches of snow this last Monday and it stayed for a couple of days. Bill got a kick out of it and it did make things look nice, but it has been quite slippery since and there have been lots of accidents. It has been raining for the last two days, so we now have more normal English weather.

We will have to move out of our pleasant little centrally heated house within a month or so and will have to find some new place. Not knowing when and if Doris and Myra will be coming back, we are somewhat uncertain as to where to move and what accommodations we will need.

Hope you are both feeling better and that your checkup was satisfactory, now.

Love, Stan

(Stan talks about the many trips he and Doris arranged with the gang to England in Part Sixteen: Travel.)

---

2. Krumkake (Norwegian), meaning curved cake, plural krumkaker) is a Norwegian waffle cookie made of flour, butter, eggs, sugar, and cream. The iron is what the krumkake batter is poured into to cook it.

3. Gommelost is a distinctive old Norwegian cheese.

Chapter 33

Henry C. Thomas

Billie's Profile of Hank Thomas

Dad met the marvelous Hank Thomas in London. Hank had gotten out of the military and loved Europe so much he asked the powers that be to give him the discharge pay and any other cash rather than pay for this flight home.

In London, he opened an antique shop, and an exclusive, private gentlemen's club that Prince Phillip frequented, named, "The Living Room." Shirley Bassey, the famous Welsh singer, was the opening act. Shirley is well known both for her powerful voice and for recording the theme songs to the James Bond films *Goldfinger* (1964), *Diamonds Are Forever* (1971), and *Moonraker* (1979). She was later given the title Dame Shirley Bassey. That's the kind of circle that Hank ran with.

Hank was also a partner in a dress store chain. He had a gorgeous flat downtown London across from Harrods and had a cottage out in Buckinghamshire. Later, he helped mother and dad find "The Danes" which was in Penn not far from High Wycombe.

When I was living in England with Dad, I was 15 and Hank, who was 30, taught me to dance the jitterbug. He was not only like a big brother, but also a charmer; good-looking and dapper to boot. After he moved to the U.S., he drove a Jaguar E-type (XK-E). Hank was flamboyant, but a classy flamboyant, and he loved life!

At our place in Farnham Royal, I remember Hank coming over some evenings after he and Dad had left the office and while I was doing my homework, Dad and Hank would drink Scotch and eat pickled pigs' feet! Hank was like a younger brother to Dad.

While in England, Dad hired him to be the office manager for DMJM. Then when Dad came back to L.A. to become a partner, Hank remained at the London office until it closed. At Dad's invitation, Hank moved to LA and worked for DMJM, facilitating the behind-the-scenes operations of public relations. This included overseeing the mailroom, the printing department and the executive dining room for which he found an excellent chef to provide wonderful lunches. In fact, he planned all their parties, buying their liquor and stocking the bars each partner had in his office.

Hank ran everything from the mailroom to anything that needed to be printed and/or and bound. Later, when I was teaching at Buckley School, Hank did all the duplicating and binding for a literary magazine I oversaw for the 4th, 5th and 6th grade English students with contributions from the lower and upper grades. With Hank's help, I came out with a book of the kids' work. Some of the famous parents whose kids attended Buckley, like Nat King Cole, Jimmy Durante, and Phillis Diller bought pages of advertising in this publication.

Hank was indispensable for many years and was probably one of the best they had. The Moes were fortunate to have Hank Thomas in their lives.

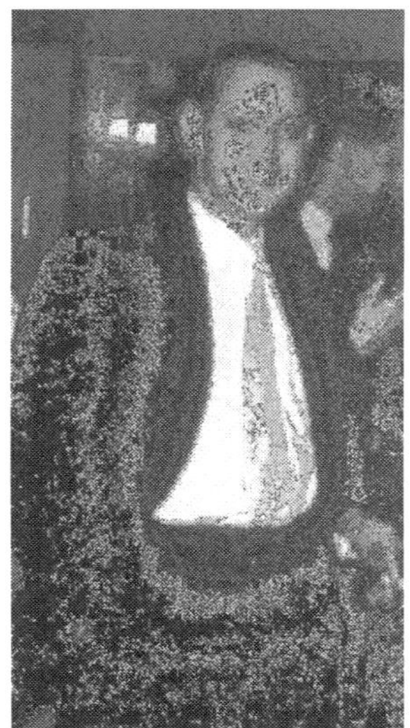

Hank Thomas

PART XII

1950s and 1960s: Thailand, Vietnam, Japan, Hawaii

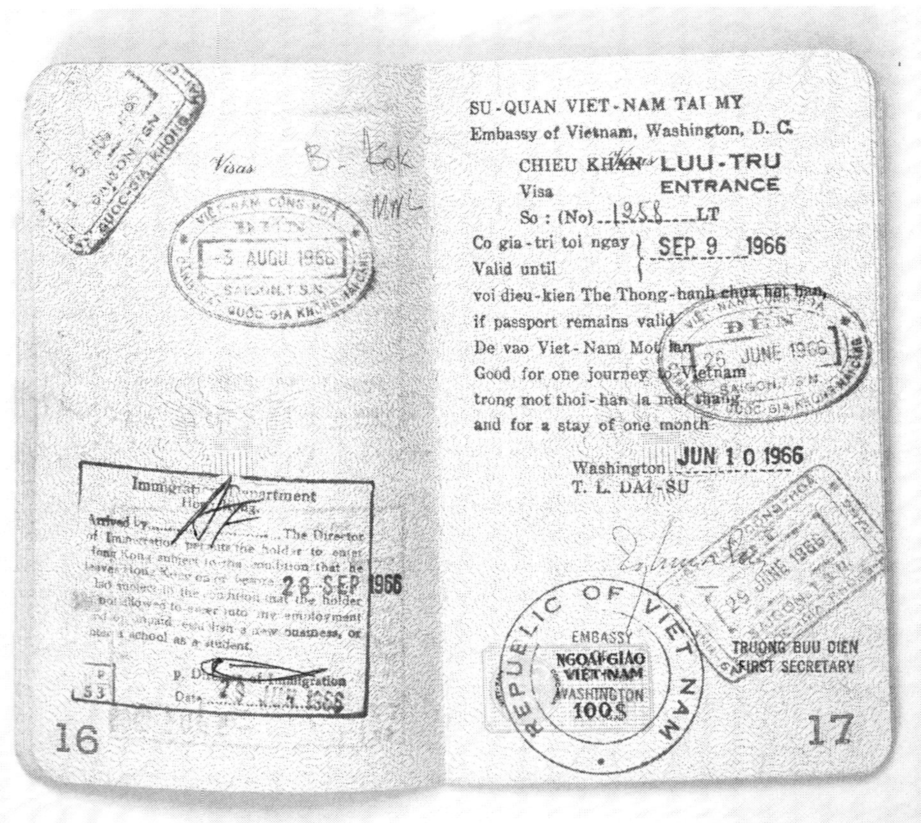
SU-QUAN VIET-NAM TAI MY
Embassy of Vietnam, Washington, D. C.
CHIEU KHAN LUU-TRU
Visa ENTRANCE
So : (No) 1958 LT
Co gia-tri toi ngay
Valid until
SEP 9 1966
voi dieu-kien The Thong-hanh chua hết han,
if passport remains valid
De vao Viet-Nam Mot lan
Good for one journey to Vietnam
trong mot thoi-han la mot thang
and for a stay of one month
Washington JUN 1 0 1966
T. L. DAI-SU
REPUBLIC OF VIET NAM
EMBASSY
NGOAI GIAO
VIET-NAM
WASHINGTON
100$
TRUONG BUU DIEN
FIRST SECRETARY
17
26 JUNE 1966
29 JUNE 1966
SAIGON. T.S.N
Visas
-3 AUGU 1966
SAIGON. T.S.N
QUOC-GIA KHONG-CANG
Immigration Department
Arrived by
The Director of Immigration permits the holder to enter Hong Kong subject to the condition that he leaves Hong Kong on or before
28 SEP 1966
and subject to the condition that the holder is not allowed to enter into any employment paid or unpaid, establish a new business, or attend a school as a student.
p. Director of Immigration
Date 29 JUN 1966
16

CHAPTER 34

Deep Involvement in Thailand and Vietnam, Hawaii and Reopening the Office in Japan

Looking Back: Thailand and Vietnam (1960s)

DMJM and I personally became deeply involved in a program set up by the U.S. government under the heading of an organization called The United States Agency for International Development (USAID). It had been set up to help many nations throughout the world that had been impacted by World War II. In addition to those, among nations that weren't deeply involved in WW 2, but did suffer upset in government, finance and so on, were nations in Asia. One country that was of interest to the U.S. was Thailand.

While, Thailand had not been involved in the war, their economy suffered and there was an urgent need for assistance in the inland areas very short of water. People were extremely poor, and so, the Thai government asked for assistance from USAID to drill some wells. Later we found that their idea was to build water wells to get water, yes, but there was hope, also, that they might run into some oil on the way. The notion that they were interested in oil, more than water, in my view, was not charitable, but the drilling for water was planned and undertaken.

The program that they set up was in an area called Khorat Plateau, reminiscent of our Mojave Desert area. There were patches of heavy jungle growth, then brush land, prairieland, and so on. A striking issue was extreme poverty.

The program was set up and DMJM got the contract. The only person who we could think of who might head up that activity was a fellow out of New York, York Peterson, who had been a county engineer up in Santa Maria, California. He was not working for me in the London office on my airport project, so I sent Peterson over to Thailand, and he went to work setting up a drilling program there for water wells.

This was not a large-scale program. The drill rigs were mounted on the back of big flatbed trucks and you could only drill a well a thousand feet deep at the most. Of course, the wells had to be equipped with casings so that when you ran into water you could get the sliding casing down the well. The program got underway and several drill rigs were set up in the northern area that extended right up to the Laos border.

One day, the driver who had to handle the little truck where Bill Shope and York Peterson were riding wasn't very alert and didn't perceive that a huge hulk coming out of the ditch—an approximately a seven-foot, 1500 pound creature was a water buffalo! The driver also failed to put on the brakes, so the truck ended up running into the poor water buffalo! Bill and York were knocked into the water with the rest. They sustained some small injuries but, fortunately, there was a hospital not too far away, operated by a religious group from the United States! The water buffalo was unharmed but had a good story to tell his kin that night!

DMJM ended up providing all the equipment for a biological laboratory – microscopes and those kinds of things. York totally healed up, but a bit weary of the project, went back to Santa Barbara to retire and Bill took over. In fact, despite the water buffalo incident, it was quite a successful program.

More projects began to arise. The operation got even bigger and these drill rig operators out in the country were quite successful in building up relationships with the local people. The locals, who had relied on water collecting in muddy ditches and ponds after the rain, now had rainwater they could get from a well with a hand-pump. In recognition of that service, the local people from about five villages collected the funds (I don't know what or how they could manage it) and built a monument in the larger of the villages as a tribute to the well-builders who had provided them with water.

Vietnam Waterways

I worked on the Vietnam waterways project. South Vietnam was a beautiful country in the eyes of visitors in the late fifties and early sixties. Despite the long war of liberation from French rule, the city of Saigon and the surrounding countryside were very pleasant and had a distinct French flavor. It was easy to understand why it was often called "The Paris of the Orient."

During the rice growing season it was a great experience to fly in from the west and see hundreds of square miles of rice waving in the wind like water. Its Minister of Agriculture, who visited the DMJM LA office once, said the country was a major rice-exporting nation. The economy was strong, and business seemed stable.

In addition to its beauty the country had a close and friendly relationship with the U.S. USAID decided to fund a contract for the improvement of the intricate system of canals and river waterways which were the main arteries for the transport of produce to the cities and the export market. The routes had been neglected since the departure of the French, who had always been careful about dredging and other maintenance operation to avoid silting and related problems.

When the war developed in Vietnam, it was very small scale in the beginning.

Billie: The Vietnamese war was from November 1955, until April 30, 1975. The US entered the war in March of 1965. My Dad was there in the late 50s.

DMJM was awarded the contract for the survey of the waterways together with the design of a maintenance program. We were to also make a study of a re-routing of the Saigon River near the city. It was a more circuitous route to the sea than was necessary.

Most of DMJM's work was done by crews assigned to work in the field. They used small boats with equipment for measuring stream size, water flow, and so on. In addition, they needed a larger boat to ferry the men and supplies back and forth from Saigon. This required a great deal of travel on the waterways since many of

Vietnamese vendors at the farmer's market

the locations were far apart and a great distance from Saigon. All the engineering data was collected and compiled in an office in Saigon.

I made frequent trips into Vietnam working with the government and our people there to get the programs underway. We assembled a crew of engineers from the Philippines and from the United States and began to check all the waterways to see where they needed to be dredged and how to go about it. It became quite a sizeable project.

North Vietnam envied South Vietnam and its prosperity and were stirring up trouble. In the beginning, the activities of the Viet Cong, as the dissident communist faction's militant members were called, were not considered to be more than a minor nuisance. We and the government looked upon our project as one of importance to the welfare of the people in the country and the nation as a whole. Why should our activities be the object of Viet Cong action?

Soon, we discovered, the operations in the field were being harassed by the Viet Cong. The South Vietnamese government did not have security forces to send to the field to protect our field crews. Instead, local village and district officers would assign armed guards to each of our crews for protection. Even when the Viet Cong did not attack us directly, they would abuse the local officials by killing them or their family members in the most brutal fashion.

In recognition of the services we were rendering to the country, the villagers along the rivers provided us with armed assistance to protect us from bandits and others. The reason this didn't work out was the Viet Cong, hearing of the assistance the U.S. was getting, slaughtered the chiefs and families of those who were assisting us, even in our peaceful mission just to dredge rivers.

As it became apparent that we must abandon the project or move our activities closer to Saigon, an event occurred which hastened our decision. On one of its frequent trips back and forth to Saigon, our larger supply boat that supplied people, equipment and food, had disappeared. It had been manned by a Vietnamese crew. We later learned from a child who had been hitch-hiking from one village to another, that the Viet Cong had taken over the boat. They had dropped the child off a long way from where the event had taken place. I never heard from any of the crew members on the boat. I assumed they were all killed by the Viet Cong.

I spent some time in Saigon working with the government officials to address these tragic incidents perpetrated by the Viet Cong. We decided to discontinue the operation totally because the price in terms of abuse to the Vietnamese people was too high. I worked to close out the project and then headed for Los Angeles to get home for Christmas, 1959.

✧ **Billie: Whenever my Dad spoke about the Vietnamese People, it was with great affection.**

Looking Back: Tokyo, Honolulu, Saigon and Bangkok (1960s)

On the way, I stopped off in Tokyo, where I hadn't been for a long time. When I got there, I visited the headquarters of the Far East Air Force and discovered that only a small group remained of the group that I had known in the early fifties. And I found that they had a rather small group headed by a colonel whom I had never met. I discovered that he was taking a Christmas vacation to help his little children set up the Christmas tree in Washington Heights, which was a military housing project in Tokyo. In 1964, this became Olympic Village Housing for the Summer Olympic Games.

I went to the colonel's home in Washington Heights and rang the doorbell. Colonel Russell Savage came to the door along with a couple of children who were part Japanese that he and his wife had adopted. We had a nice chat. I thought his wife was a little bit annoyed how he would interrupt the family activities on occasion to talk business. But during this gathering, I was able to tell about our experience in the area.

Then I was back in L.A. to celebrate Christmas. About the middle of January, I received a cable from the office of Colonel Russell Savage saying "You and DMJM have been selected to do the master planning for a new airbase for the Republic of Korea. Would you please come over at your soonest convenience to discuss details?"

I flew back to Tokyo and got a contract for master planning a base. This became quite complicated, because for a master plan, that means we had to survey the entirety of South Korea to find a suitable site for the number one air base in support of the Korean government. There were U.S. air bases scattered around the area that were manned totally by military. But this was to be a civilian as well as military airbase for the government of South Korea.

Everything went along swimmingly until Colonel Savage told me that the project manager seemed to be rather irrational in behavior and would I please do something about it. The fellow in charge had been acting strangely and he didn't know the procedure for processing people to the local authorities.

At that time, my daughter, Billie, was on summer break from Colorado State University and was surfing in Hawaii. She knew all the routines necessary to process people; she had done so when we set up the London office. So, I sent her ahead of time to Tokyo to set up and run it.

I followed Billie to Tokyo a few weeks later and let the incompetent fellow go. I had to find a project manager to take over the project and live in Japan. Phil Daniel recommended a man by the name of Sven Svenson down in Venezuela who was working for an American engineering firm from Chicago. Phil thought that Svenson would be a good candidate for project manager.

We managed to put together a team, a management system and that came to completion successfully as the years went by.

A year later, while I was in Washington, D.C., I got a call one night. The person on the other end of the phone said, "This is Colonel Curtis Stanning. We have a project that I'd like to discuss with you tomorrow in Honolulu."

"Well," I said, "That is a bit difficult. I'm in Washington, D.C.! Can you make it day after tomorrow?"

I called Jack Lipman, who was familiar with the staff and operations we had in our London office that I had set up in 1953, and asked him to meet me at the airport and get on the flight with me to fly over to Honolulu. Jack Lipman came to the airport with a portfolio full of material and we flew to Honolulu. We stayed at the Hawaiian Village Hotel where we were placed in the wing right over the kitchen, complete with annoying noises and smells! We had a giant palm tree that banged against the windows all night!

The next morning at 9:00, we arrived at Hickam Air Force Base. We walked into the meeting and met Colonel Stanning. He described, in general, what the project was all about. I described that what he wanted was exactly like the kind of stuff that I had set up in London, England, for the support of airports. At that time, I had gone for three weeks and stayed for three and a half years!

I looked around the room at a number of men in uniforms and some civilians. Lo and behold, I knew half a dozen people on a very friendly basis. We got the job. We set up offices in Saigon, Bangkok, and Hickam Air Base. We set up all the systems for feeding requirement data into the system for all the various Air Force projects in Thailand and Vietnam. It was a great success. I flew over to Bangkok, negotiated a contract for an airport. It would be the first two-million dollar contract the firm ever had. {This was around 1962-1963.}

Billie's Recollections of Working in Tokyo

I went to Tokyo the end of July, then returned to Colorado State for my senior year in early September of 1961. (I went temporary duty travel "TDY," in military planes; via Hawaii for a couple more days of surfing.) When I went to Japan, I had been given a GS rating; Government Service equivalent to a Second Lieutenant in the Air Force; so that I could live in officers' quarters and get on and off the bases as necessary to get people processed.

Dad followed me to Japan and our time together was wonderful. I shared his admiration and excitement about this special country. My summer working in Japan was a memory-maker. During the brief time Dad and I had together that summer, he made a point to take me to places and introduce me to "his Japan" outside of Tokyo. We went to Kyoto (my favorite city), to Nara, and Nikko.

Dad was a wonderful guide and my husband, Dean, and I took many trips with Dad and Mother and with Dad alone. There were more trips after mother passed.

A Letter from S.A. Moe - Imperial Hotel, Tokyo

To: Mr. + Mrs. O.A. Moe, Ross, North Dakota, USA.
March 12, 1961
Dear Mom and Dad,

After a late breakfast this morning I thought I ought to sit down and write some letters. Time has passed so fast that it is hard to realize that I've been away from home for three weeks. I had pleasure on only a two-day trip. I'll be out for at least another week.

I stopped in Honolulu for a couple of days on my way through to see some of my old friends. Neil Van Sickle (from Minot) is a Brigadier General in the A.F. in Honolulu. Had a nice chat with him and was invited out to his house. Didn't have time to go, unfortunately. We are heavily sponsored by the Air Force headquarters in Honolulu for work in this area.

After spending a couple of days in Tokyo, I discovered that I would not make much progress in estimating the work we have to do in Korea, so I flew over to Seoul and spent 4 days looking over the country. It was so rainy that we were not able to do the flying-over-the-work-area so we did what we could with cars. Not an easy way to do business. The roads are very rough and muddy. It is very desolate as the Japanese cut down every tree during their 40 years of occupation.

I've been back in Tokyo for a week. We have a suite in the old part of the Imperial Hotel. It is pleasant and quiet. The room is so full of plants and stuff that it looks like an office. We are negotiating contracts which will total over half a million dollars and which will be followed by over a million more in the span of about 3 months. Worth doing some struggling for.

I'm due in Hawaii on Thursday for a meeting with the Air Force and should be in Los Angeles on Sunday. Billie is coming home from school for Easter vacation and we all intend to go to the mountains skiing for about a week.

I may have to be back here in a few months for more negotiations. The contracts I'm working on are very specialized and I know them better than anyone else in the firm. I really can't spare the time away from the office, but we have so many people to keep busy at the home office that we must keep selling.

We are also in line for a big airfield job in Saigon. I'm hoping we will get it soon. It will be a great help. Saigon is called the "Paris of the Orient" and is a very beautiful city with very nice people, too.

Must get back to work. The weather is so nice outside, I feel terribly abused! Maybe I can do some sightseeing next week.

Hope you are all well and spring is on its way.

Love,

Stan

Billie: In Appendix Four at the back of this book, read the article in the LA Herald Examiner, August 30, 1964. Dad is quoted about working in dangerous parts of the world and how he and the DMJM staff dealt with coups in such countries as Venezuela and Korea.

Passport Stamps—1970s

Switzerland, April 4, 1970
London, England, April 18, 1970
Los Angeles, California, April 18, 1970
Singapore, May 20, 1970
Saigon, July 15, 1970
Honorio Paras, September 30, 1970
Haneda, Japan, October 1, 1970
Kimpo, South Korea, October 9, 1970
Hong Kong, October 9, 1970
Manila, Philippines, October 12, 1970
Cong-Hoa, December 1970

PART XIII

1970s and 1980s

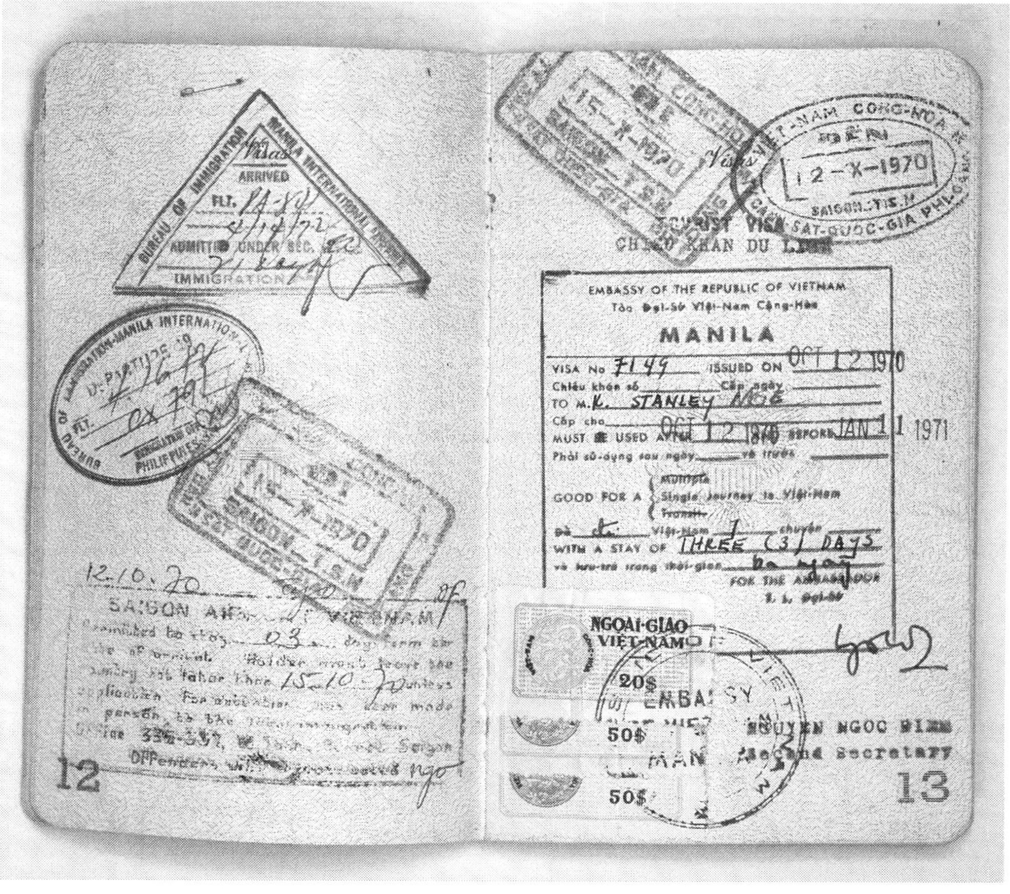

Passport Stamps—1980s

Folkestone, England, June 9, 1980
Greece, September 6, 1980
Cayman Islands, January 10, 1981
La Paz, Bolivia, May 3, 1981
Narita, Japan, September 30, 1981
Osaka, Japan, October 2, 1981
Hong Kong, October 17, 1981
Denmark, July 13, 1982
Fornebu, Norway, July 15, 1982
France, February 25, 1983
Heathrow (London), England May 16, 1983
Japan, April 9, 1984
Hong Kong, April 9, 1984
Peru, May 13, 1987
Denmark, June 27, 1988
Vancouver, BC, April 20, 1989

Note: The US stopped stamping passports upon entry in the early 80s. Some other countries followed suit. Dad still had many stamps on his passports from the fifties through the 2000s. The passports included in this book reveal only a percentage of places he traveled. Before the 1950s, Dad only needed "travel papers" issued from the government or military.

Chapter 35

Important Events of the 1970s by Billie Crouse, and the 1980s by Stan Moe

During the 1970s, Dad concentrated on major aerospace projects and special efforts at the Space Shuttle facilities in Florida and California.

He was also involved in managing the planning and design for a series of very large medical centers in Saudi Arabia. This was a particularly interesting undertaking considering the cultures he had to deal with. In addition, there were these projects:

Hospitals: Ethiopia, Egypt, Sudan
Housing: Ethiopia, Egypt, Sudan, Saudi Arabia, Okinawa
Industrial: Ethiopia, Egypt, Indonesia
Airfields: Ethiopia, Egypt, Sudan, Saudi Arabia, Okinawa
Highways: Ethiopia, Egypt, Sudan
Marine Facilities: Ethiopia, Egypt, Taiwan, Okinawa, Indonesia
Sewer Systems: Sudan, Turkey
Water Facilities: Turkey
Educational Facilities: Jordan, Korea

US Military Facilities of all types, including airfields, housing, hospitals, and marine facilities: Japan, England, Thailand, Vietnam, Okinawa

Retirement notes by Billie: Dad tried to retire three times. The first time, in 1971, he sold his interest in DMJM, but then came back as an employee after being retired six months. He consulted for DMJM off and on for another 20 years or so. In addition, over the years, he did big design projects on this drafting table for clients and family members.

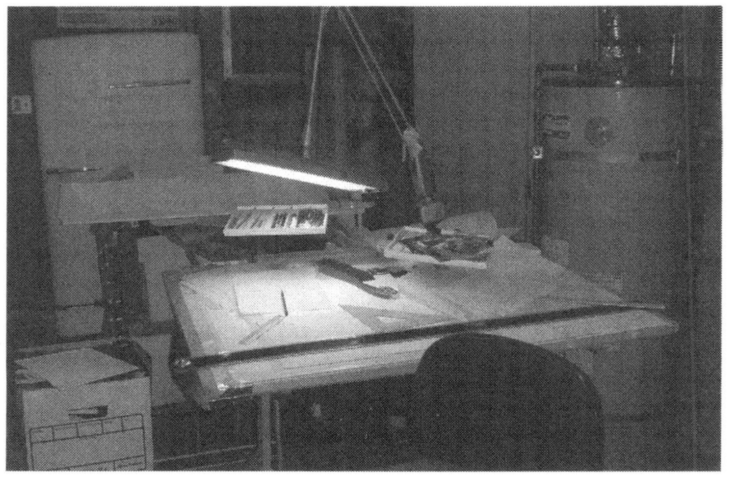

Dad's Drafting Table in the basement of our home in Los Angeles

Dad was passionate about supporting the Republican Party. He was especially involved with Reagan and active with the task force that got him elected as governor and later as president.

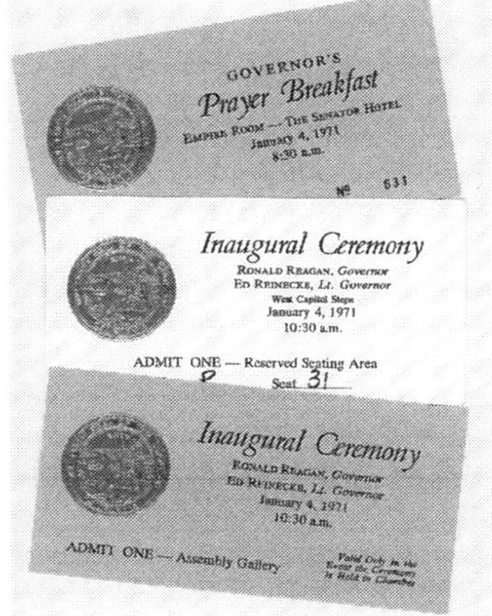

GOVERNOR'S
Prayer Breakfast
EMPIRE ROOM — THE SENATOR HOTEL
January 4, 1971
8:30 a.m.
№ 631

Inaugural Ceremony
RONALD REAGAN, *Governor*
ED REINECKE, *Lt. Governor*
West Capitol Steps
January 4, 1971
10:30 a.m.
ADMIT ONE — Reserved Seating Area
Seat 31

Inaugural Ceremony
RONALD REAGAN, *Governor*
ED REINECKE, *Lt. Governor*
January 4, 1971
10:30 a.m.
ADMIT ONE — Assembly Gallery
Valid Only in the Event the Ceremony is Held in Chamber

Invitation: Californians For Reagan – Evening of Entertainment

This event occurred at The Ambassador Hotel, October 4, 1970. Guests included: Hon. Thomas H. Kuchel, Eugene V. Klein, Mrs. Sybil Brand, George Killion, Mrs. Michael Romanoff, Armand Deutsch, Hugh Evans, Sr., Mrs. Bob Hope, Harry Karl, George Jessel, William Pereira, Jr., Mrs. Zola Siegal, and Z. Wayne Griffin.

CALIFORNIANS FOR REAGAN
cordially
invite you to attend
an evening of entertainment
with
FRANK SINATRA • DEAN MARTIN
JOHN WAYNE and BOB HOPE
honoring
GOVERNOR & MRS. RONALD REAGAN
at the
Now Grove
The Ambassador Hotel
Los Angeles, California
on
Sunday, October 4, 1970

April 17, 1975 - Kingdom of Saudi Arabia in the capital city of the Riyadh

Sweetheart,

It is a cloudy, rainy afternoon, and we have been sitting around the room without much to do and I thought it would be a good idea to bring you up to date on our activities. Our stop in Italy was pleasant and eventful. We got our work done on schedule.

We got to Riyadh at night, about midnight, and were met by Dick Meade. As usual, he found that the hotel had ignored our reservation request through the travel agent, so we stayed at Dick's house the first night. Since one of the U.S. girls in his office is a neighbor of the hotel manager, we are now pretty well set here for a while. Hotel rooms are so scarce we hear some AE people have had to sleep in taxicabs at night.

It has rained some part of every day since we arrived and is raining now. It makes it cool, but the mud on the pavement is messy. We hope to have some sun tomorrow when we get to the horse show at the airport. Dick Meade is an avid horseman—English style. So is his wife. Jumping, dressage, etc. Things are moving very slowly, but well. Everyone tries to help. Ellis Hansen and his programming people will come in on Sunday. Then we can start work in earnest.

Several DMJM people will arrive on the 25th and we can start site investigations. Good land is not obtainable in town. Due to speculation, the site is out of town in the desert nearby. We may be renting an apartment in a new building near Khalifa's office. Though we may not have many people here for very long, we will be saving $30 per day per man on hotels and will have a clean place where we can be sure of a room anytime!

April 25, 1975 (Friday)

Hon,

It is 6 o'clock in the evening. Because we are near the end of this time zone, it is now getting dark. This is the one non-working day for us, and for some of the local people in business and government offices. Though it is the equivalent of Sunday for the Muslims, we noticed a lot of activity in the more primitive native quarter when we drove through this morning. Like our stores which keep open on Sundays to extract that last dollar.

We hired a car this morning and had a driver take us to the old camel market. It is and out past some of the princes' palaces or mansions. We also drove out to a bunch of ruins in an oasis, which was once the capital before the Egyptians conquered the country in 1818. Very picturesque. The weather is warm and dry now. Quite pleasant. It will get much hotter later.

Smiles and a camera! 1980s

Tickets for the 1984 Olymic Games

Stanley's Notes on the 1980s:

Planning venues for the 1984 Olympic Games in Los Angeles provided some excitement.

Two very interesting projects afforded additional travel opportunities and management challenges during this decade. They were: directing the planning and design of an immense aircraft maintenance center in Tehran, Iran, just prior to the Shah's being exiled and deposed. Heading the development of a new "presidential" international airport in Algiers during a period when U.S. relations with Algeria were quite courteous, if not completely friendly. This project ended after 18 month's effort when the U.S. bombed Libya, a friendly neighbor of Algeria.

February 1986

Though educated and trained as both an architect and an engineer, my principal interest/responsibility was the management of large operations. I was Executive Vice President and General Manager of DMJM for many years. During this period, we grew from a moderate sized local firm to an international firm with a very large U.S. and foreign national staff.

Incidentally, the name Daniel, Mann, Johnson and Mendenhall has always been a tongue twister. The firm is now better known as DMJM or "DIMJIM." That acronym was coined by a Fortune Magazine writer who wrote an article about us in the early days of the missile programs. It was titled, "DIMJIM: Architects of the Space Age."

Fortune Magazine, August 1960

International work was one of my major areas of interest and I devoted much time to the administration of operations in project offices and branches of the company in many foreign countries during my active years with the firm.

Things have now wound down and many areas where we worked are no longer places that we would like to go or would be welcomed. These include Ethiopia, Sudan, Afghanistan, Cambodia, Vietnam and of course, Iran, where I left one month before the Shah was exiled (1979).

Airport and air base work have always been specialties of mine. This ranges from Cairo International Airport that sits on the site of Payne Field which I designed in 1943, to a new large airport in Algeria, now under construction (1986).

I have had a deep involvement in the aerospace field where I have headed up a number of project operations in the design of everything from early rocket engine test stands in the 1950s to the Titan One missile facilities throughout the U.S., to operational and maintenance facilities for the Space Shuttle, both in Florida and California.

DMJM Military and Defense Projects

Tomahawk Cruise Missile Guided System, San Diego, CA
Titan I Missile Launch, Vandenberg AFB, CA
Comsat Laboratories, Maryland
Hardened Underground Titan I Missile Silo
The Naval Aircraft Rehabilitation Facility, San Diego, CA
Rockwell Thermal Vacuum Test Chamber, Seal Beach, CA
Orbiter Maintenance and Checkout Facility, Vandenberg AFB, CA
Peace Hawk V Air Base Program, Saudi Arabia
Computer Center, Peterson AFB, CO
Space Shuttle Solid Rocket Booster, Cape Kennedy, FL
Indonesian Satellite Communication Earth Station, Indonesia
Teledyne Office and Laboratory, Northridge, CA
Military Tactical Communications Shelter
McDonnell Douglas Aeronautics Company, Huntington Beach, CA
Ship and Marine Laboratory, Carderock, MD
Lockheed Space Telescope Building, Sunnyvale, CA

PART XIV

1990s and 2000s

Passport Stamps - Stanley Moe, 1990s and 2000s

Vancouver, BC, June 20, 1991
Madrid, Spain, January 20, 1998
Madrid, Spain, September 1, 1998
Gatwick, England, April 9, 1999
Chile, (1990s)
China, (1990s)
Antarctic, (1990s)
Sorrento, Italy, (1990s)
Vancouver, BC, June 23, 2000
Birmingham, England, May 21, 2001
Madrid, Spain, May 21, 2001
Fiumicino, Italy, October 10, 2002
Taormina, Italy, October 17, 2002
China, March 25, 2002
Narita, Japan, May 7, 2003
Kansai, Japan, May 23, 2003
Heathrow (London), England, August 21, 2004
Paris, France, August 25, 2004
Frankfurt, Germany, June 16, 2005
Russia, June 23, 2005
Lisbon, Portugal, March 6, 2006
Thira, Greece, May 17, 2006
Frankfurt, Germany, May 21, 2006

Chapter 36

Items of Interest During the 1990s by Billie Crouse

The 1990s marked the bicentennial of DMJM. In anticipation of the celebration, a set of five booklets was being put together covering each decade: 1940s, 50s, 60s, 70s, and 80s. Dad had been involved in some manner in almost all the jobs since 1953 and his memory was still so sharp that he was one of the "editors"—reading and adding names and places and dates that had to be a part of the effort. It has been fun for me during this work to read Dad's letters to Mother, of course, but also to read the memos Dad wrote to all those working on the bicentennial series.

The Caboose Project, 1998-1999

For several years, Mother and Dad were involved with the Pacific Railroad Society. They both enjoyed train travel, and coming from small towns in North Dakota, they "knew" trains. In the Railroad Society, they met a fellow member named Barbara Sibert. Barbara was a real antique train-car enthusiast and had purchased a very old, rusty, torn-apart caboose: Union Pacific caboose # 25052. Dad decided he'd like to restore Barbara's caboose to its "younger glory." He undertook to help Barbara totally renovate the car; building doors, cabinets and inside trim during several months in 1998 and 1999. Half of his three-car garage was a workshop for the caboose's face lift.

Dad loved it. He would get mother up, dress and bundle her up in her wheelchair and take her to the garage to supervise his work! (Mother had had a series of strokes since 1990 and Dad was her primary caregiver.) He kept her mind stimulated by telling her about each thing he was doing.

Whenever Myra or I were visiting the folks during this time, we got to help Daddy in the garage—just like when we were little.

Years later, I contacted the Pacific Railroad Society Museum in San Dimas, California, and mailed them all Dad's notes, drawings, and photos as they had inherited the Caboose when Barbara died. If you are in California, contact the museum!

Stan in his garage workshop crafting a door for the caboose.

Stan installing the door in the caboose

PART XV

Stanley Looks Back at Stories of Risk and Adventure

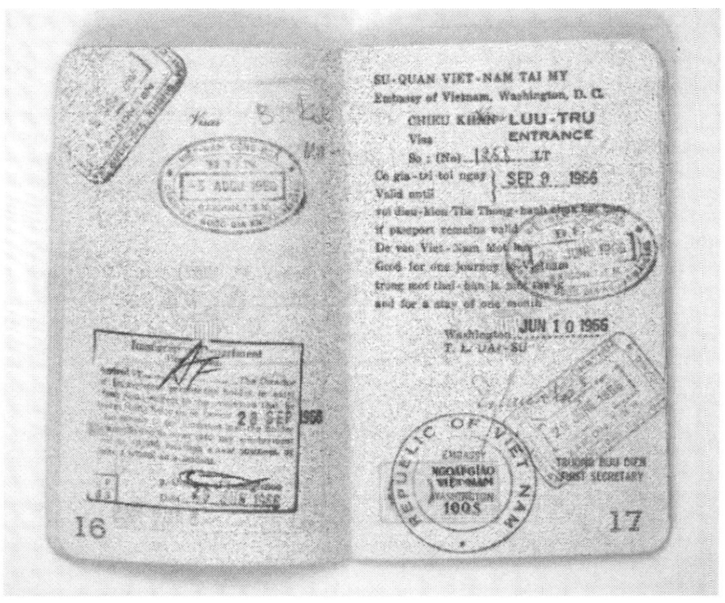

"Sometime during the night, we hear some peculiar noises. I look up and there are a couple of tall Ethiopians with spears standing above us. I thought they were giants out of my dream."

"It's quite disturbing when you go into a big stall shower that has wood slats on the floor so that you don't slip and fall, and you look at the walls and the walls are moving."

"The caterpillar was symbolic of a person who lets himself descend slowly from the sky and suddenly becomes a butterfly."

Chapter 37

Danger and a Taxicab Ride in Eritrea (1940s)

One day, Jerry Jyring said, "You know Ahma Guinea, the short fellow who works on such and such a project? He's a civil engineer and a great hunter and he'd like to take us on a hunting trip some weekend.

I said, "What do you have in mind? "

It seemed that Ahma and his son would like to go hunting with us. We would be out overnight. We would get to the hunting area late Friday night and spend Saturday in the area and return on Sunday.

I asked, "How do we get down there?"

"Well, my friend has a taxi with a stick shift and a charcoal burner."

So, Jerry and I and the driver of the taxi set out; three people in a rather small car. We pull up in front of Ahma's house. Ahma is about my height [5'6"], but his son is at least a foot taller. We're now five men in this little car, sucking in our breath.

How are we going to manage this? Then, Jerry announces that he's invited somebody else!

He shows up. Wow, okay. So, now we are six men squeezing together in this car that's feeling smaller and smaller!

I ask Jerry, "Where are we heading, Jer?"

He says, "I'm gonna check that out."

So, we take off, cozy as sardines.

We go down to an old fort. We pay a couple guys and they open up the barbed wire gates around midnight. At 2:00 in the morning, one of us asks why we're driving down this old bumpy, country road. The driver reassures us that he knows this area well. But maybe he hasn't factored in six grown man in his pint-sized car. All of sudden there's a very strange sound—the rear axle breaks!

And here we are, stranded!

Wow! So, we get out. There is nothing to do but go to sleep somewhere, and wait until morning to figure out what to do. Jerry and I are handed a blanket and are directed to find a flat piece of ground for a bed. Well, Jerry and I are about the same height. We try to sleep on the ground under a blanket so small; we have to lie spoon to spoon. He would turn over and so, then, I had to turn over and vice versa. Anyone watching us would have gotten a good laugh.

Sometime during the night, we hear some peculiar noises. I look up and there are a couple of tall Ethiopians with spears standing beside us. They must have thought we were nuts! I thought they were giants out of my dream. Anyway, they move on, the night wears on and daylight comes. Somebody's cooked a little meal (a poor excuse for a breakfast). I pick at it and then, we decide to go hunting.

"What are we going to do for guns?"

"Well," Jerry says. "I've got an American, lever-action hunting gun that I got from the recreation department."

Ahma, having been a military officer, also has access to a gun. So, we all go out and walk and walk and walk. Oh! All at once, the grass is up to our chins! Tall, thin, hard grass...WITH BUGS!

I say, "To heck with this."

I have some gauze from the first aid kit with me (it turns out, we all have some, maybe for mosquito netting). We have the presence of mind to wrap ourselves in a kind of netting to keep the bugs from biting. I take a picture of this and will later send it home.

Doris said that Billie took this photo to pre-school at University of Minnesota for "show and tell" and she said her father was a bride!

During the morning we see two fellows with a truck. Hurrah! They are British communication's officers and they have a big spool of wire in the back of their truck. They're checking up on the telephone lines that are up around here. There aren't that many telephone lines, but these officers make periodic trips through here all the time, because people would steal the wire off the poles and these fellows would climb the poles and patch the lines.

We tell them about our car. They say they're heading South but will be coming back tonight.

They were emphatic, "You gotta get back to Asmara!"

It's true, no one knows where we are! We hadn't even told anybody we were leaving. Six of us crazy people. We want to make sure they will come back to help us.

Our new friends say, "Oh, we'll come back."

Later that day, they do come back. They say, "Okay, now we're going to get you back."

"How will you get us all back?"

"We'll tow you, it's a powerful truck."

These guys take their wire and make a strong cable out of it and they loop it around the front axle of our taxi. Some of us jump at the chance to ride in the back of the truck and they tow us! But they also surprise us. One of them has a rifle and he shoots rabbits on the way back. You know, shoots out the window, stops, picks up the rabbit, moves on, then repeats.

I had not planned that we would be shooting game in this way or being towed in our driver's poor taxi, which I didn't mention had hydraulic brakes. And, in the course, during the towing, the hydraulic brake line breaks.

Anyway, we finally get somewhere near Asmara and somehow, find our way back into town.

And nobody else there ever knew about our crazy trip!

Four cans of kerosene made up my moat. **— Stan**

Chapter 38

African Adventures...with Bugs!

Now let me lay down the groundwork for this story. When I was in Africa on a project in Eritrea, I had shipped out as an employee of Johnson, Drake and Piper, a firm out of Minneapolis. The client really was the U.S. Army Corps of Engineers who was responsible for this very large project that involved Egypt, Eritrea, Sudan, and some other points that were pretty important in the World War II effort.

One day, someone came in and asked me what I knew about slaughterhouses. "Well, I don't know anything about slaughterhouses."

"Didn't you live in Minneapolis? There'd be slaughterhouses all over St. Paul." "Well, I don't know about them, anyway."

The long and short of it is: they were transporting cattle from Ethiopia, and they needed someplace to handle the processing for consumption by the British forces that were occupying Eritrea. So, I said, "What do you people have in mind?"

"We have a lot of space but it's a warehouse. I'll give you the name of the town." It was a small town outside of Asmara about four or five miles. I got a car and driver and went down and looked it over.

It's a nice compound there, very nice building. They told me to be sure to look at building number Five—that would be converted to a place for processing meat. So, I went there and looked inside. There were two big heaps, conical heaps of something.

I had an Italian with me who spoke English and I said, "What are those?"

He said, "Those are peanuts. They are sorting them here."

I asked, "What are they used for?"

He said, "I don't know."

He probably did know but wouldn't tell me.

I walked up close and looked at the pile and I saw that all of a sudden, there was motion in one of the piles. "What is that motion?" I asked.

He said. "Bugs, I guess."

Well, anyway, I looked the place over and took the measurements of the building and so on. I went back to the office the next day and I told them that I'd seen a building that was pretty small, but it might be converted to a butchery and meat processing plant.

Then I said, "Could you tell me anything more about the food processing around here in Asmara?"

He said, "There's an oil company here. They're making cooking oil."

And I said, "I wonder what they use."

He says, "I understand they are using peanuts."

So I start a little pokin' around to see if I could find anyone that could make a connection like I was making about these peanuts that were probably being processed into cooking oil that was being used throughout the area for people like ourselves…and which contained bugs."

Creepy Crawlies

So much for that one. I gotta tell you another one. A story about other critters. Insects in Africa were a nuisance. If you walk into some deep grass there were flies around and you'd have to have netting over your head or they'd just drive you crazy. You learn to stay away from grassy grounds, stay out in wide open spaces in the desert.

I found later, when I moved up to Cairo and into a rooming house near the office, there were other kinds of insects—namely cockroaches. It's quite disturbing when you go into a big stall shower that has wood slats on the floor so that you don't slip and fall, and you look at the walls and the walls are moving. Just covered with cockroaches. They seem to like it where it's nice and damp. They grew to a spectacular size.

I finally found a room where I could have a bed, and clean surroundings. One night, I'm in my bed in the corner of the room. There was a construction worker type with a bed nearby. He came in from someplace with a little lamp by his bed and he turned the light on and screamed! I thought, oh my gosh, he must have been attacked! I went over to him and he says, "Look at that!"

There were two great big cockroaches standing by his shaving brush which he hadn't cleaned off and, well, it was sitting on the table next to his lamp there, and the cockroaches were eating off of his shaving brush, like animals up at the manger eating hay!

Another time, I found a room in a place. I didn't like to run around with no clothes on in semi-private places, so I had a dressing gown type thing made out of seersucker. I would hang it up on the wall and that night I had eaten an American candy bar, which were hard to come by. On this occasion, I had the wrapper in my robe pocket. I went over to take the thing down to wear. I reached into the pocket and it was full of bugs. I got rid of that robe in a hurry.

During 1943, I would go down to Sudan and I had an encounter with ants that had gotten in my bed. I found a solution to that. I went into the kitchen of this small hotel to find some tin cans. I poured a little kerosene and set the legs of my pipe-frame cot into the cans. The ants didn't go anywhere near my bed. I was surrounded by a moat. Four cans of kerosene made up my moat.

CHAPTER 39

Goldsby's Golf Course

In 1952, Joe Goldsby was going to the U.S. from Japan with his wife, Barbara. That's the first leave they'd had since Armistice. He was one of the original groups of U.S. military who went into Japan and was assigned to go from village to village with Japanese translators to talk to the local people and try to make everything peaceful, quiet and as pleasant as possible. He'd go into homes and take over the responsibility of putting together a master plan and program of funding for the next fiscal year which would begin on the first of July, 1953. I'd see all these requests that would come in from the various commands around the world including the Philippines for various funds for vital projects.

One of them, a very dramatic one, came from the Philippines, north of Manila on the end of Luzon—and greatly famous for its Subic Bay down below which was a petroleum center that was shared by the Air Force, the Army, and the Navy. The hill country there was the site of an erosion control project. And of course, Joe Goldsby went through a very flowery description of what they were going to do. I don't know how much money they asked for, but seven years later, I was at a meeting with an Air Force general who had become a good friend when we were in England. Robert H. Curtin, at that time, was a colonel and became a major general (two stars).

I can remember Curtin telling us at a gathering that he liked to play golf and he said, "You know, it's amazing how much money you can get for erosion control. Everyone wanted to keep the landscape protected. You know, there's lots of water over here and... A great way to fight erosion is to build golf courses."

I realized that a nice sounding purpose can help get the financing.

✧ **Billie: Among Dad's stack of friends' business cards was one of Robert Harrman Curtin, Brigadier General, U.S. Air Force. I looked up his interesting story and found that he had died March 12, 2007.**

CHAPTER 40

Men Who Fly

One night, when I lived in Japan, I had a visit from a colonel from the states who had never been to Japan before. He and I were to fly down to a big port, way down in Kyushu—Nagasaki. Right near there was an air force base.

I said, "Colonel, we gotta stop at this place and that place on the way down."

The only thing they had assigned us was a CE-3 set up for military use and industrial travel. Pilots were trying to build up flying time. We landed at a base and suddenly, we heard a BANG! And then we were bouncing like crazy! My colonel friend got on the phone and called a few of the control towers, really getting into what was going on.

With a southern accent, he yelled, "Why the hell didn't ya'll tell me that you'd taken up the P-S-C?" (perforated steel planking WW2 Marston Mat). It was stacked over to one side! The plane had just bumped over the pile of PSC. Phew! What an experience!

Well, anyway, we finally got down to a base nearby Nagasaki. The Colonel said, "I'll tell you what. It was my first assignment over here from the Pentagon. I think I'm gonna find another way to travel around."

Joe Goldsby was a big man and he never would fly. When Joe told me that he and Frank Barber were going to take their leave (the first leave they had each had since they went over there right after the war) he chose to go on one of the President Line ships. When they got back from that trip, and he did come back by ship, I had been doing some flying around because every time I had a project, I seemed to be on military aircraft taking me from place to place. (This might have been sometime in the eighties.) They weren't comfortable and they didn't put a lot of stock in just how careful they were.

Sometime during the years that we knew Joe and Barbara Goldsby, who were great hosts who offered southern cooking, we often attended small dinner parties they had for people they had contact with.

At one dinner, I asked Joe, "How come you don't fly, Joe?"

"Well," he said, "I made my living before the war, flying planes. Flying circus." He'd fly the planes around and go to county fairs and all that kind of stuff. "It would take up all my time." Then he pulled out a decoration with a silkworm on it. It meant he had been saved by a parachute. He'd been flying two-engine planes when they changed over to single-engine.

Uncle Lee's Flying Stories as told to Billie

My mother's youngest brother, Uncle Lee, spent a lot of time with me because I was the first baby born in our family. He gave me several of his WW2 patches (which, in later years, I passed on to his son and daughter). I clearly remember, as a little girl, the stories of the P-38.

I loved to look at his patches and the pins that he wore on his uniform and even at age 3, 4 or 5, I'd ask him to tell me the stories about them. One that fascinated me was a pin with a worm depicted on it. He told me it was a very special worm, called a silkworm. And the reason the silkworm was so important to the Air Force was that the parachutes that saved men's lives (and thus my Uncle Lee's life) were made of silk.

He told me how he was shot down in Belgium and had to find shelter so he wouldn't get caught by the enemy and how this nice family hid him in their home for several months. (As I type this it brings tears to my eyes.)

When he got back home to America, he received many awards, but the one I liked best as a child was that silkworm pin. So, Uncle Lee told me how the silkworm makes the silk. Another thing he told me about was the Caterpillar Clubs that were for WW2 pilots who had jumped from planes. The caterpillar was symbolic of a person who lets himself descend slowly from the sky and suddenly becomes a butterfly.

Uncle Lee opened a hardware store near Grandpa Anderson's General store in Stanley which was seven plus miles from Ross. I worked for Uncle Lee during two of my college breaks. I remember counting nails and screws, which were sold in bulk back then, helping him with the annual inventory. He was a great boss. Lee spent most of his working life with Ace Hardware.

"Wasn't Uncle Don a pilot too?" Myra asked her dad.

Yes, my brother Don was a pilot and his situation was quite interesting. He decided he liked to fly. He was working as an automobile salesman before the war. They had tested the young men to see how they would do when they joined The Air Corps (1939-1947) which later became the Air Force. They'd look at a man's health and they said no to Don as he had a heart murmur and they couldn't invest the time and money if somebody's health wasn't good. So, it seemed he'd be assigned to be a soldier carrying a gun. Don was bound and determined he was going to do something else and that something was to fly!

He saved up some money and enrolled in flying school, getting enough training to get a pilot's license to fly heavy planes. Now, he went out to join the Air Corps and was accepted. He got to fly in the United States.

I asked him what kind of stuff he did.

"Well," he said, "you won't believe it." This was just about the time that the Eisenhower jacket first came out. And officers throughout the whole United States were eager to have one. Don said, "Eisenhower had one, and we will have one too," people would say. You'd be surprised how many trips I made just hauling Eisenhower jackets for that general over here and the one over there. The flights carried more, but Eisenhower jackets were a part of the cargo."

Don's one and only international assignment was an extremely dangerous one in Burma flying "The Hump." (Kathy mentions the following in her account of her father, Don Moe, in this book. "The Hump" is the nickname allied pilots gave the airlift operation that crossed the Himalayas between India and China. It was the most dangerous airlift route because they didn't have pressurized planes and they were carrying fuel. It was the only way to supply Chinese forces fighting Japan. A large percentage of pilots flying fuel to the Chinese didn't make it.)

I asked Don, "What're you doing? You're hauling stuff around over there?"

"Well, besides the fuel to China," he said, "we also hauled hay."

I said, "Hay? What for?"

"Bales of hay for Chiang Kai-shek's horses! If you're a big general, you had to have big horses and big amounts of hay!"

After the war, Don had some trouble figuring out what he would do next. He wanted to fly but needed more training in order to fly commercial planes. Back in North Dakota, he went back to the flying school where he'd trained before. He was quite upset to find that the flying school had burned down and there were no plans for miles around to build another.

Don went back into the automobile business. But he didn't go back to the company he had worked for before the war, he worked for a small company that sold Buicks. He sold one after another and by carefully saving his money, he was able to borrow enough money to buy an agency; at first, a small one, but finally, he ended up with a big one. The biggest one in Minot. He built a very good reputation and was president of Dodge Dealer's advertising. And, he got a special permit to sell both Dodge and Chrysler cars on the same property (which wasn't done back then) and he was very successful. He went on to enjoy his life; the automobile business, his wife, Helen, and daughters, Kathy and Marilyn.

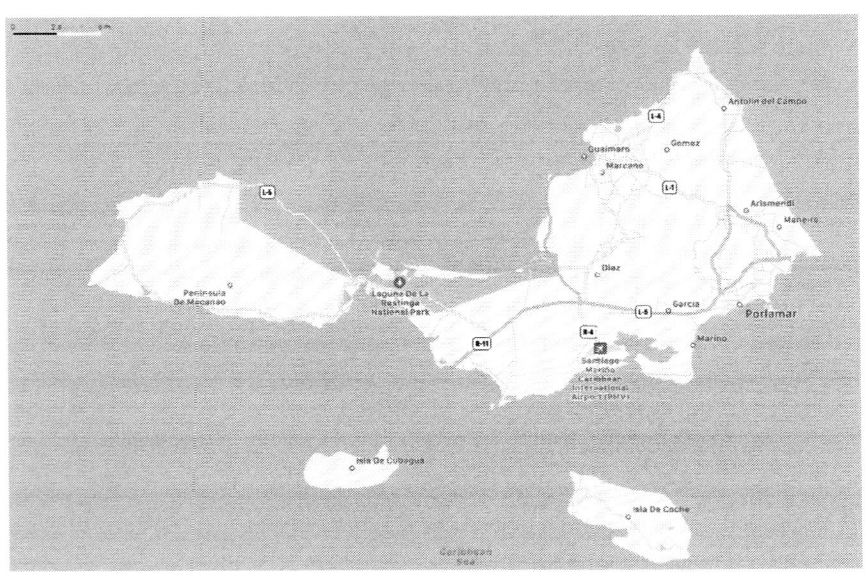

Map of the Island of Margarita, Venezuela

CHAPTER 41

Frank Sherman Story

With so many civil engineering operations scattered throughout the world they needed somebody with administrative ability and technical knowledge to coordinate international activities. I had been doing a lot of those things because I had been overseas and as general manager, I had the overall responsibility to see that things got done and done correctly. Phil Daniel had done this himself when we first set up the operations in London and Tokyo.

Tokyo was the first overseas adventure/activity the firm ever had. As time went on, a person by the name of Frank Sherman appeared on the scene in Los Angeles. Frank was a blustery type but had an attractive personality. I found that he had worked in Spain for a firm out of Chicago which happened to be the same firm that Sven Svenson had worked for in Venezuela. Sven, by the way, was working in the Tokyo office where he had taken over for me at the end of the summer of '61.

Anyway, Frank came to call on us and I hired him. Frank probably could be best described as a bull in a china shop. His blustery manner quite often did not fit very well into handling situations of management. Technically, he was very competent. We had a project in Venezuela to design and supervise the construction of a water pipeline from the coast out to the island of Margarita, a resort area. However, this area wasn't comparable to those in Los Angeles and we began to question the competence of the contractors. We wondered how well they were following the plans and so on.

So, Frank said, "I'll go out and check on 'em."

Not too much later, I got a very proper letter from a top government official about the behavior of Mr. Frank Sherman who was very insulting in his manner. I called Frank when he got back to town to find out what this was all about.

"Well," he said, "I got over there and found that the plans called for dredging—necessary to flatten the ridge on the ocean bottom in order that the pipeline would lie flat. A pipeline can't move up and down." And he said, "I found out that what they were doing wasn't right."

I said, "I don't know anything about this kind of thing."

Frank explained that he found out that to use gear where you have a pressure tank in the deep water, lessons were needed, and people needed to train on this equipment.

Frank was staying in a very nice resort hotel on the coastline of Venezuela and he went out to the hotel pool and was doing "training" in the swimming pool. This was upsetting all the elegant guests in this fancy hotel!

Then Frank went out to check the pipeline. He rented a boat. They did not have the pipeline flat, but it was going up and down hill.

Then, as Frank suspected, there was some collusion between the government officials and the contractors. Perhaps they overlooked things and maybe they were changing money back and forth. So, Frank had talked with the powers that be and made some notes.

I said, "Frank, I want you to do things that upset fewer people and then you'll get better results."

Well, shortly after that, there was a coup in Venezuela (when someone ousts the guy in charge and takes over the head of the government.) The interesting part was we got our regular monthly checks for services during all the regime changes. They never missed paying a bill.

Frank decided that he ought to look into a water-well development program in Northern Thailand. The drill rigs were scattered around the area and Frank Sherman wanted to oversee them. He could fly up to a place and get a big car and driver and go look at the area. Some of the sites were scattered quite far apart. He would just set off in a Land Rover, making a safari across the country. The interesting thing was that, though their communications by telephone were limited, there was a system that worked for people in the jungle or remote areas. They passed information by telling stories along the way—through the grapevine!

A story about a wild American engineer stopping in and seeing the water drilling operation was circulating, and Earl Young, a very competent fellow working on wells, heard it. He was living in a house trailer on the back of his truck. He was drilling two or three wells when he heard about this wild American that would be coming around with his convoy. Earl was all prepared—getting all tidied up—putting on a shirt with French cuffs, sitting at a card table under a little awning outside his trailer, waiting for Frank to come.

Frank crashed through the bushes coming into the area. He parked his car and walked up. Earl stood up and said, "Frank Sherman, I presume." You know, like Livingston was supposed to have said to Stanley when he found him in Africa? "Doctor Livingstone, I presume."

Frank poured himself a martini and Earl humored him. But Frank's bullying behavior was a constant challenge.

Finally, one day, Irv Mendenhall was quite upset by Frank's behavior because Frank had been making real loud statements that all the people back in Washington, D.C., in USAID, were "this bad thing and that bad thing, etc." Frank Sherman had said, "I want to punch the chief engineer in the nose."

You don't make statements like that when your agency is paying your bills. So, I called Frank and said, "Frank, you have to go."

He did, Frank moved on, and, low and behold, he was hired for a big convention center project in Detroit or Chicago.

Chapter 42

A Big Hunting Adventure!

The bighorn sheep head that I have in my office upstairs brings back memories of a very interesting experience. Harry Blu and I hunted together in various parts of the United States and Canada. He found a very highly regarded hunting guide and outfitter up in British Columbia. Harry and I had made reservations to fly up to Vancouver, British Columbia. Then we proceeded to a small town a little farther north where we would take a small plane and continue up to the hunting area.

Harry arrived. Everything was on schedule. There was quite a little excitement in Vancouver because I discovered, that by mistake, somebody had put my rifle in his case and it was going down the belt headed for Alaska. I retrieved it, so I had my guns. I always take two along with me. I wanted to have an extra, in case something went wrong.

We finally got up to a little town in BC and stayed the night. It was November 14th, and on the 15th, we were supposed to be going out to the small airport where a "bush pilot" would take us up to the hunting area where we'd meet the guide.

After the trip, Harry wrote the details of our adventure in an article, including this excerpt: "Leo Rutledge's hunting right in Management Area 27 includes the head-waters of the Prophet River and all but the most northern fork of the Muskwa River. No other single region in British Columbia has produced the number of record 'Stone Rams' as has the famous Prophet-Muskwa sheep range."

We looked out the window early in the morning and saw there was snow. During the night, a blizzard had come up and there was a foot or more all over the place. Things weren't working out quite the way we had hoped, so we took a taxi out to the airport to see the terminal where the private bush pilots would pick up their passengers and we discovered that there was going to be a delay. But they had radio contact with the guides up in the hunting area. After much fussing around, we finally took off in the afternoon. The sky was filled with snow as we were flying. I don't know how the pilot could even find his way around, but he did go up one river, then turned back and said, "Oh, this is the wrong river." So, we continued to fly and finally landed on a sandbar in a river. I can't remember whether we had skis on the plane in addition to wheels, but we landed and got out. It was bitter cold!

On the way we had seen wild animals; goat and sheep on the mountainsides—just waiting! When we arrived on the sandbar, the guide was there with people to take care of us. They had sleds pulled by horses to haul stuff around.

The guide said, "I'm sorry you have missed a day of hunting, but we'll try to make it up." He introduced us to two young men who were to be our personal guides. One was twenty, the other was nineteen. They didn't look very impressive to us, but anyway, they were our guides and they took the horses.

I had just had my surgery in Singapore for my prostate. It was in 1972 and I was 58.

✧ ***Dad was in Singapore on business and had serious issues with his prostate. He had a hunting trip scheduled in a few weeks and THAT trip was very IMPORTANT. He saw no reason why both could not stay on the calendar.***

Harry wrote, "We hurriedly packed what we thought we would need into two small paniers (baskets) and sent the rest of our stuff to base camp with Leo. Half an hour later, we were on the trail with our two guides, Bob Welch and Barry Thompkins and our train of ten pack horses."

Well, we spent two weeks on our horses. In addition to the horses that we rode, there were the guides' horses, and pack horses that carried all the equipment; tents, food, all the other stuff needed for the two weeks' trip. We went farther and farther up into the mountains and it continued to snow.

The outfitter apologized because he said, "I had a cook arranged who would go over to the camp in the daytime and he'd cook all the meals in the camp while you're out hunting." Well, the fella' got sick.

Since it was November, we rode even when it was getting dark. The two boys knew the areas among the trees and they quickly cleaned out an area and soon we had a tent set up; of white silk with a canvas floor. It was the main tent and primitive, but they put a little stove and other necessary things inside it, including kerosene for lamps at night. They put up another little tent for Harry and me. They cut down spruce boughs and laid them on top of the snow and then put the canvas on top of the boughs with our bedrolls on the top. It was quite an experience. They knew the area so well they even knew there was a railing through the trees where they could tie up the horses when saddling them and getting us on them.

Harry wrote, "The horses were hobbled (tied two legs together) and turned loose each night to forage on willow leaves and what grass they could paw out of the snow."

The second day we were there, the main guide said we ought to go out and get some camp meat. I said, "Like what?"

"Oh, we can find a cow moose." So, we rode and rode and all of a sudden there was a cow moose up on the hillside—a large animal. We got it, skinned it down, cut the roast out of it and the rest was left for the grizzly bears. It was interesting.

✧ ***Billie: The word "interesting" was a favorite word of Dad's. It was the response to "I'm not sure I agree," "I think I will not respond," "I don't want to talk about this anymore," and a number of other times when a response was called for but he didn't want to be the one to say more.***

We had licenses for caribou, moose, sheep, but not goat. We didn't go up quite high enough for the goat. They like rocky, and this was not rocky. This was grassy hillside and goats don't like that, they like rocks – it's more secure for them. Harry got a moose and I got a moose. The big antlers hanging out in the garage were from that hunting trip. Harry's were bigger than mine. The young guides had a tape measure and they kept notes on whose was whose. They had an organization called the Boone & Crockett Society and they ranked the size of trophies, whether they're a certain class. The one Harry got was classified in the society guidebook as being exceptional quality. I had a lesser one. The boys took the hide down too.

Another day, a bunch of caribou came through camp. Big hunting. We could have shot them right there, but we were waiting for trophies. There's a new crop of antlers every year. Moose and sheep have horns. They keep those all their life and get bigger all the time. But antelope, deer, moose, and elk—get new antlers every year.

We took off, each of us with a different guide. We could see way up high, miles or so up the mountain, that there were caribou. My guide, the nineteen-year-old, a hardworking young kid, said, "That thing up there? I think I see a trophy." I think it was a "double shovel"; the antlers look like they are shovels that stick out right over the head. Smaller antlers were on the same stem.

Then finally, the guide said, "We've gone as far as we can with the horses, the snow's too deep. We'll walk the rest of the way."

So, we lightly tied up the horses to a bush, then climbed and climbed. Finally, I got myself in a position with my own stump to hide behind. The guide said, "Pick that particular one, that's the real trophy one. You want to get him."

Something happened at that point. Some other animal scooted through the area and all of a sudden, the game were moving all over the place. That's when I fired. I shot the wrong one. Not the super trophy. I got the lesser one. I'm not licensed to shoot two. I only had a license for one. Anyway, the young kid takes an axe, cuts the antlers off, skins the thing down, and saves a roast. I can't remember just how he preserved it, but he put it on his backpack. We headed down to where the horses were. To get downhill, we used the skin with the hair, sat on the skin, and rode it down the hill to where we had left the horses.

When we got to the horses, I found that my horse had gotten unhappy with the saddle and kicked the saddle off. In the saddle back, I had left my camera and lenses for both my cameras. All were broken.

On the way down the hill, we walked behind our horses and held onto the horse's tail so we wouldn't lose our balance and fall. After we finally got down into camp, it was dark. Once there, I discovered that Harry had been successful too. He had gotten one of the big animals. The next day we were going to go for a sheep.

In the morning, we rode and rode. Again, the snow got too deep for the horses, so we walked. I couldn't believe I was doing this when I was 58 years old and right after having had prostate surgery. We saw the sheep way up there, mountainside. We had another problem, however: it had begun to rain off and on and at night there'd be avalanches where the rains fall and then sheets of snow slide down the mountains. So, we're walking up the mountain with loose shale-like rock. There's brush on occasional rocks. I was very careful with my footing. I didn't want to lose my balance. If I fell, it would be down a very steep slope. Finally, after much fussing, our guides pulled out something called a back-pack board. It was a kind of a plywood thing they strapped on. They could carry stuff on such boards. We navigated until about 4 o'clock at which time we saw two sheep.

The guide whispered, "Make up your mind what you want. Harry, you wanna take the one on the right? Stan, you take the left one. Shoot at the same time. If you shoot one ahead of the other, you'll spook then."

After a moment, I shot right down the hillside. Harry's sheep just walked away. The Guide said, "Harry, you must've missed! Stan, wait a minute, there's something wrong with Harry's gun."

The guide borrowed my rifle which was a brand-new Weathersby 300 and said, "Let me go over the hill and see what happened. We're going to get that animal before it goes away."

He fired. So, Harry shot. At that moment, I heard a racket. An avalanche was coming down the hillside. We ran about as fast as we could to get out of the way of the avalanche that also carried our two sheep as it barreled down the hillside.

Then all was quiet. This was not a great, deep slide. Just snow moving fast and sloshy. Believe it or not, we found the sheep, their feet sticking out someplace down the hill where the avalanche had lost its volume. We headed back to camp to obtain the roasts and the sheep heads for mounting.

We had three animals each. One more day would go by and finally we rode over another half day to meet with the outfitter. He had another camp way back in the woods: very nice, with bunks, a shower, and more. There must have been half a dozen hunters including Harry and myself. We settled with him on the trophies. I decided I wanted my caribou hide processed – with the hair on and I wanted my antlers from the moose and antlers from the caribou and the head of the sheep.

The trophy head was beautiful, and the horns made almost a complete circle. The meat from hunting/fishing was always eaten and the family had purses, wallets, slippers, and jackets from the hides.

All the meat had been kept cold/frozen in the snow drifts. Back in Vancouver, we went to a market, had it all cut, packed up nicely, and frozen for the trip home. We had roast sheep, moose, and caribou at home for many dinners. It kept well.

It was quite a trip. I got some nice pictures of Harry. By the way, he's a great writer. He wrote a story about our trip and sent it to some hunting magazines in hopes that it would be published.

His article appeared in an issue of *International Rifle Association* national magazine. It was a story with a photograph I took of him on horseback crossing a river there.

A couple years later, Harry said, "I really got a hot deal to get a big brown bear in Alaska-Kodiak Peninsula. It's going to cost three-thousand bucks."

And I said, "No, thanks, I don't need a bear."

Well, he went and took his wife, Hazel, along with him. I remember being at their house after that trip and seeing "his bear" as a whole hide with a head as a rug there. He had antlers and the head of a sheep. Rather like my office.

Harry and I did go on other small, deer-hunting trips down in Texas.

The Ram's head prominently placed in Stan's office

TWA

CHAPTER 43

A Striking Story!

Italy in the Spring

An overseas construction project took me to Italy on several occasions. My client had offices near the west coast of Livorno, which for the traveler, required a short flight from Rome on Air Italia or a long trip by the "Rapido," an express train. In either case, the city of Pisa was the most convenient destination, requiring only a short drive by rental car to a fine seaside hotel in Tirrenia, which was only a few miles from my client's office.

On one occasion, I had arranged my return trip to Los Angeles in the usual way. The short flight from Pisa to Rome, change to TWA for the leg to New York City, and from there to L.A. The trip would be quite leisurely, with an 8 am departure and a 5 pm arrival in LA. However, I found this was not to be the case this time.

After a leisurely breakfast at my hotel, I drove to the airport and checked in my car at the Hertz counter. The airline check-in counter was only across the lobby of the small terminal building. Because there was usually a line of travelers to check in, I felt fortunate this morning since there was no one ahead of me. I walked up, dropped my bag on the platform and produced my ticket. The airline's clerk quickly explained why there was no line. He said, "Didn't you listen to the radio? ***The airline is on strike!"*** He further said that if I were to rush to the downtown railway station, I might get the Rapido to Rome.

He called to a taxicab driver lounging by the coffee counter and said, "Luigi, rush this man to the railway station."

There ensued a hair-raising drive through the narrow streets of Pisa. We double-parked at the station. Luigi grabbed my bag and we raced across the lobby to the ticket window. They were all shuttered since everyone was having their morning coffee! Luigi rushed me to the train platform without the formality of checking with the guard at the turnstile. The Rapido was just starting to pull out. Luigi told me to buy my ticket on the train and threw my bag through an open window. I stuffed his hand with lire, jumped on the train and we were off.

The conductor was not happy about my not having a ticket but did sell me one, brightening considerably at the small tip I gave him. It had to be small because my stock of lire was diminishing. I hadn't anticipated the extra-cost items that were developing and hadn't changed dollars that morning.

My arrival at the Rome rail station presented me with new problems. I counted my lire and found that I had just enough for a taxi to someplace not too far away. Knowing that I had missed my scheduled TWA flight to NY, I decided I could go to the TWA office in downtown Rome. They had been helpful in the past and could help me with my cash problem. They would either cash a check or change money in consideration of my Ambassador Club membership. There is a sizable bank in the Rome railway station, but it was closed for some reason. Not daring to deplete my lire stock, I did not have a porter carry my heavy bag across the plaza to the taxi stand.

The TWA attendant was most helpful. They said I could get one of their flights to NY that was leaving in about an hour and a half from the Rome airport. He then also booked me on a flight from NY to LA. But no, he couldn't help me with my money problem because there was a ***bank strike***. He said he hoped I had some greenbacks and he called me a cab and instructed the driver to rush me to the airport.

We got to the Rome airport in record time and the driver was all smiles when I paid in dollars in lieu of lire. I had only very large bills, so he made out quite well.

When we got into the lobby of the terminal, I was dumbfounded to find that all the airlines' name signs had been removed from the check-in counters. The government had just decreed that only numbers would be used to identify counters and furthermore, to complicate matters, some counters were used to check in flights for more than one airline. Also, they hadn't yet installed a directory to indicate which counter to use.

I then dashed over to my usual source of help for weary travelers, the TWA Ambassador Club. Unfortunately, the hostess didn't know which counter to use for TWA check-ins. She recommended that I look at the lines and if I saw a very tall man with a leather jacket, I should get in that line as he was going to NY on the same flight I hoped to get on.

"Find a tall man with a Leather Jacket."

I found the tall man and dutifully got into line and inched forward. I kept looking at my watch and now knew that any hope to get to NY today was in vain. When I got within about fifty feet of the counter, I had another disappointment. I saw a large sign saying that the departure tax was now 1500 lire and they would only accept lire. Since I had none, I would now have to go to the money changing window. I didn't want to lose my place in line so I asked a nice matronly American lady behind me if she would watch my bag and push it forward while I went to the bank.

The bank must have been a hundred yards away. When I got there, I took out my travelers checks and asked for some lire. The clerk said he was sorry but that I had to present my passport as identification. I had left my briefcase and passport with the lady in line. Fortunately, the line had hardly moved in my absence. There were several Italian construction workers in line who were probably on their way to the Middle East and they had over-sized suitcases that created an excess baggage problem. They had to wait for their bosses to show up to pay the excess charges and the line was held up accordingly.

When I reached the counter, the attendant looked at my ticket, slapped his forehead and said, "Mama mia, you have missed your flight! It left long ago!"

I urged him to call the gate and check on the flight. He grumbled a bit, but did call and learned that, for some reason, the flight had not left and that they were expecting me.

I now had only the little formality of presenting my passport at the immigration window and I could rush to the gate. I found there was only one window open and there was a short line waiting to be checked out. A lady just ahead of me was having a problem with her papers. The immigration clerk pulled down a window shade, closed the door and headed off to check with his superiors. Though I felt it was a useless exercise, I did run the length of the concourse to reach the gate where my plane might be. In the hustle I lost my eyeglasses from my jacket pocket.

They were waiting for me at the gate and sure enough the plane was still sitting on the apron. The girls said there had been a ***baggage-handlers strike*** the hour before and so the plane had been held up! I got on board and endured the scowls of some of the other passengers who must have thought I was responsible for the delayed departure. We finally taxied to the end of the runway and were about to start the takeoff run when the captain announced that there would be a further delay since ***the air traffic controllers had called a strike!*** The flight attendants served a round of free drinks to alleviate the pain as we waited about a half hour before the strike was called off.

The flight to NY was uneventful. I loafed around the terminal at JFK for about an hour before taking my flight to LA where I arrived in time for leisurely dinner with the family. It had been a busy day and made me wonder why so many people reported on the glamour and excitement usually associated with foreign business travel.

I experienced more than two million miles of air travel before I retired, and much of it before jet aircraft were used. I visited more than one hundred countries. Generally, people, both in the United States and abroad, were quite helpful. No other mode of travel seems to have such dedicated people serving the traveling public.

PART XVI

Memories of Stan Moe from Family and Friends

CHAPTER 44

Billie's Memories of her Dad

A New Cradle for Judy: December 1941

For Christmas of 1941, when I was 2-1/2 years old, I received a doll — one that lives with me still. Her name is Judy and she has little magnets in each of her hands so she can hold bobby pins, safety pins and paperclips. Judy and I received matching wardrobes. Mother made many of my clothes and also Judy's. Judy still wears some of hers.

Judy was one of my closest friends and I loved to play with her which is apparent by her stubby fingers (I wore them down). Not only were Judy's clothes like mine, but we had the same hair-do—short, a little below our ear lobes, a slight curl at our cheeks and bangs with "a little curl, right in the middle of our foreheads."[4] She was a wonderful playmate!

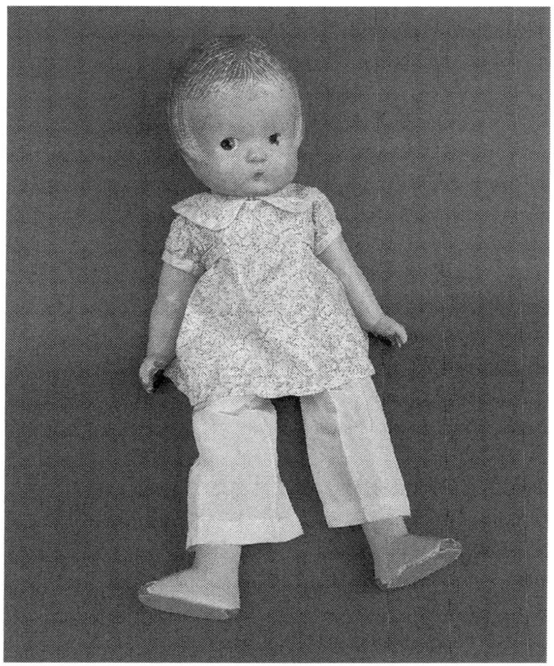

My friend Judy

4. From a nursery rhyme that goes: "There was a little girl that had a little curl right in the middle of her forehead. And when she was good, she was very good indeed, and when she was bad, she was horrid." Henry Wadsworth Longfellow

Before Daddy left for his next contract, which at Christmas of 1941 was not determined, he built an 8" x 18" toolbox for Mother to contain all the usual household tools. Mother and Daddy were both great Do-It-Yourselfers. By the time they graduated with degrees in Architecture, they had built several pieces of furniture.

The box Daddy built was raw pine joined at the corners with tongue and groove joints (tongue and groove joints allow two flat pieces to be joined strongly together to make a single flat surface). The box wasn't painted, but nicely sanded — I know, because I didn't get any slivers! There was a soft rope handle that ran from end to end. He placed all the hammers, screw drivers, wrenches, and the like in the bottom. Then, he built a tray that fit into the box which had little sections for nuts, bolts, nails, screws, and more, all neatly separated.

Sometime between Christmas and Daddy's departure for Africa the second week of January, I climbed down the basement steps and found the new, Daddy-made box on the floor next to his workbench. It was filled with all the tools it was made for. But I quickly thought of a new use for this treasure: a new cradle for Judy. I'm not sure how many trips it took, but I managed to take Judy, her blanket, and her new clothes down to the basement and place them near her "new bed." The storage tray sections were perfect for Judy's little clothes. Like any 2-1/2 year-old, I just dumped everything out on the basement floor and proceeded to arrange Judy and her clothes as I wanted. After I had had time to get Judy settled in her new bed, Daddy came down the stairs and saw his tools and nuts, bolts, and screws in a scattered pile on the floor near Judy and me. No doubt I was beaming up at him with joy in my new toy.

He stood there looking down at me and, without raising his voice, he said, "Oh, Bill!" He then just cocked his head to the side and talked with me about the new arrangements for Judy. He didn't use any stern words, but I don't remember ever using that "cradle" again after that time.

I don't know if he got the tray items separated again before he left. But I guess my brief time with the toolbox for Judy was all I needed.

About 10 days later, the second week of January 1942, Daddy left for Africa and was gone until October of 1943. As I add this cherished memory to Daddy's book, I have tears pooling in my eyes. Of course, he didn't leave because I used his toolbox for Judy. But in the 1980s, my husband, Dean, and I went to Grand Cayman for a professional counselors' retreat, and I realized that many of my life choices/challenges were made with the thought that "if I do something that might displease someone, I might get left behind." Childhood memories do play tricks on our psyches. Several years before Daddy's death, I asked him about this early 2-year-old's memory. He nodded and smiled lovingly.

We moved to Southern California in the summer of 1947. Our house was one of the early tract houses in the San Fernando Valley. All 99 of the houses, identical to one another in floorplan, were built on quarter-acre lots. The only difference between them, until Daddy made a difference to ours, was some had shutters on the front windows.

Having done extensive travel, 1941-1943, Daddy limited his travel to mostly hunting and fishing trips until the early 1950s, and this gave him plenty of time for home-bound creative projects.

Our three-bedroom one bath home was comfortable, but Daddy made creative additions. He hand built a breakfast room addition to the kitchen and a large master suite with master bath to the back of the house with sliding doors going out to the pool deck.

One of my favorite things to do with Daddy on the weekends was to "hold the boards" while he sawed by hand or with the electric table saw. My title was, "Home addition construction helper." I recall fondly and cherish the memories of those hours in the garage with Daddy, slivers and all!

Chapter 45

Myra's Memories of her Dad

My earliest memories of my dad had to do with going to his office and playing with the blueprint machine. I loved that. I didn't even mind the smell of ammonia. I must have been quite young because, later, when I was between 7 and 8, Dad was living in Japan.

Mother and Dad made sure I got a good education. I remember hearing, "You are going to get an education so you can make your own future." I started college as an astrophysics major because I wanted to be first woman astronaut. However, beginning my sophomore year of college, I discovered that I was claustrophobic! They'd have to have a rocket about the size of a coliseum before I'd be an astronaut. I changed my major to architecture and fine arts and have my degree in ceramics. One of the professors I had while I was at California State, Northridge, got us to do casting, so we developed all kinds of clay bodies, one for casting that's being used at the Northridge campus.

Dad was a very loving, giving father. Both my parents were frugal and didn't waste money. They bought us things but didn't spend money on frivolous things. Dad also instilled in us respect for the possessions we did have, so we learned to take care of them.

I've never seen my father where he wasn't in control of himself. It's not that he was all into image, but I never saw him where he was out of control with emotion. As playful and as engaged he was with life, he was also an extremely disciplined person.

I didn't want to disappoint my father. Yet, he was encouraging. He told me all my life that I could do anything I wanted to set my mind to. My dad dealt with facts, but he understood emotions. He could become very soft and gentle if you needed it. Or, he could give you a straight answer if he thought, "Yes, you should do that, or no, don't do that." He was firm on what he believed; what's good and what wasn't and why. He always said why. It wasn't just, "no you can't."

About family life, we always had dinners together when Dad was home. However, because Dad traveled so much over the years, I was closer to mom than dad.

I want to say something about my mom. She was very, very intelligent. Growing up with Mom, she could be loving but very stern as well. There wasn't a lot of grey area; she had things she approved of and things she didn't approve of. You did it her way. She was trying to keep us out of trouble, basically.

She was talented as an artist and a seamstress. She did some beautiful paintings and did a tremendous amount of sewing. I remember one time when we went to I. Magnin, and she saw this dress she loved, memorized how it was made, went home, constructed a pattern, then made the dress! She and Dad both had made furniture in their early life together.

She and Dad were a well-matched team; both in terms of intelligence, the ability to work hard, a love of travel and a keen interest in people and in the world. They were married 63 years. After raising children, they traveled extensively—all over the world. Two of their most memorable cruises were the trip on the Sea Cloud Yacht and the trip to Antarctica.

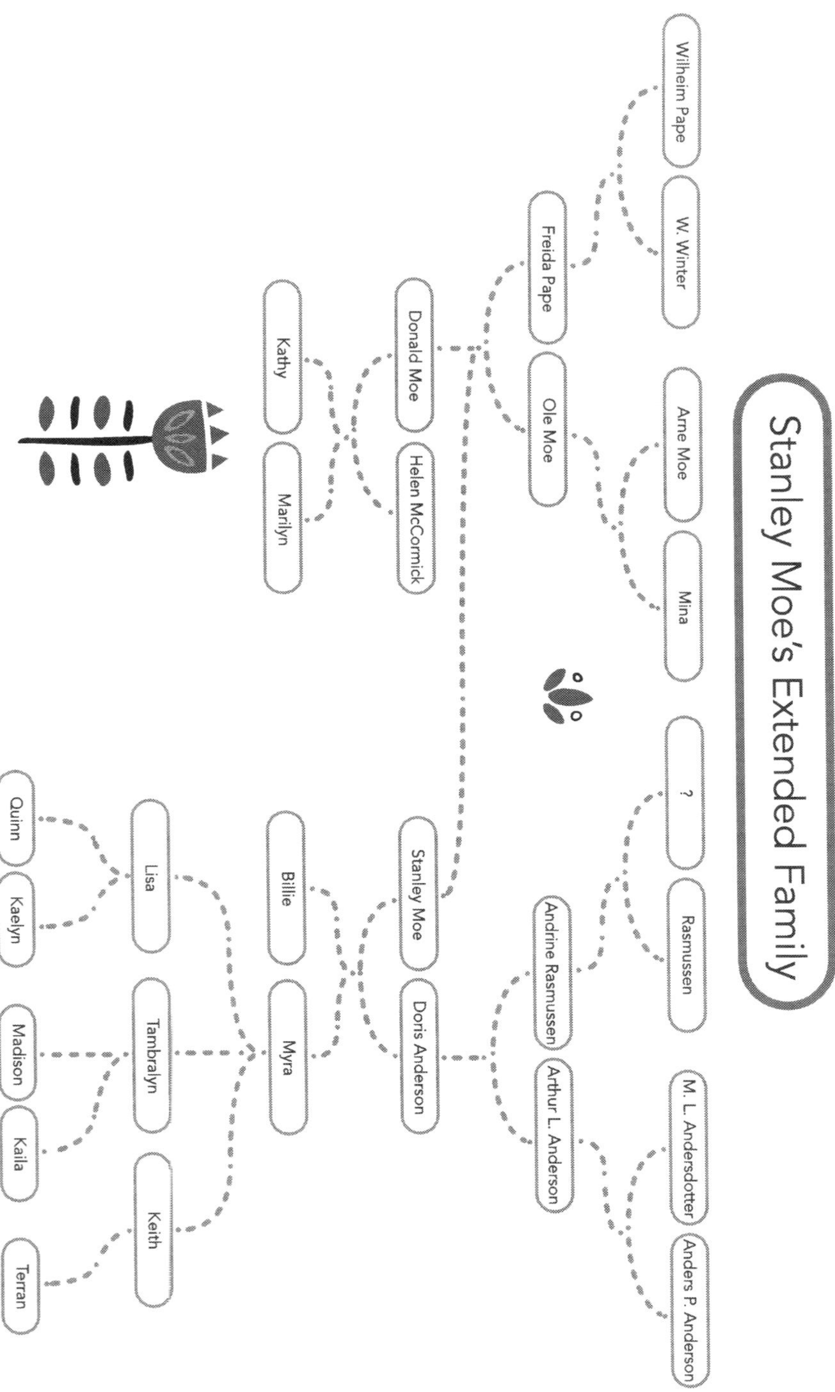

CHAPTER 46

Niece Kathy Moe Miller's Memories

My Uncle Stan was the older brother of my Dad, Don Moe. They were raised by Ole Moe and Frieda Pape Moe in North Dakota in the small towns of Ruso, Minot, and Ross. Stan and Don's grandfather, Arne Moe, emigrated from Norway along with his brother, Louis, who also settled in North Dakota, and another brother, Theodore, who settled in Canada. They worked the land as farmers.

Stan wrote beautiful accounts about his "roots" and the Moe family history in chapters one and two of this manuscript. I want to highlight some things which I feel influenced Stan's and my Don's values, and which were passed down as legacy to their children and grandchildren.

Embracing other cultures was an important value within the Moe family. One might not think that small towns in the Northern USA in the early parts of the 20th century were multi-cultural, but the towns of Ruso, Minot, and Ross had diverse populations. Stan and Don grew up in the years when the Homesteading Act was in place. The homesteaders included people from Syria and Lebanon. They were having border disputes in their countries, so, the U.S. government welcomed the people here. Those people came to North Dakota. The first mosque in North America is there in Ross—located right by their farm. There are fond memories of town picnics where the Muslim families brought baklava and other wonderful foods.

The oldest Mosque in the U.S.A. in Ross, North Dakota (photo courtesy of Kathy Moe Miller)

I think growing up there also served all of us well because it's not like growing up in some rural areas where you *only* have people from England, Scotland, Sweden, or Norway. We had all those peoples plus those from the Middle East and a lot of Native Americans. In addition, during the late fifties, the Minot Air Force base was built, bringing thousands of people and their cultures from all over the country. Because the Moe family and community was known to be very friendly, the personnel and families from the Base felt the area was welcoming and many stayed on to live there. It was the diverse culture which Stan appreciated, and as he went on to work in so many countries, his respect for diversity grew as he interacted with many different cultures.

Education was prized in our family. Arne's son, Ole (Grandpa Moe), was a stickler for education and received enough schooling to open a bank in the little town of Ross, North Dakota. Seeing how smart and capable his sons were, Ole wanted to send his eldest son, Stan, to Harvard. Then the 1929 crash occurred, and it wasn't affordable.

At age 16, however, Stan went to the University of North Dakota for two years, focusing on engineering. Stan's girlfriend, Doris, from Stanley, North Dakota (a small town 7.2 miles down the road), had now graduated from high school and was going to Macalester College in Saint Paul, Minnesota. Stan transferred to the University of Minnesota to study Architecture and incidentally, that put him closer to Doris. At that time my dad went to Minneapolis also, to finish high school while living in a missionary family that was from Ross. Dad's high school had closed in Ross because, during the depression, there was no money to pay teachers. It must have been shocking for my dad to go to such a big high school in Minneapolis after having only 30 or so in his entire school in Ross.

Things were so bad in North Dakota that many people of my parent's generation only received an 8th grade education. People were leaving town because they had no food. It was not only the depression, but the area had problems with dust, and a drought that lasted quite a few years. Fortunately, my Dad not only graduated from high school in Minneapolis, he attended the University of Minnesota to study business administration.

My maternal grandmother, Ida Nelson McCormick also felt education was important. In those days, women out on the prairie had a lot of rights and did a variety of jobs. They took care of immediate and extended family and home, worked on the farm, grew and hunted food and paid attention to their children's education. They got to vote earlier. Grandma McCormick made sure her children had a good education. My mother, for example, went to a business college for two years. My mother's father, William McCormick, a Scotch-Irish Quaker and pacifist from Quaker City, Ohio, was educated too, because in order to be an engineer on the train, one had to know how to work the train—with all the complicated engines they had back then.

During the depression, many trains came through that area because it was one of the main routes from Chicago to Seattle. The train was called ***The Empire Builder*** and was first in service June 10, 1929. My maternal grandmother, whose parents were from Sweden, started a restaurant in Stanley to cater to the train passengers that stopped there. In those days they didn't serve food on that train, but it stopped in Stanley long enough for everyone to have a good meal. All family members; from my grandmother on down, loved to cook, including Uncle Stan. His mother was an amazing cook. In addition to Grandma McCormick's talent at baking pies and cooking meals for a huge group, she was saavy enough to hire a great chef from the Chicago Athletic Club. He stayed at their restaurant for a couple of years and taught them how to make all kinds of new and interesting dishes. I remember mother talking about cream puffs that looked like swans. I still have the recipe for those cream puffs.

My husband James and I were inspired by Ole's love of education and his fluency with Norwegian. James and I lived in Norway for five years, while James was doing his PhD. He had graduated from MIT as a bio-medical engineer and his PhD work included research of spine scoliosis. In Norway, I taught at the American School, which was the Department of Defense school in Oslo. It was fun to be there. The Norwegians kept up a lot of their traditions when they moved to America. Billie still makes "lefsa" (Norwegian flatbread, made with cream, butter, flour, and principally, mashed potatoes) and I prepare a lot of Norwegian food during the holidays. I did learn Norwegian when I lived there.

Devotion to family was another important value. The brothers, Stan and Don, were very close and kept in touch throughout their lifetimes. They were both adventurous and daring. We loved to hear their stories at gatherings. Stan was a terrific storyteller, as was my Dad. One story they told concerning some work they did on the farm. It was not a prank. There were a lot of rocks out in the pastures and as kids, they would work with dynamite, breaking up the big rocks so they wouldn't damage the plows. They even once built a golf course. Then, at that time in that town, there was no indoor plumbing. The brothers said they always had to guard the outhouse on Halloween because the kids would come and tip it over.

Nowadays, kids would probably get put in jail for doing some the things they did. The fact that their parents had them out there doing such dangerous work, shows the difference in the times and in how their parents trusted them.

As the brothers grew, their sense of responsibility increased. After the bombing of Pearl Harbor, in his mid-twenties, Stan went to Africa with the Army Corp of Engineers. He designed the main airport in Cairo, Egypt. My dad was in the Army Air Corp. (The Air Force had not yet been formed. It came to be after World War II.)

During the war, Dad flew "The Hump," which is the nickname allied pilots gave the airlift operation that crossed the Himalayas between India and China. It was the most dangerous airlift route because they didn't have pressurized planes and they were carrying fuel. It was the only way to supply Chinese forces fighting Japan. A large percentage of pilots flying fuel to the Chinese didn't make it. Stan and my dad were both risk takers who had tremendous courage.

That whole generation had to do a lot of things that had never been done before. I think people growing up on the Great Plains had to learn to do for themselves. That's probably why Stan got so good at so many things. He was lucky to not only be an architect but also an engineer, which isn't true for most architects. He could always build things that would hold up. And he was a wonderful carpenter.

Uncle Stan loved to come back to North Dakota, a fact that was very appreciated, because many people, once they venture out into the larger world, didn't come back to their little home towns. Obviously, it was a special place for Stan. He got a lot of different experiences there that he wouldn't have had other places.

Stan found interesting problems in Ross. Some of the problems they had in North Dakota, Stan helped the rest of the world to fix.

He was especially talented at designing buildings that were appropriate for the climate. Stan and my Dad and their parents lived in Ross while the boys were growing up. Their father Ole, had owned a bank in Ross and when the depression hit, he lost his bank and turned to crop farming full time, but they didn't live on the farm, which was outside of town. In Ross they didn't have a grocery store or a doctor nearby, they went to Stanley to do their grocery shopping.

Stan came back and helped my dad and my mom Helen build a house in Minot. Later, he designed and built a house for his parents, also in Minot. As his parents aged, they wanted to move to a larger town with more amenities and one which was closer to our family. Stan came back from California and helped design the house that had a wonderful garden-level basement in which my grandmother could attend to her hobbies and could easily go up and down the steps. It was a very special house for North Dakota, with lots of windows reminiscent of the openness of a California house. My grandparents enjoyed living there very much.

Uncle Stan also helped design a building for my dad who was in the automobile business. Dad had one of the largest dealerships in the state of North Dakota. He needed a building where he could keep his vehicles during the winter, protected from hail, snow and other elements of the harsh climate. Stan helped design a building that not only accommodated all the vehicles but also looked pleasant and was well heated.

Stanley had a mind that could easily organize large projects. He used that ability to go on to design huge projects in many places in the world.

I was aware that Stan had offices all over the map. I would go to Washington D.C. and visit his office there. I went on "Operation Crossroads Africa" to Chad and spent some time in Cameroon, in Douala. He had an office there, too. It was amazing to think of all those different places he had offices. Crossroads Africa was for American and Canadian students to go to Africa and do projects. I'm sure that, because of Uncle Stan's wide-ranging adventures, it just seemed like the natural thing for me to do, too!

Doris Moe was a talented woman. She became an architectural interior designer and opened her own shop in Van Nuys, California. In addition, Doris made all of Billie's and Myra's clothes and she also made their home's draperies, slipcovers, and designer bedspreads. Billie and Myra were both creative, talented, and both good at making things, too. Myra got her degree in ceramics from USC and did stain glass art, quilting, embroidery and is gifted in many directions. Billie was a weaver and has done the decorating in all her family homes. Billie drew the plans to add

750 square feet to the home Stan had designed and was built before his death. All these talents were cultivated by their talented parents Stan and Doris.

The love and respect of learning, of creativity, the devotion to family, love of adventure and travel, a strong interest in other cultures, the dedication to hard work, the intention to be of effective service—all of those values Uncle Stan embodied and passed on as part of his legacy.

Stan Moe, James Miller and Kathy Moe Miller

CHAPTER 47

Granddaughter Lisa Sauers' Memories

Stanley Moe, my grandfather, was a very big part of my life. Since my father was gone most of my life due to travel, my grandfather was my father figure. He walked me down the aisle at my wedding and gave me away to my true love. It was an extremely special moment when I had my father/daughter dance with my grandfather.

Lisa's Wedding day: Keith, Myra, Lisa, Stan, and Tambralyn

When all we grandchildren were little, Grandpa took extra steps during the holidays to ensure that we still believed in Santa.

As a young girl, I loved working in his woodshop. I can still remember how his garage smelled of cut wood and oil from his woodworking machines. We made a toy chest together which I still have and see every day.

Another good memory was of picking Meyer lemons at his house and making lemonade or eating his homemade Lemon Chiffon Pie. (I have been trying to grow Meyer lemons at our house for years and they always die. I miss his lemons!)

Perhaps most gratifying for me was seeing the extreme love and joy in my grandfather's face when he was with my daughters (his great-granddaughters). Quinn and Kaelyn meant the world to him.

Quinn introduces Kaelyn to Great Grandpa

While, I don't remember any times while growing up that he "laughed," he would always smile to let you know he was proud of you and that made you feel loved and warm inside. It wasn't until his great-granddaughters came into his life that I remember him laughing. There were many times that he would laugh at the funny things my daughters would do.

Traveling the US and the world with my grandparents while listening to the historical stories my grandfather experienced in the areas we visited, was a rich experience for me.

Both my grandfather and dad traveled a lot around the world. On one of my grandfather's trips to a foreign country (I think, Singapore) he thought it would be interesting if my dad was in town at the same moment. He went to the front desk of his hotel and asked if my father was staying there. Surprisingly, my father was there at that hotel and they met up for dinner. (I always loved that story.)

When I was young, sometime between seven and ten, I told a lie to my grandparents and my grandfather caught me. I don't remember what it was, but he lectured me, and I was humiliated. He required me to write an apology letter and mail it to him.

When I was in college, I experienced the freedom of having a credit card...which was not a good thing. My grandfather had a very long and stern discussion with me about finances and advised me to pay the credit card off ASAP. It has been 30 years since our talk, and I am still debt free and only purchase items on a credit card that I can pay off each month.

If I could talk to Grandpa now, I would first say that I love him and then tell him how much his experiences continue to evolve through his great-grand-daughters. My daughters are both very interested in engineering/architecture in school and know the importance of going to a great university. One is currently looking at several top engineering/architecture schools.

If I could share some time with him again, I would like to continue to travel the world with him. There are still so many places to see and I would love to hear about the history he experienced.

Chapter 48

Granddaughter Tambralyn Peterson's Memories

My grandfather, Stanley Moe, was a very serious man. I felt that any word out of his mouth was a life lesson.

Dinner at their house was always, in my mind, a formal event. You had to change out of your daily clothes and look sharp. Grandpa went all out putting together the best meal for the family. We would all sit down at the table and wait for him to say grace. While we ate, we'd hear stories of my grandfather's past. The meal was always good, except when he cooked lutefisk (a dried cod soaked in a lye solution, then boiled or baked in butter). We had to finish everything on our plates, and yes, when lutefisk was on the menu, I would be sitting at the table for a long time. Ha ha! He loved to have ice cream for dessert with some chocolate chips.

My grandfather was a very talented builder. I would work with him in his workshop (about the size of a two-car garage) and we would build toys. For example, he and I built a wooden horse for me to play with. He made sure I was the one cutting the wood and he stood in the background directing me what to do.

It's funny, when I try to remember his stories, I often recall the ones where he had issues, where he was mugged, or when things went wrong. With those stories I feel he was telling me that the world isn't always safe, that we need to be alert.

What set my grandfather apart from other people, I think, was his generosity. When times were tough for my family, he was there to help my mom when she needed it. He also paid for two years of my college and bought me my first car. I would write him every month with words of thanks and let him know how college was going.

I admire his commitment to family. If you needed something, you could always go to grandpa, but you better make sure you had a plan for what you are going to say as he was a busy man! Grandpa was the rock in the family.

If I could do something with him now, I would have him help me build my cabin. He always had a way with woodworking and I feel he would add his unique character to some elements in my new home.

I have always liked to work with my hands, and I feel comfortable around a woodshop. I know I must have gotten this from my grandfather.

Before my grandfather passed. I had a moment with him and asked him if there were any words of wisdom, he would like to share with me.

He said, "Tammy, life is to be enjoyed!" And then he said, "I'm very proud of you for what you've accomplished."

Kaila, Tambralyn and Madison in front of a painting by Tambralyn

Chapter 49

Grandson Keith Parsons' Memories

When I was 10-years old, living in California, we took a trip with the Boy Scouts on a sailboat to Catalina Island. With my father traveling, my grandfather was the one that chaperoned me. It was a fun overnight stay. He helped me with the knots that I was learning and that was really nice.

He was largely a father figure since my dad was mainly traveling around the world. When it came down to the woodshop, taking me fishing, that one Boy Scout trip; he was a grandfather, but he was also a father figure in my life. I learned a lot of etiquette from him—be it dining room manners or how to behave in social gatherings.

I went to three of his Rotary Club luncheons. I understood and could apply the right etiquette for those events. Of course, my mom also helped with etiquette, as she enrolled me in Cotillion.

We did a lot of fishing at a place called Mt. Baldy. It was mainly rainbow trout where they would put a lot of trout into the lake and you'd just go and fish. I was taught how to clean the fish and we'd eat them for dinner.

One of the largest trips we took together happened in 2002. We traveled to Queen Charlotte Isle, which is just west of British Columbia, Canada. Stanley Moe would go every year with his Rotary fishing buddies and one of them had passed away, so, they had an open spot, and Grandpa invited me. We flew in from Vancouver to a city on the island, and from there we took a seaplane to the location, which was on the west side of the island.

For a week we fished for salmon. The company had built two barges together; one side was the restaurant and crew quarters; the other side provided the guest living quarters. They would tow those to the island during the summer and then tow them back to Vancouver at the end of the fishing season. It was a special time for a 22-year-old, to be included with Grandpa's Rotary friends.

Starting when I was a kid of about five or six, Grandfather and I did woodworking together in his shop. I remember I was with him when he got his first small jigsaw and we had a lot of fun playing with that. He taught me how to use the tools correctly and how to have respect for them.

Grandpa was a gunsmith, a shooter and hunter. Even when I was a kid, he taught me all about firearms. I learned to reload pistols, rifle rounds, shotgun shells and we'd go out to the range occasionally.

The main lesson I learned from my grandfather was: "If you think it's impossible, find another way." I've used that with automotive projects—just thinking outside the box.

When I would struggle on the job doing something, I'd just sit back, and think of it from a different angle and then be able to get it done. I'd use a tool in a way it's not designed for. Sometimes, you must do something that will take half an hour that will save you two hours in the long run.

My grandfather was a very humble man. He never bragged about anything. He's not like, "Oh, well, I did this," or "Well, I did that." I never heard him boast, ever. But he took his roles in life seriously, intent on wearing his hats, really well. He wasn't strict or stern, he wasn't like some of those stereotypical grumpy old men, *it's my way or the highway.* He would explain his views and if you didn't agree with them, tough pickles!

You know, even towards the end, my grandfather still had his wits about him. He always had his wits about him and was super interested in things. At my wedding, he was fascinated with architecture and I don't know how many pictures he took of my in-law's house because it was an actual adobe. It wasn't a house that looked like an adobe; it was actual straw and mud that they built by hand. He was so infatuated with it. He always had a camera on him, no matter what. Grandpa was always learning, being inspired and interested.

I admired my grandfather and he still inspires me. Anytime I'm working with wood, even if I'm just putting in a fence post, or, I'm cutting wood with a power saw, I always think of him. Anytime I go shooting, I always think of him. Anytime I see a Jaguar, I always think of him! I gained a lot of respect for many things from my grandfather; be it for travel, language, working with my hands and having respect for others.

Keith and daughter Terran

CHAPTER 50

Long-Time Friend Pat Gillick's Memories

Pat Gillick[5] was a general manager of the Phillies baseball team. He was a friend of Stanley Moe and his family over many decades.

"When Stan came into the room, even though he was not, in stature, a big guy, without saying a word, he took over the room."
— Pat Gillick

Billie, Stan's eldest daughter and I met at a church function when I was fifteen and we started going out in 1953. Stan was in Japan 1952 through 1953. Then, later, he did a lot of work in the Middle East.

Before I met Stanley, I'd been hearing a lot about him from his wife Doris, from Billie and Billie's sister, Myra. There were pictures of Stanley all over the house. You knew that he really existed; he had a remarkable presence. I'd heard a lot about him, that he was a wonderful guy to be around and that he had a good sense of humor—a dry humor.

Initially, when I met him in 1954, I was a bit intimidated, but immediately he made me feel comfortable. Right away I could sense his respect and that made a huge impact on me.

Stan had terrific communication skills. This is what impressed me from the onset: Stan was a good listener. And I think that's important if you're going to really hear people and understand their views. You can't do it by talking too much. In my life's work, I listened to my employees and the players carefully and that made all the difference.

The other ability he had was this: when he opened his mouth, he was prepared, and what came out of it made sense! He wasn't one of those individuals that had an ego where he had to come in and with a loud voice make himself known as the guy in charge. No, I think that when Stan came into the room, even though he was

5. "Gillick spent five years as a player in the Baltimore farm system before deciding his career was to be in baseball administration. He earned his spurs as an assistant farm director with the Houston Colt .45s in 1964 and 1965 before taking on a more involved role as a scout with Houston. Eventually he became Scouting Director of the Astros in 1974 and then with the Yankees in 1975-76. A move north in 1977 proved highly successful for both Gillick and his new club, the Toronto Blue Jays. As General Manager of the franchise, he guided the new squad through expansion to back-to-back World Series championships in 1992 and 1993. More success followed—in Baltimore, 1996 to 1998, and Seattle 2000 to 2003. He moved on to the Phillies in 2006 and ended up with his third World Series title." Kirby Arnold for The Sun, October 1, 2003. (Pat was inducted into the Hall of fame in 2011.)

not, in stature, a big guy, without saying a word, he took over the room. He was someone that people respected and a big part of that was his being a very good listener. When he did speak, everybody really got what he said, because his words were credible and had meat to them. I was to learn that he showed consistent respect for the people he worked for and the employees that he had. That way of seeing people as valuable and treating them with esteem rubbed off on me later in life.

I think what I have in common with Stan is this; I grew up with the golden rule, "Do unto others as you would have others do unto you." Consequently, I tried to treat people the way I wanted to be treated. As I said, Stan treated people with respect, and that's how people want to be treated. That's the kind of feeling that I like to give to people; that I do value them, and I do understand them.

Interestingly, I stopped calling Stan, "Mr. Moe" when I was 20 years of age. He's the one who told me to call him "Stan." I had always thought that you showed respect to your elders by addressing them as Mr. or Mrs., unless they indicated that you could drop that and just call them by their first names. When he wanted me to call him Stan, not only did I feel comfortable but also felt I was more on an equal footing with him. I, in turn, have wanted people to feel comfortable in my presence and usually ask them to call me "Pat."

I just thought of a good memory. I got married in '68 and we happened to have a team in Florida at the time. In the early 70s, Stan was working at The Kennedy Space Center. And so, my wife (also named Doris) and I went over to the Kennedy Space Center and had dinner with Stan and his Doris. At that time, they were working on different missile programs: The Atlas, the Jupiter and the Titan. Stan

Stan was working and living in Cape Canaveral, Florida

couldn't say too much from a military standpoint about what was going on, so he spoke in general terms. I got the idea that he was working on a program for the military and surmised that it was something to do with the space program or with missiles or rockets or something of that nature. In any case, Stan was such a smart man and his conversation was always tremendously interesting. We had a delightful time.

Stan and Doris had a durable and robust relationship. Even though Stan had a strong personality with immense confidence about where he was going in life, he depended greatly on his wife Doris and her considerable strengths and abilities. I believe they had a tremendous love and respect for each other. Doris understood that their separation freed him to work on important projects away from home. She knew that there had to be a stable home base for the girls to grow up in and that was her job while he was away. Consequently, he was appreciative of the fact that Doris really took care of the girls, finances, and everything at home. I think there was a tremendous amount of trust that went back and forth between them.

I believe that they both, being North Dakota people, came from very strong households with solid values, with the idea that if you work hard, you'll succeed. I think because their beliefs were along the same lines, they could debate and discuss subjects in a very, very constructive manner. I've heard them, and it was amazing. I don't think I ever really saw Stan frustrated or mad. I never saw Doris angry, either. Neither one of them let their emotions get away from them. There were never any raised voices, or any of that nature. They were running on the same track.

The parents' values and strengths affected the characters of their daughters. Billie was greatly impacted by her father. She was Daddy's girl! And, knowing Billie the best, she has that same kind of respect and caring her father had. I think Billie would have been well suited to go into the Peace Corps. She really has a huge heart for people. Both daughters inherited their parents' intelligence and sense of adventure.

Billie's husband, Dean, was a baseball fan and they lived not too far away in Albuquerque. Stan was living in California and was a huge baseball fan also. We were training in the Phoenix area and they all came for spring training because they loved to attend practices and exhibition games. It was a good time. I hadn't seen them for a while, because Billie had been in the Mid-West after she got married. It was also nice that they all had the opportunity to come over and get to meet our daughter, Kim. I hadn't seen Doris Moe since the early seventies. Here we were, twenty-six years later, over in Arizona having dinner. It was a very happy time.

At the time of that reunion, I remember saying to Stan, "We're thinking about building a house over in Toronto and I wonder if you could give me any tips or take a look at a design." He had designed their house on Plymouth Boulevard in L.A. and of course, many others.

He said to me, "I don't think I'm really qualified because I don't know your neighborhood and the style of houses there. I could design one, but it might not go with the neighborhood and fit in."

He advised us to go to a local architect that had an excellent reputation in the neighborhood and be directed by that person regarding the style of the house. That's what we did. It ended up that my Doris was the project manager working with an architect that lived just down the street from where we were. We built a house there that we were happy with, which was what Stan wanted for us.

I have always been glad that I've known a man of such integrity and life force. Stanley Moe was a great friend and role model.

Foreground: Keith Parsons, Pat Gillick and Stanley Moe
Background: Billie's husband Dean Crouse and Sam McDowell, circa 1993

Chapter 51

Phil's Son, Jim Daniel's Memories

✧ **Billie: Throughout this book, you've read the loving portrayals that Dad has written about Phil Daniel; one of the four original partners of Daniel, Mann, Johnson, and Mendenhall (DMJM). Phil became Dad's mentor, then partner and collaborator on projects throughout the world. He and Dad were great friends.**

Phil's son, Phillip J. Daniel Jr. (Jim), worked for "The Firm" from the DMJM days to the present day at AECOM, where he worked for over 35 years. At the time of this writing, Jim has recently retired from AECOM as Associate Vice President (and his long-standing services at the NASA Ames Research Center in Northern California).

Jim gives background, context and descriptions of my dad, his dad, DMJM, and the influence of these great men on his life.

My Dad, Phil, and Stan were kindred spirits. Dad had a proclivity for traveling the world, chasing and finding work all over the map. He needed people like Stan that

Phil Daniel at DMJM offices

he trusted, to go around the world and represent him, the company, the partners, and employees. As Stan demonstrated his competence beyond expectations; trust, admiration, and their personal and professional friendship grew.

I'd like to give you a little context on how DMJM was formed originally and how the pieces came together with the original partners. Dad went to USC, studying to be architect. He served in the Navy during World War II. There, he met Art Mann, who was also an architect and became the second partner in DMJM. They returned after the war and decided to "hang out a shingle" in Santa Maria, California.

As the company grew a bit more, they needed more help. Ken Johnson, who was one of Dad's fraternity brothers at USC, wanted to join. That's how they became Daniel, Mann, and Johnson. The firm moved from Santa Maria down to Los Angeles to a little building right off what is now MacArthur Park.

During the War, Dad had married Faye Mendenhall (my mother). As the business grew, the three partners (DMJ) found that they needed an engineer; a licensed professional who could "stamp" drawings. They needed someone who had the capability of an engineer for structural, civil portions of the design of the work they were getting into. Irvan Mendenhall, my mother's brother, fit the bill perfectly. He came to the firm and now there were four (DMJM).

My dad was living the business and growing it, as were Uncle Irvan, Ken Johnson, and certainly Art Mann. These were four active guys coming out of World War II intent on building roads, schools, and expanding the infrastructure of this country and as they grew, the infrastructure of other countries. They were animated, aggressive, determined, and focused professionals; hot shots going after the work, whatever it was and wherever they could. They knew they had to stay ahead of the game both domestically and internationally.

As the firm started to grow, the management and the owners had a very heavy responsibility to delegate work to people they trusted. They needed people who could be team members and could help build the business. Stan Moe had the capabilities, personality, and skillset, and beyond that, he was someone they could trust. They brought him into the firm as a compatriot, a compadre, and partner. And, God bless Stan Moe, he was certainly one of them, and they knew they were fortunate to have him as partner.

Not only was Stan Moe and all the partners, knowledgeable, skilled and proficient, but also, they all were companionable and knew how to have a good time. Their company/family picnics of the 50s and 60s were famous; held at Sunset Farms out in the San Fernando Valley in Southern California. DMJM would rent it for the day and have 100, 150, maybe 200 personnel and their families, come out for the day. They would have egg tosses, sack races, and Bar-B-Qs and just have a grand ol' time. DMJM was intent, in big and small ways, to make everybody feel a part of the larger company family.

The partners loved to socialize at each other's houses. As a kid, I remember when Stan took me for a ride in the Healy Silverstone racecar that he owned. Stan drove us kids around in this open two-seater car that, I've since found out from Billie, had an all-aluminum body, right-hand drive, fenders that could be removed when racing, two headlights right together behind the grill, a radiator that had no fan, and no top! There were only 105 of them built (hand built in England only) and no two were the same.

Norm Fugelso is taking "The Bug" for a spin
Notice the two headlights side by side inside the grill

Rear of bug before the new paint job
Note the spare tire placement inserted below a small trunk that served as the rear bumper

Interior shot of "The Bug"

Dual overhead cams and the hoses

✧ ***Billie: These hoses had to be replaced, often while in traffic, when the car over-heated and the hose split and sprayed rusty hot water on surrounding cars! Yes, I was there!***

I didn't know those car details as an eight-year-old kid, but what I did know was that Stan Moe was "cool!" He was so energetic and personable with us kids—not at all standoffish in any way, shape, or form. His innate nature was one of openness, strong interest about everything, and of friendliness.

The DMJM Family

Employees at DMJM enjoyed working for them, or might I say working with them. I know that Stan, my father, and the other partners would walk the halls. They were not owners or managers who sat up in their corner offices and pontificated or pulled out their suspenders! They were roll-up-their-sleeves, person-to-person team members. And that endeared the partners and managers to the rest of the employees.

Today, now decades later, AECOM has come to be known and respected as one of the premier Architecture/Engineering/Construction Professional Services firms in the world. The depth and breadth of its services are worldwide. AECOM, in a way, can be likened to the former British Empire in that "The Sun Never Sets" on AECOM! But few people today know the history…

AECOM Grew Out of DMJM

DMJM, its original partners, its employees were the Petri dish from which AECOM grew. Those who refer to "…when AECOM acquired DMJM…" do not know that AECOM never "acquired" DMJM. Just the very opposite. AECOM was "…envisioned, conceived, designed, drawn, engineered, and built…" by those DMJM professionals who knew, grew, and learned under the DMJM Partners. Those professionals who came after the DMJM Partners, have honored their legacy by keeping intact the integrity, the ingenuity, the camaraderie for which DMJM is lauded now within AECOM.

What did I learn from my dad and these great men? They imparted this philosophy: "Don't pat me on the back. Pat the team. Pat everybody who's involved with the project we're working on who is helping this company grow, helping all of us grow. It's not about the individual as some sort of 'star.' If you see me as special, and you want to give me a root, a toot, and a kudo, let me have the wisdom to pass that kudo on to the draftsmen on the third floor, to the guys and ladies down in the print shop, to the kids who are the gophers, to the messengers, and to the drivers in the motor pool. Those are the important people!"

When you next go to 3250 Wilshire (across from the Old I. Magnin's) to see where the DMJM office was, don't go to the Tea Room for lunch. Just walk down the street to the HMS Bounty, (directly across Wilshire Blvd from where the Old Ambassador/Coconut Grove Hotel was). Get a booth in the back, and on Friday order the Sanddabs. You just might see the ghosts of any number of The Old DMJM Officers & Crew that still "haunt" the main cabin. We anchored there through many a storm and rough sea...

HMS Bounty
(photo by Terry August)

CHAPTER 52

A Celebration of Friendship

With Grateful Nods to the LA-5 Rotary Club of Los Angeles
by Lee A. Jackman

Dinner with Stan Moe at Englefield Bay, British Columbia (photo by Lee Jackman)

"Sweet is the memory of distant friends! Like the mellow rays of the departing sun, it falls tenderly, yet sadly, on the heart."
— Washington Irving

I met Stan Moe at the Rotary Club of Los Angeles. It's important to relay the background of this branch of Rotarians: unique and elite.

In 1989, the Rotary Club of Los Angeles was a vibrant, eighty-year-old, 500-member-strong organization. Members had cachet. It was the business organization to join because it provided opportunities to network with the business elite, contribute or raise funds for the Club's numerous service projects like scholarships for local youth, and assistance for homeless centers.

The Club, called LA-5, because it was the fifth oldest Rotary Club in the world, offered individuals membership only after a lengthy and rigorous process. Applicants had to be nominated by a member in good standing. They had to have one or more face-to-face meetings with Club leaders before the board of directors would review the application. The Board of directors would hold a frank discussion about the pros and cons of extending membership, and, finally, the process would conclude with a secret ballot. To be offered membership required 100% agreement by the board. One "no" vote and the prospective member was eliminated from consideration.

Two years before, in 1987, the Supreme Court of the United States, ruled on a case brought to them regarding the Duarte Rotary Club. It seems that the Club had offered membership to three women in 1977, without being sanctioned to do so by Rotary International. The Court ruled that it was, indeed, exclusionary to preclude women from becoming Rotarians. The gates were open to the heretofore all male clubs.

The Court ruling reverberated throughout Rotary. Members, opposed to the ruling were angry and vocal, some relinquished their membership. Those in favor of including women, saw it as an opportunity, and immediately began to seek qualified women leaders for membership. It was, without a doubt, the best of times and the worst for Rotary.

In 1989, I was an executive with the Doheny Eye Institute in Los Angeles. My responsibilities included raising funds to add laboratories to one floor of the research building, thus doubling the size of the two-floor hospital building.

The owner of the construction company hired for the hospital construction project asked if I would consider joining LA-5. Great, I thought, my father was a Rotarian, so it would be nice to continue this tradition. After jumping through the proverbial membership hoops, I was inducted as a member in October 1989.

I met Stan Moe shortly after I joined the Club. He was chair of the Piscatorial Committee, responsible for arranging annual salmon fishing trips in Alaska and elsewhere. Several years after I joined the club, a new LA-5 president made the decision to change the name of the committee to the Fishing Committee. This change rankled Stan who thought it sounded common, preferring, instead, something more erudite. But he went along with the decision. At each weekly Rotary meeting, I would find him holding court at a table in the back of the Hilton Hotel Ballroom, joined by other avid fishermen.

What Stan lacked in height (he was 5' 5-1/2" tall), he made up for in presence. An impeccable dresser, he wore custom suits made of sumptuous fabrics.

"A Chinese tailor makes these for me in four days," he said, smiling. "He swings through town every six months or so."

His suits and ties were highlighted by handmade white French-cuff shirts that he donned with expensive cufflinks. His thick snow-white hair and pencil-thin mustache added pizzazz to his image. He was, in a word, distinguished. Stan was a raconteur, a soft-spoken man with a ready laugh, and his stories were endless. Time spent with Stan was continually delightful.

After his wife's death, I spoke with him every week by telephone. These conversations would inevitably turn to a common theme, our mutual interest in writing a memoir, and our shared frustration at having little motivation to get to work on it. Looking for a resolution to our shared writing block, we challenged each other.

When this tactic seemed to work, we took turns reading what we had written to the other. It was fun, and got our stagnant juices flowing again.

In the late 1990's, I called Stan to ask if my son Aaron and I could join the LA-5 fishing junket that August in Sitka, Alaska. My father had expressed his dream of taking Aaron fishing with him but had died when my son was only three. I confided to Stan, "This trip will allow me to fulfill my father's dream." He was delighted and sent me all the information I'd need, said he was sorry that he couldn't go on the trip that year, but knew how much we'd enjoy it, and wished us well. The trip was magnificent. We caught 250 pounds of salmon, cod and halibut. However, I didn't learn the real story until months later. It wasn't that Stan was unable to make the trip. He had, in fact, paid the deposit and was on the reservation list. But, when he checked on availability for us, he learned that only one spot remained, not two. In typical Stan fashion, he cancelled his reservation, thus opening up two slots, giving us the opportunity to make our dream-fulfilling fishing trip.

Two years later, Stan, my daughter Jennifer and I took an LA-5 fishing trip into the hinterlands of British Colombia, fifty miles away from civilization. We had stunning helicopter rides into and out of our floating lodge, watched majestic Bald Eagles patiently sitting on tree branches waiting for tasty entrails as the guides cleaned the day's catch, and relaxed in quiet conversation at the bar where we discussed our day over a glass of wine before turning in for a much-needed rest.

During the final five years of his life, my husband and I would join Stan and his second wife Reiko for a monthly dining experience in one of the city's fine restaurants. First, Stan would select the restaurant, the next month it was my turn. We'd join them for a glass of wine at their home before departing for an evening of fine food, storytelling, and the celebration of friendship. Stan and I were lovers of raw oysters and, if they were on the menu, we would each order a dozen. A constant presence at each of our dinners was Stan's tiny digital camera. As each course was presented, he would hoist the camera above the selection and snap a photo from just the right angle. Everyone waited for the completion of this important ceremony before they dared to lift a fork. His camera is, no doubt, filled with thousands of images of sumptuous salads with exotic toppings, entrees with flourishes of demi glaze, or desserts with spun sugar accessories.

I miss it all, the Rotary meetings, the fishing trips, the conversations, the encouraging prodding to inspire each other to write, our laughter, the good food. But, most of all, I simply miss my dear friend Stan.

April 11, 2020

✧ **Billie: I want to acknowledge that Lee Jackman was president of the LA-5 Rotary Club from 2005-2006.**

Lee Jackman, Randy Lee, and Stan Moe in Englefield Bay, British Columbia

Floating Fishing Lodge, Englefield Bay, British Columbia

Friends forever!

PART XVII

Travel!

Pre-DMJM Projects World War II and Post War: 11 Sites

- Egypt
- Nigeria
- Chad
- Sudan
- Kenya
- Ivory Coast
- Eritrea
- Ethiopia
- Liberia
- Saudi Arabia
- Yemen

Post War Projects for DMJM: 43 Sites

- Algeria
- England
- Spain
- France
- Italy
- Greece
- Turkey
- Germany
- Norway
- Jordan
- Cameroon
- Afghanistan
- India
- Iran
- Thailand
- Cambodia
- Yemen
- Saudi Arabia
- Liberia
- Ethiopia
- Eritrea
- Ivory Coast
- Philippines
- Kenya
- Sudan
- Nigeria
- Egypt
- Malaya
- Singapore
- South Viet Nam
- Taiwan
- Indonesia
- Japan
- Korea
- Guam
- Saint Vincent
- Panama
- Peru
- Bolivia
- Brazil
- Abu Dhabi
- Kuwait
- Tanzania

Personal Travel: 50 Destinations!

- Austria
- Yugoslavia
- Denmark
- Sweden
- Iceland
- Lebanon
- Sierra Leone
- Holland
- Belgium
- Luxemburg
- San Remo
- Monte Carlo
- Pakistan
- Laos
- China
- Philippines
- Caribbean (most of 26 countries)
- Australia
- Antigua
- Barbados
- Mexico
- Columbia
- Chile
- Antarctica
- Oman

Chapter 53

Personal Travel — Stories and Photographs

Letter to Barry Mountain from Stanley - April 13, 1998

Dear Barry,

In only a few days I will be on my way to visit you in Virginia. I haven't been in the area for a long time. On my previous visits, my travels were limited to the time I had left over after my business duties. This will be a pleasant change.

The itinerary you have outlined sounds great. Much of it will be completely new to me. It will be very interesting. I guess I am an incurable tourist, anyway.

Enclosed are a couple of bios on Doris and me. Nothing very exciting, but the activities have kept us busy for more than sixty years of married life, plus a few years before. I tried to keep them brief. I really wasn't very successful with brevity and the format isn't consistent. Please excuse.

Best Regards, Stanley

Barry Mountain's home in Virginia

Barry Mountain is at Dad's house seeing the work-in-progress of a rifle display case Stan made for him

Stan and Barry at Barry's home

Brochure of Kyoto: Doris and Stanley Moe on vacation in Japan

Billie: On an earlier trip to Japan someone took a photo of Mom and Dad in a tea house. A few years later when they returned to Japan, they saw their photo in this travel brochure.

Harriet Moore

The Story of Harriet Moore began in 1953. Harriet Moore was a talented, classy, Chinese lady and entrepreneur. In 1953, Dad met Harriet and her two young children in Tokyo, when she was looking for an architect who might design a Chinese restaurant for her there. Dad designed it and the restaurant was a huge success.

They stayed in touch and years later, when Harriet was living in the Los Angeles area, and had her own travel business, Dad and DMJM began using her for their travel needs, which were increasing by leaps and bounds.

With Harriet's outgoing personality, she met many people. She knew several of the notable Los Angeles restaurant owners, including Madame Wu. One of her dear friends was Madame Abe, the mother of the Japanese Prime Minister, Shinzo Abe. In fact, this special man lived with Harriet during his time attending the University of Southern California. The Prime Minister's mother traveled on many of the cruises that Dad and Reiko took.

Over the years, Dad and Mother and Harriet became good friends, and Harriet planned dozens of trips for the Moe family. Dad's 95th birthday cruise (his last) was orchestrated by Harriet. I remember Harriet saying that she too would celebrate her 95th birthday on a cruise. Several years later she did, and my husband and I, as did friends and family from around the world, celebrated with her.

Stanley and Harriet Moore

Harriet and Stan celebrating his 96 years

The Most Affordable Cruise of All

Dad and Mother were on a cruise that they felt they had been overcharged for and one night Dad was complaining to the man next to him at the bar that many of the other passengers had told him that they'd paid much less for the cruise. The man said, "Well, I can make it up to you. I have interests in this cruise but am also involved with a wonderful ship on which I can give you a free week. It is called 'Sea Cloud' and it's an antique clipper ship that holds only 64 people, and you will love it."

The Sea Cloud Yacht

Crown International Travel, Inc. (Harriet Moore's company)

BUSINESS ITINERARY FOR MR. AND MRS. STAN MOE March 31, 1972

Monday	April 10	Leave Los Angeles	Arrive Honolulu, Hawaii
Thursday	April 13	Leave Honolulu	Arrive Manila, Philippines
Sunday	April 16	Leave Manila	Arrive Denpasar, Indonesia
Thursday	April 20	Leave Denpasar	Arrive Djakarta, Indonesia
Thursday	April 27	Leave Djakarta	Arrive Singapore
Sunday	April 30	Leave Singapore	Arrive Kuala Lumpur, Malaysia
Tuesday	May 2	Leave Kuala Lumpur	Arrive Penang, Malaysia
Thursday	May 4	Leave Penang	Arrive Bangkok, Thailand
Saturday	May 6	Leave Bangkok	Arrive Rangoon, Burma
Sunday	May 7	Leave Rangoon	Arrive Delhi, India
Wednesday	May 10	Leave Delhi	Arrive Lahore
Wednesday	May 10	Leave Lahore	Arrive Islamabad
Tuesday	May 16	Leave Islamabad	Arrive Kabul
Thursday	May 18	Leave Kabul	Arrive Teheran
Saturday	May 20	Leave Teheran	Arrive Beirut, Lebanon
Sunday	May 21	Leave Beirut	Arrive Cairo, Egypt
Tuesday	May 23	Leave Cairo	Arrive Luxor
Friday	May 26	Leave Luxor	Arrive Cairo, Egypt
Saturday	May 27	Leave Cairo	Arrive Athens, Greece
Saturday	May 27	Leave Athens	Arrive Istanbul, Turkey
Tuesday	May 30	Leave Istanbul	Arrive Vienna, Austria
Friday	June 2	Leave Vienna	Arrive London, England
Friday	June 09	Leave London	Arrive Washington, DC and, on to Los Angeles!

Picture of Doris taken by Stan in Cairo

Stanley's Tour of London for "The Gang"

Because Doris and I had lived in England for a few years and had visited there frequently, we organized a tour of the United Kingdom in 1973. Four couples toured much of Southern England and Wales. In addition to ourselves, there were: Bert and Mae Larsen, Hop and Vi Layman, and Norm and Harriet Fugelso.

We drove two rental cars and followed a planned circuit of the area. We stayed in historic Inns and other interesting places. Some of the more outstanding ones I recall were:

- The Mermaiden Inn in Rye on the channel. Formally the haunt of smugglers.
- The Red Lion Inn in Salisbury. Also, the famous Haunch of Venison restaurant where we had a surprise birthday party for Norm.
- The Bull Hotel in Gerrard's Cross where we celebrated my 60th birthday party in the same private dining room where I had had my 40th birthday surprise party. Freddie, the Bartender was around for both occasions.
- Ruthin Castle in northern Wales. There we attended a medieval banquet and were serenaded by a famous Welch chorus. Dinner was delayed because another group of guests was late, so we had an overly long cocktail hour. However, we somehow did manage to survive.

- The Bear Hotel in Woodstock. This old, but fashionable inn caters to the elite from London and elsewhere. Woodstock is a village next to Blenheim Palace, the seat of the Marlborough family and where Winston Churchill was born. Bert had a pleasant visit to Churchill's grave in the small graveyard in the nearby village of Bladen. Vi gathered some blossoms there for pressing and they are still in a small frame in an easel on Doris' desk.

Our visit to London was a great success, despite the fact that our rooms in the fine Westbury Hotel on Bond Street overlooked a parking area where the empty wine bottles were noisily hauled away early each morning. But their dining room was tops and they put on a special dinner just for our group.

We thoroughly covered London's main museum. I had the pleasure of introducing Hop to the National Gallery on Trafalgar Square. Of particular note is the gallery exhibiting a large and important collection of Rubens' paintings. He is famous for his nude ladies with plump pink fannies. We noticed and admired quite a few.

English food did not enjoy a great reputation, but we dined well. Memorable occasions were a roast beef dinner at Simpson's on the Strand one night and an outstanding Beef Wellington at the Dorchester Hotel on Park Lane another time.

As novice beer drinkers, we were finally able to order our pints and half pints with some skill. We learned that the tap beer known as "bitter" (pronounced "bittah") is mild. Also, we found that a "plowman's lunch" is a large mug of beer and a basket containing homemade bread and cheese.

As they say, "All good things must come to an end." Hop and Vi as well as Bert and Mae had to go home. Norm and Harriet spent a couple of weeks more with Doris and me in exploring Northern England and Southern Scotland. We played St. Andrews and tried to sample a representative selection of the single malt whiskies produced in the area. We found the list of available examples too expensive, so we finally gave up and went back home.

Chapter 54

Adventures by Sea and Land

The Whole Family Enjoys a Maiden Voyage on The Holland American Line's ship called "The Nieuw Amsterdam," 1983

The whole tanned gang aboard the Mississippi Queen! 1987

50th Anniversary Riverboat Cruise aboard the Mississippi Queen, 1987

Stan's "Girls": Billie, Doris, and Myra

50th Anniversary Love!

CHAPTER 55

Fish Stories and Exotic Places…

Proof of a Whopper:

When fishermen get together to exchange stories, Mrs. Stanley Moe of Van Nuys, California, can probably top them all when she tells about her prize 500-pound marlin caught on a Fourth of July fishing trip at Kona, Hawaii.

Big Billfish

The fish was 11 feet 10 inches long and measured 54 inches in girth. One of the hooks had penetrated one of the eyes, which often causes such large fish to give up with less fight. It took 20 minutes to land.

Doris hooks the biggest Pacific Blue Marlin of the season in Kona

A spectator nearby was overheard to remark: "I've been fishing for Marlin for the past 14 years and never caught one. Yet, this woman caught one on her first attempt. Some people have all the luck."

Doris with her 500-pound marlin

Stan hooks a Blue Marlin in Los Cabos
Only 155 pounds—skinny!

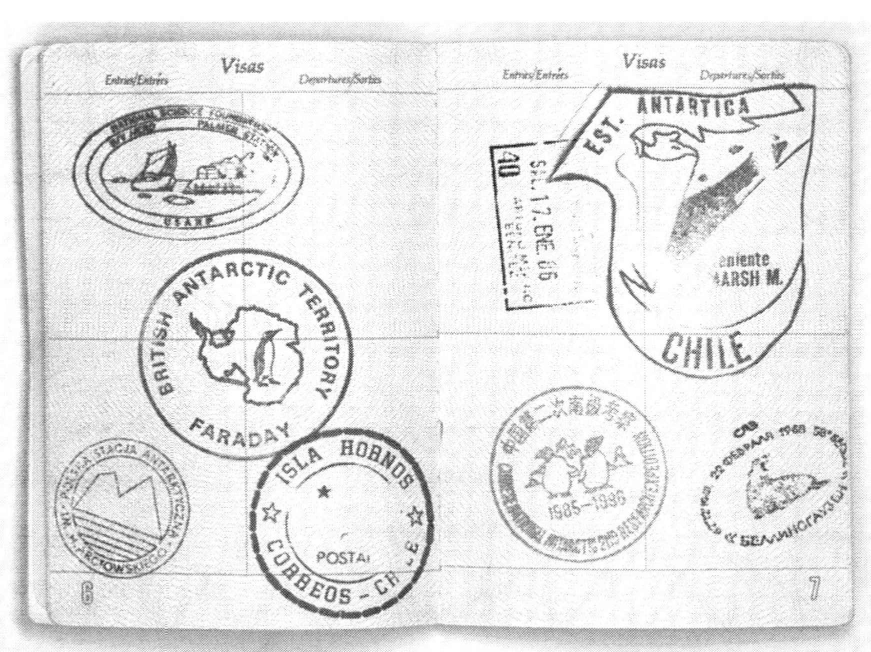

Passport to Antarctic Territory

Antarctica, in Stan's words…

Now that I am retired, my wife Doris, who is also trained as an architect, travels with me extensively. We are revisiting some of the places where I had projects years ago. We are also exploring places which have not been on our previous itineraries. Antarctica was one of those destinations—a favorite.

Excerpt: a Letter from Stanley, January 23, 1986

We just returned last week from a trip to Antarctica. During the trip we visited 15 beach locations which were reached by a small inflatable rubber boat called a "Zodiac." We stopped at Cape Horn and at numerous scientific research stations that are maintained by various countries. We are pleased to report that there are plenty of penguins, seals, rough water, ice and snow, and some of the finest and most dramatic scenery to be found anywhere in the world.

Stan at Cape Horn—a rocky headland on Hornos Island, in Southern Chile's Tierra del Fuego Archipelago. The Region is called Antártica Chilena

Mama penguin and her chicks

A curious penguin

Stan and Doris Moe had 6 decades of fun!
Much of it while traveling to exotic places

Part XVIII

Passages…

(photo by Susan Stroh)

(photo by Duane Stroh)

Chapter 56

"To Every Thing, There Is a Season."

Cairo, January 18, 1994, Letter from friend, Shafik Hakim

Dear Doris and Stan,

I appreciate very much your kind letter which made me go back 50 years. What a great time! I am sorry to hear about Jerry Jyring's passing. But, as Benjamin Franklin has said, "Our friend and we were invited aboard on a party of pleasure which is to last forever. His chair was ready first and he is gone before us."

As for our dear Doris, I pray for her to regain her health. God bless you both.

I had, since the last week of November of last year, a strong influenza and I have not felt good since then. We heard last night on our TV about the strong earthquake in the southern part of California and hope that you are safe and that it did not cause personal harm.

My dear Stan, I celebrated my 80th birthday last October. So, I am now an octogenarian. Alexandria National Iron and Steel accepted that I work in Cairo and not to be obliged to go to Alexandria. I accepted the job. Nowadays, I find myself working at least 8 hours every day—am very deep into this work. I have gone through every well and they will sign a contract next week for the installation of a new big oxygen plant with a German company.

We hope that everything goes well with you and that soon, dear Doris will be greatly improving.

With our best wishes.

Shafik

Mother Fought Long and Hard to Stay Alive with Dad by Her Side (by Billie)

Our family had 11 or 12 "last Christmases" with Mother. Dad and Mother had promised each other early in their relationship that they would never put the other into "a home." So, when Mother began having strokes about a year after she had an unnecessary mastectomy, Daddy became her caretaker for the next twelve years. I went from New Mexico to Los Angeles every 4 to 6 weeks to spend at least a week helping Dad.

During Mother's last months, during one of my help visits Dad had a serious problem with his heart. Before he got out of the hospital, he had six bypasses and came home to share Mother's round-the-clock help. Soon after his return home, Mother passed away.

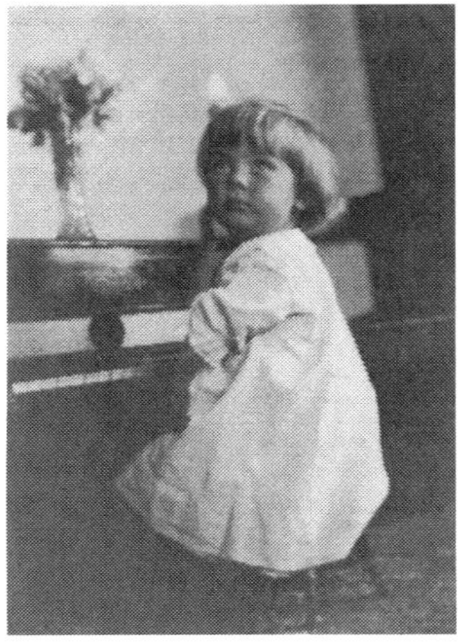

CHAPTER 57

Life Goes On

Several months after Mother's death, Dad met a lady, Reiko Izuno, through a dear friend of the family, Harriet Moore. Dad and Reiko enjoyed each other's company and a year after Mom's death, Dad and Reiko were married.

Stan and Reiko Moe cut their wedding cake 11/11/2001

Stan's beautiful girls, Billie and Myra

Stan had 9 years with Reiko

Cruises with Reiko — 2001

Christmas on Crystal Cruises: Reiko, Stan, Santa, Dean, and Billie

A Cruise for the Young at Heart — 2009

Dean Crouse, Stan Moe, Reiko Moe, & Billie Crouse
on Stan's 95th Birthday Cruise

For Dad's 95th birthday in 2009, we went on a wonderful cruise with one of the ports being Dubrovnik, Croatia. All the buildings in this old, old, beautiful, walled city on the water had clay-tile roofs. Tragically, in the 1990s, Dubrovnik was used for target practice. The United Nations stepped in and saved the city.

The wall around the city is about two and half stories high, maybe three. You walk up there to get a full view of the city and you see all the roofs that have been repaired. (The old roofs were one color, the repaired ones were another color.)

With all the crazy shooting and bombing that they did, I was told that there were no fatalities in the city. Dad and mother had been there right after the residents, ordered by the UN, started repairing the city.

Dad said, "I was here with your mother in 1994 when the bombings took place. I climbed the stairs to walk around the city."

As we're walking up this narrow stairway, one at a time, there was a lady behind us who said, "This is going to be a great view. I wish my friend had come, but she's staying below because she's too old—she's sixty!"

I said, "When you get back down, tell your sixty-year-old friend that you followed a 95-year-old up!"

She said, "Oh, my goodness, wow!"

When we got to the top, Dad said, "Having done this with your mother, I probably am not going to come back and do it again, so we're going to do this whole walk."

Stan walked the entire walk including all the steps around the walled city—at age 95!

And we did! The walk consisted of walking on little, narrow steps up the side of the massive 16th century stone walls. On top there is a walkway paved with limestone that's flat. There are little curio shops, coffee shops, and restaurants, way up high, well above the roofs of everything in the city. It was a fortress that protected the population from pirates and other enemies that approached from the Adriatic Sea.

What spunk, determination and humor Dad had!

CHAPTER 58

Saying Goodbye

After Dad and Reiko had been married for about 9 years, Dad was diagnosed with prostate cancer.

A few days before Dad passed, he was admitted to Good Samaritan Hospital in Los Angeles. The day before he died, I went with him to a lower level of the hospital for a radiation treatment. We were waiting in the hall, Dad on a gurney and I by his side.

Suddenly he raised his voice and said, "HELP ME! HELP ME!"

"I'm right here, Daddy, what can I do?"

"I'm not talking to you! I'm talking to your mother!"

Mother came to lead him to her the next morning.

The welcoming hug!

Stan: "Hey baby, let's get together in about 15 years!"

A Cruise in Memory of Stan and Doris Moe

On this cruise to St. Thomas Island, the family put Mother and Dad's ashes on wonton wrappers on which the children had drawn pictures and the adults had written memories or prayers. We let them float on the water. The fish nibbled away on the floating squares and the ashes sparkled down to the sand.

The dads and the five young girls made sandcastles and put the mixture of "Grandma and Grandpa's sand" into the castles. We all have wonderful memories. You may recall that Dad had mentioned going to St. Thomas on his way to Africa in 1942. He wrote that he wanted to take his family there one day. As I had not read Dads' diaries or letters before we did the "Ashes Cruise," it was an unknown blessing that we chose St. Thomas Island. Mom and dad had requested we do a cruise for the ashes...but God led us to St. Thomas.

Love, Billie

A Cruise in memory of Stan and Doris Moe, 2012

St. Thomas U.S. Virgin Islands
Together as a family, touring the island
This is the beach where the wonton wrappers were launched
and sandcastles were built.

Memorial Tribute

Delivered at Stanley Moe's Celebration of Life by Lee Jackman

In 1989, Stan and I met at the Rotary Club of Los Angeles. He served on the board of the club in 2005-06, when I was president. He was an avid fisherman and an email friend of mine. Stan died at age ninety-six. I delivered this tribute in the form of an email Stan might have sent from heaven.

Email sent from Stanley A. Moe from Heaven

From: Stanley A. Moe stanmoe@heaven.joy
Subject: Greetings from My New Home
Date: November 15, 2010, 10:22:50 p.m.
To: My Dear Family and Friends

Greetings! This is the first opportunity I've had to sit down and write you an email since arriving. There has been so much going on here, and I want to bring you all up to date on my recent activities.

I departed Los Angeles on October 13th, and my first-class flight couldn't have been more relaxing. It was a smooth ride, and I arrived here in what seemed like the blink of an eye. Upon landing, I was greeted by a nice young chap by the name of Gabriel, who is a professional trumpet player who moonlights as a chauffeur for newly arriving VIPs; thus, his assignment to me. Gabe met me in a shiny, new car —a gold Angelmobile—and that vehicle literally floated as we traveled along the spacious, shimmering highway leading into Paradise.

Nearing the city, flanking either side of the entrance, I was fascinated to see two mammoth gates, each about forty-feet high and encrusted with pearls. As an architect, I was intrigued by the gates and wanted to study them a bit. Unfortunately, before I was able do so, I was summoned by an officious fellow with clipboard in hand. Gabe introduced him as Saint Peter and told me that he is responsible for admitting into Paradise only those with appropriate credentials and turning away the rest. Apparently, St. Peter grows frustrated with gatecrashers whose names aren't on his list, but who try to finagle their way in anyway. Most of them are Kiwanians, I'm told. Well, as soon as St. Peter saw my name on his list and noted that I was an LA-5 Rotarian, his demeanor totally changed. He smiled, shook my hand, said I had been unanimously chosen as Piscatorial Chairman, and even asked me to call him Pete.

Gabriel then drove me to my residence, once we were safely inside the gates of the city. You should get a load of this place! From my window I can see a large blue lake, dotted with sunlight sparkles, that I've been told is abundantly filled with fish.

The entire house is made of gold and is located at the top of a high hill that overlooks a valley filled with shrubs, trees and fragrant flowers.

The accommodations are more luxurious than any I've ever seen. Bowls of fruit and honey are available everywhere, and music from the Heavenly Choir fills all of the rooms. You should see the unbelievably sumptuous meals that are served to the residents by the angels! For example, last night we had oysters on the half shell, prawns with delicious vegetables, and each plate was beautifully presented. I barely had time to eat, because I was so busy with my digital camera, taking pictures of each masterpiece that had been created! Following our meal, a few of us went out onto the veranda and everyone seemed amused by my stories as we sat, enjoying the evening and one another.

As I write this, I am sipping a glass of Chardonnay and preparing to get to bed early. Tomorrow will be an exciting day. At sun-up, LA-5 Rotarians Bill Cosko, Randy Lee and Bob Gunzel are picking me up and taking me out on that beautiful lake for a full day of fishing. I can hardly wait.

Life is good. Although I miss all of you, please know that I am happy and blessed to be in my wonderful new home. I send you my love and best wishes, until we are together again.

~ Stan

See you again...

ACKNOWLEDGEMENTS

This is not my book alone, but a book created by many. First, it is Dad's book. He was inspired to pass along his love of life by our Savior.

Over the past six years, I have worked to follow through on Dad's wish to have his diaries, love letters to Mother, correspondence with friends, some photographs, personal notes, oral memories and reflections put into a book, *The Stan Moe Memoirs.* During this time, I began by organizing his many boxes of notes. My first helper was Kirsten Andersen, my husband's oldest granddaughter, who organized all the boxes of papers from Grandpa Moe, Dad's dad, and Dad's papers into labeled decades, from 1880 to 2010. Then she began reading and typing his letters from 1941 and more—a monumental task. Thank you, Kirsten.

I then hired two graduate students from University of New Mexico who were doing graduate work in art history. Elizabeth Shores and Jana Gattshalk continued to organize and archive all of Dad's passports, paperwork and hundreds of photos.

Shirley Dunlap began reading my hundreds of typed pages and encouraged me with helpful comments. Glenn Hohnstreiter, talented professional photographer and dear friend, introduced me to Robert Laetare of The Artistic Image. Bob and fellow photographer, Leilani S.R. Brothers, beautifully photographed "historic" items and old photographs from the Moe family scrap books to add to the memoirs.

Soon, I came to realize that I needed a memoirist who had structured many memoirs as an editor and coach, and who could help find the correct construction and organization to tell Dad's story. I called a dear friend of Dad's, Lee Jackman, who I knew had written three books and she referred me to her writing coach and editor—Susan Baldwin Stroh. The book you are holding would not be possible but for Susan's skills, continuous collaborative spirit and caring. We have worked together closely on Dad's book for over a year and have come to speak the same language. Dad and she have a mutual admiration society! I truly believe Dad has been pleased with our work.

Thank you, Lee Jackman for the referral and for your marvelous written contributions to this book.

One of Susan's team members is Gwen Mackessy from Oregon—the queen of transcription. Many of my interviews and phone conversations with important people in Dad's life were recorded by Susan and sent to Gwen, who made those interviews tangible so they could be used in Dad's book.

Dear friend and neighbor Richard Siminski practiced his photography by adding to the photos that Bob and Leilani had taken. Thank you, Richard for your valuable creative additions.

The time came when I wanted to get feedback from "Readers of the memoirs." I printed up the draft of the manuscript and sent it off to Roscoe Champion, Jim Daniel, Shirley Dunlap, and Sandy Forsberg. Good readers, who know how to improve a book with specialized comments, are rare. I am grateful to you, dear

Readers, for your time and feedback. When you read this final published work, you will find your comments were heeded.

Thanks to those special friends and family who consented to have Susan interview you to get your thoughts and feelings of my dad. All of you shared your love and respect of Stanley A. Moe and he thanks you for your kind and thoughtful words. Those very special people: Myra Moe Parsons, Dad's other daughter, and his grandchildren: Lisa Parsons Sauers, Tambralyn Parsons Petersen, and Keith Parsons. Adding their wonderful memories: are Kathy Moe Miller, Dad's niece; Jim Daniel, son of Phil Daniels (a founder of DMJM and one of Dad's partners); and Pat Gillick, long time special friend of the family.

I want to thank three more of Susan's production team. First, Shawn Kelley, fine artist and graphic artist, who designed the simple family trees. Second is Theta Media Group's editor/proofreader, Cyndie Tobin, for her keen eye and meticulous sense of when clarification of terms or concepts is needed for greater reader understanding. And third, a big thank you to cover designer and typesetter, Randall Michael Tobin of Theta Media Group for designing the covers, the interior of this book, and as a final proofreader. His intent was to add to your reading pleasure visually—to keep forwarding an invitation for you to share Stanley A. Moe's adventure.

Thanks to family and friends who patiently stood by me as the surfaces of my upstairs workroom, my dining room table, my bedroom/computer room, and LIFE became cluttered (filled with budding creativity). These folks still came to visit and as needed, helped.

Thank you all for your contributions, I am greatly blessed.

Billie Crouse, co-author

EPILOGUE

Dad had so many friends, talents, interests. This book gave you an overview of what he did, saw, felt, and loved. If you knew Dad but did not find your name between the covers of this book, please take no offence. Know that Dad's knowing you helped to make him the man he was; you were a part of his "passport" that helped get him from when and where you knew him to where he evolved after 96 years.

Appendix One

Highlights of Stanley Moe's Life and Career

- Stanley Allen Moe was Born May 28, 1914, in Fargo, North Dakota
- Applied to be a sale's rep for Junior American Aircraft Company, Portland, Oregon, at age 15. (Letter dated June 10, 1929, from President of company wrote, "Dear Mr. Moe." He offered him a job as a sales rep for North Dakota. The president thought he was responding to an adult!) Stan did not accept the employment as he was going off to college.
- Graduation Exercises from Ross High School, Ross, North Dakota, May 29, 1930 (day after his 16th birthday)
- Attended University of North Dakota, 1930 to 1932
- Graduated from University of Minnesota, 1936
- Married Doris Lucille Anderson on July 25, 1937, in Stanley, North Dakota
- Daughter Billie was born July 31, 1939, in Minneapolis.
- Stan was a licensed architect in eleven states and project architect at various firms 1936–1947. From 1936-1941 he worked at several companies in Minneapolis including Rydells.
- Stan worked with the U.S. Army Corps of Engineers, working as director of design for several major military projects in Eritrea, Sudan, Egypt, and Yemen for Allied Forces; 1942–1943.
- Daughter Myra was born on April 5, 1945, in Duluth, Minnesota.
- American Institute of Architects Certificate of Membership, Feb. 14, 1947
- From 1947-1954 Stan was a partner of Moe, Larsen, Fugelso, Architects & Engineers, Van Nuys, California.
- "Moe Assumes Chamber Role in Van Nuys"—Installed as president of the Van Nuys Junior Chamber of Commerce. Valley Times News, January 21, 1949.
- "Stanley Moe named Van Nuys Man of Year." Valley Times News, (San Fernando Valley, CA) February 5, 1950, in news article.
- He became a member of Pan American World Airlines, Clipper Club, June 24, 1957, for having made valuable contributions to the advancement and public acceptance of air travel.
- Stan became a member of the Trans World Airlines, Ambassadors Club, November 4, 1957.
- October 1965, he became a member of The Far East Society of Architects and Engineers.
- Stan was one of six partners and founder-shareholders of Daniel, Mann, Johnson and Mendenhall (DMJM), one of the world's largest architectural, planning and engineering firms, 1953–1990s.

- A leading pioneer in his profession, Stan expanded architectural and engineering services to an international scale, establishing more than two dozen foreign operations around the world.
- His talents are also firmly imprinted on the U.S. Space Programs since he directed the design efforts of such space vehicles and systems as the Atlas, Jupiter, Thor, Titan I, the Lunar Excursion Module, and Space Shuttle.
- He was project director of the Space Shuttle Assembly Facility at the Kennedy Space Center, 1973.
- Stan was project director for design of the Aircraft Maintenance Complex, Iranian Aircraft Industries, 1978.
- He was project manager for the design of the major medical facilities program for the Minister of Defense and Aviation, Saudi Arabia.
- He was project manager, designing Boufarik International Airport, in Algeria, 1983.
- Stan went through initiation to become a full-fledged member of Delta XI chapter of Delta Tau Delta fraternity, October 11, 1985.
- Stan was awarded the Sioux Award from the University of North Dakota Alumni Association, University of North Dakota Homecoming, October 12, 1985.
- He received an honorary PhD, Doctor of Engineering, from the University of North Dakota, May 16, 1986.
- Stan was inducted into the North Dakota Entrepreneurs Hall of Fame, and Business Innovator of the year, 2000.
- Stan and his wife Doris were dedicated supporters of the University of North Dakota, the University of Minnesota, and the Macalester College in Minnesota. Stan also donated to the Rotary Club, to Hollywood Presbyterian church, Immanuel Presbyterian Church, and Children's Hospital of Los Angeles.
- Doris Moe died October 18, 2000.
- Stan married Reiko Izuno, November 11, 2001.
- Reiko Izuno Moe passed on May 6, 2020, in her home in Los Angeles. She is survived by her brother Masaru Izuno and niece Janet Izuno.
- Avocations included; world travel, photography, hunting, fishing, historic restoration, and woodworking.
- Stan was a loving husband, father, grandfather and great grandfather, a devoted Presbyterian and Republican.
- Stanley Allen Moe is remembered by all as a "fabulous" storyteller.
- Stanley A Moe went to be with the Father and our mother on October 13, 2010.

Appendix Two

Stanley Allen Moe State Licenses

States in Which Stanley A. Moe Was Licensed as an Architect

July 23, 1945	State of Minnesota #2458
August 28, 1947	State of California
August 1, 1962	State of Nevada #263
December 8, 1962	State of New Mexico #289
July 17, 1963	District of Columbia
December 14, 1964	Commonwealth of Virginia #1884
January 18, 1967	State of Maryland #2964-R
April 12, 1967	State of Oregon
1968	State of Connecticut #2855
July 30, 1968	Commonwealth of Mass. #2537
November 7, 1968	State of New York #10163
November 27, 1968	State of New Jersey #4953

APPENDIX THREE

DMJM

Article: "Around the World in 14 Years", p. 53-56

Excerpts reprinted courtesy of *Engineering News-Record*, copyright BNP Media, February 11, 1960, all rights reserved.

"...there is something special about DMJM, something that permitted a group of young men as unlike each other as steak and ice cream not only to guide the company's rise to the top, but to exploit bigness efficiently and continue to grow."

"That something special is the importance the partners place on personal satisfaction—that is, each working at what he likes best toward fulfilling not only professional but personal aspirations. How partners so different from each other have managed to accomplish this primary objective within the framework of cooperative organizational effort is the real DMJM success story. And it wasn't easy."

"First there were three: Philip Daniel, a hard-working, quick-on-the-decision, fun-loving extrovert; S. Kenneth Johnson, a former child-actor ("Our Gang" comedies) who's a natural-born joiner and speech-maker; and Arthur Mann, who frequently is cast as the mediator in disagreements. They started with a staff of one secretary in the small southern California town of Santa Maria in January 1946."

"Southern California was the fastest growing area of the fastest-growing state. It needed new schools, new office buildings, new industrial plants, new everything—and the three young partners, all architects, were right on the spot. Soon a 'branch' office in Los Angeles had grown into home-base, and by 1949 the partnership was no longer small business."

"The firm has used its California experience as a springboard to world-wide prominence. DMJM is currently a leader in design of missile facilities, working under the National Aeronautics and Space Agency in development of Wallops Island, VA., and with joint venture partners designing underground launching facilities for the Air Force's Titan."

"(As of this date in 1960) The firm now has a staff of 500 employees, offices in Washington, London and Los Angeles, and projects under way in Venezuela, Thailand, Honolulu and Guam. Their base of operations has also figured out to Alaska, Korea, Japan, Okinawa, India, Italy and France."

"But big business breeds big management problems—problems the three young consultants were not entirely prepared to deal with, problems that had a hand in forming ulcers for two of them, problems that almost wrecked the business before they were finally solved."

"The principal problem was that profit and expansion was not developing as efficiently as was new business, which was coming in almost faster than the partners could handle it. Business problems beyond the partners' professional experience led to personal differences. Phil Daniel was once quoted as saying: 'We knew the business needed managing, but each of us thought the other should do it, and nobody could get three votes.'"

"After everything, including psychological tests, failed, the partners turned to the management consulting firm of Booz, Allen & Hamilton, which assigned one of their men, Douglas A. Russell, to the formidable reorganizing tasks."

"Consultant Russell so impressed the partners that they took him into the firm. Thus, began a series of changes that resulted in: breaking the firm down into departments with one partner at the head of each department; bringing the engineering work inside the firm instead of subcontracting it out (Irv Mendenhall came in as the firm's first engineer-partner); writing a 'Code of Partnership Ethics' to define responsibilities, map out each partner's relationship and behavior to each other and to the firm; substituting the inefficient, often squabbling system of group decision with more direct managerial control under Douglas Russell as General Manager."

"Mr. Russell left the partnership last year to establish his own overseas development firm. In the year since Russell left, growth of the firm has continued to the point where the five partners (the original three plus Stanley A. Moe and engineer Mendenhall) have incorporated, effective at the beginning of this month."

"For the present, the five partners—now stockholder-directors—plan no changes in the effective methods of operation developed over the last several years. And they will keep the partnership organization in those states where laws prohibit corporate practice."

"As they did under their partnership organization, the five principals will hold a monthly formal meeting, with an agenda prepared in advance. Decisions have for some time been made by majority vote instead of the once required unanimity."

"The monthly meetings are augmented by an annual three-day meeting—a combination brainstorming session and confessional—at which work for the past year is reviewed, goals for the coming year are established, and all partnership problems, personal and professional, are dragged out into the open and analyzed."

"The partners consider these annual meetings vital—so vital, that for a recent one, Daniel came from Washington, Johnson from Italy, Mendenhall from Venezuela, Moe from England, and Russell from Tokyo."

"Each of the principals now has definite areas of responsibility, although earlier they had rotated jobs. Stan Moe is now Executive Vice-President and General Manager, overseeing the day-to-day details of internal organization; Phil Daniel is Executive Vice-President for commercial and systems design, and continues in charge of business development; Art Mann is Executive Vice-President for institutional facilities; Ken Johnson is Executive Vice-President for industrial and military design; Irv Mendenhall, as President, remains in charge of financial planning and certain external relationships."

"Daniel —

"Phil Daniel, in charge of business development more than any of the principals, is concerned with making the contacts that bring in new business.

"The firm's goals are developed sometimes from a five-year plan hammered out by the partners meeting together. But sometimes goals are developed more by intuition than by careful planning. This is where Daniel feels he makes the greatest contribution to the firm. It is at his insistence, for example, that DMJM is now geared to serve the European common market area, prepared to design American-type factories for Europeans.

"After receiving his architectural degree from the University of Southern California, Daniel went to work in 1938 for Louis N. Crawford, an architect in Santa Maria. In 1940 the firm became Crawford and Daniel. (The partnership came as a wedding present when Daniel married Irv Mendenhall's sister—Mendenhall at the time was still at the University of California.)"

"Mann —

"As chairman of the partnership, Art Mann prepares agendas, calls meetings and presides at the partnership sessions. Such formalities among old friends expedites the work. 'Informal meetings drag out too long,' Mann says.

"But Art Mann's contribution is more than formalizing their business relationships: Not as volatile as the others, he is generally the last to jump into an argument; frequently he's the mediator. He stabilizes the human relations among the partners; helps keep these intense individuals working together.

"A native of Glasgow, Scotland, Mann came to the U.S. as a youth and got his architectural training through the apprenticeship route. He met Phil Daniel early in World War II while both were working on the design of the Kaiser Steel plant in Fontana. They became fast friends, and the natural move was to go into business together.

"Mann oversees architectural design on schools and institutions. This work is the effort that started the partnership in 1946."

"Johnson —

"It was Ken Johnson who made the initial draft of the Code of Partnership Ethics many years ago.

"He is the partnership's 'bug' on good plans and specifications. In the early years, 90% of the firm's business was on public works. The bidding process in public works requires complete plans and specifications—change orders cost money that public works managers can see. Johnson attempts to carry the need for complete plans and specifications over into work for private clients. Here construction often proceeds at the same time as design: and cost of the resulting design changes are covered in a negotiated or cost-plus job.

"Johnson is an advocate of the total design office where all phases of the work are done in one place. Efficiency is built in, he says, because everyone knows what everybody else is doing

"Johnson was a classmate of Phil Daniel at USC, he earned degrees in architecture and civil engineering, worked as a movie-studio set designer.

"After graduation, Johnson worked for the National Park Service and as a project architect on the design of a spectacular all glass exterior ordinance building at the San Francisco Naval Shipyard before being invited to join classmate Daniel's new firm.

"It was Johnson who first suggested a branch office in Los Angeles."

"Mendenhall —

"As managing partner of the organization Irv Mendenhall oversees financing and relationships with other firms. And as the only engineer among the partners, he is in charge of all engineering efforts.

"Mendenhall served in the Seabees during World War II shortly after graduation from the University of California. After service he went into business as an engineer in his hometown, Santa Maria. Among other things he did small municipal projects for Santa Maria and surrounding communities. Mendenhall also did structural design work for the young architectural firm of Daniel, Mann and Johnson. This association developed into a partnership shortly before the Korean War.

"From this small engineering seed grew such things as DMJM's recent participation in design of the multi-million dollar Los Angeles sewage works program that centered around modification of the Hyperion treatment plant. And it led to one of DMJM's big current jobs as consultant to the Los Angeles Metropolitan Transit Authority in developing plans for rapid transit. LAMTA has no engineering staff of its own, thus DMJM is in effect a staff."

"Moe —

"Stan Moe, the fifth partner, has the title of general manager. As such, he oversees all the architect-engineer operations both for domestic and overseas work.

"It was through overseas efforts that Moe was brought into the firm. Moe, a graduate of the University of Minnesota, had his own architectural practice in the San Fernando Valley. In 1952 he joined DMJM to head an architect-engineer staff in Tokyo serving the Far East Air Force. He has long been interested in overseas work. Other early overseas assignments include work in the Middle East and a tour of duty as a civilian attached to the Corps of Engineers in Africa.

"From Tokyo, Moe went to England to administer an Air Force design program for DMJM. These two assignments were so successfully handled that, in 1955, he was made a partner."

List of DMJM projects

During his time with Daniel, Mann, Johnson and Mendenhall (DMJM), Stanley Moe was a principal owner and served as a Senior Partner, Executive Vice President, and General Manager. In addition to general administrative responsibilities, he personally directed many large design and construction projects around the world. Many of these were related to defense, industrial, and aerospace programs. Some of these were the USAF facilities at domestic and overseas locations: NASA and USAF Space Shuttle facilities in Florida and in California; airports and aircraft maintenance installations in Iran, Algeria, and elsewhere. These categories of projects included those with construction costs ranging from fifty million to several billion dollars.

Excerpted from "DMJM: Four Decades of Excellence. 1946–1986" (pamphlets prepared for 50th anniversary of DMJM.) (Far from a complete list)

1. Public Architecture

a. El Rincon Elementary School, Culver City, CA
b. Simi Valley High School, Simi Valley, CA
c. General Mail Facility, Long Beach, CA
d. Las Vegas City Hall, Las Vegas, NV
e. Mile High Stadium, Denver, CO
f. Vienna Correctional Center, Vienna, Illinois
g. Hinds County Detention Facility, Jackson, MS
h. Northlake Community College, Dallas, TX
i. Civic Plaza Expansion, Phoenix, AZ
j. University of New Orleans Event Center, New Orleans, LA
k. St. Vincent Medical Center, Los Angeles, CA
l. Veterans Admin. Psychiatric Outpatient Facility, Palo Alto, CA
m. Federal Aviation Administration Building, Hawthorne, CA
n. Santa Monica College Library, Santa Monica, CA

2. Public Works

a. Santa Marguerita Pipeline, Venezuela
b. Venice Fishing Pier, Venice, CA
c. Barbers Point Fuel Storage Facility, Oahu, Hawaii
d. Hyperion Ocean Sewer Outfall, Los Angeles, CA
e. North Central Outfall Sewer Tunnel, Los Angeles, CA
f. Seoul Metropolitan Sewerage System, Seoul, Korea
g. Containership Terminal, Port of Los Angeles, California
h. Dominguez Hills Oil Facility, Dominguez Hills, California
i. Foothills Dam, Denver, CO
j. Central Valley Water Reclamation Facility, Salt Lake City, UT

k. Doha Water Distribution Complex, Doha, Kuwait
l. S.C.E. Electrical Substation, Los Angeles, CA
m. Tehachapi Pumping Plant, Tehachapi, CA
n. Barker Dam Rehabilitation, Denver, CO
o. New Orleans Flood Control Project, New Orleans, LA
p. Donald C. Tilman Water Reclamation Plant, Sepulveda, CA

3. Military/Defense

a. Tomahawk Cruise Missile Guided System, San Diego, CA
b. Titan I Missile Launch, Vandenberg AFB, CA
c. Comsat Laboratories, Maryland
d. Hardened Underground Titan I Missile Silo
e. The Naval Aircraft Rehabilitation Facility, San Diego, CA
f. Rockwell Thermal Vacuum Test Chamber, Seal Beach, CA
g. Orbiter Maintenance and Checkout Facility, Vandenberg AFB, CA
h. Peace Hawk V Air Base Program, Saudi Arabia
i. Computer Center, Peterson AFB, CO
j. Space Shuttle Solid Rocket Booster, Cape Kennedy, FL
k. Indonesian Satellite Communication Earth Station, Indonesia
l. Teledyne Office and Laboratory, Northridge, CA
m. Military Tactical Communications Shelter
n. McDonnell Douglas Aeronautics Company, Huntington Beach, CA
o. Ship and Marine Laboratory, Carderock, MD
p. Lockheed Space Telescope Building, Sunnyvale, CA

4. Commercial Architecture

a. General Telephone Building, Santa Monica, CA
b. Manufacturers Bank Building, Beverly Hills, CA
c. Marina City Club Complex, Marina del Rey, CA
d. Hotel Meridien, Singapore
e. Portland Plaza, Portland, OR
f. The DHL Building, Redwood Shores, CA
g. Ramada Renaissance Hotel, San Francisco, CA
h. Caesar's Palace Hotel, Las Vegas, NV
i. The Royal Sonesta Hotel, New Orleans, LA
j. Transamerica Office Park, Phoenix, AZ
k. The Crowne Plaza Hotel, New Orleans, LA
l. Marriott Courtyard, Various Locations
m. The Royal Executive Park, Rye, New York
n. Encino Terrace Center, Encino, CA

5. Transportation

a. Puuloa Interchange, Honolulu, HI
b. Personal Rapid Transit System, Morgantown, WV
c. Sky Harbor International Airport, Phoenix, AZ
d. Los Angeles Int'l Airport Expansion Program, L.A., CA
e. Interstate 70 Highway, Glenwood Canyon, CO
f. New York City Rapid Transit Revitalization, New York, NY
g. C-470 Highway, Denver, CO
h. Muni Metro Turnaround Facilities, San Francisco, CA
i. MARTA 10th Street Midtown Station, Atlanta, GA
j. St. Charles Streetcar Line Revitalization, New Orleans, LA
k. Bus Maintenance and Operations Facility, Orange County, CA
l. World of Motion Pavilion at Epcot Center, Disney World, FL
m. Vancouver Advanced Light Rail Transit System, Vancouver, BC
n. Freeway I-10 Busway Project, El Monte, CA
o. Washington, DC, Metro Subway Program
p. Connecticut Route 8 and 15, Merritt Parkway, CT
q. Penang International Airport, Malaysia
r. Saudi Arabian Public Transport Co., Kingdom of Saudi Arabia
s. Mississippi River Bridge, New Orleans, LA

6. Industrial

a. IBM Office and Mfg. Complex, Burlington, VT
b. Air Research Unit 22A Mfg. Facility, Torrance, CA
c. Kmart Corp. Distribution Center, Ontario, CA
d. Sears Roebuck Catalog Order Plant, Los Angeles, CA
e. Easton Aluminum Finishing Plant, Salt Lake City, UT
f. Phoenix Newspapers, Inc., Satellite Printing Plant, Mesa, AZ
g. Gas Centrifuge Enrichment Plant, Portsmouth, Ohio
h. Coca-Cola Process and Bottling Plant, Tempe, AZ
i. Hertz Vehicle Maintenance and Turnaround Facility, L.A., CA
j. Subaru-Intermountain Warehouse and Office Facility, Aurora, CO
k. Shinko Electric Manufacturing Plant, Manteca, CA
l. Hughes Wastewater Treatment Plant, El Segundo, CA
m. Portadrill Mfg. and Office Facility, Denver, CO
n. Geothermal Steam Gathering System, Sonoma County, CA
o. Rohr Metal Processing Facilities, Chula Vista, CA
p. IBM Distribution Center, Endicott, NY

7. Landmarks

a. Ambassador College Auditorium, Pasadena, CA
b. The Superdome, New Orleans, LA
c. Fermi National Accelerator Laboratory, Batavia, IL
d. Aero Propulsion Systems Test Facility, Tullahoma, TN
e. Stanford Court Hotel, San Francisco, CA
f. The Baltimore Metro, Baltimore, MD
g. Capitol Bank of Commerce, Sacramento, CA
h. Interstate 70 Highway, Glenwood, CO

8. The Future (After 1986)

a. Canadian Int'l Centre of Commerce, Calgary, Alberta, Canada
b. Ontario Int'l Airport Terminal Area Expansion Project, Ontario, CA
c. Long Beach to Los Angeles Rail Project, CA
d. Arizona Department of Public Safety, Phoenix, AZ
e. Los Angeles Metro Rail Subway, CA
f. CEBAF—Continuous Electron Beam Accelerator Facility, Newport News, VA
g. Sacramento State U. Engineering & Computer Science Building, Sacramento, CA
h. The Fillmore Center, San Francisco, CA (completed before 1995)
i. The Resort at Squaw Creek, CA
j. Hyperion Secondary Modification Program, Los Angeles, CA
k. Lockheed Weapons System, Simulation Center, Valencia, CA
l. Jamestown Bridge, Rhode Island
m. Renaissance Tower, Sacramento, CA
n. The Royal Capitol Plaza, Honolulu, HI
o. Marriott Hotel, San Francisco, CA
p. San Jose Convention Center, San Jose, CA
q. Spinal Cord Injury Unit, V.A.M.C., Long Beach, CA
r. Renaissance Tower, Sacramento, CA
s. City/County Jail and Sheriff's Headquarters, Reno, NV
t. Arapahoe County Justice Center, CO (completed before 1995)
u. Air Force 1 Maintenance Complex, Andrews AFB, Maryland

Appendix Four

Praise for Stanley A. Moe

News Flashes from the 1960s:

Open letter of commendation and recommendation for Stanley Moe from: Rev. Thomas I. Nalbach, pastor, First Presbyterian Church, Van Nuys, CA, October 3, 1960:

"Stanley Moe is a man of sterling character and outstanding ability. As his pastor, it is my very real pleasure to give my highest commendation."

Newspaper section, Bangkok World— Tuesday, December 13, 1960. Page 8. Article: "Visiting Expert Says Thailand Has Big Chance of Industry Development"

"Mr. Moe, here on a round-the-world visit to his company's scattered international projects, said Thailand presents a real major opportunity for industrial development."

"'The situation here is unprecedented,' he said, 'because there is going to be such an abundance of power. They will have to use it and industry is the logical user. It seems to me that Thailand is sitting now about where the people on the Tennessee Valley Authority (TVA) area sat about 25 years ago.'

"Mr. Bill Shope, the company's manager here said his 14 American technicians and their 200 Thai helpers have now completed 325 exploration wells in the project they are working on in the North-Eastern plateau. Eighty percent of the wells have produced fresh water that can be used for washing, drinking, cooking and other household uses.

"'This means,' he said, 'that in four-fifths of the area, drilled wells can provide domestic water at depths of less than 200 feet. And that is in an area which the wells often dry up and where lack of water has even forced farmers to move out.'

"Mr. Moe said his company has just completed a 13-mile submarine pipeline from the mainland of Venezuela to Margarita and Cochi Islands off-shore—the longest submarine pipeline in the world. He said the company 'now feels justified' in proposing an oil pipeline across the Mediterranean from the Sahara oilfields to Europe.

"The company, which has been involved in the construction of rocket launching bases and other aspects of the missile program in the U.S., expects to play a part in putting a man into space, Mr. Moe said. He said he did not expect the U.S. to get a man into space until at least 1964.

"'In certain areas,' he said, 'the Russians appear to have advanced more than we. For instance, on thrust. But I think we are getting more useful knowledge from what we put in orbit than they are.'

"He said his company is already working on designs for space stations on the moon. Mr. Moe leaves today for Taipei, Tokyo, and Honolulu via Pan American."

Billie: Alan Shepard becomes the first American in Space, May 5, 1961.

Valley Times Today — June 29, 1962: Ground Broken for Police Building. Includes image of Stanley Moe helping to break ground for the $5 million Valley Police Headquarters Building.

Los Angeles Herald Examiner — August 30, 1964, Man's World, F-5: The New Look Engineer, Norman Dash, Herald-Examiner Staff Writer, describes Moe as "the archetypal 'new' engineer who works on projects globally regardless of politics."

"I spend about six months a year on average out of the country, flying from place to place in the northern hemisphere," Moe said.

Once in the air, Moe works out of his briefcase, substituting a soft seat for a desk—and quickly comes up with multi-million-dollar decisions.

"My biggest decision, which involved $5 million and the firm's reputation, was for the location of an airport. I thought about it all during the plane trip, and when I got off, I wired my decision. Fortunately, it was the right one."

About the most dangerous assignment for Moe's crew was in 1960 in Viet Nam, where a large force was working on the rivers and canals on that country's Mekong area.

"Our job was to make a detailed survey of their waterways, which are essential to their economy. The survey crews, made up of young Viet Nam engineers, were working with large power boats. The Viet Cong ambushed the crews and we lost two engineers, a 45-foot boat, and some boat operators."

Moe's forces also worked during a 1958 coup in Venezuela and a 1961 coup in Korea and through a Nigerian labor strike which was politically motivated.

"These things only slow us up." Moe said. "But they never bother us. What we do is stay off the streets and keep working. Although our business usually goes on as usual, we can't keep the local help from getting involved.

"Many times, it appears that the incidents are going to be bad. For example, we expected it to be nasty in Venezuela," Moe explained. "But our people weren't bothered. In fact, we submitted an invoice for a large amount of money to the government in power the day before the coup, and it was paid by the new government the day after. These people are practical and realize that business must go on as usual."

Moe, who has been involved in some 300 projects in approximately 30 different countries, never has been involved in hostile actions.

"I never had anything unpleasant occur," he said. "My stays have always been pleasant. I'm usually in a country a day before or a day after a coup. Also, we make it a practice never to get involved in street riots, and as a result, the Americans are never bothered. However, it's the French and the British who are unpopular. Very rarely do we have problems. The local people are very easy to get along with, have a lot of respect for American know-how and readily accept advice."

Retirement Plaque for Stanley Allen Moe From American Airlines, Inc.

IN APPRECIATION to Stanley A. Moe, Corporate Vice President, for more than a quarter of a century of outstanding contributions to the growth and prosperity of Daniel, Mann, Johnson, & Mendenhall. His unique professional and managerial capabilities have played a major role in the successful competition of some of the largest and most important architectural and engineering programs in DMJM's history.

His distinguished career, which began in 1936 in Minnesota, has taken him to every corner of the globe. He was responsible for setting up DMJM's Far East operations, based in Japan. Moe also directed such major projects as the U.S. Third Air Force construction programs in the United Kingdom, as well as in Europe. As Chairman of the Control Committee of a joint venture, he directed the design on the Titan I missile facilities. His co-workers will also remember his involvement in projects in such countries as Ethiopia, Egypt, Sudan, Saudi Arabia, Japan, Turkey, France, England, Vietnam, Jordan, Korea, Thailand, and Indonesia. His performance and personal charisma have touched all those who have worked for DMJM over the years. Therefore, his fellow officers wish him and Doris continued success, health, and prosperity in "retirement."

In recognition of his consistent and meritorious service
and for his many contributions to the development of
air transportation as a public service
and as a basic element of Air Power
American Airlines, Inc. hereby commissions

STANLEY A. MOE

An Admiral of the Flagship Fleet

In testimony whereof, witness my signature,
This the 9th day of May 1961

C R Smith, Fleet Admiral

Appendix Five

Currency Stan Collected Over the Years

Series of 1899

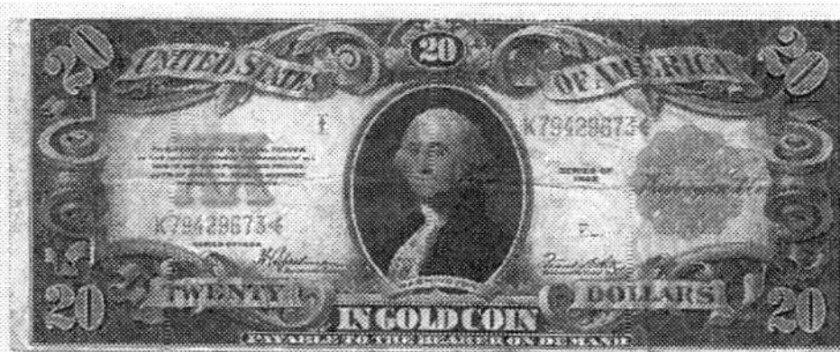

Series of 1922

Series of 1923

One dollar bill, 1923, on top,
Today's dollar size below

Made in the USA
Coppell, TX
06 November 2020

40877129R00252